LIVING AND WORKING

IN

LONDON

A SURVIVAL HANDBOOK

by

Claire O'Brien

&

David Hampshire

SURVIVAL BOOKS · LONDON · ENGLAND

First published 2000

Survival Books Limited, Suite C, Third Floor
Standbrook House, 2-5 Old Bond Street
London W1X 3TB, United Kingdom
☎ (+44) 0207-493 4244, 🖷 (+44) 0207-491 0605
✉ info@survivalbooks.net
🖳 survivalbooks.net

British Library Cataloguing in Publication Data.
A CIP record for this book is available from the British Library.
ISBN 1 901130 11 8

Printed and bound in Finland by Werner Söderström Osakeyhtiö (WSOY),
Tenhusentie 3, FIN-519000 Juva, Finland

ACKNOWLEDGEMENTS

My sincere thanks to those who contributed to the successful publication of this book, in particular Joe Laredo (author of *Buying a Home in Ireland*, Survival Books 1999) for Orientation and Earning a Living, David Hampshire (author of *Living and Working in Britain* and *Buying a Home in Britain*, Survival Books) for Somewhere to Live, Arrival & Settling In and Odds & Ends, Charles King, Karen and John Verheul, David and Sigrid O'Hara, Pat and Ron Scarborough and everyone else who contributed in any way who I have omitted to mention. Also a special thank you to Jim Watson for the superb cover, maps, cartoons and illustrations.

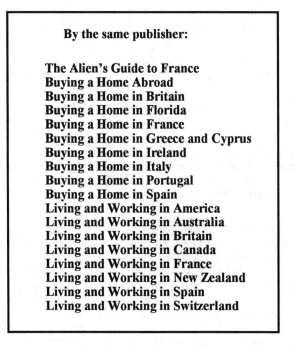

By the same publisher:

The Alien's Guide to France
Buying a Home Abroad
Buying a Home in Britain
Buying a Home in Florida
Buying a Home in France
Buying a Home in Greece and Cyprus
Buying a Home in Ireland
Buying a Home in Italy
Buying a Home in Portugal
Buying a Home in Spain
Living and Working in America
Living and Working in Australia
Living and Working in Britain
Living and Working in Canada
Living and Working in France
Living and Working in New Zealand
Living and Working in Spain
Living and Working in Switzerland

What Readers and Reviewers Have Said About Survival Books

When you buy a model plane for your child, a video recorder, or some new computer gizmo, you get with it a leaflet or booklet pleading 'Read Me First', or bearing large friendly letters or bold type saying 'IMPORTANT – follow the instructions carefully'. This book should be similarly supplied to all those entering France with anything more durable than a 5-day return ticket. – It is worth reading even if you are just visiting briefly, or if you have lived here for years and feel totally knowledgeable and secure. But if you need to find out how France works then it is indispensable. Native French people probably have a less thorough understanding of how their country functions. – Where it is most essential, the book is most up to the minute.

Living France

We would like to congratulate you on this work: it is really super! We hand it out to our expatriates and they read it with great interest and pleasure.

ICI (Switzerland) AG

Rarely has a 'survival guide' contained such useful advice – This book dispels doubts for first-time travelers, yet is also useful for seasoned globetrotters – In a word, if you are planning to move to the USA or go there for a long-term stay, then buy this book both for general reading and as a ready-reference.

American Citizens Abroad

It is everything you always wanted to ask but didn't for fear of the contemptuous put down – The best English-language guide – Its pages are stuffed with practical information on everyday subjects and are designed to complement the traditional guidebook.

Swiss News

Let's say it at once. David Hampshire's *Living and Working in France* is the best handbook ever produced for visitors and foreign residents in this country; indeed, my discussion with locals showed that it has much to teach even those born and bred in *l'Hexagone*. – It is Hampshire's meticulous detail which lifts his work way beyond the range of other books with similar titles. Often you think of a supplementary question and search for the answer in vain. With Hampshire this is rarely the case. – He writes with great clarity (and gives French equivalents of all key terms), a touch of humor and a ready eye for the odd (and often illuminating) fact. – This book is absolutely indispensable.

The Riviera Reporter

What Readers and Reviewers Have Said About Survival Books

What a great work, wealth of useful information, well-balanced wording and accuracy in details. My compliments!

Thomas Müller

This handbook has all the practical information one needs to set up home in the UK – The sheer volume of information is almost daunting – Highly recommended for anyone moving to the UK.

American Citizens Abroad

A very good book which has answered so many questions and even some I hadn't thought of – I would certainly recommend it.

Brian Fairman

A mine of information – I might have avoided some embarrassments and frights if I had read it prior to my first Swiss encounters – Deserves an honoured place on any newcomer's bookshelf.

English Teachers Association, Switzerland

Covers just about all the things you want to know on the subject – In answer to the desert island question about *the one* how-to book on France, this book would be it – Almost 500 pages of solid accurate reading – This book is about enjoyment as much as survival.

The Recorder

It is so funny – I love it and definitely need a copy of my own – Thanks very much for having written such a humorous and helpful book.

Heidi Guiliani

A must for all foreigners coming to Switzerland.

Antoinette O'Donoghue

A comprehensive guide to all things French, written in a highly readable and amusing style, for anyone planning to live, work or retire in France.

The Times

A concise, thorough account of the DOs and DON'Ts for a foreigner in Switzerland – Crammed with useful information and lightened with humourous quips which make the facts more readable.

American Citizens Abroad

Covers every conceivable question that might be asked concerning everyday life – I know of no other book that could take the place of this one.

France in Print

IMPORTANT NOTE

L ondon is huge city with many faces, a variety of ethnic groups, religions and customs, and Britain has continuously changing rules, regulations, interest rates and prices. Note that a change of government in Britain can have far-reaching effects on many important aspects of life. **I cannot recommend too strongly that you check with an official and reliable source (not always the same) before making any major decisions, or taking an irreversible course of action. However, don't believe everything you're told or read (even, dare I say it, herein).** Useful addresses and references to other sources of information have been included in all chapters and in **Appendices A and B**, to help you obtain further information and verify details with official sources. Important points have been emphasised, **in bold print**, some of which it would be expensive, or even dangerous, to disregard. **Ignore them at your peril or cost.** Unless specifically stated, the reference to any company, organisation or product in this book doesn't constitute an endorsement or recommendation. Any reference to any place or person (living or dead) is purely coincidental. There's no such city as the City of Westminster.

CONTENTS

AUTHOR'S NOTES

- Times are shown using am (latin: *ante meridiem*) for before noon and pm (*post meridiem*) for after noon.

- Unless otherwise stated, prices shown usually include VAT at 17.5 per cent and should be taken as estimates only, although they were mostly correct at the time of publication.

- His/he/him also means her/she/her (please forgive me ladies). This is done to make life easier for both the reader and (in particular) the author, and *isn't* intended to be sexist.

- Frequent references are made throughout this book to the **European Union (EU)**, which comprises Austria, Belgium, Denmark, Finland, France, Germany, Greece, Ireland, Italy, Luxembourg, the Netherlands, Portugal, Spain, Sweden and the United Kingdom, and the **European Economic Area (EEA)**, which includes the EU countries plus Iceland, Liechtenstein and Norway.

- All spelling is (or should be) English and not American.

- Warnings and important points are shown in **bold** type.

- The following symbols are used in this book: ☎ (telephone), 🖷 (fax), 💻 (Internet) and ✉ (e-mail).

- Lists of **Useful Addresses** and **Further Reading** are contained in **Appendices A** and **B** respectively.

- For those unfamiliar with the Imperial system of weights and measures, metric conversion tables are included in **Appendix C**.

- A map of the London boroughs is shown on page 20 and a map of central London is on the inside the front cover.

INTRODUCTION

London is one of the world's great cities, Europe's largest city and one of the most populous on earth – Greater London covers over 600mi² (ca. 1,500km²) and has a population of over seven million (or more, depending on how you define London). It's the seat of government and home of the British Royal Family, Britain's commercial and manufacturing heartland, the country's cultural and sporting centre, Europe's leading financial market, and the 'capital' of the English-speaking world. London is the epitome of 'cosmopolitanism', creativity, liberty and affluence, and a world leader in architecture, art, fashion, food, music, publishing, film and TV.

London is also Europe's most racially and culturally diverse city and the most cosmopolitan city in the world; one in five Londoners (over one million people) were born outside the UK and between them speak some 200 different languages. Greater London is home to almost half the ethnic minority population of Britain. Its people hail from all corners of the globe, particularly Europe and the Commonwealth countries of Africa, Asia and the West Indies, and it's a melting pot of the First and Third Worlds. Not surprisingly, London is a treasure trove of foreign culture and multiculturalism and almost anyone can feel at home there – it has some 35 foreign communities comprising over 10,000 people born outside the UK. To add to this cultural potpourri, London's resident population is swelled by a staggering over 25 million tourists a year, not to mention the hundreds of thousands of commuters who flock there daily to work.

People are drawn to London for many reasons, among which are its rich traditions, unrivalled entertainment, stimulating arts scene, and the abundance of business, career and educational opportunities. It provides more cultural activities than any other city in the world and houses the largest number of theatres, the most visited museums and some of the best known sights – history awaits you around every corner. Nowhere provides a more varied and vibrant nightlife for the young (and young at heart) than London, which is besieged by the youth of all continents. It's been called 'Swinging London' and dubbed 'the most exciting city in Europe' and the 'coolest city on the planet' (cool Britannia). A confident, cocky (Cockney) city that's constantly re-inventing itself, London is a bustling, vibrant place to live, work or study. It's also one of the world's greenest capital cities with some 1,800 parks and open spaces.

In 1999, Britain's growth rate was around 2 per cent (which is expected to increase to 3 per cent in the year 2000), inflation was around 2.5 per cent, sterling was the world's second-strongest currency and interest rates were at a 30-year low – all of which added up to a booming economy and the strongest public finances in Europe. London is Britain's main employment centre with a huge variety of job opportunities and relatively low unemployment. However, in common with most capital cities, the cost of living is high and prices (particularly property) are among the highest in Europe, although higher salaries compensate to some extent. Like all large cities, London displays stark contrasts of wealth and poverty, although few places offer such endless opportunities to make (or lose) your fortune. In London you can be anything or anyone you wish – from a pauper to a prince, a dropout or a high-flier, a punk or a poseur, famous or unknown, eccentric or conservative – London has a place for everybody.

However, in common with other major cities, London also has it share of problems and is suffering from decades of neglect. Its failings include pollution, an ageing and over-burdened public transport system, dreadful traffic congestion, substandard housing and homelessness, over-crowding, high crime (in some areas), racial tensions and all the other horrors that are part and parcel of modern life. However, it's the people – the good, the bad and the ugly – who make London what it is and give the city its unique character. Although the British can be infuriating at times, they will invariably charm and delight you with their sense of humour and idiosyncrasies.

The British people have more freedom from government interference than the people of most countries, to do, say and act any way they like, which most people take for granted. Britain is still a great civilised power (if a little frayed at the edges) and a positive influence in the world and London remains the hub of the English-speaking world. Whatever else it may be, life in London is invariably spiritually, mentally and intellectually stimulating and rarely dull, and although foreigners may occasionally complain about the Government, the British weather or parking wardens, most feel they are privileged to live and work there and wouldn't dream of leaving.

THIS BOOK

Whether you're already living or working in London or just thinking about it – this is **THE BOOK** for you. Forget about all those glossy guide books, excellent although they are for tourists – this amazing book was written especially with you in mind and is worth its weight in jellied eels. *Living and Working in London* is designed to meet the needs of anyone wishing to know the essentials of London life, whether you're from Birmingham or Berlin, Manchester or Minnesota, an immigrant, temporary worker, transferee, business person, student, retiree, long-stay visitor or even an extra terrestrial! However long your intended stay in London, you'll find the information contained in this book invaluable.

General information isn't difficult to find in London and a wealth of books is published on every conceivable subject. However, reliable and up-to-date information specifically intended for newcomers *Living and Working in London* isn't so easy to find. Our aim in publishing this book was to help fill this void and provide the comprehensive *practical* information necessary for a relatively trouble-free life. You may have visited London as a tourist, but living and working there is a different matter altogether. Adjusting to a different environment and culture and making a home in any foreign country can be a traumatic and stressful experience, and for most people Britain is no exception.

For most new arrivals in London, finding out how to overcome the everyday obstacles of life has previously been a case of pot luck. **But no more!** With a copy of *Living and Working in London* to hand you'll have a wealth of information at your fingertips. Information derived from a variety of sources, both official and unofficial, not least the hard won personal experiences of the authors, their families, friends, colleagues and acquaintances. Adapting to life in a new country is a continuous process and this book will reduce your beginner's phase and minimise the frustrations, and help you make informed decisions and calculated judgements instead of uneducated guesses and costly mistakes. **Most important of all, it will help save you time, trouble, and money and repay your investment many times over.**

Whether you're from another part of Britain or overseas, this book will prove invaluable in helping you become acclimatised and make yourself at home in London. With this book (and its sister books *Living and Working In Britain* and *Buying a Home in Britain*) you'll have all the information you need to make a period spent in London a rewarding and satisfying experience. The majority of 'foreigners' in London would agree that, all things considered, they relish living there. I trust this book will help you avoid the pitfalls of life in London and smooth your way to a happy and rewarding future in your new home.

Good luck!   **David Hampshire (Editor)**
                                                 November 1999

1.

ORIENTATION

For those who are unused to large cities, the sheer size of London can be daunting. It isn't only vast and labyrinthine, but also chaotic. Central London was originally an assortment of villages and some 250 years ago there were vast spaces between them, although today they have merged into an almost seamless metropolis. The surrounding parts of London grew mainly in the Victorian period, when the 'suburbs' were at least partly planned. Here there's more open space and the population density is generally below 7,000 people per square kilometre, compared with up to 14,000 in the city centre.

There are almost three million dwellings in London and over 14,000 new homes are built each year, which makes choosing where to live a difficult task. Any attempt to divide London into manageable and comprehensible chunks can only be partially successful. The task is further complicated by the overlap between the different artificial divisions that have been created over the years – geographical, cultural, historical, administrative and postal. The customary division of the city is marked by the River Thames, which roughly separates the northern from the southern boroughs (the administrative regions of Greater London). This pattern is broken only once, where the river cuts through the middle of Richmond, which is nevertheless generally regarded as a 'southern' borough. There's a widespread notion that north London is more pleasant than south London and that the West End is superior to the East End, but such generalisations often fail to stand up when you start looking at areas in more detail.

Historically, Greater London is a mere 35 years old and many people still consider only the central areas to be London proper, with the outer areas belonging to the surrounding ('home') counties. For example, Kingston was originally part of Surrey and Bromley was in Kent, both of which have since given their names to a London borough. Created in 1965, the boroughs are the administrative areas of Greater London, which is one of the 45 administrative regions (or 'counties') of England. There are 32 boroughs plus the City of London, which is effectively a borough but has certain peculiarities such as its own police force. (The so-called City of Westminster, on the other hand, is a borough like any other.) The boroughs vary considerably in size but each has a population of between 150,000 and 350,000, with the exception of the City of London, which has just 5,000 residents.

Unofficially, the boroughs are divided between 'inner London' (Camden, City of London, Greenwich, Hackney, Hammersmith & Fulham, Haringey, Islington, Kensington & Chelsea, Lambeth, Lewisham, Newham, Southwark, Tower Hamlets and Wandsworth) and 'outer London' (the remaining 19 boroughs). Inner London boroughs tend to be characterised by a huge gulf between rich and poor, and a wide racial and cultural mix. Outer London boroughs are more suburban with vast swathes of green belt (areas in which building is restricted) and a predominantly white (and 'white-collar') population.

Officially, each borough is divided into 'wards' (an administrative district of a parliamentary constituency), although even people who live there often don't know their names. Most people refer instead to districts which in some cases don't even appear on the map (e.g. 'Blythe Village' and 'Brackenbury Village' in the borough of Hammersmith & Fulham), but which are either named after places long since swallowed by the outward sprawl of the capital or derive from contemporary 'estate agent speak'. In many cases, these districts straddle borough or county boundaries. This situation could be further complicated by proposed administrative changes after the election of a Mayor in May 2000 and the creation of a Greater London Authority, which is expected to divide the city into 14 'constituencies' each comprising roughly two boroughs. There are other more or less arbitrary divisions also: 16 health authority areas, five police regions, four ambulance service zones and three fire brigade sectors.

The most perplexing of London's various partitions is its division into postal areas, each with a different 'postcode' that seldom bears any relationship to counties, boroughs, wards or districts. The first one or two letters signify the area of London such as E (East) or SW (south-west), although there are no south or north-east districts today, which were merged into the south-western/south-eastern and eastern districts respectively in the 19th century. As if this isn't confusing enough, the numbers following the initial letter or letters of 'London' postcodes can also be misleading. The system was based on the position of the initial letter of each sub-district in the alphabet, therefore a district beginning with the letter 'A' was given the number 1 and so on. Many people believe that the numbers indicate the distance from the centre of London, whereby logically the lowest numbers would be nearest the centre and the highest furthest out. However, this obviously isn't the case. Between 1968 and 1971, some codes gained an extra letter, e.g. parts of W1 became W1A. London's postcodes also confer status and there's a 'postcode snobbery' which not only reinforces social distinctions, but can also inflate or deflate the price of property.

Each London borough also has its own website containing a wealth of information, all of which can be accessed via http://bubl.ac.uk/uk/england/london.htm – the addresses of individual sites are www.[borough name].gov.uk, e.g. www.brent.gov.uk. Other useful sites include, www.hot-property.com/focuson/focusindex.htm, www.thisislondon.com/dynamic/lifestyle/homes/wheretolive.html and www.upmystreet.com.

Vital statistics for the 33 boroughs (shown on the map overleaf) that comprise Greater London are listed on the following pages.

BARKING & DAGENHAM

Overview: The east London borough of Barking and Dagenham was once marshland and most of it consists of terraced council houses (public housing owned by the local authority), some of which are now privately owned. The recently completed Barking Barrage has enabled development to take place along the River Roding in the south-west and there are plans to reclaim more marshland along the north bank of the River Thames over the next two decades for some four thousand new homes.

Town Hall: Barking, Essex IG11 7DU (☎ 0208-227 3181).

Postcodes: IG11, RM6 (part), RM7 (part), RM8, RM9 (part) and RM10.

Population: Barking and Dagenham is generally a rather deprived borough with a predominantly 'white' population, with just 7 per cent belonging to ethnic minorities.

Unemployment: The level of unemployment is just above the London average at 9.6 per cent, although the government is putting money into creating new job opportunities.

Crime Rate: Barking and Dagenham's crime rate is about average for London (see page 268); in other words you stand a one in nine chance of being the victim of crime.

Property: The borough's largest housing estate (a development that often refers to council or public housing), Becontree, was built in the '20s and '30s for East End workers. It consists of some 27,000 homes, mostly two and three bedroom red brick houses. Since then other council estates have been constructed to the north, but there's a relatively small amount of private housing, which is nevertheless among the cheapest in London. Barking town offers small Victorian terraced houses and as well as larger Edwardian and '20s to '30s properties. The slightly more upmarket Chadwell Heath has some semi-detached houses (semis), but over 64 per cent of properties in Barking & Dagenham are terraces (the highest proportion in London) and a further 26 per cent flats, most purpose-built.

Costs: Average house prices are the lowest in London (see page 108), while council taxes under the present Labour authority are fairly average (see page 133).

Communications: Public transport is good in most areas, particularly for commuting into central London. The tube's District Line runs through Barking, Becontree and Dagenham, and there are three overground lines: one running into London's Liverpool Street station, one to Fenchurch Street, and another from Barking to Gospel Oak near Hampstead Heath (Camden). Buses are a better bet for travelling north-south and there are good services between the towns of Barking and Dagenham. The main A13 road to Essex cuts across the southern part of the borough, while the A406, known as the 'North Circular Road', forms Barking and Dagenham's western boundary.

Schools: There are no private schools, and the borough's state schools perform poorly according to the government's 1998 league tables (see page 159).

Facilities: There's plenty of open space in Barking and Dagenham but it tends to be flat and rather dull. The largest of the borough's 16 parks, Eastbrookend Country Park in the east, boasts a lake and its own Millennium Centre, and the government is creating attractive walks along the River Roding as well as landscaping the A13. The borough is well supplied with cinemas and leisure centres, although there's only one museum, one theatre and one main library (in Barking). If you're looking for somewhere with plenty of good restaurants, Barking and Dagenham isn't for you!

Shopping: Barking is the best place for shopping, with the new Vicarage Fields centre and a 'pedestrianised' precinct. Chadwell Heath has reasonable shops, but Dagenham is best avoided.

BARNET

Overview: The outer London borough of Barnet is one of the largest. Much of its housing sprang up around the Northern tube line, which was built in the early part of the century. At the end of the line in the far north of the borough, Barnet retains its market town character. In the centre, Totteridge and Mill Hill offer some attractive parts between the main roads. To the west, Edgware and Burnt Oak aren't particularly full of character, but Hendon in the south has distant echoes of its rural past. More up-market are Finchley and Friern Barnet to the east, with Hampstead Garden Suburb in the south-east corner home to the rich and famous. In the extreme south-west of the borough are Golders Green, Cricklewood and Brent Cross.

Town Hall: The Burroughs, London NW4 4BG (☎ 0208-359 2000).

Postcodes : N2, N3, N10 (part), N11 (part), N12, N20, NW2 (part), NW4, NW7, NW9 (part), NW11, EN4 (part), EN5 (part), EN6 (part) and HA8 (part).

Population: Barnet is mainly a prosperous area with a high proportion of middle class families. Almost 25 per cent of its population belong to ethnic minorities, including London's largest Gujerati community, while Golders Green is home to the capital's biggest Jewish community.

Unemployment: The unemployment rate is below the London average at 6.6 per cent.

Crime Rate: Barnet boasts the lowest crime rate in London (see page 268).

Property: Property is fairly evenly divided between flats (38 per cent), semi-detached (31 per cent), terraces (20 per cent) and detached houses (11 per cent) and ranges from the affordable (in Edgware, Brent Cross and parts of Finchley) to the outrageously expensive (in Hampstead Garden Suburb, where London's 'Millionaires' Row', Bishops Avenue, is to be found) and includes every style from modern apartment blocks and ex-council houses to Edwardian and Georgian mansions.

Costs: House prices are just above average (see page 108), as are council taxes (see page 133).

Communications: The Northern Line remains the main public transport artery, but trains can be infrequent, slow and crowded. Barnet isn't well served by mainline trains, although one of London's two trans-Thames routes (appropriately named Thameslink) links Mill Hill, Hendon and Cricklewood to places as far south as Wimbledon and Sutton via Blackfriars station in the City. Buses run all the way into central London but there are few east-west routes.

Britain's first motorway, the M1, begins in Barnet and other main roads such as the A1 and A41 cut through the borough from north to south. The A5 runs along the boundary between Barnet and Brent, and the North Circular Road (A406) joins the M1 at the busy Brent Cross intersection. Most areas have resident parking zones.

Schools: Barnet has some of the best performing state schools in England (see page 159) as well as plenty of private schools.

Facilities: There's lots of open space in Barnet, particularly towards the border with Hertfordshire, where there are several golf courses. There are also plenty of museums (including the RAF Museum at Hendon and the Jewish Museum in Finchley), cinemas, leisure centres and libraries, and a planned arts centre in North Finchley which will provide the borough with a second theatre to add to the Bull Theatre in Barnet town.

Shopping: Barnet is second only to Westminster in terms of the number of retailers within its boundaries. Shops range from the small specialist Jewish shops (and restaurants) in Golders Green and London's only Eastern shopping centre in West Hendon, to the huge 'mall' at Brent Cross. Edgware, Finchley, Hendon and Barnet town all offer reasonable shopping.

BEXLEY

Overview: Bexley (meaning 'clearing in the box wood') is mainly suburban and often rather dull, although there are smarter areas towards its southern end and the boundary with Bromley.

Town Hall: Bexley Civic Offices, Broadway, Bexleyheath DA6 7LB (☎ 0208-303 7777).

Postcodes: SE2, SE28 (part), DA1 (part), DA5 (part), DA6, DA7, DA8, DA14, DA15, DA16, DA17 and DA18.

Population: Bexley is largely well-to-do with a predominantly white population (93 per cent), with a small Asian community centred in Belvedere).

Unemployment: Bexley has low unemployment at 5.4 per cent.

Crime Rate: With 79 crimes per 1,000 population per year, Bexley has one of the lowest crime rates in London (see page 268).

Property: A large proportion of property in Bexley is semi-detached (44 per cent – the highest percentage in London), with 30 per cent terraced, 21 per cent flats (almost all purpose-built) and only 6 per cent detached. Most properties date from the '20s and '30s and vary from the smart (around Sidcup and Blackfen in the south-west) to the shabby (around Erith in the north-east, which, however, are in line for a 'government improvement scheme'). In the centre of the borough, the town of Bexley itself is attractive, with something of a village feel, while neighbouring Bexleyheath and Welling consist mainly of typical '20s and '30s terraces and semis. In the flat marshland to the north-west, Thamesmead offers some attractive modern properties, and elsewhere there are bargains to be found among the tower blocks.

Costs: House prices are generally low and council taxes around average and (see pages 108 and 133 respectively).

Communications: The underground doesn't reach Bexley, which is, however, particularly well served by overground trains: Belvedere, Bexley, Bexleyheath, Erith, Falconwood, Sidcup and Welling are linked to various central London termini (Blackfriars, Cannon Street, Charing Cross, London Bridge, Victoria and Waterloo) and to all parts of Kent in the other direction. Bexley also has reasonable bus services.

The main A2 and A20 roads linking London with the Channel ports slice through the borough and offer escape routes into rural Kent, although they are inevitably heavy with traffic. Parking is increasingly controlled (and charged for) through resident permit zones.

Schools: There are no private secondary schools in Bexley, but several state schools perform reasonably well (see page 159) and are much sought-after.

Facilities: There are a number of hills in Bexley, as well as woods, parks and other open spaces, with golf courses in the centre of the borough and walks along the Rivers Cray and Thames. Restaurants are scarce and shopping is little more than adequate. Sports facilities are good and there are no fewer than four theatres and several museums, but only two cinemas.

Shopping: The best shops are in Bexleyheath and the worst in Erith (although it has a popular twice weekly street market); there are hardly any shops at all in Thamesmead.

BRENT

Overview: Brent, which takes its name from the river that runs through it, is a borough of various characters and is neither a typically 'inner' nor a typically 'outer' London borough. It has 'respectable' suburban districts to the north and east (around Brondesbury and Willesden Green, Dollis Hill, Kingsbury and out towards Harrow), contrasting with the dreary sprawl of Wembley to the west. Wembley, of course, is home to one of the world's most famous sporting stadiums as well as the Arena and Conference Centre, which together attract tens of thousands of visitors a week. The planned reconstruction of the stadium and regeneration of the surrounding area could make Wembley one of the newly desirable areas of London. Further east, Neasden has a partly deserved reputation for dullness (and the largest Hindu temple outside India), while Queens Park and Kilburn in Brent's south-east corner are among the capital's upwardly mobile areas.

Town Hall: Forty Lane, Wembley, Middx. HA9 9HX (☎ 0208-937 1234).

Postcodes: NW2 (part), NW6 (part), NW9 (part), NW10, HA3 (part), HA9 and HA0.

Population: Brent has the most multiracial population in London: almost 45 per cent of its residents belong to ethnic minorities, particularly Indian (mostly in the north and west), and over 70 languages are spoken in its schools. The borough also has the highest proportion of Irish-born inhabitants in London (9 per cent), mostly around Kilburn in the south-east.

Unemployment: Unemployment is high at 12.6 per cent and the borough ranks as the 20th most deprived area in England.

Crime Rate: The crime rate in Brent is around the London average (see page 268).

Property: Brent has a high proportion of flats (48 per cent), more than a third conversions, compared with 24 per cent each of terraces and semis, with a mere 4 per cent of detached houses. The flats around Queens Park are particularly attractive, being mostly in spacious, converted houses and situated close to central London.

Costs: House prices are generally below average, but vary widely, and council taxes are low (see pages 108 and 133 respectively).

Communications: Public transport in Brent is generally good. The Bakerloo and Jubilee tube lines serve most areas, but Wembley is practically the only place with overground railway stations – linking with Marylebone and Euston stations. One of London's trans-Thames rail services usefully links Wembley to Clapham Junction, Croydon and places south.

The A406 North Circular Road, which cuts the borough in half, has recently been widened but still tends to jam at peak times. The A5 runs along the boundary with Barnet. Residents' parking permits have been widely introduced in recent years, and there are particularly high fees for second and third cars.

Schools: Brent has average state schools, according to the government's 1998 league tables (see page 159).

Facilities: Apart from the Wembley Arena, which offers world-class entertainment, there are good theatres and cinemas and reasonable sports facilities (including two boules rinks) in Brent. Its 1,000 acres of open spaces include Queens Park in the south, Gladstone Park with its exotic plants in the east, Roundwood Park (venue of the largest Irish festival outside Ireland), Fryent Country Park in the north and the Brent Reservoir (known as the Welsh Harp on account of its shape) on the border with Barnet. Wembley is notable for its choice of Indian restaurants as well as for a major Asian street market in Ealing Road.

Shopping: Shopping in Brent tends to be functional, although there's a variety of ethnic shops in Kilburn, Willesden and Wembley.

BROMLEY

Overview: The largest of London's boroughs, Bromley is generally regarded as being part of Kent – particularly by its inhabitants. But in contrast to almost rural villages like Keston and Farnborough in the south, there's plenty of suburbia elsewhere. Bromley's north-west corner, which borders Lambeth, Southwark and Lewisham, has a rather depressed, inner city feel, although the government is committed to regenerating the areas around Penge, Anerley and Crystal Palace (once one of London's major attractions), which is the proposed site of a £50 million leisure complex. As you travel east, to Beckenham and Bromley town and then to Hayes and West Wickham, standards (and prices) start to rise, the most up-market parts of the borough being Chislehurst and Petts Wood in the north-east.

Town Hall: Bromley Civic Centre, Stockwell Close, Bromley BR1 3UH (☎ 0208-464 3333)

Postcodes: SE20, BR1 (part), BR2, BR3, BR4, BR5, BR6, BR7, BR8 (part), CR6 (part), TN14 (part) and TN16 (part).

Population: Bromley has a generally affluent, predominantly white population.

Unemployment: Unemployment is (with Camden) the lowest in London at 4.5 per cent.

Crime Rate: In contrast to its northern neighbours, Bromley boasts a low crime rate (see page 268).

Property: Bromley has the highest percentage of detached houses in London (18 per cent), reflecting its high proportion of well-heeled residents. Most of these houses were built during the first third of the 20th century. The remainder of properties are fairly evenly divided between semi-detached (29 per cent), terraces (25 per cent) and flats (29 per cent).

Costs: The average cost of property in Bromley is near the London average, but prices vary widely from one area to another (see page 108). Council taxes are relatively low (see page 133).

Communications: Bromley isn't served by the underground, although overground rail stations are well spread and services are good. Anerley, Beckenham, Bromley, Chislehurst, Crystal Palace, Hayes, Orpington, Penge, Petts Wood and West Wickham are variously linked to Blackfriars, Cannon Street, Charing Cross, London Bridge, Victoria and Waterloo stations. Buses are also widespread, but most won't take you anywhere near the city centre. The roads are particularly busy around Crystal Palace, where parking can also be a problem, otherwise the borough is mostly permit-free.

Schools: Bromley has some of the best performing state schools in London (see page 159), most of which, not surprisingly, are over-subscribed. There are also several private schools.

Facilities: There's plenty of open space in Bromley, as well as a variety of theatres, concert halls, libraries and museums, but just two cinemas. There are several sports centres – apart from the famous Athletics Stadium at Crystal Palace – and half a dozen golf courses. Chislehurst has a decent selection of restaurants.

Shopping: Excellent shopping facilities are to be found in Bromley town and good shops in Orpington; other towns are less well served.

CAMDEN

Overview: Camden contains some of London's smartest areas – around Regent's Park to the south-west and Hampstead to the north-east – as well as some of its seediest around King's Cross station to the south-east, one of the capital's unofficial red light districts (which is, however, part of a multi-million pound regeneration project). In the centre of the borough Camden Town itself, with its colourful markets, has recently become one of the most 'in' places in London. Bloomsbury and Fitzrovia to the south are almost as trendy, while further west Primrose Hill and Belsize Park have attractive areas.

Town Hall: Judd Street, London WC1H 9JE (☎ 0207-860 5974).

Postcodes: N6 (part), NW1 (part), NW3, NW5, NW6 (part) and WC1.

Population: Camden is the 17th most deprived area in England, yet many of the super-rich live there. Distinguished former residents include writers Charles Dickens, George Orwell, Arthur Rimbaud and Mary Shelley (author of *Frankenstein*).

Unemployment: Unemployment in Camden is high at around 12 per cent.

Crime Rate: Officially, Camden's crime rate is the second highest in London (after Westminster) with a massive 220 crimes per 1,000 population annually. In reality, however, this figure is distorted by the large influx of visitors to the borough, particularly to London's West End.

Property: The vast majority of properties in Camden are flats (86 per cent), of which over a third are conversions (i.e. converted from large houses), a further 10 per cent being terraced houses and just 4 per cent detached and semi-detached houses. Property varies from drab council blocks (in Somers Town) to elegant Georgian terraces (Camden Town) and Italianate villas (Belsize Park and Primrose Hill).

Costs: Camden has the fourth highest average property prices in London, although reasonably priced houses can be found in some areas, and the third highest council tax rates (see pages 108 and 133 respectively).

Communications: In most parts of Camden you're spoilt for choice when it comes to public transport – which is just as well, because the council is waging war on the use of cars, and parking is a problem throughout the borough. The Northern tube line serves Belsize Park, Hampstead, Tufnell Park and Kentish Town, which is also on an overground line running through Blackfriars and across the river to Wimbledon and Sutton, as well as on a route linking Richmond with east London. King's Cross/St Pancras and Euston stations are both in the borough of Camden.

Schools: Camden's state schools are only slightly above average, according to the government's 1998 league tables (see page 159), although they claim the best 1999 exam results in inner London. There's a good choice of private schools, and Camden houses much of the University of London.

Facilities: There's no shortage of leisure facilities in Camden, which includes part of London's 'theatreland', as well as the British Museum and the British Library in its new home at St Pancras. Hampstead Heath lies within the borough as does part of Regent's Park, and there are plenty of other green spaces including Primrose Hill, Parliament Hill and Kenwood. Camden has a vast choice of excellent restaurants.

Shopping: For shoppers, there's everything from crafty Covent Garden and ethnic Camden Market (actually five separate markets with a total of over 1,000 stalls) to the computer-heaven of Tottenham Court Road.

CITY OF LONDON

Overview: The most ancient part of London, dating back to Roman times, 'the City' measures just one mile by one mile and is often referred to as 'The Square Mile' for that reason. This is the financial heart of London and, until quite recently, it consisted of almost nothing but banks and office buildings. Even today, outside working hours, it's a quiet place, with many shops, pubs and restaurants closed in the evenings.

Town Hall: The Guildhall London, The Corporation of London, PO Box 270, London EC2 2EJ (☎ 0207-606 3030).

Postcodes: EC2 (part), EC3 and EC4.

The City of London is unlike the other 32 boroughs in that it's governed by a corporation, which has existed since the Middle Ages, and has its own police force – the City of London Police.

Population: Although some 350,000 people work in the City, its resident population is a mere 5,000 – most of them wealthy.

Crime Rate: The City of London isn't covered by the Metropolitan Police, therefore there are no crime figures to compare with other boroughs.

Property: Virtually all the property (99 per cent) in the City of London is purpose-built flats. The largest development is the Barbican, dating from the '70s – a concrete maze broken up by occasional green spaces and ponds – but there are also luxury flats around St Paul's cathedral and Fleet Street, now deserted by the newspapers in favour of Docklands.

Costs: Not surprisingly, the City's few properties are among the most expensive in London, although council tax rates are the third lowest in the capital (see pages 108 and 133 respectively).

Communications: Being in the centre of London, the City is naturally well served by public transport and has no fewer than eleven tube stops and four overground termini: Blackfriars (serving north London, the Midlands and the north of England as well as south London, Sussex, Hampshire and Dorset), Cannon Street (serving south-east London and Kent), Fenchurch Street (serving the East End and Essex) and Liverpool Street (serving Essex and East Anglia). It isn't, however, a place where cars are welcome. Not only is road access to the City restricted by the police (as a result of IRA bombings), but there's no resident parking and car parks can cost £12 per day or more.

Schools: There's only one state school in the City, a high-performance primary school (see page 159), although there are three private schools.

Facilities: The Barbican has its own Arts Centre (incorporating a theatre, concert hall, museum, art galleries and cinemas) as well as being home to the Guildhall School of Music and Drama. The Museum of London is nearby. There's just one public leisure centre in the City, but umpteen private 'health clubs' for those who can afford them. Green spaces are few and small. Like its shops, the City's restaurants cater mainly for the local office population and choice is limited in the evenings.

Shopping: Shops cater mostly for the working population, with the exception of the famous Petticoat Lane market (actually in Middlesex Street on the border with Tower Hamlets).

CROYDON

Overview: The outer London borough of Croydon has more than its fair share of drab parts – not least much of Croydon town itself in the centre of the borough – as well as some smarter suburban areas to the south.

Town Hall: London Borough of Croydon, Taberner House, Park Lane, Croydon CR9 3JS (☎ 0208-686 4433).

Postcodes: SE19, SE25, SW16 (part), CR0, CR2, CR3 (part), CR5, CR7 and CR8.

Population: Almost 20 per cent of Croydon's population belong to ethnic minorities, mostly Asian and Afro-Caribbean.

Unemployment: Unemployment is low at 6.1 per cent, many people commuting into central London or working locally, particularly in Croydon town.

Crime Rate: Croydon has a slightly higher crime rate than its outer London neighbours, but below the London average (see page 268).

Property: Croydon has an even mix of flats (31 per cent), terraces (34 per cent) and semi-detached or detached houses (35 per cent). Large Victorian properties predominate around Upper Norwood and South Norwood in the north, many converted into flats. Thornton Heath and Norbury to the north-west have mostly flats. Shirley Hills, south-east of Croydon town, is one of the borough's smartest areas and there are attractive semi-detached and detached houses around Purley, Selsdon and Coulsdon to the south. The best parts of Croydon town are on the east and south sides.

Costs: Average house prices are lower than in Bromley, Merton or Sutton (see page 108), and council tax rates around average (see page 133).

Communications: There are no tube stations but excellent rail services through Croydon town north to central London and south to Gatwick airport. A new scheme called Tramlink, due to be completed in 2000, will connect parts of Croydon laterally with the edge of Bromley to the east and with Sutton and Merton to the west. Most bus routes stop short of the city centre. The A23, which becomes the M23 south of Croydon, runs south into Surrey and Sussex.

Schools: Croydon's state schools offer only average performance (see page 159), but there's a good selection of private schools.

Facilities: There are lots of parks in the borough, including Lloyd Park near Croydon town, South Norwood Country Park, Happy Valley Park near Coulsdon and the North Downs in the south. There's a fine house and garden at Norwood Grove near Upper Norwood with splendid views. The borough has a reasonable selection of cinemas, libraries, museums and leisure centres, and Croydon town boasts the new Clocktower arts centre as well as the Fairfield Halls. There are probably more golf courses in Croydon than in any other London borough. There are some interesting restaurants in Crystal Palace and Upper Norwood; Croydon town is surprisingly not such a good place for eating out.

Shopping: A great deal of money is being spent on Croydon town's shopping centres, which are among the best outside central London. Otherwise shopping in the borough is rather uninspiring.

EALING

Overview: Ealing boasts interesting buildings, good shops, plenty of open space and good public transport. The borough as a whole is being promoted as a tourist and business destination. Ealing town in the centre is much sought-after, but Bedford Park in the south-east corner is the most expensive area. Acton in the east is less smart but seems to be on the up.

Town Hall: Perceval House, 14-16 Uxbridge Road, London W5 2HL (☎ 0208-579 2424).

Postcodes: W3, W5, W7, W13, UB1, UB2, UB5 and UB6.

Population: Ealing's population is mostly middle class. Almost a third of the residents belong to ethnic minorities and the borough has London's biggest Indian population (centred in Southall, where there's also a significant Afro-Caribbean community).

Unemployment: Unemployment is near the London average at 9.5 per cent.

Crime Rate: Ealing's crime rate is about average for London (see page 268).

Property: Some 42 per cent of properties in Ealing are flats, 35 per cent terraces, 19 per cent semi-detached houses and just 3 per cent detached houses. Property in Ealing town is largely Victorian, as it is in Acton, where some attractive converted flats are to be found. West Acton has mock Tudor houses and flats, and North Ealing is mainly Edwardian. Near the A40 (Great West Road), Southall in the west and Greenford and Northolt in the north consist of mostly boring '30s semis. West Ealing and Hanwell are among the cheapest areas.

Costs: House prices are comparable with neighbouring Hounslow, but council taxes are relatively low (see pages 108 and 133 respectively).

Communications: One of Ealing's main attractions is its excellent train and tube links. The Central Line runs east-west across the middle of the borough and the Piccadilly Line north-south. Acton and Ealing are on an overground route into London Paddington and Acton is also linked by rail to Richmond and the City Airport in Docklands. The A40 runs across the north of the borough, linking it to central London and Birmingham, but, like all London's arterial roads, it's often badly clogged. The A406 North Circular Road, which cuts through Ealing from north to south, is notoriously busy at Hanger Lane (which is a bottleneck).

Schools: Ealing's state schools are no better than average, according to the government's 1998 league tables (see page 159), and there are some private schools.

Facilities: There are plenty of theatres, cinemas and leisure centres in the borough, but poor library provision. There's also lots of open space, particularly in the north, where there are fine views from Horsenden Hill, and a surprising number of golf courses. Attractive walks can be found along the River Brent and the Grand Union Canal in the south-west of the borough. Shops are good in Ealing and dull in Acton, although the latter are due for a face-lift. Southall has many excellent Indian restaurants and there's also a wide range of restaurants in Acton and Ealing.

Shopping: There's a large choice of shops in Ealing, where you can find all the usual high street names and a number of shopping malls. Most of the rest of the borough has uninspiring shopping, with the exception of Southall, which has a wealth of Indian shops selling everything from spices to saris and excellent indoor and outdoor markets.

ENFIELD

Overview: London's most northerly borough, Enfield is a mixture of salubrious suburbs in the west and grim council estates in the east, although the industrial areas around Edmonton and Ponders End are being regenerated. The smart parts are Palmers Green, Oakwood, the rather twee village of Winchmore Hill and Hadley Wood – the most expensive part of Enfield where the odd celebrity may be spotted. In the centre is Enfield town itself, which is more of a county town than a London suburb.

Town Hall: Civic Centre, Silver Street, Enfield, Middx. EN1 3XY (☎ 0208-366 6565).

Postcodes: N9, N13, N14 (part), N21, EN1, EN2 (part), EN3, EN4 (part) and EN7 (part).

Population: Enfield's population is mostly white (only 14 per cent belong to ethnic minorities), but there's a significant Indian and Afro-Caribbean population in Enfield town.

Unemployment: Unemployment is low at just 4.9 per cent.

Crime Rate: The borough's crime rate is below average at 96 crimes per 1,000 (see page 268).

Property: There's everything from grand detached houses in the north-west to grim tower blocks in the east. But even Edmonton and Ponders End have their Victorian terraces and '30s semis. In fact terraces make up 42 per cent of properties in Enfield, flats (which are mostly purpose-built) 32 per cent, semi-detached houses 20 per cent and detached houses the remaining 5 per cent.

Costs: House prices are around the London average, similar to those of neighbouring Brent, and council taxes around average (see pages 108 and 133 respectively).

Communications: Only the west of the borough is served by the tube; the Piccadilly Line stops at Southgate and Oakwood. Otherwise there are overground rail services from Moorgate and Liverpool Street stations to most parts of the borough. Few buses make the slow journey to central London. The main A10 bisects Enfield north-south and the A406 North Circular Road cuts east-west across its southern end.

Schools: Slightly below average state schools (see page 159) are supplemented by good private and selective state schools.

Facilities: Enfield has a reasonable selection of theatres, cinemas and leisure centres as well as several parks: Trent Park Country Park in the west, Whitewebbs Park and Forty Hall Country Park in the north, and Lee Valley Park (as well as the River Lee and a chain of reservoirs) in the east. Towards the Hertfordshire border is the vast open space of Enfield Chase. Enfield has a rather unexciting choice of restaurants.

Shopping: Enfield town has good shopping and there are a number of antiques shops in Winchmore Hill. In contrast, Southgate is dull and Edmonton Green has some of the worst shops in London.

GREENWICH

Overview: Greenwich is a curious mixture of the historic and the futuristic, the grand and the derelict. Despite Greenwich town being one of London's principal tourist attractions with its Observatory, National Maritime Museum and Royal Naval College, the borough as a whole is the 11th most deprived area in England. The government is addressing the problem by spending money – most conspicuously on the Millennium Dome project and transport links to it, but also on a riverside 'revival programme' at Woolwich. An area of waste land near Deptford Creek at the extreme west of Greenwich is being developed with luxury flats, hotel, arts centre and a cruise ship terminal.

Town Hall: Wellington Street, Woolwich, London SE18 6PW (☎ 0208-854 8888).

Postcodes: SE3, SE7, SE9, SE10, SE18 and SE28 (part).

Population: Some 15 per cent of the population belong to ethnic minorities.

Unemployment: Unemployment in Greenwich is high at 13.4 per cent.

Crime Rate: Greenwich's crime rate is fairly high at 139 per 1,000 inhabitants (see page 268).

Property: Property ranges from grand Victorian and Georgian houses in Blackheath and West Greenwich, small Victorian terraces in East Greenwich, Shooters Hill and Plumstead to the east, and '60s tower blocks in Thamesmead in the north-east. Some of the cheapest properties in London are to be found among the council estates of Abbey Wood in the south. Some 42 per cent of properties in Greenwich are flats (the great majority purpose-built), 39 per cent terraced houses, 16 per cent semi-detached and just 3 per cent detached houses. Most detached houses are found in Kidbrooke (centre) and Charlton (north), the latter enjoying good views across the River Thames to Docklands.

There's a considerable amount of development taking place in Greenwich: up to 1,500 new homes are to be built in the Millennium Village on Greenwich's so-called peninsula (its north-west corner, which protrudes into a bend in the River Thames) near the Dome, and there are plans for 2,500 more along Gallions Reach to add to the recently built starter homes at Thamesmead North. Several interesting buildings in and around Woolwich are being renovated and converted into housing.

Costs: Greenwich has some of the city's cheapest property (see page 108), although average prices are similar to neighbouring Bromley, and it has the second highest council taxes (see page 133) in London (only Islington's are higher).

Communications: Greenwich is to be linked to the underground network by the Docklands Light Railway and Jubilee Line extensions. Overground train services are better in some areas than others; Thamesmead, for example, is more than two miles from a station. Bus services are little better, although there are routes across the river to the city centre and the river bus service is expected to be revived. Greenwich is at the end of the A2, the main road from northern Kent, and is bisected north-south by the A205 South Circular Road before it comes to a dead end at the river. Parking is virtually impossible around Greenwich town, particularly at weekends.

Schools: Greenwich has some of the worst performing state schools, not only in London but in the whole of England (see page 159), although there are some good private schools.

Facilities: As well as the attractions of Greenwich town (see above), the borough has many parks, woods and open spaces: Oxleas Woods in the east, Greenwich Park and Blackheath in the west, and Avery Hill near Eltham in the south-west. There are numerous leisure centres but few theatres and cinemas. The Blackheath Concert Halls do their best to rival those in Croydon and central London. Most of the best restaurants are to be found in Eltham and Greenwich town.

Shopping: Shopping facilities in Greenwich are no better than average, although there are some interesting shops in Eltham and Greenwich town.

HACKNEY

Overview: Hackney stretches from the City to Haringey and shares with neighbouring Islington such inner city problems as high unemployment and crime rates and poor schools. In response to these, the government is injecting money into Dalston, Haggerston, Hackney Wick and Hackney town itself.

Town Hall: Mare Street, London E8 1EA (☎ 0208-356 3000).

Postcodes: E5, E8, E9, EC2 (part), N1 and N16.

Population: Hackney is the country's fourth most deprived area, although it's trying to revive itself and attract artists and small businesses as well as middle-class homebuyers. Almost half of the population live in council houses, but some parts – particularly adjacent to Islington – have recently become quite trendy, particularly Stoke Newington. There's a substantial Turkish population in Hackney as well as a large orthodox Jewish community around Stamford Hill and Clapton.

Unemployment: Hackney has London's highest level of unemployment at 21.5 per cent.

Crime Rate: Hackney has one of the highest crime rates in London at 179 crimes per 1,000 population (see page 268).

Property: The borough has a good deal of council property including ugly tower blocks, some of which are due to be demolished. Some of the best property is to be found by the Regent's Canal in the south, around Victoria Park (which is actually in Tower Hamlets) to the east and in De Beauvoir Town to the west. There are some large Victorian houses around Stamford Hill to the north and Clapton to the east. Warehouses and factories are being converted into flats in Shoreditch and Hoxton in the south. Flats account for the vast majority of properties in Hackney (77 per cent) and a further 20 per cent are terraced houses. Just 2 per cent of properties are semi-detached and fewer than 0.5 per cent are detached houses, most of these in and around Stoke Newington.

Costs: There's some cheap property but average prices are surprisingly high (see page 108), as are council taxes (see page 133).

Communications: Incredibly, there's only one tube station in Hackney – Old Street on the Northern Line on the Islington boundary, but the borough does have reasonable rail links into Liverpool Street, except in the south-west corner. There's also an overground route running east-west through Dalston, Hackney and Homerton. Fortunately, bus services are good, although most roads are clogged with traffic.

Schools: Hackney is bottom of the boroughs when it comes to schools, both its primary and secondary state schools being among the worst performing in the country (see page 159). There are just a few private schools, which are run by the local Jewish community.

Facilities: Inhabitants of Hackney have access to lovely Victoria Park in Tower Hamlets and to the Regent's Canal. In Clissold Park, near Stoke Newington, there are even deer, but Hackney Marsh consists mostly of football pitches.

Varied entertainment facilities include live circus, art cinemas and the famous Hackney Empire theatre. There are also lots of art galleries and many resident artists open their studios to the public. Hackney has four leisure centres as well as other sports facilities, and the Stoke Newington West Reservoir is to be converted into a water sports centre. Stoke Newington is the place to eat out in Hackney, although there are also plenty of restaurants in Shoreditch and a number of Turkish restaurants elsewhere.

Shopping: Shopping facilities are adequate, the most interesting shops being near Victoria Park (arts and crafts), Stamford Hill (Jewish) and Stoke Newington (ethnic).

HAMMERSMITH & FULHAM

Overview: Hammersmith & Fulham started to become fashionable in the '80s and is now solidly respectable. The smarter areas – Hammersmith, Fulham, Parsons Green, Hurlingham, Sands End and the exclusive Chelsea Harbour – are in the south near the river and in the east along the border with Kensington & Chelsea. The further north you go, through Shepherds Bush towards White City and Wormwood Scrubs, the scruffier the borough becomes. In fact, these three areas are the centre of a multi-million pound government regeneration scheme.

Town Hall: King Street, London W6 9JU (☎ 0208-748 3030).

Postcodes: NW10 (part), SW6, W6, W12 and W14 (part).

Population: Despite the 'Yuppie-land' reputation of parts of the borough (particularly Fulham), Hammersmith & Fulham is the 18th most deprived area in England.

Unemployment: The unemployment rate is around the London average at 9.1 per cent.

Crime Rate: The crime rate is on the high side at 163 crimes per 1,000 population (see page 268).

Property: Hammersmith & Fulham has a similar property mix to Hackney with just 3 per cent detached and semi-detached houses, 24 per cent terraces and 72 per cent flats, almost half of which are conversions (compared with just a fifth in Hackney). West Kensington and Barons Court in the centre of the borough have mostly flats, as do Sands End in the southeast, although here the buildings are modern. Nearby Chelsea Harbour is an '80s development of exclusive flats, shops, restaurants and a five-star hotel surrounding a small marina with access to the River Thames. In the southwest around Fulham and Parsons Green are mostly Victorian terraces – those along the river at Hurlingham having distinctive terracotta facings. All this is in stark contrast to the unsightly council estate at White City in the north.

Costs: Average house prices are the fifth highest in the capital (see page 108). Hammersmith & Fulham has the sixth highest council tax rates in London, in contrast to neighbouring Kensington & Chelsea, which has the fourth lowest (see page 133).

Communications: The District, Piccadilly, Central and Hammersmith & City/Metropolitan tube lines all run through the borough, but there are virtually no overground train links (two lines run along the boundary with Kensington & Chelsea, stopping at West Brompton). Bus services are generally good, but there's invariably heavy traffic on and around the A4, which cuts across the centre of the borough. Hammersmith & Fulham contains no fewer than three major football grounds (Chelsea, Fulham and Queen's Park Rangers) as well as the Olympia Exhibition and Conference Centre, which can cause severe congestion of the transport system.

Schools: According to the government's 1998 league tables, Hammersmith & Fulham has average state secondary schools but poor primary performance (see page 159). There's a reasonable selection of private schools.

Facilities: The borough boasts several well-known theatres (Apollo Hammersmith, Lyric and Riverside Studios), but only one mainstream cinema. There isn't much in the way of museums either, although the 'museum borough', Hounslow, is next-door. There are few open spaces and the largest area, Wormwood Scrubs (adjacent to the eponymous prison), is uninteresting. By way of compensation there are attractive walks along the River Thames and three leisure centres. Fulham, Parsons Green, Hammersmith and Shepherds Bush all have a good selection of restaurants, pubs and wine bars.

Shopping: The smartest shops are along the New Kings Road in Fulham and at Chelsea Harbour. Hammersmith and Shepherds Bush have extensive but not very user-friendly shopping centres. There are six-day markets in the North End Road east of Hammersmith and in Goldhawk Road in Shepherds Bush.

HARINGEY

Overview: Haringey is less popular than its southern neighbours, Islington and Camden, and is generally considered as part of inner London. Some of

London's wealthiest citizens can be found in Highgate in the south-west and some of its poorest in Tottenham in the north-east. The government is pouring millions into new housing, shops and leisure facilities in the latter area.

Town Hall: Civic Centre, High Road, Wood Green, London N22 4LE (☎ 0208-975 9700).

Postcodes: E5, E8, E9, N4, N6 (part), N8, N10 and N16.

Population: Almost a third of the borough's inhabitants belong to ethnic minorities, with significant Afro-Caribbean, Asian, Greek and Turkish communities.

Unemployment: Unemployment is high at 13.6 per cent and, despite affluent areas such as Highgate, Haringey ranks as the 13th most deprived area in England.

Crime Rate: Haringey has an above average crime rate (see page 268) with a particularly high risk of robbery.

Property: Haringey has 52 per cent flats (almost half of which are conversions), 41 per cent terraced houses, 5 per cent semi-detached and just one per cent detached. There are some lovely Georgian residences among the mix of properties in Highgate, which is marginally less expensive than Hampstead in neighbouring Camden, and splendid Edwardian properties in Muswell Hill, Alexandra Palace and Crouch End in the west. In the north, Wood Green, Noel Park and their more up-market neighbour Hornsey offer Victorian terraces, while up-and-coming Finsbury Park in the south-east has plenty of large conversion flats. Housing in Tottenham in the north-east mostly consists of drab council estates, but Victorian and Edwardian terraces can also be found. The cheapest properties are around White Hart Lane, where Tottenham Hotspur football club has its ground.

Costs: House prices in Haringey are near the average for the whole of London, but the range is exceptionally wide (see page 108). Council taxes are the fourth highest in London (see page 133).

Communications: The Victoria and Piccadilly tube lines run through the borough, but some parts (e.g. Muswell Hill) are a good walk from a station. Two overground rail routes run north-south through the borough – one centrally, the other down the eastern side – and a third runs east-west across the southern part of the borough. There are good bus services to central London. The A1 cuts across the south-west corner of the borough and the A10 forces its way up through the east end. There's only one controlled parking area, in Wood Green.

Schools: Only Tower Hamlets and Hackney have worse performing state schools (see page 159), but there are a few private schools.

Facilities: Haringey is reasonably well provided with theatres, cinemas, museums and sports facilities and boasts the recently rebuilt Alexandra Palace exhibition centre in Alexandra Park, which provides fabulous views over London. Haringey's many other open spaces include Finsbury Park in the south, Highgate Woods in the south-west and the River Lea on the border with Waltham Forest. There's a reasonable choice of restaurants, particularly Turkish and Greek around Finsbury Park, Hornsey and Wood Green.

Shopping: There's a large mall at Wood Green and reasonable shopping in Highgate, Hornsey and Finsbury Park, but the best shops are in Muswell Hill and Crouch End. A new retail centre is planned for Tottenham, where there are several interesting Afro-Caribbean shops.

HARROW

Overview: Most people in Harrow actually believe they live in Middlesex, even although Middlesex ceased to exist in 1965 and isn't marked on any current map. Harrow is famous for its public school – which is actually in Harrow-on-the-Hill, the smartest part of the borough. Elsewhere there's dull '20s and '30s suburbia, which stretches from South Harrow in the south through Harrow town and Wealdstone to Harrow Weald in the north. Further out still, around Stanmore in the north-east and Pinner in the north-west, are more open areas.

Town Hall: Civic Centre, Station Road, Harrow, Middx. HA1 2XF (☎ 0208-863 5611).

Postcodes: HA1, HA2, HA3, HA5 (part), HA7 and HA8 (part).

Population: Harrow is 30 per cent 'ethnic', with a large Indian population and a Jewish community centred on Stanmore, although the majority of inhabitants are white-collar workers who commute into the city centre.

Unemployment: Unemployment in Harrow is low at 5.7 per cent.

Crime Rate: Harrow's crime rate is the third lowest in London (see page 268).

Property: Harrow boasts one of the highest levels of owner-occupied property in Britain. Harrow-on-the-Hill in the south-east of the borough has mostly Victorian and Edwardian properties, many converted into flats. There are some attractive modern flats to be found among the inter-war semis in and around Harrow town just to the north, and bargain buys to be had in South Harrow (south-west) and Wealdstone (centre). In the north-west, Pinner and Hatch End offer semi-detached and detached '30s Tudor-style houses as well as more modern townhouses. Stanmore to the north-east boasts some of the borough's grandest properties as well as more modest semis and detached houses. Overall, Harrow has a high proportion of semi-detached houses (39 per cent) with a further 11 per cent detached. The remainder are equally divided between flats (27 per cent) and terraced houses (23 per cent).

Costs: Harrow's has average house prices (see page 108) for London, although they vary greatly, and council tax rates are also around average (see page 133).

Communications: The Bakerloo, Jubilee and Metropolitan tube lines run through the western and eastern parts of the borough. In the centre,

Harrow and Wealdstone are linked by overground trains to London Euston as well as being on the trans-Thames route to Clapham Junction and places south, while Harrow-on-the-Hill is linked to London Marylebone. Buses are good for local journeys but won't take you into central London. There are no major roads through Harrow but plenty of traffic, and there's controlled parking in most areas.

Schools: In common with just one other London borough (Merton), Harrow has a three-tier school structure with primary, middle and high schools. Even more unusually, the high schools cater for up to 16 year-olds only and the only sixth form college in the borough is a private one for girls. Nevertheless, Harrow's schools generally perform well (see page 159). The famous Harrow School caters for boys only (boys whose parents are *very* wealthy).

Facilities: Harrow has a below average selection of theatres, cinemas, museums and galleries, just one leisure centre, although it's the largest in north London, and few golf courses. There's plenty of open space, however, with more than 50 parks including Bentley Priory Nature Reserve and woodland at Stanmore and Harrow Weald on the edge of Hertfordshire, as well as one of London's few working farms at Pinner. Good views can be had from Harrow-on-the-Hill. There's a reasonable selection of restaurants in Harrow town, Harrow-on-the-Hill and Pinner.

Shopping: The new shopping centre in Harrow town is claimed to be one of London's 'top ten'. Otherwise, Harrow-on-the-Hill and Pinner have attractive shops, but Wealdstone and Stanmore are a let-down.

HAVERING

Overview: London's easternmost borough and the only one with a border outside the M25 orbital motorway, Havering offers more space between its houses than any other borough. Havering Atte Bower in the far north is more or less in the country, and there are marshes in the south around industrial Rainham by the River Thames. The main towns are in the centre and west: Hornchurch and Upminster, which grew up around the District tube line, and Romford (on the border with Barking & Dagenham), which is Havering's commercial and administrative centre.

Town Hall: Main Road, Romford RM1 3BD (☎ 01808-772222).

Postcodes: CM14 (part), RM1, RM2, RM3, RM4 (part), RM5, RM7, RM9 (part), RM11, RM12, RM13, RM14 and RM15 (part).

Population: Havering has the lowest proportion of ethnic minorities of any London borough (a mere 3 per cent).

Unemployment: Unemployment is low at 5.2 per cent, but Havering isn't particularly affluent.

Crime Rate: The crime rate is the second lowest in London after Barnet (see page 268).

Property: Havering has the lowest percentage of flats of any borough (just 18 per cent – almost all purpose-built), 32 per cent terraces, 40 per cent semi-detached houses and 10 per cent detached. There's a mixture of Victorian and '30s terraces, converted and modern flats in Romford. Gidea Park to the east is one of London's garden suburbs, dating from the early years of the 20th century, and boasts some elegant Edwardian houses. The '50s council estate at Harold Hill in the north-east is now more than half privately owned and there are bargains to be found here. Hornchurch and Upminster offer attractive properties in a variety of styles.

Costs: Havering enjoys the third lowest average property prices in London (see page 108) but has average council tax rates (see page 133).

Communications: Elm Park, Hornchurch and Upminster are on the District tube line. Upminster is also served by overground trains into Liverpool Street and Fenchurch Street. Romford, Gidea Park and Harold Wood in the north are on the Liverpool Street Line and Rainham in the south is linked to Fenchurch Street. Elsewhere, cars are the order of the day, as few bus services reach the city centre. The A12 cuts through the northern part of the borough, the A13 through the southern part and the M25 makes a brief appearance in the east.

Schools: Havering has well performing state schools (see page 159) but no private schools.

Facilities: There are two cinemas and two leisure centres in the borough but just one theatre and no public museums or galleries. Compensation is the amount of open space, including several parks and golf courses. The attractive River Ingrebourne virtually bisects the borough from north to south. From a culinary point of view, Havering is something of a desert.

Shopping: There's nothing much in the way of shopping centres outside Romford, which isn't exactly in the premier league itself.

HILLINGDON

Overview: London's second largest borough, Hillingdon covers the whole of the western end of the capital, but for the most part it's more like the Home Counties than London, with swathes of green belt (areas in which building is restricted) and expanses of suburbia. (Like the inhabitants of Harrow and Hounslow, most Hillingdon residents think they still live in Middlesex.)

Town Hall: Civic Centre, High Street, Uxbridge UB8 1UW (☎ 01895-250111).

Postcodes: HA4, HA5 (part), HA6 (part), TW6, UB3, UB4, UB7, UB8, UB9 (part), UB10, UB11 and WD3 (part).

Population: Hillingdon is very much commuter-belt with a high proportion of white-collar workers and few non-whites.

Unemployment: Unemployment is low at 5.1 per cent.

Crime Rate: The crime rate is around average for London (see page 268).

Property: Hillingdon's smartest areas are in the north-east: Eastcote, Ruislip, Northwood and Northwood Hills. This is Metroland, so-called because it grew up around the Metropolitan Line 'underground' (although it runs mostly above ground here) and memorably satirised by poet John Betjeman. The borough becomes progressively less salubrious as you move south, through Ickenham village, Uxbridge (the borough's administrative capital) to Hillingdon, Hayes and West Drayton. But government spending is revitalising these parts, particularly Uxbridge, where a massive new shopping centre is planned. Hillingdon boasts the second-highest proportion of detached houses (14 per cent) in London. Of the remainder, 35 per cent are semi-detached and 28 per cent terraced houses, with 24 per cent flats (almost all purpose-built). Much of the property is in the '30s suburban style – if it can be called a style. Victorian terraces can be found in Uxbridge to the west and Hayes in the south-east.

Costs: Average property prices in Hillingdon are relatively low and there are inexpensive houses to be found here (see page 108). Council taxes are slightly above average for London (see page 133).

Communications: Hillingdon is well served by both underground and overground trains. The top half of the borough has three tube lines (Hammersmith & City /Metropolitan, Central and Piccadilly) as well as an overground line through Northolt Park and Ruislip. The bottom half has two train lines running into London Paddington, plus another branch of the Piccadilly tube line. Heathrow airport is also served by the non-stop link Heathrow Express from Paddington. There are no regular bus services to central London. Three major roads cut across Hillingdon from east to west – the A4 and M4 in the south and the A40 in the centre – so in theory it's a good place to escape the city from (in theory, because all three roads are often jammed with traffic). Even more convenient for escapees is Heathrow airport itself.

Schools: State primary schools perform well, secondary schools are only average according to the government's 1998 league tables (see page 159), but there are several good private schools in the north.

Facilities: Amazingly, there's only one cinema in the whole borough, but Hillingdon has a good supply of leisure centres and other sports facilities (Uxbridge even has a dry ski slope!) as well as several theatres, museums and galleries. Hillingdon is also well endowed with open space and borders the Chiltern hills to the west and Ruislip Woods, which is claimed to be the largest uninterrupted stretch of woodland in London. The Grand Union Canal, which runs across the borough between the M4 and A40 through mostly industrial areas, isn't as picturesque as it might sound.

Shopping: Uxbridge is the main shopping centre in Hillingdon, where a new shopping centre is planned, although much of it is fairly downmarket (apart from Windsor Road), as is Hayes. More interesting shops can be found in Ruislip and Northwood.

HOUNSLOW

Overview: Hounslow stretches all the way from Hammersmith & Fulham to Surrey. Like the people of Hillingdon and Harrow, most of Hounslow's inhabitants believe they live in Middlesex. Unfortunately, much of the borough lies directly under the path of planes landing at or (if the wind is from the east, as it occasionally is) taking off from Heathrow airport. Nevertheless, it has attractive areas, particularly at its eastern end (around Chiswick and Bedford Park), which borders the River Thames and boasts some of the most picturesque riverside views in London.

Town Hall: The Civic Centre, Lampton Road, Hounslow TW3 4DN (☎ 0208-862 5070).

Postcodes: W4, TW3, TW4, TW5, TW7, TW8, TW13 and TW14.

Brentford in the north-east is in line for a multi-million pound transformation from industrial site to trendy enclave, complete with luxury riverside flats, hotels, restaurants, shops and offices.

Population: Hounslow has a significant Indian population (25 per cent of the borough's residents are ethnic minorities) and is mostly a white-collar area.

Unemployment: Unemployment is low at 6.7 per cent.

Crime Rate: The crime rate in Hounslow is high – higher than that of the inner London boroughs of Lewisham and Wandsworth (see page 268).

Property: Hounslow has an even mix of property types with 33 per cent detached and semi-detached houses, 31 per cent terraces and 36 per cent flats (mostly purpose-built). Like neighbouring Hillingdon, Hounslow has more than its fair share of '30s developments, the worst of which are found around Feltham, Hanworth and Heston in the west. To the north, around Osterley Park, are more interesting properties. Chiswick in the east has Victorian and Edwardian terraces as well as Victorian semis and detached houses. The centre of Hounslow town also has Victorian terraces.

Costs: Average property prices are on the high side, while council taxes are average (see pages 108 and 133 respectively).

Communications: Only the north-east corner of the borough is served by the tube – the Piccadilly and District lines. Other parts are well served by the South West Trains network. As in many other outer London boroughs, there are no regular bus services into central London. Running east-west through much of Hounslow are the A30, the A4 and (often directly above it) the M4.

Schools: Overall, state school performance is similar to that of neighbouring Hillingdon, but Hounslow's primary schools come a lowly 82nd in the 1998 league tables compared with Hillingdon's 39th (see page 159). Some high-performance secondaries and a good choice of private schools both in Hounslow and in nearby Ealing and Richmond help redress the balance.

Facilities: Hounslow is home to several stately homes including Chiswick, Gunnersbury, Osterley Park and Syon Houses with their accompanying parks and gardens. More open space is provided by Hounslow Heath between Hounslow town and Hanworth. The borough has no shortage of leisure centres, plus two cinemas and two theatres. Chiswick is the borough's restaurant capital.

Shopping: Hounslow town is the main shopping centre with an airy indoor mall and there are attractive and unusual shops in Chiswick. Brentford and Feltham are best avoided – at least until their promised face-lifts are completed.

ISLINGTON

Overview: Until 30 years ago Islington was run-down and undesirable. Today it's one of London's most trendy boroughs – and property prices have risen in proportion. There remain very poor areas, although the council is pouring money into revitalising the worst of them.

Town Hall: Upper Street, London N1 2UD (☎ 0207-226 1234).

Postcodes: EC1, N1 (part), N5, N7 and N19.

Population: Almost 20 per cent of Islington's population belong to ethnic minorities and there's a large Italian population around Clerkenwell. It's also known for its fashionable people, particularly left-wingers.

Unemployment: Islington is the 10th most deprived area in England and unemployment is high at 14 per cent.

Crime Rate: Islington has a relatively high crime rate (see page 268).

Property: Islington has the second-lowest proportion of detached and semi-detached houses in London (less than 1.5 per cent). Some 16 per cent of properties are terraced houses, the remaining 82 per cent being flats (more than a third conversions). In the extreme south of the borough, on the City border, are converted warehouses, council blocks and Georgian terraces in Clerkenwell and Finsbury (not to be confused with Finsbury Park a few miles further north in Haringey). Highbury and Islington in the centre are the smartest areas with attractive Georgian and Victorian terraces, although property becomes less desirable the further east you go. In the north of the borough, Tufnell Park and Upper Holloway offer a mixture of council property, Victorian terraces and grander detached houses.

Costs: Islington has the sixth highest average house prices in London as well as the capital's highest council tax rates (see pages 108 and 133 respectively). Even for the cheapest house on the market you would pay over £600 a year in taxes.

Communications: Islington is poorly served by trains: the Northern (tube) Line barely touches the south-west corner of the borough and the Piccadilly Line cuts across the north-west corner only. The main railway line from the north of England into Moorgate makes just three stops in the borough. Bus services, on the other hand, are good. The A1 cuts the borough in half vertically and traffic is particularly bad around Archway. At almost £100 a year, residents' parking permits are the most expensive in London.

Schools: Islington has the worst performing state secondary schools in London (the 4th worst in the country); its primary schools aren't much better (see page 159) and there's only one private school in the borough.

Facilities: If you like open spaces, Islington isn't for you, as it has less than any other London borough. Only the Regent's Canal, which runs across the centre of the borough, and Highbury Fields in the north-east offer any escape from buildings. On the other hand, Islington is one of the best places in the capital for fringe theatre. It's also the home of Sadlers Wells, famous for opera and ballet, and the theatres and cinemas of London's West End are nearby. There are no fewer than seven leisure centres in Islington, as well as other sports facilities. There are plenty of restaurants, particularly in Clerkenwell, Holloway and Islington town, where Upper Street has almost nothing but eating places.

Shopping: Shopping facilities are generally no better than average, although Islington town has some unusual shops.

KENSINGTON & CHELSEA

Overview: More than two-thirds of Kensington & Chelsea is a conservation area and the borough boasts some of the most attractive buildings in London. Not surprisingly, they're also some of the most expensive to buy. Kensington & Chelsea is also crowded, particularly in summer when tourists flock to its museums and galleries. Colville is London's most densely populated area with 20,000 residents per square kilometre.

Town Hall: Hornton Street, London W8 7NX (☎ 0207-937 5464).

Postcodes: SW3, SW5, SW7, W8, W10, W11 and W14 (part).

Population: The population of Kensington & Chelsea is among London's most affluent, although it has its share of deprived areas. There's a smaller proportion (16 per cent) of people from ethnic minorities than anywhere else in inner London, although there's a significant Afro-Caribbean community in North Kensington and Notting Hill, scene of an annual carnival over the August Bank Holiday weekend (if you choose to live there, you'll either have to join in the fun or get out of town).

Unemployment: Unemployment is among the lowest in London at just 4 per cent.

Crime Rate: Although the official crime rate is high, figures are distorted by the influx of non-residents to the borough (see page 268).

Property: Some 84 per cent of properties in Kensington and Chelsea are flats and it's the only borough in London where the number of conversions exceeds the number of purpose-built flats. Of the remaining 16 per cent, 14 per cent are terraced houses and just 2 per cent semi-detached or detached. Elegant properties in Chelsea (south), South Kensington (centre) and Knightsbridge (east) contrast with shabby Earls Court (west) and North Kensington (north). In between, Notting Hill has become one of London's trendiest areas and property prices have risen accordingly. Earls Court is gradually being tidied up and North Kensington is the target of recent public and private investment.

Costs: Average house prices in Kensington & Chelsea are the highest anywhere outside the City, although it has one of the lowest council tax rates in London (see pages 108 and 133 respectively).

Communications: The Central, Circle, District and Piccadilly tube lines all run through the borough. Only Chelsea is a long way from a tube stop. Kensington/Olympia is also served by an overground rail route between Clapham Junction to the south and Willesden Junction to the north as well as by a second trans-Thames line linking the north and south of England. Bus connections to the city centre are good and both the A4 and M40 Westway run east-west through the borough. Parking, however, can be a problem, even outside your own home.

Schools: Kensington & Chelsea has reasonably well performing state schools (see page 159) and a good selection of private secondary schools.

Facilities: If Westminster is London's 'theatreland', Kensington & Chelsea is its 'museumland'. The Science Museum, Natural History Museum and Victoria & Albert Museum are all crowded into a small area between Earls Court and Knightsbridge. There are also plenty of cinemas, although fewer theatres and leisure centres. Open space includes Kensington Gardens and Holland Park as well as numerous 'garden squares', to which access is usually for residents only. If there isn't a restaurant to suit you in Kensington & Chelsea, you're extremely hard to please.

Shopping: Kensington & Chelsea is also something of a shoppers' paradise, having the Kings Road, Kensington High Street and the Portobello Road within its boundaries, plus many interesting shops in Notting Hill and along the Fulham and Old Brompton Roads.

KINGSTON-UPON-THAMES

Overview: The borough of Kingston protrudes deep into Surrey along its southern border. Indeed to most people, Kingston is in Surrey rather than in London. Kingston town in the north-west dominates the borough. Once an attractive market town, Kingston has been developed almost out of recognition – and more developments are planned.

Town Hall: Royal Borough of Kingston, Guildhall, High Street, Kinston-upon-Thames, Surrey KT1 1EU (☎ 0208-547 5757).

Postcodes: KT1, KT2, KT3, KT5, KT6 and KT9.

Population: Kingston is inhabited mostly by middle-class, white-collar workers and just 10 per cent of the population belongs to ethnic minority groups. The largest of these is Indian and there's a significant Korean population around New Malden.

Unemployment: Kingston has among the lowest unemployment rate in London at around 3 per cent.

Crime Rate: The crime rate in Kingston is lower than the London average (see page 268).

Property: Kingston has the third highest proportion of detached houses in London (13 per cent). A further 32 per cent are semi-detached, 21 per cent terraced and 34 per cent flats. The northern half of the borough is mostly a mass of '30s housing, with some Victorian and Edwardian properties by way of contrast. South of the A3 the housing thins out into fields as London gives way to Surrey. The most attractive properties are found in the north-east around Coombe, where large detached houses predominate. The least attractive areas are Tolworth and Chessington in the south.

Costs: Average house prices in Kingston are around the London average, while council tax rates are below average (see pages 108 and 133 respectively).

Communications: No tube lines reach as far as Kingston, but the borough is reasonably well served by the overground rail network, linking the south and south-west of England with London Waterloo. The A3 cuts across the middle of the borough on its way to Portsmouth on the south coast. As with most outer London boroughs, bus routes stop short of the city centre, although services are good within Kingston itself and there are coach links with both Heathrow and Gatwick airports.

Schools: Outside the City, Kingston has the best performing state schools in London – in fact the third best secondary schools in the country (see page 159), which inevitably means strong competition for places. There's also a good choice of private schools.

Facilities: There's a fair amount of open space, particularly in the south, but the most attractive parks – Richmond, Bushy, Hampton Court and Wimbledon Common – are in neighbouring boroughs. Kingston is also poorly served with entertainment facilities, having just one cinema and no theatres (although there are plans to build one in Kingston town). By way of compensation there are four leisure centres and Chessington World of Adventures – Surrey's answer to Disneyland. Kingston town is the best place for eating out, although for the adventurous there are one or two Korean restaurants in New Malden.

Shopping: Kingston town is a Mecca for shoppers with its unique Bentalls department store and centre, plus branches of most leading chains. Elsewhere in the borough shopping facilities are more run-of-the-mill.

LAMBETH

Overview: Lambeth is in the process of recovering from years of inefficient local government, and an ongoing regeneration programme has so far been only partially successful. Scene of rioting in 1981, Brixton (in the centre of the borough) is well on the way to becoming one of the newly trendy areas of London, joining neighbouring Clapham to the west. Nearby Stockwell Park and Tulse Hill in the east are doing their best to catch up.

Town Hall: Brixton Hill, London SW2 1RW (☎ 0208-547 5757).

Postcodes: SE11, SE24 (part), SE27, SW1 (part), SW2, SW4, SW8 (part), SW9 and SW16 (part).

Population: Almost a third of its inhabitants belongs to ethnic minorities, with a large Afro-Caribbean population centred on Brixton and a substantial Portuguese community in Stockwell and Vauxhall.

Unemployment: The 12th most deprived area in England, Lambeth has a high level of unemployment at 14.8 per cent.

Crime Rate: Lambeth has a poor crime record with 180 crimes per 1,000 population annually, including the highest rate of burglaries and the second worst rate of violent crimes and robberies in the capital (see page 268).

Property: Some 70 per cent of properties in Lambeth are flats (22 per cent conversions), 22 per cent are terraces, 6 per cent semi-detached and 1 per cent detached houses. The few properties along the River Thames in the north enjoy views of the Houses of Parliament. Most of the properties in Kennington in the north-east (where ex-council flats are to be found), Stockwell in the north-west, Brixton and Clapham are Victorian. Clapham – Lambeth's most expensive area – also boasts attractive Georgian houses. There are more Victorian terraces in West Norwood and Gipsy Hill in the south-east and typical '30s semis around Streatham in the south.

Costs: There are some cheap properties in Lambeth, although overall prices (see page 108) are average for London. Council tax rates are below average (see page 133).

Communications: Only the north and west of the borough are served by the underground (Northern and Victoria lines). Other parts can be reached by various overground services: Brixton, Denmark Hill, Streatham, Tulse Hill and Norwood by services out of Victoria; Vauxhall and Clapham from Waterloo (which is in the far north-east of the borough). Clapham is also linked to Willesden Junction north of the River Thames, while Streatham and Tulse Hill are on the trans-Thames line running through Blackfriars to the north. (Note that Clapham Junction station is in neighbouring Wandsworth.) Bus services are generally good, but roads are busy, particularly around Clapham (where the A3 Portsmouth road meets the A205 South Circular) and Vauxhall in the north-west.

Schools: Lambeth's schools are fairly well down in the government's league tables, particularly for secondary education (see page 159). There are no private primary schools and only one private secondary school.

Facilities: Lambeth is home to London's largest arts complex, now called the South Bank Centre, comprising three concert halls, three theatres, a gallery, the National Film Theatre and the Museum of the Moving Image. As if that weren't enough, there are cinemas in Waterloo, Clapham, Brixton and Streatham, the Imperial War Museum, the Old and Young Vic theatres, four leisure centres, four swimming pools, an ice rink and the Oval cricket ground. On the other hand, a few small parks (Kennington Park, Brockwell Park and Streatham Common) are the best Lambeth can offer in the way of open spaces, although West Norwood and Gipsy Hill in the south-east enjoy superb views. Clapham is the best place for eating out, although the area around Waterloo station and the South Bank is improving.

Shopping: Shopping in the borough is generally unexciting. The biggest choice of and the most unusual shops are to be found in Brixton.

LEWISHAM

Overview: Like Lambeth, Lewisham has only a short stretch of River Thames frontage, along its northern boundary. Many parts of the borough are somewhat down-at-heel, but it does have smart areas, particularly Blackheath in the north-east, and its worst parts (Deptford and Lewisham town centre) are being regenerated thanks to government money.

Town Hall: Catford Road, London SE6 4RU (☎ 0208-695 6000).

Postcodes: SE4, SE6, SE8, SE12 (part), SE13, SE14, SE23, SE26 and BR1 (part).

Population: Just under 25 per cent of Lewisham's population belongs to ethnic minorities, the largest being Afro-Caribbean (around Deptford and Lewisham) and Turkish.

Unemployment: The unemployment rate is above the London average at 11.6 per cent and Lewisham is the 14th most deprived area in England, although there are affluent areas, in particular Blackheath and parts of Lee near the Greenwich border.

Crime Rate: Lewisham's crime rate is neither high nor particularly low for London (see page 268).

Property: Just 2 per cent of properties in Lewisham are detached houses, 9 per cent semi-detached, 37 per cent terraced and 52 per cent flats (a third conversions). Deptford, by the river, was once an industrial area and is overshadowed by ugly '60s tower blocks. However, there are inexpensive ex-council properties to be had as well as some attractive Victorian houses. Large (and affordable) Victorian properties are also to be found in Brockley, New Cross and Lewisham town just to the south, as well as around Forest Hill and Sydenham in the south-west corner of the borough. In the centre, Catford and Hither Green offer more modest Victorian and Edwardian terraces. By the time you reach Grove Park in the south-east, these have given way to the ubiquitous '30s semis of outer London.

Costs: Average house prices (see page 108) are low in Lewisham, although the range of prices is greater than almost anywhere else in the capital. Council taxes are average (see page 133).

Communications: The tube barely stretches into Lewisham, the East London Line reaching only as far south as New Cross, but the Docklands Light Railway is to be extended to Lewisham town in time for 'the Millennium' (year 2000). The rest of the borough is served by overground trains only; a line running north-south through the extreme west of the borough links Sydenham, Forest Hill and Honor Oak Park to London Bridge and Charing Cross stations. A few buses reach into the city centre, while others link the borough with neighbouring Bromley. Lewisham is criss-crossed by main roads: the A2 and A20 roads linking central London with Kent converge in the northern part of Lewisham, the A205 South Circular Road cuts across the southern part of the borough and the A21 splits it from north to south.

Schools: State school performance is generally poor (see page 159), although there are a few private schools to choose from.

Facilities: Lewisham can boast at least 40 parks and gardens, although all except Blackheath are small; there are fine views to be had from the hills leading to Crystal Palace in the south-west corner of the borough. The borough has only one cinema and one museum, but boasts four leisure centres and several theatres. The widest selection of restaurants is found in Deptford and Blackheath.

Shopping: In theory, Lewisham town is the best place for shopping, but there are more interesting shops in Deptford and Blackheath,

MERTON

Overview: Unusually, Merton's most sought-after areas (and most of its open spaces) are in the north of the borough, nearest central London. This is Wimbledon, famous for its annual tennis tournament in late June/early July. Wimbledon Village is the smartest part, but Merton Park to the south is also attractive.

Town Hall: Civic Centre, London Road, Morden, Surrey SM4 5DX (☎ 0208-543 2222).

Postcodes: SW19 (part), SW20, CR4 and SM4.

Population: Some 16 per cent of the population belongs to an ethnic minority, mostly Indian or Afro-Caribbean.

Unemployment: Unemployment is low at 6.6 per cent.

Crime Rate: Merton has a similar crime rate to neighbouring Kingston at 96 per 1,000 population per year (see page 268).

Property: Merton has 4 per cent detached houses, 13 per cent semi-detached, 48 per cent terraced and 34 per cent flats. Wimbledon and South Wimbledon in the northern part of the borough are mainly Victorian. Raynes Park in the south-west offers Edwardian terraces, while Morden in the south is mostly '30s semis with some inexpensive houses on the St Helier Estate.

Costs: There's a huge range of house prices in Merton (a small flat can cost anything from £60,000 to £400,000 depending on the area) and average prices are on the high side, as are council tax rates (see 108 pages 133 and respectively).

Communications: Surprisingly, two tube lines reach right down into Merton – the District line, which terminates at Wimbledon in the west of the borough, and the Northern line, ending at Morden in the south. Wimbledon and Raynes Park are also on an overground line into Waterloo, while other parts of Merton are served by trains that run via Blackfriars and northwards as far as Yorkshire. The new Tramlink line, due to be completed in 2000, will connect Wimbledon, Merton, Morden and Mitcham with Croydon and the western part of Bromley. The A24 is the only major road, cutting through Merton on its way to Surrey.

Schools: Merton is one of only two London boroughs (Harrow is the other) that have a three-tier state system instead of the usual primary/secondary structure. Its state schools' performance is below average (see page 159) but there are some good private schools and the best selection of nurseries, both state and private, in London.

Facilities: Most of Wimbledon Common is within the borough of Merton, as are Wimbledon Park, Merton Park and Mitcham Common, and there are pleasant walks along the river Wandle. Merton has a reasonable selection of theatres, concert venues, museums and leisure centres, but only one cinema. Restaurants are rather thin on the ground everywhere except for Wimbledon Village, the 'in' place to eat out in Merton.

Shopping: Outside Wimbledon, which has an attractive and up-market retail centre, shopping in Merton is a pretty unexciting experience.

NEWHAM

Overview: Newham has the dubious distinction of being the second most deprived area in England and the most deprived in London, although the government is spending millions on Stratford and Canning Town – chiefly in relation to the Jubilee Line extension – and Newham as a whole claims to be 'London's fastest improving borough'. The south of the borough, along the River Thames, contains the largest of the old London docks, which have not yet been redeveloped to the extent of the smaller docks in neighbouring Tower Hamlets..

Town Hall: East Ham, London E6 2RP (☎ 0208-557 8759).

Postcodes: E3 (part), E6, E7, E13, E15 and E16.

Population: Newham has a higher proportion (nearly 50 per cent) of inhabitants from ethnic minorities than almost anywhere else in London, with particularly large Afro-Caribbean and Asian populations.

Unemployment: Unemployment is high at 15.3 per cent.

Crime Rate: The crime rate is high, even for London (see page 268).

Property: Newham has the second highest proportion of terraced houses in London (57 per cent), with 39 per cent flats, 3 per cent semi-detached and just 1 per cent detached houses. There's some unusual Victorian property between the docks and the river and new housing is being built around Beckton just to the north of the docks. Otherwise, it's rather a dull borough architecturally, with long rows of late 19th century/early 20th century terraces. Larger Victorian houses can be found in East Ham in the centre of the borough and Stratford in the north-west, as well as around Forest Gate in the north – probably the best part of Newham. There are plans to build 1,000 new homes at Silvertown by the river.

Costs: Newham has the second lowest average house prices in the capital (after Barking & Dagenham), although council tax rates are around the London average (see pages 108 and 133 respectively).

Communications: Unlikely as it may seem, Newham can boast an international airport – London City Airport, whose runway occupies a strip of land between two huge docks. The top part of the borough is served by the Hammersmith & City/Metropolitan and District lines, the lower part by the Docklands Light Railway (DLR) and the eastern end of the Jubilee Line (due to be joined with the western end in time for 'the Millennium'). Two overground lines run through Newham from east to west: one crossing the top of the borough en route to Liverpool Street station, the other running into Fenchurch Street station but stopping at West Ham only. A third overground service links London City Airport with Richmond via north London. A few bus services connect with central London. The main road through the borough is the A13, which cuts across it east to west.

Schools: Newham's state primary schools are just one from the bottom of the government's 1998 league tables; its secondary schools perform a little better, but are still poor compared with those of neighbouring Waltham Forest and particularly Redbridge (see page 159).

Facilities: Newham has little open space, its few parks tending to be small, although there are walks along the River Lea and Bow Creek in the west. The regeneration of Stratford is to provide the town with a theatre and cinema; otherwise there are few cultural facilities in the borough. On the other hand, there are unusually good sporting facilities, including three leisure centres (and a fourth scheduled for East Ham), water sports in the Royal Docks and a dry ski slope at Beckton.

Shopping: Newham isn't a known for its shopping, although Green Street in Stratford is good for Asian food and wares (particularly Indian) and there are some good street markets.

REDBRIDGE

Overview: Redbridge is neither deprived nor particularly affluent, although it has plenty of smart areas. Generally, the eastern part of the borough is more working class and the west more middle class, with particularly well-to-do areas around Woodford and Wanstead. Although there's a town of Redbridge, the borough's 'capital' is Ilford in the south (curiously, IG postcodes derive from it), the borough taking its name from the brick bridge linking Ilford with Wanstead and Woodford.

Town Hall: High Road, Ilford IG1 1DD (☎ 0208-478 3020).

Postcodes: E11 (part), E18, IG1, IG2, IG3, IG4, IG5, IG6, IG7, IG8, IG18 and RM6 (part).

Population: More than 20 per cent of Redbridge's inhabitants belong to ethnic minorities, with a substantial Asian population, particularly in the east. There's also a considerable Jewish community in and around Gants Hill in the centre.

Unemployment: Unemployment is just above the London average at 10.5 per cent.

Crime Rate: The crime rate in Redbridge is among the lowest in London (see page 268).

Property: Property in Redbridge consists of 4 per cent detached houses, 22 per cent semi-detached, 48 per cent terraces and 26 per cent flats (a quarter conversions). In the south around Ilford there are mainly Victorian and Edwardian terraces, as in shabby Goodmayes and Seven Kings to the east (where there are nevertheless bargains to be found). Further north, around Gants Hill and Clayhall, are the usual '30s suburban semis, while the Hainault area in the north-east consists mainly of council estates (where good buys can also be had). The west boasts larger, semi-detached and detached properties.

Costs: Redbridge has fairly low average house prices and average council tax rates (see pages 108 and 133 respectively).

Communications: Redbridge is served by the Central tube line, which reaches as far as Epping in Essex. The only overground service runs across the south of the borough, through Ilford and Goodmayes, linking them with London's Liverpool Street station. A few buses go as far as the city centre. The M11 (Redbridge's main escape route to the country) encroaches on the north-west corner of the borough. Other main roads are the A12, which cuts the borough in half from west to east, and the A406 North Circular in the west and south-west. Most of Redbridge still has 'permit free' parking.

Schools: Redbridge's state secondary schools (including two grammar schools) rank 5th in London and 10th in England according to the government's 1998 league tables; its primary schools, on the other hand, are only just in the top third in the country (see page 159). There's also a good selection of private schools.

Facilities: There are three leisure centres, two cinemas and a theatre in the borough, but no museums or galleries. Known as the 'leafy suburb', Redbridge has plenty of open space (a third of the borough is Green Belt land), particularly in the north-east, where Hainault Forest offers wildlife and good views. Nearby are two golf courses and riding facilities as well as water sports on Fairlop Water. The choice of restaurants is rather limited.

Shopping: The main shopping centre is Ilford, although there are interesting shops in Woodford Green and Wanstead.

RICHMOND-UPON-THAMES

Overview: Richmond is the only borough that's divided by the River Thames. One of London's greenest boroughs, it includes Hampton Court Park, Bushy Park, Old Deer Park, Kew Gardens and Richmond Park (the capital's largest, complete with herds of deer). Like neighbouring Hounslow, however, northern parts of Richmond suffer from the continual drone of aircraft landing at Heathrow.

Town Hall: Civic Centre, York Street, Twickenham TW1 3BZ (☎ 0208-891 1441).

Postcodes: SW14, KT8, TW1, TW2, TW10, TW11 and TW12.

Population: Just 3 per cent of the population belongs to ethnic minorities in this largely white and white-collar borough.

Unemployment: Richmond is one of London's most affluent boroughs with low unemployment of 6.5 per cent.

Crime Rate: Richmond enjoys one of the lowest crime rates in London (see page 268).

Property: The mix of properties in Richmond is close to the outer London average, with 8 per cent detached houses, 23 per cent semi-detached, 31 per cent terraces and 38 per cent flats. A high proportion of buildings are Victorian, from Castlenau and Barnes in the north-east corner, past East Sheen and Richmond Hill (the borough's most desirable area) and across the river to Hampton Wick and Teddington. There are also many attractive Georgian properties; the inevitable '30s semis don't start until Hampton and Whitton (the cheapest part of Richmond) in the extreme south-west. Kew in the far north offers everything from turn-of-the-century to contemporary.

Costs: Richmond has both high property prices and high council tax rates (see pages 108 and 133 respectively).

Communications: As far as trains are concerned, Richmond is best served by the overground network. Richmond town itself is also at the end of both the rail route to the East End via north London and the District tube line. There are no bus services to the centre of London, but it's possible to get to Westminster by boat. The A205 South Circular Road cuts across the north-east part of the borough and the A316 (the extension of the M3) runs across the top to join it. Several parts of the borough have controlled parking.

Schools: Richmond has some of the country's best performing state primary schools, although its secondary schools are generally less outstanding (see page 159).

Facilities: Richmond is richly endowed with parks (see above) and historic houses (most notably Hampton Court Palace on the Surrey border), while Kew Gardens in the north-west incorporate the famous Royal Botanical Gardens. The borough also has three leisure centres and other sports facilities, including several golf courses, and there are three cinemas and two theatres in Richmond town.

Shopping: Richmond has many interesting small shopping centres and plenty of restaurants (and Kingston is nearby).

SOUTHWARK

Overview: Southwark is a borough of contrasts: in the north-east, the once industrial areas of Bermondsey and Rotherhithe are being rediscovered; in the west, formerly run-down Camberwell is fast becoming the borough's answer to Brixton and Notting Hill; in the centre, Peckham's grim tower blocks are being pulled down as part of a multi-million pound face-lift; and in the south there's the ultra-smart village of Dulwich.

Town Hall: Peckham Road, London SE5 8UB (☎ 0207-525 5000).

Postcodes: SE1, SE5, SE15, SE16, SE17, SE21, SE22 and SE24 (part).

Population: A quarter of Southwark's population belongs to ethnic minority groups, the largest being Afro-Caribbean, Turkish and Vietnamese.

Unemployment: The 8th most deprived area in England, Southwark has a high level of unemployment at 16.8 per cent.

Crime Rate: In terms of crimes per resident, Southwark has the worst record of all the London boroughs. According to Metropolitan Police statistics you're more than twice as likely to be the victim of crime in Southwark as in neighbouring Bromley (see page 268).

Property: Some 76 per cent of properties in Southwark are flats and a further 19 per cent terraced houses, with just 4 per cent semi-detached and 1 per cent detached houses. Bermondsey in the north consists mostly of council estates, but former warehouses are gradually being converted into flats (or 'lofts', as they are known). New houses are to be found in Rotherhithe in the north-east, while The Borough in the north-west and The Elephant & Castle, Camberwell, Peckham and Nunhead in the centre and Dulwich in the south offer Victorian, Edwardian and Georgian properties – varying enormously in price!

Costs: Southwark's average house prices are significantly lower than other inner city areas but council tax rates are relatively high (see pages 108 and 133 respectively).

Communications: Only the northern part of Southwark is served by the tube network, the Bakerloo and Northern lines reaching The Elephant & Castle and the Jubilee Line extension due to stop at Bermondsey. On the other hand, overground trains run from various parts of the borough into London Bridge, Blackfriars and Charing Cross. Bus services into central London are also good, although inevitably slow. The A205 South Circular passes through Dulwich, and The Elephant & Castle is effectively a huge roundabout.

Schooling: Southwark is the fourth worst London borough in terms of the overall performance of its state schools, according to the government's 1998 league tables (see page 159), but there are plenty of private schools to choose from.

Facilities: Government and Lottery money is allowing Southwark to regenerate its stretch of River Thames frontage with the reconstruction of the Globe theatre, a modern art gallery in the old Bankside power station and a new footbridge across the river. Elsewhere, there are two mainstream cinemas, five leisure centres and numerous museums and galleries (including the world's first wine museum!). Most of Southwark's open space is in the south, in and around Dulwich, although there are a few parks and gardens in the north. There's a variety of restaurants in Southwark, particularly in Dulwich and East Dulwich.

Shopping: Southwark's main shopping centre is the rather unsightly complex at The Elephant & Castle. Elsewhere, shopping facilities are mostly uninspiring.

SUTTON

Overview: Sutton calls itself the 'greener, cleaner borough' and is one of London's most affluent boroughs, having more in common with neighbouring Surrey than London 'proper'. The smartest areas are Carshalton Beeches (centre), North Cheam (north-west), South Sutton town (west) and Belmont (south-west). Cheaper parts include St Helier in the north and Beddington in the east.

Town Hall: Civic Offices, St Nicholas Way, Sutton, Surrey SM1 1EA (☎ 0208-770 5000).

Postcodes: CR0 (part), CR4, KT4, SM1, SM2 (part), SM3, SM5 and SM6.

Population: Just 6 per cent of Sutton's inhabitants belong to ethnic minorities and most of the population is well-to-do.

Unemployment: Unemployment is the lowest in London at below 3 per cent.

Crime Rate: Sutton has one of the lowest crime rates in the capital (see page 268).

Property: Sutton has 11 per cent detached houses, 27 per cent semi-detached, 29 per cent terraces and 33 per cent flats (the great majority purpose-built). Properties built in the '20s and '30s predominate the further south you go, although there are some Victorian and Edwardian houses in Sutton town as well as on a large council estate in St Helier to the north, where bargains can be found. Victorian terraces can also be found in Wallington and Beddington to the east and in the 'village' of Carshalton in the centre. Here and in North Cheam there are some 16th century properties, while Beddington and Sutton town offer modern homes.

Costs: Somewhat surprisingly, average property prices in Sutton are relatively low – similar to neighbouring Croydon – but council tax rates are on the high side (see pages 108 and 133 respectively).

Communications: Sutton is beyond the reach of the tube network, but has good overground rail services. Buses will take you to the shopping centres of Kingston or Croydon but not to central London. Main roads include the A24 and A217, both running north-south, and traffic generally – as in most parts of London – is slow.

Schools: After Kingston, Sutton has the best performing state secondary schools in London (the fourth best in England), although the highest performers are selective schools; its primary schools, on the other hand, aren't even in the top third in the country (see page 159). There are also a fair number of private schools.

Facilities: Sutton's leisure facilities are limited to one cinema, two theatres, two leisure centres and a smattering of historic houses. But, as you might expect, there's plenty of open space including Beddington Park in the east and Cheam Park in the west, the latter adjoining Nonsuch Park just across the Surrey border. Croydon, Cheam and Carshalton are the best bet for eating out.

Shopping: The borough's main shopping centre is Sutton town, although it offers little competition to nearby Croydon. There are also some attractive shops in Cheam and Carshalton.

TOWER HAMLETS

Overview: Taking its name from the historical association between the Tower of Londothe riverside hamlets that once surrounded it, Tower Hamlets claims to be 'the fastest-changing place in Britain'. Financial and media businesses are moving there from the City, the Jubilee Line extension is to link the East End to the West End, and the Spitalfields area (traditionally the centre of London's wholesale clothing industry) is fast establishing itself as an artistic quarter. It's estimated that 50,000 new jobs will be created within the borough by the year 2005. At the centre of this transformation is Docklands, previously an area of disused docks and derelict warehouses and now a thriving business centre.

Town Hall: Tower Hamlets has no central town hall. Contact the Information Centre, 18 Lamb Street, Spitalfields market, London E1 6EA (☎ 0207-364 4970).

Postcodes: E1, E2, E3 (part) and E14.

Population: Once the home of intrepid seafarers such as Walter Raleigh and Captain Cook, Tower Hamlets is now home to the UK's largest Bangladeshi community – almost 25 per cent of its inhabitants – as well as Vietnamese and Somali refugees.

Unemployment: The population as a whole is said to have the highest average salary in the UK, yet unemployment is among the highest in London at 19.7 per cent and the borough ranks as the sixth most deprived area in England and the third highest in London.

Crime Rate: Tower Hamlets has one of the highest crime rates in London (see page 268).

Property: Tower Hamlets has the smallest proportion of detached and semi-detached houses outside the City of London (1 per cent). Some 14 per cent of properties are terraces and the remaining 85 per cent flats (almost all purpose-built), many council owned. This means that there are bargain ex-council properties to be found, particularly in Spitalfields and Whitechapel in the west and in Bethnal Green in the north-west. Stepney in the centre of the borough is almost all council property and there are some particularly unsightly council blocks in Bromley (not to be confused with Bromley town in the borough of Bromley) and Poplar in the east. In the north-east, Bow offers attractive Victorian and Georgian houses and the Spitalfields/ Whitechapel area is spawning 'loft' conversions, which are already prevalent in Wapping and Limehouse in the south-west. Here and on the Isle of Dogs (not an island at all, merely a bend in the river) construction is still going on so it can be rather like living on a building site.

Costs: Tower Hamlets has surprisingly high average property prices and average council tax rates (see pages 108 and 133 respectively).

Communications: Tower Hamlets has some of the best rail connections of any London borough. No fewer than five tube lines (Central, District, Hammersmith & City/Metropolitan, East London and the Docklands Light Railway) run in various directions through the borough. By the year 2000 the Jubilee Line extension will make a sixth. The overground line from Fenchurch Street station to parts of Essex also crosses the borough, and the service from Liverpool Street station to Cambridge cuts across its north-west corner. Bus services are better in the north than the south but Tower Hamlets is no place for car owners; there's nowhere to park without paying, even outside your own house.

Schools: Only Hackney has worse performing state schools than Tower Hamlets, according to the government's 1998 league tables (see page 159), although nowhere in London offers more state nurseries for the under fives.

Facilities: Good sports facilities (including five leisure centres) compensate for a shortage of cinemas (none) and theatres (one). The London Arena on the Isle of Dogs hosts pop concerts as well as exhibitions, and the capital's top tourist attraction, the Tower of London, is just within the borough's boundary (in the extreme west). Apart from Victoria Park in the north-east, Tower Hamlets has little green space to offer. What it does have in abundance is water – not only the River Thames, but the River Lea, the Regent's and Hertford Union Canals and, of course, the old docks. Tower Hamlets isn't noted for its restaurants, with the exception of some good ethnic eating places.

Shopping: Tower Hamlets' shopping facilities are rather patchy, but it has colourful markets such as Brick Lane (Shoreditch), Roman Road (Bow) and the famous Petticoat Lane (actually in Middlesex Street on the border with the City).

WALTHAM FOREST

Overview: Waltham Forest is one of London's 'in-between' boroughs – neither affluent nor impoverished, neither fashionable nor conservative – but it has its attractions nevertheless, not least historic Epping Forest. Its administrative and geographical centre is Walthamstow, to the south of which are the former working class areas of Leyton and Leytonstone, and to the north the smart suburb of Highams Park. Standard outer London suburbia takes over in the far north around Chingford before the border with Essex.

Town Hall: Forest Road, Walthamstow E17 4JF (☎ 0208-527 5544).

Postcodes: E4, E10, E11 (part) and E17.

Population: Unusually for an outer London borough, Waltham Forest has a high proportion (almost 25 per cent) of residents belonging to ethnic minorities, particularly Afro-Caribbean and Pakistani.

Unemployment: Unemployment is above the London average at 10.6 per cent.

Crime Rate: The official crime rate in Waltham Forest is about average for London at 115 crimes per 1,000 population annually (see page 268).

Property: Around 48 per cent of properties are terraced houses, 11 per cent semi-detached and 2 per cent detached. The remaining 39 per cent are flats. Leyton and Leytonstone in the south are mainly Victorian terraces, as is Walthamstow itself, where conversion flats are also plentiful. In the north are the inevitable '30s semis of Chingford, mixed with some more attractive Victorian and Edwardian properties. A similar combination is found in Highams Park, which is nevertheless the borough's most sought-after area.

Costs: Waltham Forest offers some of the cheapest property in London, but its council tax rates are among the highest in the capital (see pages 108 and 133 respectively).

Communications: Tube services are limited here. The Central Line serves only Leyton and Leytonstone in the south, and the Victoria Line terminates at Walthamstow. The Barking to Richmond overground line also passes through Leyton and Walthamstow, northern parts of the borough only being reached by a line from Liverpool Street terminating at Chingford. The M11, which currently peters out in neighbouring Redbridge, is being extended south-west through Waltham Forest and into Hackney. Other major roads through the borough include the A406 North Circular, which cuts across the centre, and the A11/A12 in the south-east corner. Residents' parking permits are in force in Walthamstow and Chingford.

Schools: The government's 1998 league tables put Waltham Forest firmly in the bottom third of the league in terms of the overall performance of its state schools, although secondary schools do marginally better than primary (see page 159). There are a few private schools.

Facilities: There's just one cinema in the borough, but live entertainment can be had at the Waltham Forest theatre and the Walthamstow Assembly Hall and there are four leisure centres to choose from. Lloyd Park near

Walthamstow is home to the William Morris Gallery but is otherwise uninspiring. The most attractive open space is what's left of Epping Forest in the east, the opposite side of the borough offering expanses of water in the shape of a chain of reservoirs. Apart from a few unusual restaurants, eating out is uninspiring.

Shopping: Walthamstow is the borough's shopping centre with a new complex planned and a daily High Street market that claims to be the longest in Europe. Elsewhere shopping facilities are at best adequate.

WANDSWORTH

Overview: Wandsworth is one of the most 'upwardly mobile' of London's boroughs; once working class Battersea – where the council has spent millions on regeneration and developers have moved in – has recently become a trendy place to live.

Town Hall: Wandsworth High Street, London SW18 2PU (☎ 0208-871 7660).

Postcodes: SW8 (part), SW11, SW12, SW15, SW17, SW18 and SW19 (part).

Population: Wandsworth has an increasingly middle-class population with a relatively large ethnic community.

Unemployment: The unemployment rate is below average at 7.2 per cent.

Crime Rate: Wandsworth's crime rate is slightly worse than average for London (see page 268).

Property: Typically for an inner London borough, Wandsworth has 2 per cent detached houses, 5 per cent semi-detached, 30 per cent terraced and 63 per cent flats (almost a third of which are conversions). Most of the detached houses are to be found in Putney in the south-west, Southfields in the centre and Wandsworth Common in the north-east, while most semis are in Tooting in the south-east, where much of the property is Edwardian (as it is in Putney and Earlsfield in the south).

Costs: Average house prices are on the high side, but Wandsworth boasts the lowest council tax rates in England, let alone London, and barely more than a third of Islington's (see pages 108 and 133 respectively).

Communications: Two tube lines run through Wandsworth: the District line, slicing north-south through the centre of the borough, and the Northern line, cutting across its south-eastern corner. Britain's busiest railway station, Clapham Junction, is also in Wandsworth, providing overground rail links not only with the whole of the south of England but with the north as well. Wandsworth isn't the best place to live for car owners as the A3 and A205 South Circular merge in an almost constant traffic jam right in the centre of the borough and parking is restricted in many areas.

Schools: Overall, the performance of Wandsworth's state schools is comparable with that of Waltham Forest's, although Wandsworth's primary schools rate higher than its secondary schools (see page 159). There's a good choice of private schools and plenty of nurseries, both state and private.

Facilities: Wandsworth is poorly supplied with entertainment facilities: one theatre, one cinema and a small museum. The borough's impressively ugly landmark, Battersea Power Station (which ceased to be used decades ago) still stands empty despite several attempts to transform it into an entertainment centre. However, Wandsworth has plenty of parks and commons including Battersea Park and Wandsworth Common in the north-east, Tooting Common in the south-east, and Putney Heath in the south-west as well as parts of Clapham and Wimbledon Commons (see Lambeth and Merton). Beautiful Richmond Park is just next door. When it comes to eating out, Wandsworth residents are spoilt for choice with umpteen ethnic restaurants in Battersea, Putney and Wandsworth town.

Shopping: Shopping facilities are improving with a new centre in Putney and another planned in Wandsworth town. Some unusual shops are also to be found in Tooting.

WESTMINSTER

Overview: The City of Westminster, as it's properly called (although it's a borough like any other), contains most of London's most frequently visited places: Buckingham Palace, the Houses of Parliament, Leicester Square, Piccadilly Circus and Trafalgar Square, to name but a few. Not surprisingly, these areas are among the most expensive in the capital, although Westminster also has less salubrious parts. These are mainly in the north-west around Paddington, where redevelopment is in the pipeline, but also (for different reasons) in Soho in the east – traditionally London's sleaze centre but also an 'in' place to live.

Town Hall: Westminster City Council, City hall, 64 Victoria Street, London SW1E 6QP (☎ 0207-641 6000).

Postcodes: NW8, SW1, W1, W2 and W9.

Population: The extreme affluence to be found in some areas is in stark contrast to the quite severe deprivation in others. Almost 25 per cent of Westminster's population belongs to ethnic minority groups, notably Afro-Caribbean and Middle Eastern. There's also a large Jewish community in the north of the borough and London's greatest concentration of Chinese in Soho.

Unemployment: The unemployment level is near the London average at 9.7 per cent.

Crime Rate: On paper, Westminster's crime rate of 384 crimes per 1,000 population annually seems appalling and is easily the highest in London (see page 268). In reality, however, the figure is highly distorted by the large number of non-residents (particularly foreign tourists) falling victim to petty crime while visiting the borough.

Property: Some 90 per cent of properties in Westminster are flats (a third conversions), leaving just 9 per cent terraces and 1 per cent each of detached and semi-detached houses. There are flats of various styles (and prices) in Soho, Covent Garden (east), Marylebone (north-east), Pimlico (south) and Westminster itself (south-east). Maida Vale (north) and St John's Wood (north-east) offer some attractive properties near the Regent's Canal, but the crème de la crème is to be found in Mayfair (centre) and in Knightsbridge and Belgravia (south-west), where Eaton Square is reputed to be London's smartest address. Apart from Paddington, the cheapest properties are in Bayswater (west) and West Kilburn (north-west).

Costs: Not surprisingly, Westminster's average property prices are among the highest in London (behind only Kensington & Chelsea and the City), surprisingly its council tax rates are the second lowest in the capital after Wandsworth (see pages 108 and 133 respectively).

Communications: Westminster is in the heart of tube-land, so getting around isn't a problem. With Paddington, Charing Cross and Victoria stations also in the borough, getting out of London (at least in a westerly or southerly direction) is also straightforward – the new Heathrow Express route out of Paddington is particularly handy for those wanting to escape the country! There are also plenty of bus routes to choose from, but not surprisingly, traffic is generally at a crawl and parking is a nightmare.

Schools: State primary schools in Westminster rate reasonably highly in the government's 1998 league tables; its secondary schools, on the other hand, are among the worst in the country (see page 159). There are, however, some good private schools.

Facilities: Westminster is home to London Zoo, Madame Tussaud's, the Planetarium, the National and National Portrait Galleries, the Tate Gallery, the Royal Opera House, the Royal Albert Hall and the Wigmore Hall, not to mention over 40 theatres and more cinemas than you can shake a stick at. London's four most famous parks – Hyde Park, Regent's Park, Green Park and St James's Park – and the most attractive reaches of the Regent's Canal are also found within the borough. As if all that weren't enough to keep its residents (and millions of visitors) entertained, Westminster has four leisure centres and the best-used libraries in the capital. As with shops, Westminster is blessed with some of London's most exclusive eating places.

Shopping: When it comes to shops, Westminster has a veritable cornucopia of facilities, including Harrods, Covent Garden, Oxford Street and Regent Street.

2.

GETTING THERE & AROUND

Getting to London from most countries is relatively easy as it's served by all the world's major airlines and by a direct rail connection from Brussels and Paris, and there's also a regular ferry service to Britain from a number of European countries. London has five international airports (City, Gatwick, Heathrow, Luton and Stanstead), which between them provide services to all major domestic and international destinations. London is the hub of air, rail and road communications in Britain and, as you would expect, has excellent connections with the rest of the country. London is also at the centre of a extensive network of motorways.

London has a comprehensive public transport system encompassing suburban trains, underground (tube) trains, buses and river ferries. Getting around London by tube and train is relatively fast and convenient, although travel by bus or car is slow due to interminable traffic jams. Although Britain killed off its trams many years ago, a number of light rail transit and supertram systems have been built in recent years (Docklands Light Railway) or are planned (Croydon Tramlink). It's also easy to get around central London by bicycle (although you'll need a smog mask!) or even on foot, particularly in the central area which is surprisingly compact. (The best way to get to know – and enjoy London – is to wander the streets at random.) However you plan to get around London, one of your first acts should be to buy a good street map, such as the excellent street plans produced by the Geographers A-Z Map Co.

Despite more people using public transport in London than in any other European city – London has the world's largest rail and tube network – it has the most expensive public transport of any capital city in Europe, with fares around four times higher than in Rome and some 15 times more expensive than Budapest. Public transport is, however, cheaper if you're able to take advantage of the wide range of discount, combination (e.g. rail, bus and underground), season and off-peak tickets available.

For the purposes of public transport, London is divided into six concentric fare zones stretching 12mi (19km) from the centre. The central area is designated zone 1, while the outer suburbs are in zone 6, and ticket prices depend on how many zones you travel through. You can buy a ticket for a single or day return trip, although a **Travelcard**, which is valid on the underground (tube), the Docklands Light Railway (DLR), buses and suburban trains, provides better value if you're planning to use public transport extensively. Travelcards offer unlimited tube travel for one day, seven days, one month or one year, and you can limit them to specific zones if your journey won't cover the whole network.

If you're travelling into London by rail, your ticket can also include a Travelcard supplement so that you can use it for onward travel on the tube and buses. If you need a Travelcard (also called a **Seasonal Travelcard**) for seven days or more or a child rate ticket for someone under 16, you will require a free **Photocard** for which you need a passport-size photograph and proof of age for children.

It isn't essential to own a car if you live in central London, where a car is a liability and parking is prohibitively expensive if you don't have a private garage. If you commute into London from one of the outer boroughs or surrounding counties it will almost certainly be faster by public transport, although you may need a car to get to your local railway or tube station. In common with most major cities, London is plagued by chronic traffic problems and most roads are permanently jammed with traffic, making travel by car slow and frustrating. Parking in central London is at best difficult (and expensive) and at worst impossible. During rush hours, from around 7.30 to 9.30am and 4.30 to 6.30pm, Mon-Fri, traffic flow is painfully slow, particularly in central London, where the average traffic speed is around 10mph (it takes as long to cross London by car as it did 200 years ago in a horse and cart!).

However, although public transport, both from a convenience and environmental point of view, is a better option than attempting to get around by car, services are often stretched to breaking point, particularly during peak hours and the summer tourist season. Most experts believe that the only long-term solution to the city's traffic problems, and that of urban Britain in general, is to impose stiff costs on people bringing cars into city centres or to 'pedestrianise' central areas completely, while simultaneously making a massive investment in public transport.

A wealth of information about public transport is published by borough councils, local transport authorities and transport companies, many of which are mentioned in the relevant section in this chapter.

ARRIVING BY AIR

London is one of the busiest air transport hubs in the world and you can fly there from practically any country. Whether you're travelling to London from Dublin, Denver or Delhi, if you travel by air you'll arrive at one of London's five international airports: Heathrow, Gatwick, Stansted, Luton and City (in order of size and passenger numbers). With the exception of the small City airport, all are situated some distance outside the city and entail a 20 to 60 minute journey into the centre.

London's Airports

Heathrow airport (☎ 0208-759 4321, 🖳 www.baa.co.uk) is located 15mi (24km) south-west of the city centre and is the world's busiest airport, handling over 60 million passengers a year. Over 90 airlines are based here, spread over its four sprawling terminals that are almost airports in their own right. Terminal 1 (mainly short-haul British Airways flights) is close to terminals 2 (European services of non-British airlines) and 3 (non-British long-haul services) in the centre of the Heathrow complex, while terminal 4 (British Airways intercontinental and Concorde flights) is a few miles further south. An application to build a fifth terminal is being considered (approval is expected late in 2000), which will take at least four years to build.

The new high-speed **Heathrow Express** rail service is by far the quickest and easiest way to get to central London. The airport has two stations, one for Terminals 1, 2 and 3 and another for Terminal 4, operating direct trains to London's Paddington station. The single fare is £10 and the journey takes around 20 minutes, with trains running every 15 minutes between 5.10am and 11.40pm. Alternatively, you can take the cheaper (and slower – 50 to 60 minutes to Piccadilly Circus) **underground** into central London for £3.30 (£1.60 for under 16s); trains run between 5.30am and 11.30pm. Information is available from London Transport Travel Centres at Heathrow's tube stations. There's also an **Airbus Heathrow Shuttle** service (☎ 0207-222 1234) operating every 15 minutes between 5am and 10.30pm to 23 central London destinations (the journey time is 60 to 80 minutes and tickets cost £6, or £3 for under 15s).

The journey by taxi costs upwards of £35 and the journey time is from 45 minutes to well over an hour, depending on the traffic congestion. You can book a cheaper minicab in advance from a company such as **Airport Transfers** (☎ 0207-403 2228), which serves all London's airports, or book the **Airbus Hotel Shuttle** (☎ 0208-400 6656, ☐ book@airbus.co.uk) which will pick you up in a minibus and ferry you to the door of any central London hotel for £12. If you arrive in the dead of night you can catch the hourly **night bus** (N97) to Trafalgar Square; a leisurely trip of around 75 minutes and a bargain at just £1.50 for a single fare.

Gatwick airport (☎ 01293-535353, ☐ www.baa.co.uk) is situated 30mi (50km) to the south of London and is the capital's second-largest airport, operating two terminals (North and South) linked by a monorail service. International flights are handled by both terminals, while most domestic flights are serviced by the South terminal only. Exceptions include British Airways flights to and from Aberdeen, Edinburgh, Glasgow and Manchester, and Brymon Airways flights to and from Newquay and Plymouth, which operate from the North terminal.

Gatwick Express (☎ 0990-301530, ☐ www.gatwickexpress.co.uk) operates a 24-hour train service between the airport's South terminal and Victoria station in central London (trains run every 15 minutes during the day and evening, and every hour between 1.45am and 4.35am). The journey takes 30 minutes and tickets, which you can buy on the train, cost £10.20 one way. **Connex South Central's** slower trains cover the same route for a slightly lower fare of £8.20. There are also **Thameslink** trains from Gatwick serving other London stations including Blackfriars, City Thameslink, Farringdon, King's Cross Thameslink and London Bridge.

A cheaper but much slower option – the journey takes 90 minutes – is the **Flightline 777 Bus** (☎ 0208-668 7261) which runs every one to two hours between 5am and 8pm to London's Victoria Coach Station. Tickets cost £7.50 single (under 15s half price and under 5s free). Alternatively, you can book the **Airbus Hotel Shuttle** (☎ 0208-400 6656, ✉

book@airbus.co.uk), which will take you from the airport to the Gatwick Express, pick you up at Victoria and ferry you to the door of any central London hotel by minibus (fee £18). A **taxi** from Gatwick to central London costs at least £50 and takes as long as a bus.

Stansted airport (☎ 01279-680500, 🖳 www.baa.co.uk) is located 34mi (60km) north-east of the capital. It's the newest of London's airports and the fourth largest in the UK in terms of passenger numbers, serving 66 scheduled destinations and the home base of around 25 scheduled airlines. It has two terminals for domestic and international flights respectively and handles a range of flights within the UK, the Irish Republic and most European countries (including Turkey and Israel). The fastest way to get to central London from Stansted is by train via the **Stansted Express**, which takes 45 minutes to Liverpool Street station in central London (single fare £10.40). Trains depart every 30 minutes from 8am to 8pm and hourly from 8pm to midnight and between 6 and 8am. There's no service between midnight and 6am. Alternatively, you can catch the **Flightline 777 bus** to Victoria coach station for £9 (under 16s half-price); it takes around one hour and 40 minutes and stops at Hendon, Finchley or Marble Arch en route. A taxi costs over £50 for a journey of around an hour.

Luton airport (☎ 01582-646 0000, 🖳 www.london-luton.com), situated around 30mi (50km) north-west of central London, is London's fastest-growing airport. It handles scheduled (around two-thirds of the total) and charter flights to a wide range of destinations in the UK and Europe, and is a favourite departure point for British holidaymakers. It opened the second of its two terminals in October 1999. Trains from **Luton Airport Parkway** offer a direct link from the airport to King's Cross Thameslink station. A cheaper (£7) and slower journey is via a **Green Line 757 coach** (see page 80) to Victoria Coach Station. Coaches leave at 40 minutes past each hour and the trip takes 90 minutes. A taxi to central London from Luton isn't advisable as it takes over an hour and costs at least £70.

City airport (☎ 0207-646 0088, 🖳 www.londoncityairport.com) is the smallest of London's five airports and is situated just 9mi (14km) east of London's centre in the old Docklands district. Only domestic and European flights operate from here and the airport courts its largely business clientele by offering the fastest check-in and arrival times in Europe (so they claim). The airport serves popular business destinations within the UK such as Dundee, Edinburgh, Manchester and Sheffield, as well as a number of European destinations including Amsterdam, Antwerp, Basel, Berne, Brussels, Dublin, Dusseldorf, Frankfurt, Geneva, Le Havre, Luxembourg, Lugano, Malmo, Paris, Rennes, Rotterdam and Zurich.

Silvertown & City Airport railway station (**Docklands Light Railway**) is a ten minute walk from the airport and you can catch a train into the centre around every 20 minutes, interchanging with the tube system. An **Airbus** service operates every ten minutes between 6.50am and 9.10pm weekdays, 7.30am to 1.10pm on Saturdays and 11am to 9.10pm on

Sundays, costing £4 for the half-hour trip to Liverpool Street station. **Taxis** to the City take up to 40 minutes and cost around £15.

Some airlines flying into London have negotiated discount rates for onward travel by coach, so it's advisable to retain your airline ticket and ask for information when you arrive. If you're part of a group and finances permit, you can charter a private helicopter to get to London – prices vary, for example the 20-minute trip from Gatwick to London costs around £850 plus VAT. Contact Biggin Hill Helicopters (☎ 01959-540803, 🖳 www. bhh.co.uk/charter.htm) or Fast Helicopters Ltd. (☎ 01264-772508, 🖳 www.fast-helicopters.co.uk) for information and rates.

ARRIVING BY SEA

Regular car and passenger ferry services to Britain operate year round from ports in Belgium, Denmark, France, Germany, Holland, Iceland, Ireland, Spain and Sweden. The proportion of passengers travelling to and from Britain by sea has reduced considerably since the early '60s due to the reduced cost of air travel and competition from Eurotunnel (see below) and Eurostar trains. The major ferry companies providing international services are P&O (which also operates as P&O Stena Line on some routes) and Brittany ferries, which dominates the routes in the western Channel (Caen, Cherbourg, Roscoff and St Malo) with around 40 per cent of the market. Hoverspeed operates a hovercraft service from Dover to Calais and catamaran (Seacat) services on the same route, plus Folkestone to Boulogne and Dover to Ostend. A larger Hoverspeed superseacat service operates from Newhaven to Dieppe.

Some ferry services operate during the summer months only, e.g. May to September, and the frequency of services varies from dozens a day on the busiest Dover-Calais route during the summer peak period, to one a week on longer routes. Services are less frequent during the winter months, when inclement weather can also cause cancellations. Most Channel ferry services employ large super ferries with a capacity of 1,800 to 2,000 passengers and 700 cars. Ferries carry all vehicles, while hovercraft carry all vehicles except large trucks and buses. All operators, except Hoverspeed, offer night services that may be cheaper. Berths, single cabins and pullman seats are usually available, and most ships have a restaurant, self-service cafeteria, a children's play area and shops. Generally, the longer the route, the better and more comprehensive the facilities provided, which may make it worthwhile considering alternative routes to Dover-Calais. Although Dover-Calais is the shortest route and offers the most crossings, ships on longer routes are generally less crowded and more relaxing.

Le Shuttle: Eurotunnel started operating their shuttle car train service from Folkestone (access to the Eurotunnel terminal is via the M20 motorway, junction 11a) to Coquelles, near Calais, in 1995. The shuttle provides a 15-minute service during peak periods, taking just 35 minutes.

One of the advantages (in addition to the short travel time) of Le Shuttle is that you can remain in your car isolated from drunken soccer fans and screaming kids. Fares are similar to ferries, e.g. in 1999 a peak (summer) club class return cost around £340 and an off-peak (January to March) return £170, for a vehicle and all passengers. It's advisable to book in advance (☎ 0990-353535), although if you arrive earlier than planned you can travel on an earlier train providing there's space. Don't expect to get a place in summer on the 'turn up and go' service, particularly on Fridays, Saturdays and Sundays. Demand is lighter on services from France to Britain, when bookings may be unnecessary. Trains carry all 'vehicles', including cycles, motorcycles, cars, trucks, buses, caravans and motorhomes.

If you arrive in Britain by sea, you will need to travel on to London by train (see below) or, if you bring a car with you, by road (see page 87).

ARRIVING BY TRAIN

Since the opening of the Channel tunnel in 1994, London has had a direct rail connection with the continent of Europe with the introduction of the Eurostar train service to Brussels, Lille and Paris. Since the start of Eurostar services, some 25 per cent of travellers have switched from air to rail for journeys from London to Brussels and Paris. If you're travelling to or from central London it's the most convenient and comfortable way to travel. There's also a special excursion to Disneyland Paris and a Saturday ski train to Bourg St Moritz and Moutiers during the winter ski season.

London Waterloo to Paris Gare du Nord takes three hours and you can get to Brussels in 2 hours 40 minutes. Eurostar trains operate at speeds of up to 185mph on the continent, while in Britain trains still use the standard railway lines on which speeds are restricted. However, when the new high-speed rail link is inaugurated in around 2003, trains will run at much faster speeds (eventually operating from a new terminal at St Pancras station), and the journey time to Paris will be cut to 2 hours 20 minutes and to just 2 hours to Brussels.

Standard fares are more expensive than standard-class flights, but special offers are frequently available. A range of special fares are offered, including discovery special, weekend return, apex weekend, pass holder (for holders of international rail passes), senior return, youths (under 26) and groups. In late 1999 the cost of a standard plus return to Paris was £249, although special deals were available from £79 (weekend day return). For reservations ☎ 0990-186186; fare details and timetables are also available on the Internet (www.eurostar.com).

Britain's Rail Network

Originally built in the 19th century to bring goods and supplies into London from the provinces, Britain's railway infrastructure is out-dated and underfunded, with high prices, and frequent delays at the top of most Londoners' list of travel complaints. British Rail was privatised in 1997, and passenger services in the UK are now operated by some 25 separate private companies which have been awarded franchises to operate services in certain regions or on particular routes. Under privatisation, the track, stations and depots on Britain's railways are owned by **Railtrack**, which is responsible for the network's upkeep and maintenance.

As many people feared, far from improving a bad service, privatisation has led to increased fragmentation of the network and has often resulted in companies blaming one another for bad service. Travel in peak periods is to be avoided, when packed trains (often standing room only) cause considerable discomfort for those commuting into central London from the suburbs and outlying country areas. Londoners call it 'the rush hour', but it actually extends to over two hours both morning and evening. If you're fortunate enough not to be tied to the nine-to-five routine, you should avoid using London's transport system between 7.30 and 9.30am and from 4.30 to 6.30pm at the very least.

Since privatisation there hasn't been a clear distinction between 'mainline' rail services running between major cities and regional/local services. A company may offer either or both services on its routes. Suburban or local trains stop at most stations along their route, while long distance trains are express services that stop at major towns only and often include 1st or 'executive' class carriages. While it's usually possible to buy a meal on long-distance trains, either in a restaurant car or from a buffet, suburban trains usually offer just a snack trolley service or nothing at all. Toilets are provided on trains on all but the shortest services, but shouldn't be used when a train is in a station. British trains usually include carriages for smokers, although they're becoming rare as it becomes less socially acceptable to smoke in public. There are stiff fines for smoking in a non-smoking carriage and the guards (and other passengers) will look at you askance if you dare place your feet on the opposite seat.

Although a number of companies may be involved, you can buy 'through' tickets to stations on a different company's network; the price shouldn't vary, irrespective of where you purchase your ticket, although individual train companies sometimes offer reduced fares on their own routes. For example, between London and Peterborough you can buy a normal ticket valid on all train operators' services, or a cheaper ticket that's valid only on WAGN (West Anglia Great Northern) services. If you were to travel through London, e.g. from Brighton to Inverness in Scotland, the normal return fare would be £106.40. The Great North Eastern Railway (GNER), however, are currently offering a cheap return fare from London to Edinburgh for £30, although you would then have to look around for the cheapest tickets between Brighton and London (Connex) and Edinburgh and Inverness (Scotrail or GNER) to complete your journey. Depending on the special offers available, you may obtain a better deal by purchasing separate tickets for different 'legs' of a long journey.

There's a bewildering array of different-priced tickets available, including child tickets, family tickets, youth discounts (16-to-25 year olds), and discounts for the over 60s and disabled people, as well as special holiday and advance purchase excursion (Apex) tickets. Some tickets require the purchase of a special annual 'railcard', which entitles you to discounts each time you buy a ticket. If you're a regular train commuter, you can buy a weekly, monthly or annual point-to-point season ticket, for which you need a passport-sized photo. If you're taking a long journey by train, bear in mind that buying a ticket doesn't guarantee you a seat on any particular train unless it's reserved in advance. If you know what time you plan to travel it's advisable to reserve a seat, particularly during holiday periods and at weekends.

Information about tickets is available from information and ticket offices at stations. To check the times of trains, journey times and other information you can consult **Railtrack's Travel Timetable** on the Internet (www.railtrack.co.uk/travel/timetable) and also book tickets via **The Trainline** (www.thetrainline.com), where you input your start and destination stations and are given a listing with a full itinerary, plus any alternative routes.

London is the hub of most long-distance railway travel in the UK, although the old emphasis on bringing goods and passengers into the city, with trains from each corner of the UK arriving at their own specific terminus in the capital, has given way to a more diffused system. **Virgin Trains**, for example, treats Birmingham as the hub of its nation-wide network rather than London. However, long-distance trains arriving in London still terminate there, and if you want to continue to another provincial destination you must change trains and continue your journey from another mainline station.

London's Main Railway Stations

London has many main railway stations including Charing Cross, Euston, King's Cross, Liverpool Street, Marylebone, Paddington, St Pancras, Victoria and Waterloo, each serving a different region (or regions) of Britain.

Euston station opened in 1837 and was completely redeveloped in the '60s. From here you can catch long-distance trains to North Wales, the North of England and parts of Scotland. **King's Cross** station is the starting point for trains to East Anglia, the East Midlands, Yorkshire, the north-east and Scotland. This is the place to go if you fancy a day trip to the historic university city of Cambridge or wish to visit the Scottish capital, Edinburgh.

Liverpool Street station is the gateway to an extensive rail network to East Anglia, including the historic city of Norwich, the port of Harwich and the coastal resort of Clacton. Originally completed in 1875 and recently refurbished at a cost of £150 million, it still has many fine Victorian features along with a huge modern shopping centre. **London Bridge** station operates trains to Kent and Sussex and to Gatwick airport. From **Marylebone** station, Chiltern Trains operate a service via the West Midlands to Birmingham, while from **Paddington** station in the west of London, Great Western Trains run services to the west of England, the Cotswolds and South Wales. Currently undergoing a £63 million development, the station also has check-in desks for customers planning to travel on the Heathrow Express (see page 66).

Next door to King's Cross is the beautiful Gothic **St Pancras** station, from where you can catch a train to Bedfordshire, Northamptonshire, the East Midlands and Yorkshire, terminating at Leeds. This station is also used by commuters in Hertfordshire. St Pancras is also set to become the new terminal for Eurostar services to Paris and Brussels (see **Waterloo** below). **Victoria** station is the main gateway to the south and south-east of the country. Many commuters catch the train home to the Surrey suburbs from here and it's also the place to catch a train to Gatwick airport or for a day by the sea at Brighton. **Waterloo** station connects the capital to the south of England and to Europe via the **Eurostar** service (see page 69) through the Channel Tunnel. Nearby **Charing Cross** station has fast trains to south-east England including Dover, Folkstone and Ramsgate. Other less important mainline stations include **Blackfriars**, **Cannon Street** (both serving south-east England), and **Fenchurch Street** (serving Essex). There are also dozens of smaller railway stations throughout London's suburbs.

Suburban Trains: London's suburban rail network is concentrated to the south of the city where the underground service peters out. Travelcards (see page 64) are valid on this network and you can also purchase a Network Card for £20 that provides a one-third discount on suburban tickets for one year. Most lines are used by commuters in south-east England, living in what's known as the 'stockbrocker belt' (from where hundreds of thousands of workers commute into London each day). In addition to the many suburban lines that terminate at a London mainline station, there are also two over-ground railway lines traversing central London.

On the **Silverlink Line** there's a 15-minute service between Richmond and North Woolwich via Hampstead, Camden and Islington, and the **Thameslink** service operates trains north-south from the Luton area in Bedfordshire via King's Cross and London Bridge to Brighton on the south coast, via Wimbledon and Gatwick. It often pays to investigate routes taken by 'alternative' lines – railway enthusiast Dan Wilson has brought some surprising anomalies to light. For example "very few Londoners know that you can get to Hounslow 10 minutes faster from Waterloo on South West Trains than on the Piccadilly Line," he says, "or that Cannon Street on Connex SE is so near to the Bank station that it can be regarded as an interchange for the Central, Northern and DLR lines as well as the Circle Line."

National Rail Enquiries provide an enquiries hotline (☎ 0345-484950), which is the best and fastest way of obtaining information about connections, timetables and, in particular, fares. Alternatively, some of the best nation-wide railway information on the Internet is provided by **UK Railways on the Net** (www.rail.co.uk).

Station Facilities

Most main railway stations have restaurants, buffets and snack outlets; the standard of food has improved since privatisation, although prices can be high. Smaller stations sometimes have vending machines for snacks, sweets and drinks. Only large London stations have wash and brush-up facilities, although most provide basic toilet facilities (sometimes for a fee) and many have baby changing rooms. All stations have payphones, most accepting phonecards and coins, and most larger stations provide instant 'passport' photo machines. Car parking is provided at most country and suburban stations, although there's a high level of theft of (and from) cars parked at railway stations, so don't leave your CD collection on the back seat!

Many stations and airports have luggage lockers or 'left luggage' offices and you can usually find a trolley to wheel your bags around, although porters are rare these days. Disabled passengers can use the wheelchairs available at major railway stations and most trains have special facilities for their storage. Shops are provided at most central London stations and some large termini, e.g. Liverpool Street, have full-size shopping centres with banking facilities.

Light Rail Systems

It's interesting to reflect that a new generation of trams are making a comeback in Britain after the original pre-war systems were killed off earlier this century. The most recent development of London's transport system has been the introduction of **Light Rail** systems, sometimes known as super trams or tramlink systems. Familiar to Americans as 'transits' or 'streetcars' and to Europeans as trams, these train systems are different from traditional railways. Short trains or 'trams' run as single or articulated units on tracks laid along streets, in cuttings or on elevated platforms. They usually stop more frequently than conventional trains, even where there's no driver. Fuel-efficient (they're electrically powered), quiet and non-polluting, they also help to reduce traffic congestion on London's busy roads. There's a fascinating website (www.lrta.org) that offers everything you could ever want to know about light rail systems.

The **Docklands Light Railway (DLR)** in London was one of the first success stories in this regenerated transport arena. Treated as part of the underground network (see below) with regard to fares, the DLR covers the whole Docklands area and beyond, from Tower Gateway to Beckton, Stratford to the Isle of Dogs, Greenwich and Lewisham. It's also an excellent way to see some of the most interesting parts of London, where old meets new in a redeveloped and regenerated landscape, or to visit Greenwich's Millennium Dome. London's docks once served the busiest port in the world, while now they are home to many of London's workers and to industries such as Britain's major newspapers, which moved from Fleet Street to the Canary Wharf development in the '80s.

The DLR has three lines – **red** running north-south, **green** running from east to west and the **Beckton** line starting at Poplar station (red line) and running 5mi/8km to the east – and interchanges with both the main overground railway system and the tube. The network is being extended to south-east London and north Kent. Unusually for light rail systems, the DLR uses modern station designs with high level platforms. Trains are driver-less and remotely operated from the permanently staffed control centre located at Poplar. Facilities for disabled passengers are excellent, with all stations having wheelchair access. Most stations are also unmanned, although they are equipped with closed-circuit TV for security reasons. Like underground stations, all DLR platforms have train indicators showing the destination of trains and their estimated arrival times.

DLR offer a 'Sail & Rail' ticket that provides a day's unlimited travel on the DLR plus a riverboat trip from either Westminster or Greenwich Pier. Information about the DLR is available from DLR Customer Service (☎ 0207-363 9700 and the Internet (www.dlr.co.uk), where a map (reproduced opposite) is also available (www.xs4all.nl/~dodger/routes.htm).

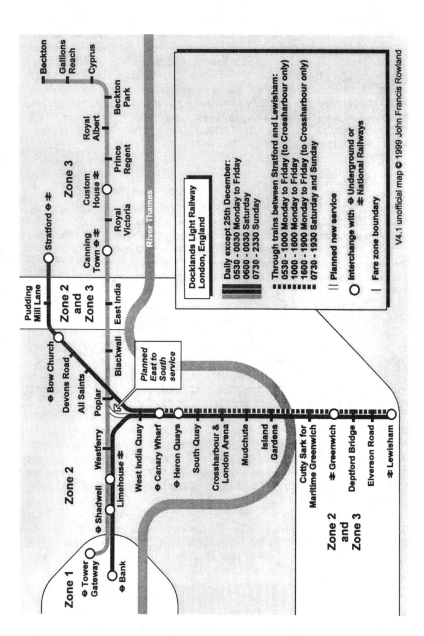

Docklands Light Railway
London, England

Daily except 25th December:
0530 - 0030 Monday to Friday
0600 - 0030 Saturday
0730 - 2330 Sunday

Through trains between Stratford and Lewisham:
0530 - 1000 Monday to Friday (to Crossharbour only)
1000 - 1600 Monday to Friday
1600 - 1900 Monday to Friday (to Crossharbour only)
0730 - 1930 Saturday and Sunday

‖ Planned new service

◯ Interchange with ⊖ Underground or ⇥ National Railways

| Fare zone boundary

V4.1 unofficial map © 1999 John Francis Rowland

Beckton
Gallions Reach
Cyprus
Beckton Park
Royal Albert
Prince Regent
Custom House ⇥
Royal Victoria
Canning Town ⊖ ⇥
Stratford ⊖ ⇥

Zone 3

River Thames

Pudding Mill Lane
Zone 2 and Zone 3
East India
Blackwall

⊖ Bow Church
Devons Road
All Saints
Poplar

Planned East to South service

West India Quay
⊖ Canary Wharf
⊖ Heron Quays
South Quay
Crossharbour & London Arena
Mudchute
Island Gardens

Westferry
Limehouse ⇥
⊖ Shadwell

Zone 2

⊖ Tower Gateway
⊖ Bank

Zone 1

Cutty Sark for Maritime Greenwich
⇥ Greenwich
Deptford Bridge
Elverson Road
⇥ Lewisham

Zone 2 and Zone 3

Another light railway system, the Croydon Tramlink, is under construction in the south London borough of Croydon. It will incorporate both on-street platforms built into the pavements, making for easy access, and former rail platforms at stations where it connects with conventional rail. It will provide a circular system around Croydon's town centre with links to Wimbledon, New Addington, Elmers End and Beckenham. Units – it's undecided whether to call them trains or trams – will be powered by overhead conductor wires and run smoothly along streets or disused railway lines. The first service on the system was due to begin at the end of 1999. A map of the Croydon Tramlink system is available on the Internet (www. croydon.gov.uk/tramlink/routemap.htm).

UNDERGROUND (TUBE)

In most European countries, an underground train system is called a metro system, while in the USA it's the subway. In London the vernacular is the 'tube' – a term derived from the tube-shaped tunnels through which the trains run under the city. Outside the central areas (and even within some of them) trains actually run above ground – something which, not surprisingly, many first-time visitors to the city find confusing! The London underground system is the oldest (parts of it have been around since the 1860s) and largest in the world, and during World War II stations were used as bomb shelters. The tube operates almost 500 trains, has over 270 stations and handles some 2.5 million passenger journeys a day. Given the congestion above ground, London without its tube would be unthinkable and it's easily the fastest and most convenient way to get around the city and its suburbs.

Although few Londoners have much good to say about it, the tube is nowhere near as bad as some people would have you believe. Despite hot, sticky and airless conditions in some older parts of the network, there are other areas, such as the recently opened Jubilee Line extension to Greenwich, which are clean, efficient and air-conditioned. Nevertheless, like most of Britain's rail network, the tube desperately needs a huge investment to overcome the backlog of neglect and to modernise it, and privatisation (or a public-private partnership) has been suggested as a means of providing the necessary funds. However, refurbishment of the Northern Line is underway and further modernisation and extensions are planned.

The tube network is shown on free maps (see the map inside the back cover) available at stations, London Transport Information Centres and on the Internet (www.ukguide.org/london/londonmap.html). The network has 11 separate lines (strictly speaking the Docklands Light Railway – see page 73 – is classed as part of the tube network), each of which is colour-coded on the tube map, e.g. yellow for the Circle Line, green for the District Line, red for the Central Line and so on. This makes it easy to follow your route and find your way to the correct platform. Some larger stations have electronic route planners where you input the name of your destination station and the shortest route is displayed; there's something similar on the **Subway System of London** website (http://metro.ratp.fr:10001/bin/select/ english/united-kingdom/london) and **Subway** (http://3lib.ukonline.co.uk/ subway.htm).

Although the tube is most widely used in the centre of the city, where it provides a useful alternative to fighting your way through the gridlocked London traffic, it also includes extensive coverage of the suburbs to the north, east and west of the city. There are fewer lines and stops south of the River Thames, where commuters tend to use the main rail network. The tube operates for some 20 hours a day, until around 00.30am – it varies depending on the day of the week, the station and the line. If you miss the last tube, don't panic but find a taxi or, if your budget doesn't permit it, a night bus (see page 80).

A typical tube station has an entrance above ground, indicated by the London Transport 'bull's eye' logo of a red circle with a horizontal line through the middle. Put your cigarette out before going any further, as for safety reasons smoking isn't permitted anywhere on the network. Neither are you allowed to drop litter – it was a build-up of litter beneath the escalators which caused an horrific fire at King's Cross station in the '80s – or take flash photographs. Security is tight, so don't leave your bags unattended or staff might treat them as 'suspicious packages' or suspected bombs.

On entering a station you must buy a ticket before commencing your journey – there's a £10 fine if you're caught travelling without one. You can buy tickets from machines and from ticket windows at most stations. Most machines provide change and if a machine runs out of change it will display a message telling you to deposit the exact fare. It's advisable to carry some change when travelling on the tube, as queues at ticket windows in central London can be long.

Like all London's public transport, the tube network is divided into (six) fare zones. The city centre is designated zone 1, while the outer suburbs such as High Barnet in the north or Upminster in the east are in zone 6. The price of your ticket depends on how many zones you travel through: they range from a not-very-good-value £1.40 for a single-zone journey (even if you're going only one or two stops – when it's probably quicker to walk anyway!) to a more reasonable £3.40 for a journey across all six zones. You can buy a ticket for a single or day return trip, although a **Travelcard** (also valid on London's buses and many over-ground trains) offers better value if you're going to be using the system more extensively. They offer unlimited travel for one day (after 9.30am), a weekend, seven days, one month or one year, and you can limit them to specific zones if your journey won't cover the whole network. If you're exploring the central area and expect to be making a lot of short journeys, buy a carnet of ten tickets for £10, but bear in mind that you cannot travel outside Zone 1 without buying another ticket.

Most central London stations have automatic ticket barriers that speed up the flow of passengers from the concourse to the platforms. Once you have your ticket, insert it into the slot on the front of the machine. It will pop out at the top and as you take it the gates will open to let you through. If you have problems, there's usually a member of staff nearby to help; special gates are provided for wheelchair users, those with children in pushchairs or bulky luggage. Once through the barrier, access to platforms is via escalators (moving staircases) or lifts, although some stations have stairs only. Escalators can be tricky if you have young children with you, so fold pushchairs before you start and take extra care. Stand on the right – those in a hurry (half of London) like to stampede past you on the left – and hold the moving handrail at the side. If you have young children, you may need to help them to jump on and off at the right moment. One last fashion note – stiletto heels and long skirts can be a menace on escalators. There's nothing worse than being carried inexorably to the top or bottom of an escalator with your foot firmly wedged in the metal grooves or your hem caught in the mechanism!

Once safely at the bottom of the shaft, make sure you're following the signs to the right line in the right direction, e.g. Northern Line southbound or Piccadilly Line westbound. There are electronic displays on platforms that tell you the time until the next train and its destination. Note that on many lines, trains can have more than one destination on the same line (i.e. a number of branches) and some trains terminate before the end of the line. Train doors open and shut automatically or you may be required to press a button near the door to open them.

The tube system can become *very* crowded, particularly at peak hours (around 8 to 9.30am and 5 to 6.30pm, Mondays to Fridays) so it's advisable to avoid these times if you can. Standing in a train that's packed to the doors can be an uncomfortable and claustrophobic experience, and packed platforms and trains are a haven for pickpockets (and gropers), so keep a tight hold on your valuables. The District Line is the busiest, although the shorter Victoria Line carries more passengers per mile, with Victoria and Oxford Circus the two busiest stations on the network.

At quiet times, tube travel can be moderately relaxing, providing you keep an eye on the frequent stops and don't miss your destination or interchange point! Each carriage has seats, although priority should be given to the elderly, pregnant, disabled or those laden with children or heavy bags. If you don't get a seat it's wise to hang on tight, as trains can hurtle through twisting tunnels at an alarming rate and it's easy to find yourself tumbling into the lap of a surprised stranger. There are plenty of bars as well as handles or 'straps' that dangle from the ceiling for support (a passenger suspended from a strap is said to be 'strap-hanging' in London tube parlance). If you've forgotten your book or cannot manage your strap along with your daily newspaper, you can amuse yourself by reading the advertisements, studying your fellow passengers or trying to spot 'ghost stations': deserted and disused stops on the line. Watch for the British Museum station just west of Holborn on the Central Line; it was closed in

1933 but is still visible from passing trains, as is St Mary's station (closed 1938) between Whitechapel and Aldgate East on the District Line.

If you have children with you keep a firm grip of them, as it's easy to become separated in the crush on a train or platform. You should also stand well back from the platform edge as it's possible to fall or be pushed onto the live rail or under the wheels of an approaching train (the wind in the stations can be surprisingly strong as trains force pockets of air along the tunnels). When you arrive at your destination, follow the directions to the exit. In central London you'll probably have to negotiate more escalators or lifts and another set of automatic barriers. If your ticket has expired the machine will 'swallow' it so that it cannot be used again.

There are London Transport (LT) centres throughout central London at Euston, King's Cross, Liverpool Street, Oxford Circus, Piccadilly Circus, Victoria and St James's Park rail/tube stations and at Hammersmith Bus Station (plus Heathrow Airport). LT centres provide extensive information about the tube network plus bus services and the Docklands Light Railway. Business hours vary, but there's also a 24-hour hotline (☎ 0207-222 1234) and a recorded information line (☎ 0207-222 1200). London Transport publishes a booklet about facilities for disabled passengers, called *Access to the Underground*, available free from ticket offices or from LT's special Unit for Disabled Passengers (☎ 0207-918 3312, minicom 0207-918 3012). *Access in London* by Gordon Couch, William Forrester and Justin Irwin (Quiller Press, 1996) also provides details of the most accessible tube stations and step-free routes for wheelchairs.

The Internet positively pulsates with tube-related websites, both official and enthusiastically amateur. Some of the best are the **Official London Underground Site** (www.londontransport.co.uk/underground/index.htm), **Carter's Unofficial Guide to the London Underground** (www.geocities. com/CollegePark/3812) and **Going Underground** (http://victorian.fortune city.com/finsbury/254/index.html).

BUSES

When you mention a London bus, most people immediately conjure up the image of the old Routemaster: post-box red double-deckers with a roving conductor or 'clippie' to take your fare and a rear platform you can hop on and off. The youngest of these are now thirty years old and they are gradually being replaced with cheaper-to-run, one-man buses. You board at the front and pay the driver, so the new buses also tend to be slower – it's advisable to have the correct change ready, which on some buses is mandatory. New buses are also trickier to negotiate if you have heavy bags or pushchairs to manage, as the entrance is narrow and there's no helpful conductor around to give you a hand.

Travelling by double-decker bus can be one of the most pleasurable and scenic ways to get around the capital (or out to the suburbs), providing you don't try to do it during the rush hour when progress can be painfully slow and it may be quicker to walk! Fares are low, with tickets starting at 70p and going up to £1.20 and a standard 40p fare for children under 15. Most bus routes accept **Travelcards** (see page 64) or you can buy a one-day bus pass for £2.80 that's valid for all six travel zones.

To catch a bus, first find a bus stop on the right side of the road for the direction you want to go. Bus stops are roadside poles with a red sign at the top. Many are request stops, which means you need to put your arm out to hail the bus as it approaches or it won't stop. There are many different routes serving the same stops, so look at the front of the bus for an indication of its destination or study the bus routes in advance by picking up a free bus map and timetable from a London Transport centre (see page 79). Alternatively, have a look at the **Greater London Bus Map** Internet site (http://homepages.which.net/~m.harris/).

The regular red bus service runs between 6am and midnight, after which a **Night Bus** service comes into operation. These buses have numbers prefixed with the letter 'N' and all routes radiate outwards from Trafalgar Square, so that's the place to head for if you've missed the last tube or 'day' bus and cannot afford a taxi home. They run approximately every hour and charge a flat fare of £1.50 regardless of the distance travelled. You can use a weekly Travelcard (see page 64) on night buses, but for some reason daily, family and weekend Travelcards are invalid.

The outer suburbs of London within a 40mi (64km) radius are serviced by **Green Line** buses (☎ 0208-668 7261, 🖳 www.greenline.co.uk), most of which leave from Victoria Coach Station in Eccleston Street. Travelcards can be used on some Green Line bus services.

RIVER FERRIES

One method of getting around London that's often overlooked is river transport. If your daily route to and from work follows the line of the River Thames this is a pleasant way to travel. **London River Services/LRS** (☎ 0207-918 4753) is a recent subsidiary of London Transport, which aim to develop river passenger transport by providing new river piers and boat services. One of the main reasons is to make it easier for visitors to get to the riverside site of the Millennium Dome in Greenwich, but there's also a longer-term strategy to 'promote and co-ordinate river boat services on the River Thames.' To this end, LRS has recently acquired seven piers: Bankside, Embankment, Greenwich, Temple, Tower, Waterloo (formerly Festival) and Westminster. It's also building a new pier at Blackfriars, making eight in all. Other piers on the river are in private or local government ownership.

The **Central London Fast Ferry** operates between Waterloo and Rotherhithe via Westminster, Embankment, Blackfriars, Bankside, London Bridge City, Tower and Canary Wharf. It uses 60-passenger capacity boats which passengers board via hinged ramps leading to the covered fore deck. Disabled passengers have a separate access door leading directly from the fore deck to a dedicated area set aside for wheelchairs.

There are also a number of other services intended for tourists. Two dedicated services, the **Millennium Express** from Waterloo and Blackfriars to the Millennium Dome and the **Greenwich Shuttle** from Greenwich to the Dome began on 1st January 2000 and will continue while the Dome remains open. There are also a variety of other services both up and down river, some operating year round. Details of routes, fares and timetables for all services are available on the Internet (www.londontransport.co.uk/info/river_00.htm) or you can call London's 24-hour travel information hotline (☎ 0207-222 1234).

TAXIS

If you like the idea of being chauffeured direct to your destination, then stick out your arm and hail one of London's famous, purpose-built 'black cabs', officially called 'Hackney Carriages'. Taxis are licensed by the Metropolitan (London) police and each cab has a license number plate and the driver (cabby) wears a badge bearing his driver number. London taxis cover a vast area of around 610mi² (1,580km²) stretching well into the outer suburbs.

Taxis are relatively expensive in Britain, although they are cheaper than in some other European countries. They have a strictly regulated scale of fares and charges, to which it's customary to add a tip of around 10 per cent. There's a minimum charge of £1.40 for roughly the first 450 metres or two minutes and 20p for each additional around 225 metres or 45 seconds (a lot of time is spent stuck in traffic, hence the charge for time). There are extra charges for additional passengers and baggage, and surcharges for evenings between 8pm and midnight, nights, weekends and public holidays. There are also business class cabs in London with more luxurious seats, soundproofing and a telephone (and higher rates than standard cabs).

If fares have recently gone up and the meter hasn't yet been adjusted to show the new rates, an 'additional fares' list is displayed inside the cab. You can be sure you'll be safe in one of these taxis and nor will you be cheated. Although they aren't a cheap mode of transport (unless three of four people plan to share their roomy interior), a licensed cab driver won't usually take anything but the shortest route between two points (unless he does so to avoid traffic congestion). Before obtaining his license, a cab driver must undergo a long training period and pass a stiff exam on what's known as 'The Knowledge' – an encyclopaedic test of London's geography. Cabbies vary from grimly silent to downright loquacious, and many won't hesitate to tell you their opinions on every topic under the sun. Just nod and smile.

Most drivers are more than pleased to help disabled passengers and wheelchairs can usually be stored inside the cab along with any luggage. Although most cabs are black, they also come in other colours, including *Financial Times* pink and *Evening Standard* 'newsprint' pattern, although they all have a yellow 'For Hire' sign at the front and a white numbered license plate on the back. If you want to book a cab in advance, call **Radio Taxicabs** (☎ 0207-272 0272), **Dial-a-Cab** (☎ 0207-253 5000) or e-mail the **Licensed London Taxi Booking Service** (✉ sttaxi@aol.com). If you have a complaint about a taxi driver, contact the **Public Carriage Office** (☎ 0207-230 1631) with the number of the offending cab and the driver's badge number.

In addition to regular taxis, you can also take a minicab, which, unlike regular taxis, cannot be hailed in the street and must be booked by phone. (It's illegal for minicabs to ply for hire in the street like licensed taxis, although some do.) Minicabs are cheaper than licensed taxis, but you have no guarantee that the driver will be reliable, honest or know his way around. There's no official training scheme for minicab drivers and there are dozens of companies available, so the best way to find a good one is to ask someone you trust. Phone for a minicab in advance and agree the price to your destination before commencing your journey, as few have meters. If you're female and worried about your personal safety late at night, you might want to consider **Ladycabs** (☎ 0207-254 3501), which employ women only. **Freedom Cars** (☎ 0207-734 1313, ✉ freedom.cars@virgin.net) or **Q-Cars** (☎ 0207-622 0011, ✉ qcars@dircon.co.uk) can both provide a minicab driven by a gay man or woman.

In addition to taxi services, many taxi and minicab companies operate private hire (e.g. weddings or sightseeing), chauffeur and courier services, and provide contract and account services, e.g. to take children to and from school.

DRIVING IN LONDON

You need nerves of steel and the patience of Job to drive in central London – and it also helps to be a little crazy. Not only will it cost you dearly in terms of time, petrol (among the most expensive in Europe), insurance and headache pills, it's also virtually impossible to find affordable parking (see below) in the central area. Few central London properties have garages or off-road parking, although you may be fortunate enough to find a house or apartment with a residents' parking scheme (see page 87). Very few employers provide workplace parking in central London and when they do it's usually for an elite few only. Parking meters are for temporary stays of up to two hours and private car parks for the seriously rich only. An additional hazard is having your car stolen. The number of cars stolen in London is the highest (per capita) in Western Europe and if you work or live in London and park your car there, you have a one in four chance of having it stolen or broken into.

Congestion on London's roads and the resulting air pollution has reached nightmare proportions in recent years. Getting anywhere by private car takes eons, and an accident at a busy intersection can cause long tailbacks or even gridlock throughout the city. There has been a widespread debate about traffic congestion in recent years and various measures have been introduced to limit its effects, ranging from special bus and cycle lanes to help speed traffic, and punitive parking fees to discourage driving in the city. However, these measures have, so far, had little impact.

If you think you cannot live without a car in London, you can gain some first-hand experience of the nightmare by hiring one for a week or two. Many people soon realise that they're better off without one and use public transport (and the occasional taxi) to get around; over 50 per cent of those living in central London don't own a car, along with some 40 per cent of Greater London's residents. To hire a car you need at least one year's driving experience and must be aged at least 21 or 25, depending on the rental company. European Union driving licences are valid indefinitely in the UK, while most other licences are valid for one year, after which the nationals of many countries must pass a British driving test. The major car hire companies in London include Avis (☎ 0990-900500), British Car Rental (☎ 0207-255 2339), Europcar BCR (☎ 0207-255 2339) and Hertz (☎ 0990-996699). Shop around, as hire charges vary considerably. Disabled drivers can hire vehicles with hand controls from Hertz and other national car hire companies and specialist companies such as **Wheelchair Travel** (☎ 01483-233640) based in Guildford (Surrey), 32mi/51km south of London.

If you break down anywhere in the UK, you can obtain roadside assistance if you're a member of a motoring organisation such as the **Automobile Association/AA** (☎ 0800-444999), **Royal Automobile Club/ RAC** (☎ 0990-722722) or **Green Flag National Breakdown** (☎ 0800-001313), Membership costs between £40 to £140 per year, depending on the level of cover required. Valuable advice and assistance about driving in the UK is available on the Internet at **Driving Online** (🖳 www.driving.co.uk). If you aren't used to driving in Britain, you would also be advised to buy a copy of the *Highway Code*, available from any bookshop. Finally, bear in mind that UK speed limits are 30mph (48kph) in urban areas, 60mph (96kph) on unrestricted single carriageway roads (outside towns), and 70mph/113kph on motorways and dual carriageways. It's also useful to remember that traffic drives on the left-hand side of the road!

Parking

Parking in central London is expensive, prohibitively so if you drive into the city every day. On-road parking (waiting) restrictions in Britain are indicated by yellow lines at the edge of roads, usually accompanied by a sign indicating when parking is prohibited, e.g. 'Mon-Sat 8am-6.30pm' or 'At any time'. If no days are indicated on the sign, restrictions are in force every day including public holidays and Sundays. Note that, unlike many other European countries, Britain doesn't have a cavalier attitude towards illegal parking and the authorities rarely (if ever) turn a blind eye to it. Yellow signs indicate a continuous waiting prohibition and also detail times when parking is illegal, while blue signs indicate limited waiting periods. Yellow lines provide a guide to the restrictions in force, but the signs must always be consulted. The following road markings are in use in London and its suburbs:

Road Marking	Prohibitions
white zig-zag line or studded areas	no parking or stopping at any time (e.g. next to a zebra crossing)
double yellow lines	no parking at most or all times (it may be possible to park on double yellow lines during some periods, but if in doubt, don't)
single yellow line	no parking for at least eight hours between 7am and 7pm (e.g. from 8.30am to 6.30pm) on four or more days a week
broken yellow line	restricted parking shown by a sign

Red lines indicate a red route, which came into operation in London in 1991 to speed up traffic. A single red line means you aren't permitted to stop between the hours of 7am and 7pm (or as indicated by a sign) from Mondays to Fridays, except for loading or unloading. Special parking bays are marked in red, where parking is strictly limited. A double red line indicates no stopping, loading or parking at any time. If you park illegally on a red route, your car will be towed away in the blink of an eye. Loading restrictions for loading and unloading goods may be shown by one, two or three short yellow lines marked diagonally on the kerb and a sign. For more information consult the *Highway Code.*

In most towns there are public and private off-road car parks, indicated by a sign showing a white 'P' on a blue background. Parking in local authority (council) car parks usually costs from around 20p for a half-hour or hour. Parking in short-term (local authority) car parks may become progressively more expensive the longer you stay and can cost as much as £5 for over five hours parking. However, parking is generally cheaper (per hour) the longer you park, up to a maximum of around nine hours.

Off-Road Private Car Parks: Parking in a private central London car park costs as much as £4 an hour or up to £45 per day (monthly and annual season tickets are usually available for commuters). National Car Parks (NCP), Britain's largest car park operator, has a number of 24-hour car parks in central London including the following: 21 Bryanston Street, W1 (☎ 0207-499 7050); 2 Lexington Street, W1 (☎ 0207-734 0371); and Arlington Street, SW1 (☎ 0207-499 3312). A free map of NCP car parks is available from NCP, PO Box 4NH, Bryanston Street, London W1A 4NH (☎ 0207-499 7050). In many areas there are short-stay and long-stay car parks. Fees may be the same for short stays of up to two or three hours, beyond which rates at short-stay car parks are much more expensive. If you commute into London it's cheaper to drive to a convenient railway station, where parking costs around £2 to £3 a day, and take a train into central London. Weekly, monthly and annual season tickets are usually available at rail and underground stations. Parking in public car parks and at meters may be free on Sundays and public holidays, so check the notice *before* buying a ticket.

Parking meters: The maximum permitted parking period at meters varies from 30 minutes to two hours. Meter-feeding is illegal. You must vacate the parking space when the meter time expires, even if it was under the maximum time allowed, and you may not move to another meter in the same group. Meters normally accept a combination of 5p to 20p coins, and are usually in force from 7am until 7pm, Mondays to Fridays, and from 7am to 6pm on Saturdays (check meters to be certain). Sundays are usually free. Meters at railway stations and airports may be in

use 24-hours a day. Don't park at meters that are suspended as you can be towed away. If you remain at a meter beyond the excess charge period, you will be liable for a fixed penalty handed out by a police officer or by London's infamous and much reviled traffic wardens. Parking meters are being phased out and replaced by pay-and-display parking areas.

Pay-and-display: These are parking areas where you must buy a ticket from a machine and display it behind your windscreen. It may have an adhesive backing which you can peel off and use to stick the ticket to the inside of your windscreen or a car window. Parking costs 20p or 30p an hour in most areas and machines usually accept all coins from 5p to £1. When you have inserted sufficient coins for the period required, press the button to receive your ticket. Pay-and-display parking areas usually operate from 7am until 7pm, excluding Sundays and public holidays. A new pre-paid parking scheme (called Easypark) is in operation in some towns where you buy a card costing from £3 to £125 (gold card), which is used to pay for parking in special machines (like using a phone card). Cards are sold at post offices, shops, garages and council offices. In some towns a 'scratch and display' parking scheme is in operation, where you buy vouchers and scratch off panels to show the month, day, date and time of arrival (and display the voucher in your car's window).

Parking Fines: The fine for illegal parking depends on where you park. There's usually a fixed penalty ticket of £40 or £60 (50 per cent discount if you pay within 14 days) for parking illegally on a yellow line. Parking in a dangerous position or on the zig-zag lines or studded area near a pedestrian crossing results in a higher fine, plus three penalty points on your driving licence. Penalties for non-payment or overstaying your time in a permitted parking area (e.g. at a parking meter or in a pay-and-display area) are set by the local authorities who issue parking tickets. In Westminster, which operates a 'reign of terror' against motorists, you may be hit with an £80 fine for over-staying your time at a £4 an hour parking meter!

You shouldn't even *think* about parking illegally, for example, in a residents' only area, on a double yellow line or at an expired meter, as your car could be clamped or towed away in the blink of an eye. (In one notorious case a woman's car was seized by bailiffs and sold at auction to pay a £30 fine while she was on holiday. Of the auction proceeds of £3,500 – £1,500 below its market value of £5,000 – she eventually received £1,700.) You must then pay a substantial fee (e.g. over £100) before your car is released, plus a fine. A car pound won't release your car until you've paid and will accept cash or a guaranteed cheque only. All car pounds charge a daily storage fee after the first 24 hours of around £12 a day. You cannot be towed away from a pay-and-display area or a parking meter (unless the parking bay is suspended). If you believe that you have been treated unfairly there's a Parking Appeals Service (PO Box 3333, London SW1Y, ☎ 0207-747 4700).

Clamping: Illegal parking can result in your car being 'clamped', where a large metal device (a clamp) is clamped onto one of its wheels, thus preventing you driving it away. Over 3,000 cars are clamped each week in London and 2,000 are towed away. If you find yourself in this predicament, phone the **Clamping and Vehicle Section's** 24-hour hotline (☎ 0207-747 4747) for instructions. If you've been clamped, you'll have a lengthy wait even after you've paid the fine (some boroughs allow you to pay over the phone by credit card, while others insist that you pay in person). Companies say they will unclamp your car within four hours of receiving your payment, but they won't give you a precise time. If they do unclamp it and you don't remove the car quickly, i.e. within an hour, they're quite within their rights to reclamp it and the whole process starts all over again. If you're in the habit of parking illegally, you can join the Car Clamp Recovery Club (☎ 0208-777 2287), who will recover your car for you for an annual fee of £50.

Cars parked at meters aren't usually clamped unless a parking bay is suspended, the meter was 'fed' with coins, or a car has stayed two hours beyond the period paid. Note also that the owners of private car parks or private land can also clamp a car parked illegally and can set their own charge to remove clamps (e.g. £100 or more). It's inadvisable to park on private land, particularly where there's a 'clamping' sign, as private clamping is widespread throughout Britain, although it's often illegal. Many 'cowboy' clamping companies clamp and tow away cars that are legally parked and charge up to £250 a time to free them. You will be pleased to note that most clampers and towers *really* enjoy their work, despite the universal abuse they attract!

Whether parking restrictions exist or not, when parking on a road, be careful where you park as you can be prosecuted for parking in a dangerous position and could also cause an accident. If your car contributes to an accident you may need to pay damages. Take care in car parks, as accidents often occur there and they may not be covered by your car insurance. Parking on pedestrian footpaths is illegal everywhere. Note that parking in towns with your hazard warning lights on makes no difference if you're parked illegally. Wherever you drive in Britain, keep a supply of coins handy for parking meters.

Residents' Parking: Most central London residents (those whose postcode lies within a controlled parking zone) can obtain a residents' parking permit that provides inexpensive local (on-street) parking in designated spaces. Any resident whose postcode lies within a controlled zone can apply for a permit from his local council by providing proof of identity and residence (usually a council tax bill). Charges vary as they are set by local borough councils, e.g. Hammersmith and Fulham charges £50 per year or £28 for six months. There are also special permits for disabled drivers who are permitted to park in reserved spaces, park free at meters and in car parks, and to ignore many on-road parking restrictions.

Information about parking regulations throughout London (including how to appeal against parking tickets) is available from the **Parking Committee for London** (New Zealand House, 80 Haymarket, London SW1Y 4TE, ☎ 0207-747 4700, 🖳 www.open.gov.uk/park/parkhome.htm) or you can obtain a copy of the *London Parking Atlas* (Pathmedia) showing parking areas throughout central London.

Travelling to London by Road

The web of motorways leading into London intersect with the M25, London's orbital motorway, and continue towards the city centre. After crossing the M25, traffic heading into London can suddenly become less congested, as much of the long-distance and road freight traffic peels off to head for the Channel ports and other destinations. However, this is more than compensated for by local traffic and commuters driving into London from the outer suburbs. The unexpected surge in local traffic took the planners of the M25 completely by surprise. The motorway was intended to consolidate the motorway system around the capital, drawing long distance traffic away from the centre. However, it attracted a huge volume of local traffic, as a result of which long stretches have had extra lanes added, increasing the number of carriageways from three to four (mainly in the south-western section between the intersections with the M4 and M23).

Arriving in London from the north-west, the M40 becomes the A40 and is dual carriageway all the way to Regent's Park, while further to the north the M1 pushes some way into London ending at an intersection with the North Circular, the original (and now inner) London ring road. From here, follow either the A41 for Regent's Park and the West End, or peel off the M1 one exit before it ends and merge with the A1 which takes you further east to Islington and the City. The A41 is one of the better roads leading into the city centre but, because it brings you into the heart of London's leisure and shopping areas, it can get clogged at unexpected times, for example, going *into* London in the early evening. The A10 is a good road from the north until it hits the North Circular, after which traffic speeds fall considerably. The M11 enters London from the north-east, also terminating at the North Circular at the same point as the A12 from the east. However, there's no fast road on which to continue, leaving several miles of congested East End high streets before you reach the City.

South of the river, road access to the centre is frustratingly complicated. There are almost no fast roads in from the south-east, the best being the A2 and A20. Both of these leave you with Hobson's choice of either entering the Blackwall Tunnel under the river, from which you'll emerge still some way from the City and even further from the West End, or heading further west up the Old Kent Road before crossing the River Thames. Either way is likely to consist of a lengthy crawl through congested urban streets. Major routes in from the south-west are slightly better, but not much. The M23 arrives from the south and finishes soon after its intersection with the M25, becoming dual carriageway for a few miles but soon degenerating into another crawl through a mass of crowded suburban high streets towards the centre.

From the south-west, the A3 and M3 are completely separate roads, both of which continue as dual carriageways some distance towards the centre of London after reaching the M25 (the M3 becomes the A316). Entry to London from the west is via the M4, which runs to Chiswick in west London before merging with London's urban sprawl. The M4 is one of Britain's busiest and most congested motorways, carrying London's traffic from prosperous industrial towns such as Slough and Reading, the tourist traffic for Windsor and the West Country, and swarms of taxis and coaches going to and from Heathrow airport.

International bus services to and from Britain are provided by a number of companies including Eurolines, Eurobus and Hoverspeed services, with regular services to around 200 destinations in Europe and Ireland. Most international services operate to and from Victoria Coach Station (☎ 0207-730 3466, bookings 0207-730 3499), Buckingham Palace Road (Victoria), although some operate directly from the provinces.

Cycling in the City

Short of walking, cycling is the cheapest way to get around in central London and one of the fastest. It's also potentially the most dangerous. If the traffic doesn't flatten you first, any positive benefits on physical fitness may be offset by the adverse effects of air pollution. Always wear a smog mask with a proper air filter as well as a safety helmet, and don't try this mode of transport at all unless you're an experienced cyclist. Carrying children on the back of a bike in London's heavy traffic isn't advisable, but if you must do it, ensure that they're also fitted with helmet and mask and are securely strapped into an approved child seat. When you park your bicycle, make sure that you lock both the frame and the wheels to an immovable object or it's unlikely to be there when you return.

All this is discouraging for cycling enthusiasts in London, who need to head out to the suburbs to enjoy it in relative safety. Unfortunately, many modes of public transport won't carry bicycles. Restrictions on suburban railways vary, so phone to check before attempting to take your bike on the train. The Docklands Light Railway has a blanket ban on bikes and only four tube lines (the District, Circle, Metropolitan and Hammersmith & City) allow them, but only outside peak hours. Other tube lines allow them on overground sections only, i.e. those in the outer suburbs.

However, things may be about to change. For over twenty years the **London Cycling Campaign** (228 Great Guildford Business Square, 30 Great Guildford Street, London SE1 0HS, ☎ 0207-928 7220, 💻 www.cerbernet.co.uk/lcc) has been trying to promote the rights of cyclists in London. The crisis in London's transport system is widely acknowledged and the London boroughs are setting up a network of 1,200mi (1,931km) of cycle routes throughout the capital, with the help of government funding. Routes (marked by blue signs showing a bicycle) bypass the major thoroughfares, usually taking fairly direct routes through residential areas that are unsuitable for heavy traffic. Companies are beginning to encourage their employees to cycle to work and there are increased facilities for cycle parking at workplaces and elsewhere. The London Cycling Campaign publishes *On Your Bike: Guide to Cycling in London*.

So why not buy yourself a bike? If you want to get a taste of what it's like first, you can hire one for £5 to £10 a day or around £30 per week from a number of sites in central London (a deposit is necessary). Try the **London Bicycle Tour Company** at 1a St Gabriel's Wharf on the South Bank (☎ 0207-928 6838), which also organises cycle tours, or **Bikepark** at 14 Stukely Street, Covent Garden (☎ 0207-430 0083). This excellent shop provides comprehensive services to cyclists such as repairs, left luggage and even showers! Alternatively, you can hire a motorbike or moped for £20 to £80 per day, £130 to £400 per week, depending on its size and power. This is usually inclusive of insurance, breakdown cover, tax, helmet and unlimited mileage. One company you can try is **Scootabout** in King's Cross (☎ 0207-833 4607).

3.

SOMEWHERE TO LIVE

In most areas of London, there's a wealth of accommodation, both to rent and buy, in every price range. However, prices in central London are astronomical and finding property at an affordable price is difficult. Unless you're wealthy, you'll invariably find that you'll need to compromise to find a home you like. For example, you'll probably need to pay more than you had planned, buy or rent a smaller home than you would like or live in a less desirable area. You may also need to live further from the centre and possibly further away from public transport and other amenities than you would wish. Before choosing somewhere to live it's advisable to check the present and planned public transport services, particularly if you will be commuting to a job in central London or one of its suburbs. If you're buying you'll find that a planned improvement in local public transport – such as a new tube or rail extension – offering a fast journey time into central London will have a dramatic effect on property values.

Renting isn't as common in Britain as it is in many other European countries, and some 70 per cent of Britons own their own homes – one of the highest figures in Europe (Britain also has the highest ownership of second homes in Europe). The average age of first-time buyers is around 27, one of the lowest in the world, due mainly to easy access to mortgages and the large loans (as a percentage of a property's value) offered by lenders. Four out of five people in Britain live in houses rather than flats (apartments) and most Britons aren't keen on apartment living or townhouses and want their own detached houses with a garden and garage. Nevertheless, the vast majority of Londoners live in apartments!

Most Londoners don't live in central London but in the numerous suburbs, where life's still largely community based. Many people who work in London commute into the city from the surrounding (home) counties, with thousands travelling from even further afield. Wherever you are in the suburbs, you're never far from a traditional 'parade' of shops selling the essentials of life, and all areas provide amenities such as schools, health and leisure facilities. Much of London's suburbia is characterised by row upon row of brick terraced houses, mainly built in Victorian times to provide housing for the rapidly growing population, or tree-lined avenues of endless semi-detached properties dating from the '20s and '30s. The price of this kind of typical suburban architecture varies considerably depending on the area, although prices in London are generally much higher than in other parts of Britain. As with all large cities, there's a huge variation in housing quality and price.

In late 1999, the average price of a home in London was around £185,000 in central London and £120,000 in Greater London, although many properties are sold for seven figure sums. Cheaper properties tend to be found in unfashionable 'working class' suburbs mainly situated south of the river in districts such as Clapham and Streatham, or in the East End away from the Docklands, although even here prices have risen dramatically in recent years. Note, however, that the cheaper areas generally have poor housing stock and are subject to the typical inner city problems of neglect, poverty, unemployment and high crime rates.

Britain had a booming housing market in the '80s, which culminated in average prices rising by 30 per cent annually in 1988/89, when the most desirable properties rose by 50 to 100 per cent in a single year! However, during the recession in the late '80s and early '90s the country experienced an unprecedented collapse in property values, which left almost two million owners with negative equity (where the amount owed on the mortgage exceeds the value of a property). Negative equity was widespread in London and the south-east, where over 25 per cent of owners were affected in some areas. The shock of falling home values hit the British particularly hard, as they traditionally view buying a house as an investment rather than a home for life (as is normal in most of the rest of Europe). In recent years there has been a strong recovery in property values in most regions. In 1999 prices were rising by up to 30 per cent a year in some parts of London, although the average rise was around 15 per cent.

Most property in Britain is owned freehold, where the owner acquires complete legal ownership of the property and land and his rights over it, which can be modified only by the law or specific conditions in the contract of sale. Most houses, whether detached, semi-detached, terraced or townhouses, are sold freehold. However, unlike most other countries, apartments in London aren't usually owned outright under a system of co-ownership, but are 'leasehold', with a lease of, for example, 99 to 999 years (see page 109).

A number of books are published specifically for house hunters in London, including *Where to Live in London* by Sara McConnell (Simon & Schuster) and *The New London Property Guide* by Carrie Segrave (Mitchell Beazley). However, if it's inspiration you're after, buy a copy of *The London Magazine* (see **Appendix A**) which is packed with enticing pictures of beautiful (and *very* expensive) London homes.

BRITISH HOMES

British homes are usually built to high structural standards and whether you buy a new or an old home, it will usually be extremely sturdy. There are stringent planning regulations in most areas regarding the style and design of new homes and the restoration of old (listed) buildings. Britain offers a vast choice of properties (few countries have such a variety of housing), including some of the most luxurious and expensive homes in the world. At the bottom end of the market they are likely to be terraced or semi-detached houses, whereas more expensive homes are detached and are built on a half or one acre (2,000 to 4,000m²) plot. In recent years Britons have taken to apartment living in London and other cities (often more out of necessity than choice), many of which are tasteful conversions of old buildings that have been converted into luxurious loft apartments. Many single people live in huge apartments or large houses and generally people live in as much space as they can afford.

The British usually prefer older homes with 'charm and character' to modern homes, although you often find pseudo period features such as wooden beams and open fireplaces in new homes. Some new luxury homes are built to modern standards using reclaimed materials, thus offering the best of both worlds. Although new properties may be lacking in character, they are usually well endowed with modern conveniences and services, which cannot be taken for granted in older properties. Standard fixtures and fittings in modern houses are more comprehensive and generally of better quality than those found in old houses. For example, central heating, double or triple-glazing and efficient insulation are standard in new houses and are essential in Britain's climate. Central heating may be gas (the most common) or oil-fired, or a home may have electric night-storage heaters. Air-conditioning is rare in Britain, although many luxury apartments and houses have what's called comfort cooling, air cooling, or a climate controlled refrigerated air system. Swimming pools are rare in Britain, although indoor pools are becoming more popular in large luxury homes.

In the last decade or so, apartment and townhouse conversions have been common throughout the country and include former stately homes, hospitals, schools, churches, mills, warehouses, offices and factories. Barn conversions are also popular (and *very* expensive), although rare due to the lack of barns (you can also have a 'barn' home built from new). Loft conversions are popular due to their high (cathedral) ceilings and general spaciousness.

Old homes: Old homes usually refer to pre-1940; homes built prior to 1900 are often referred to as period homes, e.g. Georgian or Victorian. Older, larger homes often contain a number of interesting period features such as high ceilings, fireplaces, sash windows, panelled doors, elaborate staircases, attics, cellars, alcoves and annexes. Fireplaces are usually a principal feature in most old houses, even when central heating is installed. Floors in old homes are often made of wood, which may be polished, although they are more likely to be carpeted. Walls are either painted or papered (in older homes the walls are more likely to be papered). Most older, smaller homes (e.g. semi-detached and terraced houses) were often built without modern conveniences such as central heating, double glazing, fitted kitchens and proper bathrooms, although most have been modernised and contain similar 'mod cons' to new homes. However, in some old homes that haven't been modernised there may be no bath or shower room or even an inside toilet! If a home has gas central heating, it will usually also have a gas water heater (otherwise it will have an electric immersion heater).

Modern Homes: Modern homes are built in a vast range of styles and sizes, from small studio and one-bedroom apartments and townhouses, to huge luxury 'executive' detached homes on large plots and luxury penthouse apartments. Most new homes in England are built with brick and block cavity walls, and only some 10 per cent are timber frame construction.

New houses are usually (but not always) built to higher standards than older houses and include thermal insulation, double glazing, central heating and extensive ventilation. They also usually contain a high level of luxury features such as tiled kitchens, deluxe bathroom suites, fitted wardrobes, fitted kitchens with cookers and refrigerators (possibly also dishwashers and microwave ovens), smoke and security alarms, and optional co-ordinated interior colour schemes. Refrigerators and stoves are usually quite small in British homes. Modern homes usually have a separate utility room off the kitchen where the washing machine and dryer are stored. A modern home has at least one full bathroom (in luxury homes all bedrooms may have en suite bathrooms) and a separate toilet or shower room. British homes rarely have shower rooms and no bath. Most modern homes, except flats, also have garages.

The most common kinds of homes in Britain include the following:

Bedsit: A studio flat with one room for living and sleeping.

Bungalow: A single-storey detached or semi-detached house. Popular with the elderly as they have no stairs.

Cottage: Traditionally a pretty, quaint house in the country, perhaps with a thatched roof (although the name is often stretched nowadays to encompass almost anything except a flat). May be detached or terraced.

Detached house: A house that stands alone, usually with its own garden (possibly front and rear) and garage.

Flat: An apartment or condominium, usually on one floor. A block of flats is an apartment building, high-rise tower block, or possibly a large house that has been converted into flats.

Houseboat: These are popular in some cities (with waterways!) and modern houseboats are luxurious and spacious. One of the drawbacks is finding a suitable mooring, which costs over £2,000 a year in London.

Maisonette: Part of a house or apartment block forming separate living accommodation, usually on two floors with its own outside entrance.

Mews house: A house that's converted from old stables or servants' lodgings (usually 17th to 19th century) which is the town equivalent of a genuine cottage. These are common in London, although expensive.

Mobile (park) home: A pre-fabricated timber-framed home that can be moved to a new site, although most are permanently located on a 'home park'.

Period property: A property built before 1900 and named after the period in which it was built, e.g. Elizabethan, Georgian or Victorian.

Semi-detached house: A detached building containing two separate homes joined in the middle by a common wall.

Stately home: A grand country mansion or estate, usually a few centuries old, many owned by Britain's oldest titled families and open to the public.

Terraced house: Houses built in a row of three or more, usually two to five storeys high.
Townhouse: Similar to a terraced house but more modern and larger, often with an integral garage.

RELOCATION CONSULTANTS

If you know what sort of property you want, how much you wish to pay and where you want to buy or rent, but don't have the time to spend looking, e.g. you live abroad, you can engage a relocation agent or property search company to find a home for you. This can save you considerable time, trouble and money, particularly if you have special or unusual requirements. Many relocation consultants act as buying agents, particularly for overseas buyers, and claim they can negotiate a better deal than private buyers (which, if true, could save you the cost of their fees).

Some specialise in finding exceptional residences costing upwards of £250,000. Agents can usually help and advise with all aspects of house purchase and may conduct negotiations on your behalf, organise finance (including bridging loans), arrange surveys and insurance, organise your removal to Britain and even arrange quarantine for your pets (see page 271). Most agents can also provide a comprehensive information package for a chosen area, including information about employment prospects, health services (e.g. local hospitals), local schools (state and private), shopping facilities, public transport, sports and social facilities, communications, and amenities and services.

Agents charge a fee of 1.25 to 1.5 per cent of the purchase price (or up to 2 per cent in London) and a retainer of between £300 and £1,000 payable in advance. The retainer is deducted from the fee when a property is purchased, but if no deal is done it's usually non-returnable. To find an agent contact the Association of Relocation Agents (ARA), PO Box 189, Diss IP22 1PE (☎ 01359-251800, 💻 www.relocationagents.com) or look in the Yellow Pages under 'Relocation Agents'. Some companies offer a 'free property locator service' in central London such as RUMC Ltd., 21 Grafton Street, Mayfair, London W1X 3LD (☎ 0207-491 8977, ✉ rumc@btinternet.com).

If you just wish to look at properties for sale in a particular area, you can make appointments to view properties through estate agents (see page 113) in that area and arrange a viewing visit. However, you must make *absolutely certain* that agents know exactly what you're looking for and obtain property lists in advance.

RENTED ACCOMMODATION

Renting accommodation is advisable for people who will be staying in London for one or two years only (when buying isn't usually practical) or those who don't want the trouble, expense and restrictions involved in buying a home. Unlike in most other European countries, there isn't a strong rental market in Britain (less than 10 per cent of private properties are rented in Britain, compared with around 20 per cent on the continent), where families traditionally prefer to buy rather than rent. There's a chronic shortage of good rental properties in London and properties with three or more bedrooms located in good areas are in short supply everywhere. Furthermore, rental accommodation can be prohibitively expensive and the quality of properties often leaves a lot to be desired, particularly at the lower end of the market. **You should be aware that renting accommodation is a jungle in Britain, which has one of the most unregulated letting markets in Western Europe and there's little consumer protection against unscrupulous agents and landlords.**

One of the reasons for the unpopularity of renting in Britain is that it has traditionally been relatively easy to obtain a 95 or even 100 per cent mortgage with repayments over 25 or 30 years (see page 125). This means that it's usually cheaper or no more expensive to buy a home in Britain than it is to rent. According to research done by the Abbey National Bank, renting is around 35 per cent more expensive than buying a home over the long term and people who rent a house 'waste' an average of £85,000 over 25 years! Owners can also make a tax-free profit (or a tax-free loss!) in a relatively short period, as no capital gains tax is paid on the profits from the sale of your principal home. Many people who cannot afford to pay a high mortgage often let a room (or rooms) to reduce the cost.

The 1988 Housing Act deregulated new lettings in the private sector. Since January 1989 new lettings were generally of two kinds: an **assured tenancy** (abolished in 1996) with a long-term security of tenure or an **assured shorthold tenancy** for a fixed period of at least six months (see **Rental Contracts** on page 103). These changes were intended to encourage greater choice and competition in the rental market. Unlike many other countries, 95 per cent of rental properties in Britain are let furnished. The reason is historical, because until January 1989 landlords had much greater protection under the law if properties were let furnished, although this is no longer the case. The furniture and furnishings in many rental properties vary from fair to terrible, except for the rare luxury property that's let for a fixed term by owners spending a period abroad.

Rental property can usually be found in two to four weeks in most areas, with the possible exception of large houses (four or more bedrooms), which are rare and *very* expensive. Family accommodation in particular is in short supply in London, with the possible exception of luxury homes with astronomical rents. Most people settle for something in the suburbs or country and commute to work. Note that if you need to travel into London each day, you should be prepared to spend at least an hour or more travelling each way.

Most rented property is let through letting agencies or estate agents, who charge between £25 and £150 for 'administration', taking up references, drawing up tenancy agreements and making an inventory. You must usually pay one month's rent in advance, depending on the type of property and the rental agreement, plus a deposit against damages equal to one to two months rent. When you agree to rent a property you're usually asked for a holding deposit of between £50 and £200 before an agreement is signed (this should go towards your rent but is often simply an additional fee). Some letting agents charge an up-front fee of around £100 to house hunters with the promise of finding them accommodation, in return for which they simply supply a list of 'vacant' properties often just taken from newspapers. You shouldn't pay a letting agent an up-front fee to find you a property, which is, in any case, illegal.

Agents usually have a number of properties available for immediate occupancy and lists are normally updated weekly. You should have no problem finding something suitable in most areas if you start looking at least four weeks prior to the date when you wish to take occupancy. Most letting agents require a reference from your employer (or previous employer if you have been less than one year with your current employer) and bank, and possibly a credit reference. Copies of audited accounts and status are required for company lets. Agents may ask to see a foreign resident's police registration certificate (see page 251).

Your deposit should be put into a savings account in your name and the name of the agent or landlord, although this is rare (if it isn't and the letting agent goes bankrupt, you will lose your deposit). If possible, you should deal only with a member of the Association of Residential Letting Agents (ARLA) or the National Association of Estate Agents (NAEA), both of which insist that members have a bonding scheme or professional indemnity cover to safeguard rental income and deposits. However, agents are totally unregulated in Britain and you may have no option but to deal with a 'cowboy'.

Local Housing Aid or Advice Centres offer advice concerning finding somewhere to live and usually handle both private and council house problems. Contact your local council for information. A Citizens Advice Bureau can also offer advice regarding the legal aspects of letting and a tenant's rights. In some towns and cities there are council-run housing aid centres where you can obtain free advice on housing problems. There are also a number of useful books published detailing the legal rights and duties of both landlords and tenants including the *Which? Guide to Renting and Letting* (Which? Books).

Single Accommodation

Finding accommodation in London that doesn't break the bank is a huge problem for young people and students (and anyone not earning a fortune). For many the solution is a bedsit, flatlet, lodgings or sharing accommodation with others, officially termed 'houses in multiple occupation' (HMOs). Single accommodation also includes hostels (including student and youth hostels), guesthouses, lodgings, bed and breakfast, and cheap hotels, although these usually provide relatively expensive temporary accommodation only. Don't expect any 'luxuries' in inexpensive accommodation as the standard is generally poor, particularly in areas where demand is high.

The standard of rental accommodation is at its worst in HMOs such as bedsits, studios, shared houses and properties with shared facilities. In an English House Conditions Survey in 1996 it was estimated that around 20 per cent (much higher in London and other major cities) of all privately rented homes were unfit for human habitation. In fact, at the bottom end of the market Britain has among the worst rental accommodation in Western Europe which may include faulty plumbing, poor sanitation, decrepit furniture, insect and rodent infestations, dangerous wiring and unsafe gas appliances. There's little or no control over landlords who get away with almost anything, although legislation has been proposed that will lay down minimum standards and include a registration scheme.

You must be over 18 to hold a tenancy agreement and young people usually find it harder to find a rental property than more mature people, due to the usual arguments that the young are unreliable, noisy, poor, itinerant and untidy (etc.). If you're seeking cheap accommodation, you may find it more difficult in September when the new term starts and students are looking for accommodation. Before taking on long-term accommodation, you may wish to check the council tax rate in the borough (see page 133).

Bedsits: If you prefer to live on your own, but don't want to pay a lot of rent (who does?), the solution may be a bedsit (also called a studio). A bedsit usually consists of a furnished room in an old house, where you live, eat, sleep and sometimes cook. If separate cooking facilities are provided, you must usually share them with someone else (or a number of people). You must also normally share a bathroom and toilet, provide your own linen (sheets, blankets and towels), and do your own laundry and cleaning. Bedsits offer privacy but can be lonely and depressing. A single bedsit costs from around £50 in the provinces and from £75 a week in London. Double bedsits are also available costing from around £75 in the provinces and from £100 a week in London. Slightly up-market from a bedsit is a flatlet or studio flat, which may have its own bath or shower and toilet, and sometimes a separate kitchen or kitchenette (a tiny kitchen). The rent for a studio apartment is around 50 per cent higher than for a bedsit.

Lodgings: Another possibility is to find lodgings (also called digs) in a private home, which is becoming increasingly common as many people are forced to take in lodgers to pay their mortgages. This is similar to bed and breakfast accommodation, except that you're usually treated as a member of the family and your rent normally includes half-board (breakfast and an evening meal). In lodgings you have less freedom than a bedsit and are required to eat at fixed times, but you will at least have some company. Lodgings are often arranged by English-language schools for foreign students. A boarding house is similar to lodgings where the owner takes in a number of lodgers and may provide half-board or cooking facilities. Lodgings or a room in a boarding house cost from around £50 in the provinces to £75 a week in London, for a room with breakfast. With breakfast and an evening meal, the cost ranges from around £75 in the provinces to £100 a week in London.

Shared Accommodation: For many young people and students, sharing accommodation is the answer to high rents. Sharing usually involves sharing the kitchen, bathroom, living room, dining room and possibly even a bedroom. Sharing also usually involves sharing all bills (in addition to the rent) including electricity, gas and telephone, and may also include sharing food bills and cooking. Some landlords include electricity and gas (plus heating) in the rent. The cleaning and the general upkeep of a house or apartment is also usually shared. As always when living with others there are advantages and disadvantages, and success depends on the participants' ability to live together in harmony.

If you rent a property with the intention of sharing, you should ensure that it's permitted in your contract. The cost of sharing a furnished apartment varies considerably depending on the size, location and amenities. A rough guide is from around £50 (single) to £75 (double) in the provinces and from £75 a week in London with your own bedroom. Note that shared accommodation in many areas is in old, run-down houses where even the living and dining rooms have been converted into bedrooms. You may also be sharing with the owner, which can be a bit inhibiting. Flat-sharing is commonplace in London where many newspapers and magazines contain advertisements for flat-sharers, such as the *Evening Standard, Loot* and *Time Out*, the free *Midweek* magazine available from tube stations on Thursdays and a multitude of free expatriate publications such as *TNT* magazine (also available from tube stations). **Capital Radio** publishes a weekly flat-share list available from their foyer at 30 Leicester Square, WC2 on Thursdays.

Rental Costs & Standards

Rental costs vary considerably depending on the size (number of bedrooms) and quality of a property, its age and the facilities provided. Not least, rents depend on the neighbourhood and the suburb or county, and are generally lower the further you are from the centre of London. Rents are high in London, particularly when you consider that renting can cost more than buying a home in many areas. Rents vary from around £300 per month for a tiny bedsit (studio) apartment to £2,000 or more for a three or four-bedroom detached house or luxury apartment in a desirable area. It may be possible to find cheaper, older apartments and houses for rent, but they are rare, generally small and don't usually contain the conveniences that are standard in a modern home, e.g. no central heating or double glazing (heating in old houses can be highly 'eccentric'). If you like a property but think the rent is too high, you should try to negotiate a reduction or ask an agent to put an offer to the owner. In addition to the rent, tenants must pay for utilities such as gas, electricity and phone, and also water if it's metered.

Kitchens normally contain an oven with a grill, refrigerator (usually small), fitted kitchen units, and occasionally a dishwasher and a separate freezer. Many houses don't have basements or utility rooms, so washing machines (usually provided) and dryers are located in the kitchen. Many houses have lofts and garages that are often used for storage. Most have baths (but not enough hot water to fill them!) and may have a separate shower or an *en suite* shower or bathroom. Often shower attachments are run from a bath and don't have a separate power pump, which means that the water trickles out. Bathrooms occasionally contain a bidet. In general, British plumbing is better than that found in many countries, although Americans won't be impressed. All modern houses have central heating (see page 117), although it's rare at the bottom end of the market. An airing cupboard (linen closet) is common and usually contains the hot water boiler. Unfurnished apartments and houses usually have light fittings in all rooms, although there may be no bulbs or lampshades. Fitted wardrobes in bedrooms are rare in older homes and curtain rails aren't provided unless they are built-in. Most houses, whether furnished or unfurnished, are fully or partly carpeted.

Many flats are parts of old houses that have been modernised and converted into apartments. At the bottom end of the market, many properties have dreadful furnishings, e.g. flowery wallpaper which may 'match' the equally awful three-piece suite, with sickly green carpets and brown bathroom suites (or vice versa). Up-market (i.e. expensive) property may, however, be furnished to a high standard. In furnished accommodation you usually need to provide your own bedding and linen, although crockery, kitchen utensils and most household appliances are usually provided. It may be possible to 'throw out' the owner's or landlord's tatty furniture and replace it with your own (but you may have to pay to store it).

The table overleaf shows the average weekly rents (1998) in each London borough, listed in alphabetical order.

Rents:

MONTHLY RENT (£)

Borough	Flats		Houses	
	S–1	2–3	1–2	3–4
Barking & Dagenham	400–475	525–575	550–600	650–900
Barnet	450–800	575–1,100	800–875	875–2,000
Bexley	325–475	400–650	450–550	550–1,000
Brent	425–1,250	600–1,350	700–1,600	750–1,650
Bromley	375–875	575–875	575–875	750–3,000
Camden	525–1,450	875–1,850	1,475–2,200	1,325–4,350
City of London	750–1,350	1,350–2,200	N/A	N/A
Croydon	325–750	475–950	475–950	550–3,000
Ealing	450–1,000	550–1,500	550–1,100	725–2,000
Enfield	400–575	500–700	600–800	650–1,750
Greenwich	300–650	450–1,000	450–800	500–1,300
Hackney	575–750	600–1,000	650–2,175	875–1,750
Hammersmith & Fulham	600–2,175	875–3,450	1,300–1,550	1,650–2,200
Haringey	450–875	650–1,100	725–875	875–1,575
Harrow	525–700	750–1,000	800–900	1,300–2,000
Havering	375–400	450–525	475–600	550–1,000
Hillingdon	400–600	600–2,000	550–900	700–2,500
Hounslow	425–1,300	650–2,000	550–1,750	850–2,000
Islington	650–1,300	1,100–1,750	900–1,750	1,510–2,000
Kensington & Chelsea	650–2,175	1,200–3,500	2,175–3,500	2,600–5,500
Kingston	550–700	700–850	800–900	950–1,500
Lambeth	450–875	600–1,650	800–1,300	1,000–2,250
Lewisham	350–1,000	525–1,500	550–1,300	700–3,000
Merton	400–750	550–1,750	500–1,500	700–2,000
Newham	350–475	500–550	550–600	600–800
Redbridge	350–700	525–850	550–900	600–2,000
Richmond	450–1,300	650–300	575–2,500	750–3,500
Southwark	400–675	650–1,300	750–1,125	950–2,200
Sutton	350–550	550–750	550–750	600–1,250
Tower Hamlets	525–1,750	700–1,350	1,050–1,100	1,100–1,750
Waltham Forest	400–750	575–900	700–900	800–2,000
Wandsworth	550–800	950–2,175	1,000–1,550	1,600–4,000
Westminster	550–3,500	1,050–8,750	1,100–6,500	2,000–9,000

Note: S = Studio, 1 = one bedroom, 2 = two bedrooms, etc.

Rental Contracts

When you find a suitable house or apartment to rent, you should insist on a written contract with the owner or agent, which is called a tenancy or rental agreement. Make sure that you obtain a rent book, which is used to record all payments made. If you don't have a rent book, always pay by cheque and insist on a receipt. Your contract may include details of when your rent will be reviewed or increased, if applicable. When you wish to leave rented accommodation you must give at least one month's notice in writing, unless it's within the first six months of an assured shorthold tenancy (see below), in which case you must pay the rent to the end of the period. If your landlord wants you to leave, the notice he must give you depends on your agreement with him and whether your tenancy is covered by the law. It's a criminal offence for your landlord to harass you in any way in an attempt to drive you out. Under the Housing Act (1988) the following kinds of rental agreements and tenancies were created, which provide tenants with fewer rights than previously and make evictions easier for landlords:

Assured tenancy: An assured tenancy is a tenancy for an indefinite period and doesn't need to be in writing. The landlord cannot live on the premises and providing you pay the rent and take care of a property, you cannot be asked to leave. Your landlord must apply to a county court and must have a good reason to evict you, e.g. unpaid rent, damage to the property or its contents, or you must have otherwise broken your contract with him. However, if he offers you similar accommodation, needs the property for himself, or a mortgage lender requires vacant possession in order to sell it, a court may serve you with written notice to leave. The rent cannot be increased until one year after you have signed a contract and if you don't agree with the increase you can ask the council's Rent Assessment Committee to set a fair rent. **Note that under the Housing Act (1996), assured tenancies are no longer legal for new lettings.**

Assured shorthold tenancy: An assured shorthold tenancy is a tenancy with a fixed time limit, for which a written rental agreement is necessary, clearly stating that it's an assured shorthold tenancy. There was previously an initial minimum let of six months, although a shorter term can now be agreed between the landlord and tenant. You cannot terminate your agreement (or be evicted) during the initial period and thereafter, you or your landlord must give two months notice in writing to terminate the agreement. Under an assured shorthold tenancy you have the right in certain cases to ask the Rent Assessment Committee to set a fair rent, but only during the first six months of the tenancy. Under the Housing Act (1996), all new tenancies have automatically been short-hold tenancies unless rents are over £25,000 a year or other arrangements (such as company lets) are agreed in writing.

No agreement: If you haven't an agreement with your landlord, you're protected under the law and have the same rights as an assured shorthold tenancy (see above) if your landlord doesn't live on the premises. Always try to obtain a tenancy agreement and retain evidence of all payments to your landlord. If, after taking up residence, you're offered a holiday let, licence agreement or tenancy with board and service, you should refuse and contact a Citizens Advice Bureau for advice. These agreements provide you with no security and few legal rights as a tenant.

Flat-sharers: The law regarding flat-sharing is more complicated and it's simpler when one person is the tenant and sub-lets to the others, which must be permitted by the tenant's agreement. It's possible for all sharers to be joint tenants with one tenancy agreement (in which case they are jointly and severally responsible) or individual tenants with individual tenancy agreements. Whatever the agreement, you should have just one rent book and pay the rent in a lump sum. It's usually the occupants' responsibility to replace flatmates who leave during the tenancy.

Fair Rents: A tenant in an assured shorthold tenancy can ask the local Rent Assessment Committee for help in ensuring that his rent isn't too high. Your complaint will be investigated and your rent could be lowered or raised (if it's decided the rent is too low). If you have been overcharged, the landlord can be ordered to repay the excess as far back as two years. Information concerning rent allowances, rent rebates, fair rents and housing benefits is contained in a series of free housing booklets published by the Department of the Environment and available from rent (registration) offices, local authorities, Citizens Advice Bureaux and housing advice centres.

Deposits: Usually a deposit equal to one or two months rent (the maximum permitted by law) must be paid for an assured shorthold tenancy. This should be repaid when you leave, providing there are no outstanding claims for rent, unpaid bills, damages or cleaning. Always check a contract to find out who holds the deposit and under what circumstances it will be returned, and obtain a receipt. Note than many agents and landlords will go to almost any lengths to avoid repaying a deposit and tenants in Britain lose £millions to landlords and letting agents who refuse to repay deposits when a lease expires. Often a landlord will make a claim for 'professional' cleaning running into hundreds of pounds, even when you leave a property spotless. If the landlord fails to return your deposit you should threaten legal action and if this has no affect you should take him to the small claims court.

Don't sign a contract unless you're sure you fully understand all the small print. Ask one of your colleagues or friends for help or obtain legal advice. English law usually prevents you from signing away your rights; nevertheless, it pays to be careful. Note that most rental agreements forbid the keeping of pets. In order to avoid disputes, the agreement should spell out in detail who's responsible for maintenance, e.g. appliances, building, decoration and garden. If you have any questions regarding your rental agreement or problems with your landlord, you can ask your local Citizens Advice Bureau for advice. They will check your rental agreement and advise you of your rights under the law.

BUYING PROPERTY

Buying a house or apartment in Britain has traditionally been an excellent investment, although this was severely tested in the '90s during much of which a property investment was anything but as safe as houses! However, most people still find buying preferable to renting, depending, of course, on how long you're planning to stay in London and where you're planning to live. If you're staying for a short term only, say less than two years, then you may be better off renting (see page 96). If you're planning to stay for longer than two years, have a secure job and can afford to buy, then you should probably do so, particularly as buying a house or apartment is generally no more expensive than renting and you could make a sizeable profit.

Contracts: When buying property in England, prospective buyers make an offer subject to survey and contract. Either side can amend or withdraw from a sale at any time before the exchange of contracts (when a sale is legally binding). In a seller's market, gazumping, where a seller agrees to an offer from one prospective buyer and then sells to another for a higher amount, is rampant and *isn't illegal*. There are proposals to speed up the home buying process (see below), which would reduce the risk of gazumping, although many people believe that following the example of Scotland and many other countries, where a contract is legally binding once an offer has been made and accepted, is the only way to stamp it out altogether. On the other hand, in a buyer's market a buyer may threaten to pull out at the last minute unless the seller reduces the price (called 'gazundering').

The conveyancing process in Britain is among the slowest in the world, with the average time required to complete a sale twice as long as in many other countries. A new law is to be introduced in the year 2000 to speed up the home buying process (to four weeks or less), which will require vendors to produce a 'seller's pack' (at a cost of between £350 and £500). This will include commissioning a survey, collecting the title deeds and conducting local council searches, before putting a home on the market. It's hoped that this will reduce the risk of gazumping. In a sellers' market your chances of being gazumped are high (in 1999 it was blamed for wrecking one in seven deals) and it's so prevalent that you can take out insurance against being gazumped after having paid for a survey and legal fees.

Information: There are numerous books on the subject of buying a home including *Buying a Home in Britain* by your author David Hampshire (published by Survival Books). There are also many magazines published in Britain for homebuyers, including *What Mortgage*, *Mortgage Magazine*, *What House* and *House Buyer*, which contain the latest information about mortgages and house prices throughout Britain. Up-market properties are also advertised in glossy magazines such as *The London Magazine* and national broadsheet newspapers such as *The Sunday Times*. Homebuyer Events Ltd., Mantle House, Broomhill Road, London SW18 4JQ (☎

0208-877 3636) organise regular property shows in Britain. Most building societies and banks publish free booklets for homebuyers, most of which contain excellent (usually unbiased) advice.

HOUSE PRICES

Britain generally has a fairly buoyant property market in most regions, although in recent decades it has been prone to boom and bust cycles. The first boom came in the early '70s, when prices jumped by around 90 per cent in three years to over £11,000 in 1973. The next big increases came at the end of the '70s, when prices rose steadily until skyrocketing in the late '80s. However, the boom years of the late '80s (when property values were doubling every few years in some areas) ended in a disastrous collapse during the recession of the early '90s, when many people lost their homes when mortgage interest rates soared to over 15 per cent. It took almost ten years for house prices to return to what they were at the end of the '80s; in 1998 the average property price was around £65,000, which was about the same as in 1989, although by autumn 1999 it had climbed to over £75,000.

Property prices in London are the highest in Britain and among the highest in Europe, although overall British house prices are below those in Germany, Ireland, the Netherlands and Norway. In late 1999, the average property price was around £120,000 in Greater London and £185,000 in central London, where many properties are sold for seven figure sums (see the table on page 108 for prices in individual boroughs). The cheapest properties tend to be found in unfashionable 'working class' suburbs mainly situated south of the River Thames in districts such as Clapham and Streatham, or in the East End away from the Docklands, although even here prices have risen dramatically in recent years. Note, however, that the cheaper areas generally have poor housing stock and are subject to the typical inner-city problems of neglect, poverty, unemployment and high crime rates.

In 1999, Britain was in the midst of one of the biggest property booms of all time, inspired by a shortage of property and low mortgage rates (in 1999, you could buy a home for twice the price in 1990 and still have lower mortgage payments). However, it was a highly selective boom that varied considerably depending on the region. House prices in London are now astronomical, with a small old-fashioned, one-bedroom apartment costing around £100,000 and a two-bedroom apartment in a new development costing £300,000 or more. (The cost of office space in central London has also soared and in mid-1999 was the second most expensive in the world after Tokyo, at around £50 per ft²/£550 per m².) For the price of a two-bedroom apartment in London you can buy a substantial three or four-bedroom detached house almost anywhere else in the country. However, it's expected that the sheer quantity of homes being built in some areas of London will eventually put a brake on prices.

In London in 1999 there were over ten prospective buyers for each property, which has led some sellers to invite sealed bids, with winning bids up to double the guide price. Buyers have had to move fast in recent years, as good properties at realistic prices were being snapped up by cash buyers as soon as they came onto the market. Not surprisingly, first-time buyers are finding it hard to get their foot on the property ladder. If you're anxious to climb onto the bandwagon, bear in mind that while many analysts expected the boom to last a number of years, others feared a crash was imminent. However, you need to take what the 'experts' say with a pinch of salt as virtually nobody saw the boom coming and even fewer will see the bust coming until it's upon us – if indeed, there's a crash at all!

As with most things, higher-priced houses, e.g. over £250,000 (which outside London are usually termed executive or prestige homes by developers), generally provide much better value for money than cheaper houses, with a proportionately larger built area and plot of land, better build quality, and superior fixtures and fittings. Most semi-detached and detached houses have single or double garages included in the price. When property is advertised in Britain, the number of bedrooms and bathrooms is given and possibly other rooms such as a dining room, lounge (living/sitting room), study, breakfast room, drawing room, library, playroom, utility, pantry, cloakroom, cellar and conservatory. More expensive properties often simply list the number of reception rooms (e.g. lounge, dining room, study, drawing room, etc.).

The total living area in square feet or square metres is almost never stated in ads., although knowing the size of house you want saves a lot of house-hunting time. For most people the size (total area) is much more important than the number of bedrooms. The average size of new homes in inner London is: one-bedroom apartment (650ft²/60m²), two-bedroom apartment (850ft²/80m²), three-bedroom apartment (1,300ft²/120m²), four-bedroom house (2,000-2,500ft²/185-230m²) and five-bedroom house (3,000-3,500ft²/280-325m²).

The table overleaf gives an indication of house prices in 1998 in the London boroughs. Note that in most cases, prices vary considerably depending on the particular area in which a property is located (in some cases a different street or postcode can make a huge difference). The cost per square foot can vary by up to 400 per cent, depending on the location. The boroughs have been listed according to the average purchase price (least expensive first) of a two-bedroom dwelling, which is shown in column six.

House Prices:

HOUSE PRICE (£ '000s)

Borough	Flats (beds)		Houses (beds)		Average
	S–1	2–3	1–2	3–4	2 bed
Barking & Dagenham	30–50	40–60	40–75	65–200	52
Newham	30–50	40–70	55–70	65–150	57
Havering	25–75	45–175	60–85	70–200	66
Bexley	40–60	55–100	45–100	60–200	66
Waltham Forest	35–65	45–80	75–100	80–250	67
Lewisham	30–150	55–300	75–200	100–200	69
Croydon	30–75	55–100	60–120	75–500	71
Redbridge	35–75	50–80	85–140	85–275	73
Sutton	30–65	50–90	60–100	75–375	74
Greenwich	25–85	45–200	55–200	60–400	77
Bromley	30–90	50–145	60–145	85–425	81
Hillingdon	35–80	60–225	60–130	90–300	81
Enfield	35–60	50–200	65–150	75–350	81
Brent	40–115	70–190	90–200	100–340	86
Haringey	30–125	75–300	75–225	80–350	91
Harrow	40–250	100–200	150–200	200–275	93
Lambeth	25–130	75–300	85–260	180–450	94
Barnet	40–100	80–300	60–120	120–400	96
Kingston	50–85	85–150	110–130	100–300	96
Hackney	30–90	70–160	85–165	125–300	97
Hounslow	45–150	60–250	60–275	80–300	99
Merton	40–170	60–400	65–250	80–300	100
Ealing	40–120	55–180	75–170	95–300	100
Southwark	30–110	60–225	85–225	95–375	100
Wandsworth	40–135	80–300	130–275	160–400	126
Tower Hamlets	30–150	55–225	110–160	130–350	127
Richmond	50–150	75–250	100–275	110–450	147
Islington	60–140	155–200	175–350	160–450	152
Hammersmith & Fulham	45–280	120–1.750	200–250	170–600	164
Camden	65–200	125–500	200–500	300–1M	169
Westminster	60–300	100–750	140–550	175–1M	201
Kensington & Chelsea	70–300	150–800	275–400	350–1,000	234
City of London	75–180	150–250	N/A	N/A	N/A

Note: S = Studio, 1 = one bedroom, 2 = two bedrooms, etc.

LEASEHOLD APARTMENTS

Most property in Britain is owned freehold where the owner acquires complete legal ownership of the property and land and his rights over it, which can be modified only by the law or specific conditions in the contract of sale. Most houses, whether detached, semi-detached, terraced or townhouses, are sold freehold. However, this doesn't apply to flats (apartments), which are usually sold leasehold where 'ownership' is limited to the life of the lease, for example, 80 to 100 years for an old building and up to 999 years for a new building (unlike in most other countries, where apartments or condominiums are owned outright under a system of co-ownership).

Most apartments in London are sold leasehold and a property can change hands several times during the life of a lease, although when the lease expires, the property reverts to the original owner (the freeholder). When buying a leasehold apartment, the most important consideration is the length of the lease, particularly if it has less than around 50 years to run, in which case you will have difficulty obtaining a mortgage. Most experts consider 75 years to be the minimum lease you should consider. Leases often contain special terms and conditions which should also be taken into account.

It's sometimes possible for lessees to buy the freehold of their apartments and they may have a statutory right of first refusal if the landlord plans to sell. A lease may also be renewable, which must usually be contained in the leasehold agreement. In 1993 the Leasehold Reform, Housing and Urban Development Act gave certain lessees the right to acquire the freehold or a lease for a further 90 years. This right is available to tenants who have lived in a property for the preceding three years or three of the previous ten years, when the original lease was for 21 years or longer and the ground rent is above a certain threshold. For information contact the Leasehold Enfranchisement Advisory Service (☎ 0207-493 3116), which provides free advice and maintains lists of valuers and solicitors specialising in leasehold properties. If you sell a lease that was drawn up prior to 1996, you must ensure that your solicitor includes an indemnity in the contract that allows you to pass liability for any debts on to the new leaseholder, otherwise you could be held liable – this anomaly was abolished in the Landlord and Tenants (Covenants) Act of 1995.

Apartments are common in London and other cities, but rare elsewhere, particularly in small towns, where they are unpopular and tend to be budget accommodation. In recent years many old properties, including stately homes, hospitals, warehouses, offices and factories have been converted into luxury apartments, which have proved extremely popular in London and other cities where houses are rare and prohibitively expensive. Although there's often little choice if you want to live in a city, many young professionals prefer to live in apartments rather than houses. So called 'mega-apartments', i.e. huge open plan apartments, and loft apartments with double or triple height 'cathedral' ceilings are popular in London as are penthouses, some of which sell for £5 million (£1,000 per ft²) or more in London. They are often an emotive purchase, where you pay dearly for the panoramic views.

New apartments (particularly in London) are invariably lavishly appointed, which is essential nowadays if they are to sell well. The best apartments are beautifully designed and fitted, with developers vying with each other to design the most alluring interiors. These include designer kitchens complete with top quality appliances; en suite bathrooms with separate showers; fitted carpets; built-in wardrobes; ceramic floors in kitchens and bathrooms; and telephone and TV points (including cable) in all rooms. Luxury apartments often have a discreet system that allows you to control the temperature, lighting, security, music and TVs. Many luxury apartments and houses also have air-conditioning or what's called comfort cooling, air cooling or a climate controlled refrigerated air system.

Modern developments often have a leisure complex with swimming pool and gymnasium, sauna, Jacuzzi, tennis courts, plus secure parking and landscaped gardens. Sports facilities are often the clincher in an inner-city development. Some developments also have an in-house medical centre, business centre, private meeting rooms for residents' exclusive use, a restaurant and a bar. Security is a key feature of most developments, which may have a 24-hour caretaker/concierge, CCTV surveillance and a security entry system with entry phones (some even have a video entry system that takes a picture of callers who press your door button when you aren't at home!).

Before buying an apartment it's advisable to ask the current owners about a development. For example, do they like living there, what are the charges and restrictions, how noisy are other residents, are the recreational facilities easy to access, would they buy there again (why or why not?), and, most importantly, is the development well managed? You may also wish to check on your prospective neighbours. An apartment that has other apartments above and below it is generally more noisy than a ground or top floor apartment. If you're planning to buy an apartment above the ground floor, you may wish to ensure that the building has a lift. The ground or garden level apartments (along with the penthouse) are more prone to theft and an insurance company may insist on extra security before they will insure a property. Note that upper floor apartments are both colder in winter and warmer in summer, and may incur extra charges for the use of lifts. Apartments under the roof may also have temperature control problems (hot in summer, cold in winter), although they enjoy better views.

Cost: Prices of apartments vary considerably from as little as £20,000 for a studio or one-bedroom apartment in a small rural town to £100,000 for a small old-fashioned, one-bedroom apartment in London and £300,000 or more for a new two-bedroom apartment. Prices in London, where many apartments are purchased by investors, have risen considerably in recent years and in 1999 were £600 to £700 per ft² (£6,500 to £7,500 per m²) in prime areas. The price often includes a year's free membership of a health club. Bear in mind that amenities such as a health club or gymnasium don't come cheap and there are often high service charges, e.g. £4,000 a year, which may, however, include hot water and heating.

Cheaper apartments are available in London's Docklands and south of the River Thames, where loft conversions can be purchased for around £250 per ft² (£2,700 per m²). Apartments in London are a good investment and have excellent letting potential, always assuming that the rental market doesn't become saturated. Penthouses sell like hot cakes, although few people can afford the astronomical prices (often in the £millions). The best-selling apartments are spacious with at least two bedrooms and good views. Note that in popular developments you must usually buy off plan long before a development is completed – but don't expect it to be completed on time or even to be given a completion date!

In an older development, you should check whether access to private grounds and a parking space are included in the lease. Garages and parking spaces may need to be purchased separately. If you're buying a resale property, check the price paid for similar properties in the same area or development in recent months, but bear in mind that the price you pay may have more to do with the seller's circumstances than the price fetched by other properties. Find out how many properties are for sale in an old development; if there are many on offer you should investigate why, as there could be management or structural problems. If you're still keen to buy, you can use any negative aspects to drive a hard bargain. Note that apartments aren't universally popular, particularly one-bedroom apartments, and can be difficult to sell.

Service Charges: Apartment owners pay service charges for the upkeep of communal areas and for communal services. Charges are calculated according to each owner's share of the development and a proportion of the common elements is usually assigned to each apartment owner depending on the number and size of apartments in a development. Ground floor owners don't usually pay for lifts and the amount that other owners pay depends on the floor (those on the top floors generally pay the most because they use the lifts most). Service charges include such things as road and pathway cleaning; garden maintenance; cleaning, decoration and maintenance of buildings; caretaker; communal lighting in buildings and grounds; water supply (e.g. swimming pool, gardens); insurance; administration; and fees for communal facilities such as a health club or gymnasium. Service charges may also include heating and hot water. Buildings insurance is provided by the freeholder, but you're usually required to have third party insurance for damage you may cause to other apartments, e.g. through a flood or fire.

Always check the level of service charges and any special charges before buying a community property. Fees are usually billed monthly or biannually and adjusted at the end of the year (which can be a nasty shock) when the actual expenditure is known and the annual accounts have been finalised. If you're buying an apartment from a previous owner, ask to see a copy of the service charges for previous years, as owners may be 'economical with the truth' when stating service charges, particularly if they are high. Fees vary considerably and can be relatively high (e.g. £4,000 a year or more) for luxury developments with a high level of amenities such as a health club and swimming pool. They may also increase annually. An apartment block with a resident caretaker will have higher community fees than one without, although it's preferable to buy in a block with a caretaker. If a management company is employed to manage and maintain an apartment block, the service fees will be higher but the building will also usually be maintained better. High fees aren't necessarily a negative point (assuming you can afford them), providing you receive value for money and the development is well managed and maintained. The value of a leasehold apartment depends to a large extent on how well it's maintained and managed.

Disputes over service charges can be acrimonious, although they are usually confined to old buildings. Under the 1996 Housing Act, leaseholders can take disputes over service charges or bad management to a Leasehold Valuation Tribunal (LVT), with a panel comprising a solicitor, a valuer and a third experienced person, as these disputes are no longer decided by the courts. In the past landlords used threats of expensive court action to intimidate owners into paying higher fees. Many landlords have increased their service charges significantly in recent years, which often bear little or no relationship to actual costs, and many people have been hit by high charges for major repairs (see below). It's essential when buying a leasehold property to take legal advice and have the lease checked by a solicitor.

Maintenance & Repairs: If necessary, owners can be assessed an additional service charge to make up for any shortfall of funds for maintenance or repairs. You should check the condition of the common areas (including all amenities) in an old development and whether any major maintenance or capital expense is planned for which you could be assessed. Beware of bargain apartments in buildings requiring a lot of maintenance work or refurbishment. Most developments have a sink or reserve fund to pay for major expenses, which is funded from general service charges.

Ground Rent: Ground rent is a nominal rent for the land on which an apartment block is built and is usually around £100 a year. The lease should indicate whether the ground rent is fixed or whether it can be reviewed after a certain period.

Covenants & Restrictions: Covenants are legally binding obligations of the freeholder and leaseholder to do or refrain from doing certain things, while restrictions are regulations governing how leaseholders are required to behave. Restrictions usually include such things as noise levels; the keeping of pets; renting; exterior decoration and plants (e.g. the placement of shrubs); rubbish disposal; the use of health clubs and other recreational facilities; parking; business or professional use; and the hanging of laundry. Check the regulations and discuss any restrictions that you're unsure about with other residents. Permanent residents should avoid buying in a development with a high percentage of rental units, i.e. units that aren't owner-occupied, although you may have little choice in London.

GARAGES & PARKING

A garage or private parking space isn't usually included in the price when you buy an apartment in Britain, although private parking may be available at an additional cost, possibly in an underground garage. Modern townhouses, semi-detached and detached homes usually have a garage or car port. Smaller homes usually have a single garage, while larger 'executive' homes often have integral double garages or garaging for up to four cars. Parking isn't usually a problem when buying an old home in a rural area, although there may not be a purpose-built garage.

When buying an apartment or townhouse in a modern development, a garage or parking space may be available as an extra, although the price can be high, e.g. £20,000 for a space in an underground garage. Note that the cost of an optional garage or parking space isn't always recouped when selling, although it makes a property more attractive to buyers and may clinch a sale. In suburban and rural areas, a garage is essential and a double garage is even better. The cost of parking is an important consideration when buying a property in London or its suburbs, particularly if you have a number of cars. It may be possible to rent a garage or parking space, although this can be prohibitively expensive in London. Bear in mind that in a large development, the nearest parking area may be some distance from your home. This may be an important factor, particularly if you aren't up to carrying heavy shopping hundreds of metres to your home and possibly up several flights of stairs.

Without a private garage or parking space, parking can be a nightmare, particularly in central London. In many areas of London it's necessary to obtain a resident parking permit from the local council to park on public streets, although this doesn't guarantee you will be able to find a parking space! Free on-street parking can be difficult or impossible to find in London and is inadvisable for anything but a wreck. A lock-up garage is important in London, where there's a high incidence of car theft and thefts from cars, and it's also useful to protect your car from climatic extremes such as ice, snow and extreme heat.

ESTATE AGENTS

Most property in Britain is bought and sold through estate agents (they aren't called real estate agents, realtors or brokers in Britain) who sell property on commission for owners, although an increasing number of people are selling their own homes. Property sold by estate agents is said to be sold by private treaty, a method of selling a property by agreement between the vendor and the buyer, either directly or through an estate agent.

Although there are nationwide chains of estate agents in Britain, e.g. covering England and Wales, most agents are local and don't have a nationwide listing of properties in other regions. There's no multi-listing system in Britain, as there is, for example, in North America, and agents jealously guard their list of properties from competitors. If you wish to find an agent in a particular town or area, look under estate agents in the local Yellow Pages (available at main libraries in many countries), check the Internet (see below) or hire a relocation agent (see page 96) to find you a home. Many estate agents are also letting and management agents.

Internet: You can search for an estate agent or property on the Internet, which has come a long way in recent years and is expected to dominate the market in the next decade (in the USA some 70 per cent of homes are advertised on the Internet). It's particularly useful when you're looking for a property from abroad, when the Internet can be a good place to start and allows you to peruse property lists at your leisure. Some agents offer virtual viewing whereby you can take a guided tour around a property via your computer.

Among the many good websites available are (in no particular order) www.propertylive.co.uk, www.houseweb.co.uk, www.findaproperty.com, www.homedirectory.com, www.property-seeker.co.uk, www.realestate. com, www.hot-property.com/scripts/lootsite.dll, www.fish4homes.co.uk, www.home2view.co.uk, www.propertyfinder.co.uk, www.propertycity.co. uk, www.homes-on-line.com, and www.faronsutaria.co.uk (which is a multi-lingual site). Most of the above sites aren't dedicated to single agents and many allow you to search for homes and agents throughout Britain, e.g. by location and price. Many estate agents produce free newspapers and magazines containing details of both old and new houses, and colour prospectuses for new property developments.

Always choose an estate agent who's a member of a professional organisation, such as the National Association of Estate Agents (NAEA, ☎ 01926-496800, ⌨ www.naea.co.uk). You should also check whether an agent is a member of the Ombudsman Scheme for Estate Agents (☎ 01722-333306), whose members must abide by a code of practice and to whom you can complain if you have a problem.

UTILITIES

Utilities is the collective name given to electricity, gas and water companies (and usually also includes telephone companies). All Britain's utility companies have been privatised in the last decade or so, which was quickly followed by increased prices and worse service. However, in the last few years, most people have been able to choose their electricity and gas supplier and the increased competition has led to lower prices, with many companies promising savings of around 10 per cent to switch companies. Many companies now provide both electricity and gas and offer contracts for the supply of both fuels, often called 'dual fuel', which may result in a discount (although you may be better off buying from separate companies). You can find the cheapest supplier of electricity, gas and water on the Internet (www.buy.co.uk), although you should carefully compare rates, standing charges and services before changing your supplier.

Electricity

The electricity supply in Britain is 240 volts AC, with a frequency of 50 hertz (cycles). This is suitable for all electrical equipment with a rated power consumption of up to 3,000 watts. For equipment with a higher power consumption, a single 240V or 3-phase, 380 volts AC, 20 amp supply must be used (in Britain, this is installed only in large houses with six to eight bedrooms or industrial premises). Power cuts are rare in most parts of Britain, although some areas experience many a year. Electricity companies pay compensation for a power cut lasting longer than 24 hours, but nothing for cuts of less than 24 hours (which includes 99.9 per cent of cuts).

If you move into an old home in Britain, the electricity supply may have been disconnected by the previous electricity company and in a brand new home you will also need to have the electricity connected. In the last few years householders have been able to choose their electricity company from among British Gas, Eastern Energy, Eastern Electricity, East Midlands Electricity, Independent Energy, London Electricity, Manweb, MEB, Northern Electric & Gas, Norweb, Scottish Hydro-Electric, Scottish Power, SEEBOARD, Southern Electric, SWALEC, South Western Electricity and Yorkshire Electricity. Most companies cover the whole country, while a few cover certain regions only.

You should allow at least two days to have the electricity reconnected and the meter read after signing a contract with an electricity company. There's usually a charge for connection. If you're in Britain for a short stay only, you may be asked for a security deposit or to obtain a guarantor (e.g. your employer). You must contact your electricity company to get a final reading when you vacate a property.

Complaints: If you have any complaints about your electricity bill or service, contact your local electricity company. If you don't receive satisfaction, contact the Office of Electricity Regulation (Offer), Hagley House, Hagley Road, Edgbaston, Birmingham B16 8QG (☎ 0800-451451 or 0121-456 2100) or the Electricity Consumer Council, 5th Floor, 11 Belgrave Road, London SW1V 1RB (☎ 0207-233 6366).

Gas

Mains gas is available in all but the remotest areas of Britain. However, you may find that some modern houses aren't connected to the mains gas supply. If you're looking for a rental property and want to cook by gas, make sure it already has a gas supply (some houses have an unused gas service pipe). If you move into a brand new home you must have a meter installed in order to be connected to mains gas (there may be a charge for this, depending on the gas company). In some remote areas without piped gas, homes may have a 'bottled gas' (e.g. Calor Gas) cooker. If you buy a house without a gas supply, you can usually arrange to have a gas pipeline installed from a nearby gas main. You're usually connected free if your home is within 25 metres of a gas main, otherwise a quotation is provided for the cost of the work involved. A higher standing charge is made for properties in remote areas.

Gas was previously supplied by British Gas throughout Britain, which was the monopoly supplier to some 19 million homes. However, since May 1998, everyone in England, Scotland and Wales has been able to choose from up to 26 gas supply companies. Depending on where you live, up to 17 companies may compete for your business including Amerada, Beacon Gas, British Fuels, British Gas, Calortex, Eastern Natural Gas, Energi from Norweb, Independent Energy, London Electricity, Midlands Gas, North Wales Gas, Northern Electric & Gas, ScottishPower, Southern Electric Gas, SWALEC Gas, York Gas and Yorkshire Electricity. In 1998 almost all the new companies were cheaper than British Gas and millions of households had left British Gas for one of its competitors. Among the cheapest suppliers in London are Independent Energy and London Electricity. If your new home already has a gas supply, simply contact the company of your choice to have the gas supply reconnected or transferred to your name (there's a connection fee) and the meter read. You must contact your gas company to get a final meter reading when you vacate a property.

For further information and a wide range of gas brochures, contact your local gas company. If you have a complaint about your gas bill or service and you don't receive satisfaction from your gas company, you can contact the Office of Gas Supply (Ofgas), Stockley House, 130 Wilton Road, London SW1V 1LQ (☎ 0207-828 0898) or the Gas Consumers Council, Abford House, 15 Wilton Road, London SW1V 1LT (☎ 0207-931 0977). See also **Heating** on page 117.

Water

The water industry in England and Wales was privatised in 1989, when ten regional water companies were created to provide water and sewerage services (there are also a further 18 local water-only companies). You're unable to choose your water company (as you are your electricity and gas companies), which have a monopoly in their area. Less than 10 per cent of households in England and Wales have water meters, where you're billed for the actual water used (plus a standing charge). For all other households, water and sewerage rates are based on the rateable value of a property (although rates were abolished in April 1990 and have been replaced by the council tax).

Water companies include an annual standing charge of from £25 to £40 (for both water and sewerage), which is the same for all properties, plus a variable charge based on the rateable value of your property if you don't have a water meter. If you have a water meter installed, water is charged by the cubic metre. Bills, which usually include sewerage, are sent out annually and can usually be paid in full, in two six-monthly payments or in ten instalments. In some areas, water and sewage are handled by separate companies and homeowners receive bills from each company. Since water privatisation in 1989, water bills have increased by some 40 per cent in real terms. The cost of water varies depending on the local water authority, with the most expensive water companies charging almost double the cheapest. The average unmetered annual water and sewerage bill in 1998-99 was around £250.

If you have a complaint that you cannot resolve with your water company, you should contact you local Customer Service Committee or the Office of Water Services (OFWAT), Centre City Tower, 7 Hill Street, Birmingham B5 4UA (☎ 0121-625 1300).

HEATING & AIR-CONDITIONING

Central heating, double or triple-glazing and good insulation are standard in new houses and are essential in Britain's climate. Around 80 per cent of British homes have central heating (including all new homes) or storage heater systems, most of which also provide hot water. Central heating systems may be powered by oil, gas (the most common), electricity (night-storage heaters) or solid fuel (e.g. coal or wood). Whatever form of heating you use, you should ensure that your home has good insulation including double glazing, cavity-wall insulation, external-wall insulation, floor insulation, draught-proofing, pipe lagging, and loft and hot water tank insulation, without which up to 60 per cent of heat goes straight through the walls and roof. Many companies advise and carry out home insulation, including gas and electricity companies, who produce a range of leaflets designed to help you reduce your heating and other energy bills.

The cheapest method of central heating is gas (indicated in ads. as GCH or GFCH), which is estimated to be up to 50 per cent cheaper than other forms of central heating and hot water systems, particularly if you have a high-efficiency, condensing boiler. Many homes have storage heaters that store heat from electricity supplied at the cheaper off-peak rate overnight and release it to heat your home during the day. If an apartment block is heated from a central system, radiators may be individually metered so you pay only for the heating used, or the cost of heating (and hot water) may be included in your service charges. If you wish to install heating in your home, you should use a company that's a member of the Heating and Ventilating Contractor's Association, 34 Palace Court, London W2 4JG (☎

0345-581158 or 0207-229 2488), who operate a guarantee scheme for domestic heating.

You can reduce your heating and other energy bills by saving energy. For information contact your gas or electricity company or your local Energy Advice Centre (☎ 0800-512012). Wasting Energy Costs the Earth (PO Box 200, Stratford-upon-Avon CV37 9ZZ, ☎ 01908-672787) can provide details of energy surveyors in your area who will perform an energy survey for £50 to £100, depending on the size of your property. Information about energy efficiency is also available from the National Energy Foundation, 3 Benbow Court, Shenley Church End, Milton Keynes MK5 6JG (☎ 01908-501908, ✉ nef@natenerg.demon.co.uk).

Air-Conditioning: Although summer temperatures can be above 30°C (86°F), British homes rarely have air-conditioning and aren't usually built to withstand the heat. However, in recent years many luxury apartments and houses have been built with cooling systems such as comfort cooling, air cooling or a climate controlled refrigerated air system. If you want to install air-conditioning you can choose between a huge variety of systems including fixed or moveable units, indoor or outdoor installation, and high or low power. An air-conditioning system with a heat pump provides cooling in summer and economical heating in winter. Note, however, that there can be negative effects if you suffer from asthma or respiratory problems.

MOVING HOUSE

After finding a home in Britain it usually takes just a few weeks to have your belongings shipped from within continental Europe. From anywhere else it varies considerably, e.g. around four weeks from the east coast of America, six weeks from the US west coast and the Far East, and around eight weeks from Australasia. Customs clearance is no longer necessary when shipping your household effects from one European Union (EU) country to another. However, when shipping your effects from a non-EU country to Britain, you should enquire about customs formalities in advance. If you're moving to Britain from a non-EU country, you must provide an inventory of the things that you're planning to import. If you fail to follow the correct procedure you can encounter problems and delays and may be charged duty or even fined. The relevant forms to be completed by non-EU citizens depend on whether your British home will be your main residence or a second home. Removal companies usually take care of the paperwork and ensure that the correct documents are provided and properly completed (see **Customs** on page 249).

It's advisable to use a major shipping company with a good reputation, e.g. a member of the British Association of Removers (BAR). For international moves it's best to use a company that's a member of the International Federation of Furniture Removers (FIDI) or the Overseas

Moving Network International (OMNI), with experience in Britain. Members of FIDI and OMNI usually subscribe to an advance payment scheme providing a guarantee. If a member company fails to fulfil its commitments to a client, the removal is completed at the agreed cost by another company or your money is refunded. Some removal companies have subsidiaries or affiliates in Britain, which may be more convenient if you encounter problems or need to make an insurance claim.

You should obtain at least three written quotations before choosing a company, as costs can vary considerably. Moving companies should send a representative to provide a detailed quotation. Most companies will pack your belongings and provide packing cases and special containers, although this is naturally more expensive than packing them yourself. Ask a company how they pack fragile and valuable items, and whether the cost of packing cases, materials and insurance (see below) are included in a quotation. If you plan to do your own packing, most shipping companies will provide packing crates and boxes. Shipments are charged by volume, e.g. the square metre in Europe and the square foot in the USA. If you're flexible about the delivery date, shipping companies will quote a lower fee based on a 'part load', where the cost is shared with other deliveries. This can result in savings of 50 per cent or more compared with an individual delivery. Whether you have an individual or shared delivery, obtain a delivery date in writing, otherwise you may need to wait weeks or months for delivery!

Be sure to fully insure your belongings during removal with a well-established insurance company. Don't insure with a shipping company that carries its own insurance, as they will usually fight every penny of a claim. Insurance premiums are usually 1 to 2 per cent of the declared value of your goods, depending on the type of cover chosen. It's prudent to make a photographic or video record of valuables for insurance purposes. Most insurance policies cover for 'all-risks' on a replacement value basis. Note that china, glass and other breakables can usually be included in an 'all-risks' policy only when they're packed by the removal company. Insurance usually covers total loss or loss of a particular crate only, rather than individual items, unless they were packed by the shipping company. If there are any breakages or damaged items, they should be noted and listed before you sign the delivery bill (although it's obviously impractical to check everything on delivery). If you need to make a claim, be sure to read the small print, as some companies require clients to make a claim within a few days, although seven is usual. Send a claim by registered mail. Some insurance companies apply an 'excess' of around 1 per cent of the total shipment value when assessing claims. This means that if your shipment is valued at £25,000, a claim must be for over £250.

If you're unable to ship your belongings directly to Britain, most shipping companies will put them into storage and some allow a limited free storage period prior to shipment, e.g. 14 days. **If you need to put your household effects into storage, it's important to have them fully insured as warehouses have been known to burn down!** Make a complete list of everything to be shipped and give a copy to the removal company. Don't include anything illegal (e.g. guns, bombs, drugs or pornographic videos) with your belongings as customs checks can be rigorous and penalties severe. Provide the shipping company with *detailed* instructions how to find your British home from the nearest motorway or trunk road and a telephone number where you can be contacted.

After considering the shipping costs, you may decide to ship only selected items of furniture and personal effects and buy new furniture in Britain. If you're importing household goods from another European country, it's possible to rent a self-drive van or truck. Note, however, that if you rent a vehicle outside Britain you usually need to return it to the country where it was hired. If you plan to transport your belongings to Britain personally, check the customs requirements in the countries you must pass through. Most people find it isn't advisable to do their own move unless it's a simple job, e.g. a few items of furniture and personal effects only. It's no fun heaving beds and wardrobes up stairs and squeezing them into impossible spaces. If you're taking pets with you, you may need to get your vet to tranquillise them as many pets are frightened (even more than people) by the chaos and stress of moving house.

Bear in mind when moving home that everything that can go wrong often does, therefore you should allow plenty of time and try not to arrange your move from your old home on the same day as the new owner is moving in. That's just asking for fate to intervene! If your British home has poor or impossible access for a large truck you must inform the shipping company. Note also that if furniture needs to be taken in through an upstairs window you will usually need to pay extra. See also **Customs** on page 249 and the **Checklists** on page 253.

MOVING IN

One of the most important tasks after moving into a new home is to make an inventory of the fixtures and fittings and, if applicable, the furniture and furnishings. When you have purchased a property, you should check that the previous owner hasn't absconded with any fixtures and fittings that were included in the price or anything which you specifically paid for, e.g. carpets, light fittings, curtains, furniture, kitchen cupboards and appliances, garden ornaments, plants or doors. It's common to do a final check or inventory when buying a new property, which is usually done a few weeks before completion. Note the reading on your utility meters (e.g. electricity, gas and water) and check that you aren't overcharged on your first bill. The meters should be read by utility companies before or soon after you move into a resale property, although you usually need to organise this yourself.

It's advisable to obtain written instructions from the previous owner concerning the operation of appliances and heating and air-conditioning systems; maintenance of grounds, gardens and lawns; care of special surfaces such as wooden or tiled floors; and the names of reliable local maintenance men who know a property and are familiar with its quirks. Check with your local town hall regarding local regulations about such things as rubbish collection, recycling and on-road parking.

HOME SECURITY

When moving into a new home it's often wise to replace the locks (or lock barrels) as soon as possible, as you have no idea how many keys are in circulation for the existing locks. This is true even for brand new homes, as builders often give keys to sub-contractors. In any case, it's advisable to change the external locks or lock barrels periodically, particularly if you let a home. If they aren't already fitted, it's advisable to fit high security (double cylinder or dead bolt) locks. It pays to look at your home through the eyes of a burglar and remedy any weak points. Many modern developments have intercom systems, CCTV, alarms, security gates and 24-hour caretakers. In areas with a high risk of theft (e.g. most areas of London), your insurance company may insist on extra security measures and the policy may specify that all forms of protection must be employed when a property is unoccupied. If security precautions aren't adhered to, a claim can be reduced or even dismissed. It's usually necessary to have a safe for insured valuables, which must be approved by your insurance company.

You may wish to have a security alarm fitted, which is usually the best way to deter thieves and may also reduce your contents insurance (see page 124). It should include all external doors and windows, internal infra-red security beams (movement detectors), activate external and internal lights, and may also include a coded entry keypad (which can be frequently changed and is useful for clients if you let a home) and 24-hour monitoring – with some systems it's even possible to monitor properties remotely from another country via a computer.

New high-tech alarms can be purchased that broadcast a personal message, e.g. "there's an intruder in the house at number XX, please call the police". With a monitored system, when a sensor (e.g. smoke or forced entry) detects an emergency or a panic button is pushed, a signal is automatically sent to a 24-hour monitoring station. The duty monitor will telephone to check whether it's a genuine alarm (a password must be given) and if he cannot contact you, someone will be sent to investigate. Alarms should be approved by the National Approval Council for Security Systems/NACOSS (☎ 01628-37512).

You can deter thieves by ensuring that your home is well lit and not conspicuously unoccupied. External security 'motion detector' lights (that switch on automatically when someone approaches); random timed switches for internal lights, radios and televisions; dummy security cameras; and tapes that play barking dogs (etc.) triggered by a light or heat detector may all help deter burglars. In remote areas it's common for owners to fit two or three locks on external doors, alarm systems, grills on doors and windows, window locks, security shutters and a safe for valuables. You can fit UPVC (toughened clear plastic) security windows and doors, which can survive an attack with a sledge-hammer without damage, and external steel security blinds (which can be electrically operated), although these are expensive. A dog can be useful to deter intruders, although he should be kept inside where he cannot be given poisoned food. Irrespective of whether you actually have a dog, a warning sign with a picture of a fierce dog may act as a deterrent. If not already present, you should have the front door of an apartment fitted with a spy-hole and chain so that you can check the identity of visitors before opening the door. Bear in mind that prevention is better than cure, as stolen property is rarely recovered.

If you vacate your home for an extended period, it may be obligatory to notify your caretaker, landlord or insurance company, and to leave a key with the caretaker or landlord in case of emergencies. One way to avoid burglaries when you're away is to employ house sitters. Home insurance companies usually offer discounts for owners who employ house sitters – you should, in any case, tell your insurance company if you employ a sitter. There are a number of companies including Home Match (☎ 01962-856631), Home and Pet Care (☎ 01697-478515), Homesitters (☎ 01926-630730) and Housewatch (☎ 01279-777412). Check that housesitters are experienced and have been vetted. Companies charge a daily fee (e.g. £20 or £25) plus travelling expenses, a daily food allowance (e.g. £5 per day), and extras for looking after pets such as dogs and cats.

If you have a robbery, you should report it immediately to your local police station, where you must make a statement. You will receive a copy, which is required by your insurance company when you make a claim. When closing up a property for an extended period, you should ensure that everything is switched off and that it's secure.

Another important aspect of home security is ensuring that you have early warning of a fire, which is easily accomplished by installing smoke detectors. Battery-operated smoke detectors can be purchased for around £5 or less (they should be tested periodically to ensure that the batteries aren't exhausted). You can also fit an electric-powered gas detector that activates an alarm when a gas leak is detected. See also **Crime** on page 266.

BUILDINGS INSURANCE

For most people, buying a home is the biggest financial investment they will ever make. When buying a home, you're usually responsible for insuring it before you even move in. If you take out a mortgage to buy a property, your lender will usually insist that your home (including most permanent structures on your property) has buildings insurance from the time you exchange contracts and are legally the owner. If you buy the leasehold of an apartment, buildings insurance will be arranged by the owner of the freehold. Even when it isn't required by a lender, you would be extremely unwise not to have buildings insurance.

Buildings insurance usually includes loss or damage caused by fire; theft; riot or malicious acts; water leakage from pipes or tanks; oil leakage from central heating systems; flood, storm and lightning; explosion or aircraft impact; vehicles or animals; earthquake, subsidence, landslip or heave; falling trees or aerials; and cover for temporary homelessness, e.g. up to £5,000. It usually includes all permanent fixtures and fittings such as baths, toilets, fitted kitchens, bedroom cupboards and interior decoration, i.e. anything that cannot reasonably be removed and taken with you when moving house. Some insurance companies also provide optional cover to include trees and shrubs damaged maliciously or by storms. Note that there may be an excess, e.g. from £25 or £50, for some claims, which is intended to deter people from making small claims. Buildings insurance should be renewed annually and insurance companies are continually updating their policies, so you must take care that a policy still provides the cover required when you receive a renewal notice.

The amount for which your home should be insured for isn't its current market value, but the cost of rebuilding it should it be totally destroyed. This varies depending on the type of property and the area, for example an inexpensive terraced house could cost twice its market value to rebuild whereas a more expensive detached property may cost a lot less than its market value to rebuild, due to the high value of the land. There's generally no deduction for wear and tear and the cost of redecoration is usually met in full. Note that buildings insurance doesn't cover structural faults that existed when you took out the policy, which is why it's important to have a full structural survey done when buying a home.

The cost of buildings insurance varies depending on the insurer, the type of building and the area, and is calculated per £1,000 of insurance, e.g. from £1 per £1,000 of cover per year in an inexpensive area to between £2 to £4 (or over £4 in London) in more expensive areas. Therefore, insurance on a property costing £100,000 to rebuild usually costs from £100 to £400 a year. In recent years, increased competition has reduced premiums. Shop around as many people can reduce their premium by half (but don't believe the advertising blurb, as some companies that claim to save you money actually charge more).

Insurance for 'non-standard' homes such as those with thatched roofs, timber construction, holiday homes, old period properties and listed buildings is usually much higher. The highest level of cover usually includes damage to glass (e.g. windows and patio doors) and porcelain (e.g. baths, washbasins and WCs), although you may have to pay extra for accidental damage, e.g. when your son blasts a cricket ball through the patio window. Always ask your insurer what *isn't* covered and what it will cost to include it (if required). Shop around a number of companies and agents and compare rates (you can do this on the Internet via www.find.co.uk/insurance, www.intersure.co.uk, www.screentrade.com and www. swinton.co.uk).

A booklet entitled *Buildings Insurance for Home Owners*, including a valuation table, is available from the Association of British Insurers (56 Gresham Street, London EC2V 7HQ, ☎ 0207-600 3333). British insurance companies are covered by the Policyholders' Protection Act (PPA), which guarantees that in the event of an insurance company going bust, 90 per cent of the value of any outstanding claims will be met.

Buildings insurance is often combined with home contents insurance (see below), when it may be termed household insurance, although it may be cheaper to buy buildings and home contents insurance separately.

HOME CONTENTS INSURANCE

Home contents insurance is advisable for anyone who doesn't live in an empty house. Burglary and house-breaking is a major problem in Britain (particularly in cities) and there's a burglary every minute somewhere. Although there's a lot you can do to prevent someone from breaking into your home, it's virtually impossible or prohibitively expensive to make your home completely burglar-proof without turning it into a fortress. However, you can ensure you have adequate contents insurance and that your most precious possessions are locked in a safe or safety deposit box. Around one in four homes in Britain have no home contents insurance.

Types of Policy: A basic home contents policy covers your belongings against the same sort of 'natural disasters' as buildings insurance (see page 122). You can optionally insure against accidental damage and all risks. A basic contents policy doesn't usually include such items as credit cards (and their fraudulent use), cash, musical instruments, jewellery (and other valuables), antiques, paintings, sports equipment and bicycles, for which you normally need to take out extra cover. You can usually insure your property for its second-hand value (indemnity) or its full replacement value (new for old), which covers everything except clothes and linen (for which wear and tear is assessed) at the new cost price. Replacement value is the most popular form of contents insurance in Britain; it's best to take out an index-linked policy where the level of cover is automatically increased by a percentage or fixed amount each year.

Premiums are dependent largely on where you live and your insurance company. All companies assess the risk by location based on your postcode. **Check before buying or renting a home as the difference between low and high-risk areas can be as much as 500 per cent!** The difference between premiums charged by companies for the same property can also vary by as much as 200 per cent. Annual premiums are usually calculated per £1,000 of cover and range from around £2 to £3 in a low-risk area to between £10 and £15 in a high-risk area. Although many homeowners in high-risk areas would be willing to forego theft insurance, insurance companies are unwilling to offer this, because premiums would be substantially reduced if theft was omitted (theft is a convenient excuse to load premiums). Your premiums will also be up to 100 per cent higher if you live in a flood-prone area (over one million homes in Britain are at constant risk from flooding).

There are two ways to insure your possessions: 'sum-insured' (where you calculate the cover you need and the insurer works out the premium based on the cover required) and 'bedroom-rated' policies (where you pay a set premium based on the number of bedrooms in your home). Take care that you don't under-insure your house contents (including anything rented such as a TV or video recorder) and that you periodically reassess their value and adjust your premium accordingly – half of all homeowners are thought to underestimate the value of their home contents. Your contents should include everything that isn't part of the fixtures and fittings and which you could take with you if you were moving house. If you under-insure your contents, your claim may be reduced by the percentage by which you're under-insured. It's common for those with valuable belongings to inadvertently under-insure them; don't forget antiques, designer clothes, jewellery, art, collections, etc.

With a bedroom-rated policy the insurance company cannot scale down a claim because of under-insurance, however, you're usually better off calculating the value of the contents to be insured. Some companies have economy (e.g. for struggling authors), standard and deluxe rates for contents valued, for example, from £10,000 to £40,000. You can take out a special policy if you have high-value contents, which may be cheaper than a standard contents policy. However, this usually requires a valuation costing around £300 and therefore isn't worthwhile unless your home contents are worth over £50,000. **Always list all previous burglaries on the proposal form, even if nothing was stolen.**

MORTGAGES

Mortgages (or home loans) in Britain were traditionally provided by building societies, which were created as savings banks for people saving to buy a home. Nowadays, in addition to building societies, you can obtain a home loan from high street and foreign banks (including offshore banks), insurance companies, mortgage companies (including direct mortgage companies), local authorities and even employers. Competition to lend you money is fierce and homebuyers in Britain have a greater variety of home loan finance available than elsewhere in Europe.

When looking for a mortgage it's important to shop around and compare deals. Most high street banks and building societies offer similar deals and you may get a better deal from a small regional building society, although they may not offer fixed rate mortgages. Major lenders often conceal the best deals, which may be available only through mortgage brokers. Although brokers may not provide independent advice, they can save you money and may be able to offer lower rates, free valuations and more generous cashbacks due to inducements offered by lenders to encourage them to push their products. **It's highly advisable to obtain independent advice before taking out a mortgage in Britain, as mortgage mis-selling is widespread.**

Income: You can usually borrow up to 3.75 times your gross (pre-tax) salary or 2.75 times the joint income of a couple. For example, if you earn £25,000 a year and your wife £20,000, you would qualify for a £123,750 mortgage. Note, however, that this varies depending on the lender and some will provide only 3.25 times your salary plus the salary of a partner, while others lend on the basis of 'affordability', which may allow you to borrow much more than 3.75 times your salary. Many people in London and the south-east of England pay between 40 and 50 per cent of their net income in mortgage payments, while in other parts of the country it has fallen to below 30 per cent. Most lenders will give you a 'conditional' decision over the phone and will provide a written 'mortgage promise' that you can show sellers to prove that you're a serious buyer. If you're an employee in steady employment, Britain is one of the easiest countries in the world in which to obtain a mortgage. Foreign residents are assessed on the same basis as Britons, although a newcomer without a credit history in the UK may be unable to obtain as high a loan-to-value as a long-term resident.

Loan-to-Value (LTV): The loan-to-value is the size of the mortgage as a percentage of the price or value of a property. An £80,000 mortgage on a house worth £100,000 is equal to a LTV of 80 per cent. In Britain, most borrowers can obtain 90 to 95 per cent mortgages and some lenders offer 100 per cent mortgages (in 1999 some lenders were offering up to 125 per cent mortgages!). In many other European countries, loans are usually limited to between 50 and 75 per cent of a property's value (the average loan to homebuyers in most European countries is around 60 per cent of the value of a property). Hence the average age of first-time buyers in Britain is around 27, compared, for example, with the mid to late thirties in Germany and Italy. Note, however, that the larger the deposit you can pay (as a percentage of the value), the wider the choice of mortgages and deals available to you.

Interest Rates: In recent years the cost of a standard variable-rate mortgage has fallen considerably and in late 1999 was below 7 per cent (from a peak of over 15 per cent in 1988), the lowest rate for over 40 years, with most lenders offering even lower short-term rates to new customers. Many experts expect sterling base rates (5.5 per cent in November 1999) to come into line with the Euro base rate (which was just 3.5 per cent in late 1999) during the next few years. Rates would be even lower if the difference between the rate at which lenders borrow and the rate they charge homeowners hadn't grown over the last few years (profit margins on mortgages in Britain are around double those in many other countries). As the base rate fell to 5 per cent in spring 1999, many lenders refused to pass on cuts to borrowers, ostensibly to protect savers, because when mortgage rates are cut the interest paid to savers must also be reduced. On a £100,000 interest-only mortgage, savings would be £485 a year if your interest rate was 0.5 per cent lower, £970 (1 per cent), £1,455 (1.5 per cent), £1,940 (2 per cent), £2,425 (2.5 per cent) and £2,910 (3 per cent).

An important aspect of a mortgage is how interest is calculated, which may be daily, monthly or annually. Daily is the best method for borrowers, as when you make payments (or overpayments) they take effect immediately. With a repayment mortgage, payments include part interest and part capital repayments, and when interest is calculated annually, the outstanding debt doesn't decrease daily or even monthly but once a year. This results in you paying interest on money you have already repaid, which has been called downright dishonesty or usury by many analysts. Some lenders claim they cannot calculate interest daily, as it's too expensive to upgrade their computer systems!

The gross monthly payments per £1,000 borrowed for repayment and interest-only mortgages over 20, 25 and 30 years are shown overleaf:

Interest Rate	Repayment Mortgage*			Interest-Only
(%)	20 Years	25 Years	30 Years	Mortgage#
4.00	6.13	5.33	4.82	3.33
4.25	6.27	5.48	4.97	3.54
4.50	6.41	5.62	5.12	3.75
4.75	6.55	5.77	5.27	3.96
5.00	6.69	5.91	5.42	4.17
5.25	6.83	6.06	5.58	4.37
5.50	6.97	6.21	5.73	4.58
5.75	7.12	6.36	5.89	4.79
6.00	7.27	6.52	6.05	5.00
6.25	7.41	6.67	6.22	5.21
6.50	7.58	6.83	6.38	5.42
6.75	7.71	6.99	6.55	5.62
7.00	7.87	7.15	6.72	5.83
7.25	8.02	7.31	6.88	6.04
7.50	8.17	7.48	7.06	6.25
7.75	8.33	7.64	7.23	6.46
8.00	8.49	7.81	7.40	6.67
8.25	8.65	7.97	7.58	6.87
8.50	8.81	8.14	7.75	7.08
8.75	8.97	8.31	7.93	7.29
9.00	9.13	8.48	8.11	7.50
9.25	9.29	8.66	8.29	7.71
9.50	9.46	8.83	8.47	7.92
9.75	9.62	9.00	8.66	8.12
10.00	9.79	9.18	8.84	8.33

* **Repayment Mortgage:** To calculate your mortgage repayments using the above table, simply find the payment that applies to your mortgage rate and term and multiply it by the amount of your mortgage. For example if you borrow £75,000 at 6.75 per cent over 25 years your monthly repayments will be £6.99 x 75 = £524.50.

Interest-Only Mortgage: This column applies only to the interest on your mortgage and the cost of the investment element (e.g. endowment, ISA or pension) of your mortgage that's intended to pay off the capital at the end of the loan period must be added.

Term: The usual home loan period in Britain is 25 years on repayment mortgages and 40 years for interest-only mortgages linked to an endowment, ISA or pension. Note that reducing the term, say from 25 to 20 years, will save you a lot of money, e.g. £12,000 in interest on a £50,000 repayment mortgage. Most mortgages allow you to pay off lump sums at any time, which can also save you thousands of pounds in interest and reduce the term of your loan. For example, a lump sum payment of £5,000 results in a saving of £17,948 on a 20-year mortgage at 7.7 per cent and a payment of £10,000 a saving of £32,551. There are usually minimum lump sum payments, e.g. £500 or £1,000, and lenders may credit lump sum payments immediately, monthly or annually. There are usually penalties with fixed rate loans.

Fixed or Variable Rate: You can generally choose between fixed and variable rate mortgages, where the interest rate goes up and down depending on the base rate. Those who cannot afford an increase in their mortgage repayments are better off with a fixed-rate mortgage where the interest rate is fixed for a number of years (e.g. one year to the whole mortgage term), no matter what happens to the base rate in the meantime. The longer the fixed-rate period, the lower the interest rate offered. If interest rates go down, you may find yourself paying more than the current mortgage rate, but at least you will know exactly what you must pay each month. To judge whether a fixed-rate mortgage is worthwhile, you must estimate in which direction interest rates are heading (a difficult feat even the experts cannot manage). The standard variable rate is usually around 1.5 per cent above the base rate. Building societies typically offer standard variable rate mortgages that are around half a percentage point below high street banks. Some 60 per cent of loans are fixed rate deals and many experts recommend that lenders fix rates to avoid being hit by a rise in the cost of borrowing.

Fees: There are various fees associated with mortgages. All lenders charge an arrangement fee (also called a completion, booking or reservation fee) for establishing a loan, which is either a fixed amount or a percentage of the loan. This is usually from £150 to £400 and is paid when you apply for a loan or when you accept a mortgage. This has been branded a rip-off by mortgage brokers and others in the loan business, particularly as some 20 per cent of purchases fall through and lenders keep the fee. Some lenders charge an up-front application fee and a completion fee when you accept the mortgage. Mortgage brokers may also levy a fee, e.g. 1 per cent of the value of the loan or a fee starting at around £300 to find you a deal. Always check whether fees are refundable if the purchase falls through. There's usually a valuation fee of around £200 and the lender's legal fees, although many lenders now waive these.

Types of Mortgages: Once you've calculated how much you wish to pay for a home, you must decide what kind of mortgage you want. Although there are many different mortgages on the market, all fall into two main categories: repayment and interest-only. Most interest-only mortgages are linked to an endowment (**which should be avoided like the plague!**), investment (such as an ISA) or a pension plan. It's beyond the scope of this book to describe all the various types of mortgages available, but one kind deserves a special mention: flexible or current account mortgages.

Flexible or Current Account Mortgage: One of the most profitable innovations for homebuyers in recent years has been the flexible or current account mortgage (also called an 'all-in-one' account), where you operate your mortgage as a current account within certain limits. With a current account mortgage you have your salary paid into your mortgage account, which automatically reduces your mortgage debt and saves you interest until you withdraw money (interest is calculated daily). You also earn the same interest rate on your savings as you pay on your mortgage and you can borrow additional funds at any time at the same interest rate you pay for your mortgage.

Analysts agree that these accounts are difficult to beat and if you make full use of the account you could save tens of thousands of pounds and pay off your borrowing as fast or slowly as you wish. A typical £100,000 25-year mortgage could be paid off within 17 years with a flexible mortgage, which are expected to become the standard mortgage in the future. Among the lenders offering this kind of loan are Virgin One (☎ 08456-000001, 🖳 www.virgen-direct.co.uk), First Active (☎ 800-550551) and Kleinwort Benson (☎ 0800-317477), although not all allow over payments, payment holidays, a cheque book and borrow back (one that does is the Virgin One Account).

Foreign Currency Mortgages: It's possible for some lenders to obtain a foreign currency mortgage, e.g. in Euros, Swiss francs, US dollars, Deutschmarks or Japanese yen. All these currencies have historically low interest rates and have provided huge savings for borrowers in recent decades. However, you should be cautious about taking out a foreign currency mortgage, as interest rate gains can be wiped out overnight by currency swings. Most lenders advise against taking out a foreign currency loan unless you're paid in a foreign currency (such as Euros), and some lenders will make this a condition of a loan. Euro loans are available for expatriates paid in Euros. This offers lower interest rates than sterling, but usually requires a higher deposit (e.g. 30 per cent) and a high booking fee, e.g. £500.

The lending conditions for foreign currency home loans for UK residents are stricter than for sterling loans and are generally granted only to high-rollers (those earning a minimum of £40,000 or £50,000 a year) and may be for a minimum sum of £100,000 and a maximum of 60 per cent of a property's value. If you take out a foreign currency loan with an offshore bank, switching between major currencies is usually permitted. When choosing between a sterling loan and a foreign currency loan, make sure that you take into account all charges, fees, interest rates and possible currency fluctuations. However you finance the purchase of a home in Britain, you should obtain professional advice from your bank manager and accountant.

Advice & Information: Whatever kind of mortgage you want, you should shop around and take the time to investigate all the options available. One way to find the best deal is to contact an independent mortgage broker. Mortgage advice offered by lenders is often misleading and biased and not to be trusted (surveys have found that the mis-selling of mortgages is widespread among high street lenders). The best independent advice is found in surveys carried out by publications such as *Which?* magazine (see **Appendix A**), which accepts no advertisements, and daily newspapers. The best variable, fixed-rate and discount mortgage rates are published in Sunday newspapers such as *The Sunday Times, The Sunday Telegraph, The Observer* and *The Independent on Sunday*, and in monthly mortgage magazines such as *What Mortgage* and *Mortgage Magazine*. You can also make comparisons on the Internet (e.g. www.moneynet.co.uk, www.money extra.co.uk, www.ftquicken.com, www.hot-property.com/mortgages, www. propertycity.co.uk and www.moneyworld.co.uk).

COUNCIL TAX

The council tax is a property-based tax that replaced the reviled poll tax (or community charge) in 1993, which itself replaced property rates in 1990 in England and Wales. The council tax is a local tax levied by local councils on residents to pay for such things as education, police, roads, waste disposal, libraries and community services. Each council fixes its own tax rate, based on the number of residents and how much money they need to finance their services.

The amount payable depends on the value of your home, relative to others in your area, as rated by your local council (not necessarily the market value). Properties in England are divided into the following bands:

Band	Property Value
A	up to £40,000
B	£40,001-£52,000
C	£52,001-£68,000
D	£68,001-£88,000
E	£88,001-£120,000
F	£120,001-£160,000
G	£160,001-£320,000
H	over £320,000

The tax payable varies considerably depending on the borough or county where you live. In London boroughs, council tax in 1998/99 varied from £212 to £608 for band A to between £638 and £1,824 for band H (see the table on page 133). You can find out what the council tax is in any town in England and Wales via the Internet (www.upmystreet.com).

The tax includes payments for the county, borough or district council; the local police, fire and civil defence authorities; and possibly a 'special expenses' payment in certain areas. It can usually be paid by direct debit from a bank or building society account, by post with a personal cheque, in person at council offices, by credit card, or at a bank or post office. Payment can be made in a lump sum (for which a reduction may be offered) or in ten instalments a year, from April to January. In recent years, council tax has increased due to inadequate funding from central government and many councils have also been forced to cut services to meet their budgets. Taxes increased by 5 to 10 per cent in many parts of England in 1999.

The full council tax assumes that two adults are living permanently in a dwelling. If just one adult lives in a dwelling (as their main home), the bill is reduced by 25 per cent. If a dwelling isn't a main home, e.g. it's unoccupied or is a second home, the bill is reduced by 50 per cent. Exempt dwellings include those that are unfurnished (exempt for up to six months); undergoing structural alteration or major repair (exempt for up to six months after completion); are left empty for specific reasons (e.g. the occupier is in hospital, a nursing home or prison, or is a student); or are occupied by people under 18 years of age only.

Certain people aren't counted when calculating the number of adults resident in a dwelling, e.g. full-time students and 18 and 19 year-olds who have just left school. If you or someone who lives with you has special needs arising from a disability, you may be entitled to a reduction in your council tax bill. Those receiving Income Support (social security) usually pay no council tax and others on low incomes have their bills reduced. You can appeal against the assessed value of your property and any errors due to exemption, benefits or discounts.

All those who are liable for council tax must register with their local council when they take up residence in a new area and are liable to pay council tax from their first day of residence. A register is maintained by councils containing the names and addresses of all people registered for council tax, which is open to public examination. If you don't want your name and address to appear on the register you can apply for anonymous registration. New arrivals in Britain must register with their local council after taking up residence in Britain or after moving house. When moving to a new county or borough, you may be entitled to a refund of a portion of your council tax.

The table opposite shows annual council tax rates (to the nearest £1) for 1999/2000 in the 33 London boroughs. Note that tax levels bear no relation to the price of property, e.g. Kensington & Chelsea and Westminster have some of the highest house prices, but among the lowest council tax charges.

Council Tax Rates:

BOROUGH	A	B	C	D	E	F	G	H
					BAND			
Barking & Dagenham	£492	£574	£656	£738	£902	£1,066	£1,230	£1,476
Barnet	£507	£592	£676	£761	£930	£1,099	£1,268	£1,522
Bexley	£500	£583	£667	£750	£917	£1,084	£1,250	£1,500
Brent	£452	£528	£603	£674	£829	£980	£1,131	£1,357
Bromley	£447	£521	£596	£670	£819	£968	£1,117	£1,340
Camden	£598	£697	£797	£897	£1,096	£1,295	£1,494	£1,793
City of London	£357	£417	£476	£536	£655	£774	£893	£1,072
Croydon	£505	£590	£674	£758	£926	£1,095	£1,263	£1,516
Ealing	£469	£547	£625	£703	£860	£1,016	£1,172	£1,407
Enfield	£488	£570	£651	£733	£895	£1,058	£1,221	£1,465
Greenwich	£589	£687	£785	£883	£1,080	£1,276	£1,472	£1,767
Hackney	£526	£614	£702	£790	£965	£1,141	£1,316	£1,579
Hammersmith & Fulham	£551	£643	£735	£827	£1,011	£1,195	£1,378	£1,654
Haringey	£598	£698	£798	£898	£1,098	£1,297	£1,497	£1,796
Harrow	£525	£613	£700	£788	£963	£1,138	£1,313	£1,575
Havering	£527	£614	£702	£790	£966	£1,041	£1,317	£1,580
Hillingdon	£509	£594	£679	£764	£933	£1,103	£1,273	£1,527
Hounslow	£530	£619	£707	£795	£972	£1,049	£1,326	£1,591
Islington	£608	£709	£811	£912	£1,115	£1,317	£1,520	£1,824
Kensington & Chelsea	£382	£446	£509	£573	£700	£827	£954	£1,146
Kingston	£529	£617	£705	£794	£970	£1,147	£1,323	£1,587
Lambeth	£428	£499	£571	£642	£785	£927	£1,070	£1,284
Lewisham	£485	£566	£647	£728	£890	£1,051	£1,213	£1,456
Merton	£522	£610	£697	£784	£959	£1,133	£1,307	£1,568
Newham	£470	£548	£626	£704	£861	£1,018	£1,174	£1,409
Redbridge	£500	£583	£667	£750	£917	£1,083	£1,250	£1,500
Richmond	£556	£649	£742	£834	£1,020	£1,205	£1,391	£1,669
Southwark	£539	£629	£719	£809	£988	£1,168	£1,348	£1,617
Sutton	£499	£582	£665	£749	£915	£1,081	£1,248	£1,497
Tower Hamlets	£449	£524	£599	£674	£824	£974	£1,123	£1,348
Waltham Forest	£560	£654	£749	£840	£1,022	£1,214	£1,400	£1,681
Wandsworth	£247	£288	£329	£370	£452	£534	£616	£740
Westminster	£233	£272	£311	£350	£428	£506	£583	£700

4.

EARNING A LIVING

There are over 250,000 businesses in London employing some three and a half million people (2 million men and 1.5 million women). The vast majority of businesses are small, with almost 90 per cent employing less than 25 people and just 10 per cent with a turnover of over £1 million. Compared with the UK as a whole, London has a high proportion of self-employed people, which has risen sharply in recent years. Between spring 1997 and spring 1998, an additional 17,000 men and 16,000 women registered as self-employed in London, and there are now almost 50 per cent more self-employed women in London than there were a decade ago (the overall increase is 10 per cent). This trend looks set to continue, with large companies 'downsizing' and 'outsourcing', and an increasing number of small businesses being set up to provide services for them.

Despite a vast labour market and inflated salaries, London has higher unemployment than the UK as a whole, at just over 8 per cent compared with 6 per cent nationally, although most people with good qualifications or experience have little trouble finding a job. In fact, many Europeans find that job opportunities in London (and Britain in general) far outweigh those in their home countries. Note, however, that if you don't automatically qualify to live in Britain, for example as a national of a European Economic Area (EEA) country (see page 11), obtaining a work permit will probably be more difficult than finding a job.

Average earnings in London have always been significantly higher than the UK average, although the cost of living is also higher (see page 265). Men in manual (blue-collar) jobs earn around 12 per cent more than the UK average, while those in non-manual (white-collar) occupations earn almost 30 per cent more (the figures for women are 15 and 27 per cent respectively). This is largely a reflection of the high earnings in the financial and business services sectors, and the high salaries paid to managers and administrators generally. The highest paid workers in London earn over 35 per cent more than their counterparts elsewhere in the UK, and earnings in professional and technical occupations are 45 per cent higher than the UK average.

Over the past few decades there has also been a shift (throughout the UK, but more marked in the capital) away from manufacturing towards service industries. Today, London's job market is dominated by financial and business services (39 per cent) followed by other services industries such as education, social work and health (16 per cent); distribution, hotels and catering (14 per cent); transport, storage and communications (10 per cent); public administration and defence (5 per cent); and other industries (6 per cent). Manufacturing now makes up just 10 per cent of London's GDP, most of which is concentrated in just a few areas.

What little is left of London's manufacturing industry is confined largely to the boroughs of Hackney and Barking & Dagenham, the latter being the only London borough to have a higher proportion (31 per cent) of employees in manufacturing than the UK average (18 per cent), thanks largely to the Ford car plant at Dagenham. Other boroughs with a significant manufacturing industry include Brent (mainly food and drink), Haringey (footwear, printing and publishing, drink, food and tobacco, metal goods, motor vehicles, rubber and plastic products, timber and wooden goods), Tower Hamlets (mainly clothing and printing), Merton and Waltham Forest.

The highest concentration of service industries is to be found in a 'corridor' across north and central London incorporating the boroughs of Barnet, Camden, City, Westminster, Kensington & Chelsea, Hammersmith & Fulham, and Wandsworth, where over 90 per cent of jobs are in the service sector. Certain areas also concentrate on specific business sectors, for example the City of London is (of course) mostly finance and insurance, a sector which is also on the increase in neighbouring Tower Hamlets. Docklands (in Tower Hamlets) is still being developed and will comprise over half a million square metres of office and retail space by the time building is completed. The workforce of Canary Wharf alone is expected to total around 100,000 by the year 2006. On the other side of central London, Hammersmith & Fulham has recently become the focus of the media and entertainment industries, and in Kensington & Chelsea there are opportunities in the pharmaceutical and cosmetics industry, creative and media work, leisure and tourism. Cultural and media jobs are also available in Lambeth.

QUALIFICATIONS

The most important qualification for working in London is the ability to speak fluent English. Once you have overcome this hurdle you should establish whether your trade or professional qualifications and experience are recognised in Britain. If you aren't experienced, British employers usually expect studies to be in a relevant discipline and to have included work experience. Professional or trade qualifications are necessary to work in many fields in Britain, although these aren't as stringent as in many other European Union (EU) countries.

Theoretically, all qualifications that are recognised by professional and trade bodies in one EU country should be recognised in Britain. However, recognition varies from country to country and in some cases, foreign qualifications aren't recognised by British employers or professional and trade associations. All academic qualifications should also be recognised, although they may be given less prominence than equivalent British qualifications, depending on the country and the educational establishment where they were earned.

All EU member states issue occupation information sheets containing a common job description with a table of qualifications, which are published in the various languages of the member states. These cover a large number of trades and professions and are intended to help someone with the relevant qualifications look for a job in another EU country. In most jobs and trades, member states are already required to recognise qualifications and experience obtained elsewhere in the EU. To obtain a comparison of British qualifications and those recognised in other EU countries contact the Qualifications and ITOs Branch, Department for Education and Employment, Overseas Labour Service, Moorfoot, Sheffield S1 4PQ (☎ 0114-275 3275, 🖥 www.dfee.gov.uk/ols).

JOB HUNTING

When looking for a job in London, it's advisable not to put all your eggs in one basket and to spread your net far and wide – the more job applications you make, the better your chances of finding the right job. Contact as many prospective employers as possible, either by writing, telephoning, or calling on them in person. Whatever job you're looking for, it's important to market yourself correctly and appropriately, which depends on the type of job you're after. For example, the recruitment of executives and senior managers is handled almost exclusively by consultants, who advertise in the British quality national press (and also abroad) and interview all applicants prior to presenting clients with a shortlist. At the other end of the scale, manual or part-time jobs requiring no previous experience may be advertised at Jobcentres, in local newspapers and in shop windows, and the first suitable, able-bodied applicant may be offered the job on the spot.

Your method of job hunting will depend on your particular circumstances, qualifications and experience and the sort of job you're looking for, and may include the following:

- Contacting the **Employment Service** (see below) and visiting local **Jobcentres** (see page 139).

- Registering with private **recruitment consultants and employment agencies** (see page 140).

- Obtaining copies of British daily and weekly **newspapers**, most of which have 'positions vacant' sections on certain days (see page 141).

- Surfing the **Internet** (see page 142), where there are literally hundreds of sites for jobseekers including corporate websites, recruitment companies and newspaper job advertisements.

- Checking **TV Teletext** job services (on BBC, ITV and Sky).

- Making applications directly to **companies** in London. You can obtain a list of companies operating in a particular field from trade directories, such as *Kelly's* and *Kompass*, copies of which are available at reference libraries in London and **British Chambers of Commerce** overseas. Most medium to large companies also advertise job vacancies on the Internet.

- **Networking**, basically getting together with like-minded people to discuss business, which is a popular way of making business and professional contacts in Britain. It can be particularly successful for executives, managers and professionals when job hunting.

- Asking **relatives, friends or acquaintances** working in London whether they know of an employer looking for someone with your experience and qualifications.

If you're already in London, you can contact or join expatriate social clubs, churches, societies and professional organisations, or your country's chamber of commerce. Many good business contacts can also be made among expatriate groups.

RESOURCES

Among the best resources for those seeking employment in London are the Employment Service, Jobcentres, recruitment agencies and consultants, newspapers and other publications, and the Internet.

Employment Service

The Employment Service (☎ 0207-211 3000, 💻 www.employmentservice. gov.uk) provides a number of services and programmes to help new job-seekers, unemployed people (particularly long-term unemployed people), those with disabilities and others who may need extra help in finding a job. A new service, Employment Service Direct, allows jobseekers to find a job for the price of a local phone call (☎ 0845-606 0234, textphone 0845-6055 255, 9am to 6pm weekdays and 9am to 1pm Sat). The Employment Service provides most of it services through Jobcentres (see below).

Jobcentres

Jobcentres (written as one word) are government offices run by the Department of Education and Employment where local companies advertise job vacancies and where the unemployed can obtain information about government employment and training schemes. The vast majority of jobs advertised in Jobcentres are manual or low paid and they don't usually include managerial or professional positions (or jobs for 16 to 18-year-olds, which are advertised in careers' centres). Jobs are displayed on boards under headings such as building, clerical, domestic, drivers, engineering, factory, hairdressing, hotel and catering, industrial, motor trade, nursing, office, receptionists, temporary, shops and latest vacancies (where new vacancies are initially posted). Most Jobcentres provide details of all kinds of vacancies, although some offices specialise in certain industries, e.g. the Denmark Street Jobcentre in Camden (☎ 0207-853 3200) specialises in hotel and catering jobs. You can search for a Jobcentre via the Employment Service website (www.employmentservice.gov.uk).

Jobcentres are generally self-service, although staff are on hand to provide advice and help when required. If you find a job that's of interest, write down the reference number and take it to one of the staff, who will tell you more about it and arrange an interview if required. You can register with a Jobcentre by completing a card and providing details of the kind of job you're looking for. If the Jobcentre doesn't deal with your profession or industry, they should be able to tell you about other sources of information. When a job comes in that matches your requirements, you will be informed. However, don't rely on this method but check the boards regularly, as new jobs are displayed each morning and good jobs don't remain vacant for long. You can usually check on new vacancies by telephone. Note also that London boroughs have their own employment centres or 'job shops' where jobs with the local council are advertised (jobs may also be advertised in the Internet).

Employment Agencies & Consultants

Private employment agencies and recruitment consultants (also known as head-hunters) abound in London where they outnumber pubs and restaurants. Most large companies are happy to engage consultants to recruit staff, particularly executives (head-hunters account for around two-thirds of all top-level executive appointments in Britain), managers, professional employees and temporary office staff (temps). Most agencies specialise in particular fields or positions, e.g. computer personnel, accounting, executives and managers, sales staff, secretarial and office staff, catering, engineering and technical, nursing, industrial recruitment and construction, while others deal with a range of industries and professions.

Some agencies deal exclusively with temporary workers such as office staff, baby-sitting, home care, nannies and mothers' helps, housekeeping, cooks, gardeners, chauffeurs, hairdressing, security, cleaners, labourers and industrial workers. Nursing agencies are also fairly common (covering the whole range of nursing services including physiotherapy, occupational and speech therapy and dentistry), as are nanny and care agencies. The largest agencies in London include Adecco, Alfred Marks, Brook Street, Kelly Services, Manpower, Prime and Reed Employment, all of which have offices throughout the city.

Employment agencies make a lot of money from finding people jobs, so providing you have something to offer, they'll be keen to help you (if you're an accountant or a computer expert, you may get trampled in the rush to find you a job). If they cannot help you, they'll usually tell you immediately and won't waste your time. A list of agencies specialising in particular trades or professions can be obtained from the Federation of Recruitment and Employment Services (36-38 Mortimer Street, London W1N 7RB, ☎ 0207-323 4300), which represents some 5,500 recruitment offices. To find your local agencies look in the Yellow Pages under 'Employment Agencies'. Many local newspapers have an 'Employment Agency Directory' and agencies also advertise jobs via TV teletext and the Internet (see page 142).

Newspapers and Magazines

The national newspapers all have 'situations vacant' or 'appointment' sections, some of which specialise in particular fields or industries on certain days, e.g. Monday's *Guardian* for sales, marketing, PR and secretarial, Wednesday's *Times* for secretarial, and Thursday's *Daily Telegraph* for technical and managerial, sales and marketing. The Sunday broadsheet newspapers such as the *Observer, Sunday Telegraph* and *Sunday Times* also have 'appointments' sections for management staff and professionals. Most newspapers also list all jobs advertised on the Internet, e.g. www.jobs unlimited.co.uk (*Guardian*) and www.careerlink. co.uk (*Daily Mail*).

The London *Evening Standard Classified* (☎ 0207-938 3838) is published on a Friday (£1.20). Each area of London has local (free) newspapers and magazines, most of which also contain recruitment sections, and many London boroughs have business magazines or newsletters, e.g. Croydon Marketing and Development Ltd. publish an information sheet, *Croydon – The Facts* (☎ 0208-686 2233, 🖳 www.croydon.gov.uk/index-working.htm). The **Federation of Jobseekers** (☎ 0800-320 588/ 0207-323 4300) publishes lists of jobs in different sectors (£3.75 each).

A number of free newspapers and supplements for jobseekers aged 21-45 are also published in London, including *Girl About Town, Midweek* (men), *Ms London* and *Nine to Five* (men), all of which are published on Mondays by Independent Magazines (UK) Ltd. (7-9 Rathbone Street, London W1P 1AF, ☎ 0207-636 6651, 🖳 www.londoncareers.net). Others include *Metro London* (☎ 0207-651 5200), a free daily (Mon-Fri) newspaper aimed at commuters travelling into London; *TNT* and *Southern Cross* (☎ 0207-373 3377), free magazines targeted at Australians and New Zealanders living in London containing a wealth of ads. from employment agencies; and *Just the Job* (✉ justthejob@standard.co.uk) distributed free with the *Evening Standard* on Mondays. Most of the above are distributed free at train and tube stations and other outlets such as newsagents, pubs, and newspaper dispensing machines in central London.

Placing an advertisement in the 'Situations Wanted' section of a local newspaper in London may also prove fruitful and if you're a member of a recognised profession or trade you could place an advertisement in a newspaper or magazine dedicated to your profession or industry.

The Internet

The Internet is fast becoming one of the most important resources for both job hunters and employers. In addition to those listed below, don't neglect newspaper websites (where jobs advertisements are usually listed) and company websites – many companies receive as many as half of all their job applications via advertisements placed on their websites. Listed below are some of the many websites for those seeking a job in London:

- www.badenochandclark.com (a recruitment consultant specialising in accountancy, banking/financial services, law and IT jobs)

- http://cafe.sdc.uwo.ca/joblistings (lists jobs for students)

- www.careermosaic-uk.co.uk (has a database of vacancies world-wide plus details on hundreds of the world's top employers – you can also post your CV online for employers to peruse)

- www.dotjobs.co.uk (for jobs throughout the UK in the IT and technical sectors)

- www.gradunet.co.uk (for graduate jobs throughout the UK and abroad)

- www.jobmart.co.uk (a basic job search site)

- www.jobs-by-email.co.uk (lists up to 3,500 jobs in various categories in the UK and abroad)

- www.jobserve.com (claims to be the UK's largest source of IT vacancies)

- www.jobsite.co.uk (lists vacancies in all sectors advertised by top European companies and recruitment agencies – claims to be the UK's premier Internet recruitment site)

- www.jobstop.co.uk (general site for advertisers and jobseekers)

- www.london.hrdc-drhc.gc.ca/jobbank/index_e.html (lists jobs in London)

- www.londoncareers.net (lists selected jobs advertised in the free weekly magazines – see page 141 – *Girl About Town*, *Midweek*, *Ms London* and *Nine to Five*, including information for overseas applicants)

- www.manpower.co.uk (Manpower Recruitment Services' site)

- www.monster.co.uk (a search engine for both job seekers and employers)

- www.peoplebank.com (a database of vacancies and CVs which matches jobseekers with employers)

- www.prospects.csu.ac.uk (for graduate jobs and postgraduate study)

- www.reed.co.uk (Reed Recruitment's site on which you can post your CV and search for suitable jobs or careers)

- www.stepstone.co.uk (a general and European job search site)
- http://taps.com (a general UK and international job search site)
- www.uk.topjobs.net (lists elite jobs in the UK)

Each London borough also has its own website containing information on jobs, all of which can be accessed via www.bubl.ac.uk/uk/england/london.htm; the addresses of individual sites are www.[borough name].gov.uk, e.g. www.brent.gov.uk. Particularly useful for job-hunting are Haringey's (www.investinharingey.org.uk), Hackney's (http://jobline.hackneylink.org.uk) and Newham's (www.newham.gov.uk/jobops/jobs.asp).

SELF-EMPLOYMENT & DOING BUSINESS

Anyone who's a British citizen, an EEA-national, or a permanent resident can work as self-employed in Britain, which includes partnerships, co-operatives, franchise and commission-only jobs, or a private business. There have traditionally been fewer restrictions and red tape for anyone wanting to start a business or work as self-employed in Britain, although this has changed in recent years with a veritable tidal wave of employment legislation emanating from both the British government and the European Union. Many experts believe that red tape is strangling enterprise, so much so that many companies pay consultants a retainer just to be kept informed of new legislation! You must be particularly wary of employment legislation, which can be *very* expensive if you fire an employee and are subsequently sued for unfair dismissal.

However, this doesn't deter most people and Britain is traditionally a country of enterprise and entrepreneurs, where the business climate positively encourages self-employment and business creation. The key to starting and running a successful business is exhaustive research, research and yet more research. If you want to join London's growing legions of self-employed, you need to carefully select the area in which to establish your business. Each borough, naturally, claims special advantages and is keen to attract entrepreneurs who will stimulate the local economy. Consequently there's no shortage of information and advice (most of it free) on all aspects of starting and developing a business, either in London as a whole, a particular region, or individual boroughs.

General Information

The organisations listed below provide general information about doing business in London.

- **Business Link London** (⌨ www.businesslink.co.uk) provides independent advice, information and support services, including benchmarking, market research, consultancy subsidies, seminars and training courses. There are eight regional offices: central (☎ 0207-316 1000), city partners (☎ 0207-324 2700), east (☎ 0208-432 0400), north (☎ 0208-447 9422), north-west (☎ 0208-901 5000), south (☎ 0208-315 6666), south-west (☎ 0208-780 6500) and west (☎ 0208-577 1010), which can be contacted directly or via the Business Link London switchboard (☎ 07000-405060).

- The **Department of Trade and Industry** (☎ 0207-215 5000, 🖳 www. dti.gov.uk) provides a wealth of information and publications for budding entrepreneurs.

- **Greater London Enterprise** (☎ 0207-403 0300/0207-815 6930) provides support for smaller companies through loans, advice and training.

- The **London First Centre** (☎ 0207-925 2000) is the inward investment agency for London, providing a free and confidential service to companies considering London as a business location. It provides a general introduction to London and a complete relocation service, from assistance with company registration to identifying the best location and finding premises. It can also introduce companies to potential partners and investors.

- The **London Regional Supply Network** (☎ 0207-203 1953) links buyers and suppliers to help companies obtain the most competitive supplies and help suppliers find outlets and opportunities. Supported by the DTI, the RSN provides free and impartial information.

- The **Prince's Youth Business Trust** (☎ 0207-543 1234) provides financial and other assistance to those aged 18–30 starting a business.

Organisations that can help once your business is established include:

- The **London Chamber of Commerce and Industry** (☎ 0207-248 4444) is the largest business organisation in London, whose members range from small retailers to large 'blue chip' companies. It seeks to help businesses succeed by representing and promoting their interests and expanding their opportunities, through providing members with business information, co-ordinating trade missions, and organising training and networking events.

- The **London Growth Fund** provides low interest loans to companies that have been trading for at least a year and wish to expand. For information contact Greater London Enterprise (see above).

Regional Organisations

There are seven Training and Enterprise Councils (🖳 www.tec.co.uk) in central London which run networking events and providing training and business support services through local chambers of commerce, Business Link offices, enterprise agencies and other local organisations:

- **AZTEC** (☎ 0208-547 3934, ✉ info@aztec-iip.co.uk) is the Training and Enterprise Council (TEC) for south-west London covering the boroughs of Merton, Kingston and Wandsworth.

- **Focus Central London TEC**, Centre Point, 103 New Oxford Street, London WC1A 1DR (☎ 0800-243 9433 or 0207-896 8484, 🖳 www.focusnet-works.com) is the largest training and enterprise council in the country. It provides information on trends and forecasts for the central London labour market and helps new and existing businesses with recruitment and training of staff, managing their human resources and obtaining national 'Investor in People' standards.

- **London East TEC** (☎ 0208-432 0000) is the Training and Enterprise Council for the eastern boroughs of Barking & Dagenham, Havering, Newham, Redbridge, Tower Hamlets and Waltham Forest.

- **North London TEC** (☎ 0208-447 9422, ✉ post@nltec.co.uk) covers the boroughs of Barnet, Enfield and Haringey.

- **North West London TEC** (☎ 0208-901 5000) covers the boroughs of Brent and Harrow.

- **SOLOTEC** (☎ 0800-800222 or 0208-313 9232) is the new name of the South London Training and Enterprise Council, covering the boroughs of Bexley, Bromley, Croydon, Greenwich, Lewisham and Sutton.

- **West London TEC** (☎ 0208-577 1010, ✉ info@wltec.co.uk) covers Ealing, Hillingdon, Hounslow and Richmond.

Other regional organisations offering advice and information include the following:

Central: The **Portobello Business Centre** (PBC) in North Kensington (☎ 0207-460 5050) is central London's leading enterprise agency, specialising in providing advice to new businesses in various sectors including media, fashion, catering, design, building and craft manufacturing. PBC also provides information on sources of funding and runs training programmes.

East: The **Business Enterprise Exchange** (☎ 0208-215 0700) is funded by the European Commission to help small and medium-size enterprises (SMEs) to develop. ELSBC (☎ 0207-377 8821) provides a business start-up service.

North: The **Barfield Group** (☎ 0208-447 1000) provides business support services in north London and operates a business start-up loan scheme called Team 2. Most programmes are funded by the North London TEC and are therefore free to those who meet the qualifying criteria. The **Global Trade Centre** helps small and medium size businesses to develop and consolidate international trade links. **London Ventures** is a venture capital fund created by Midland Bank in partnership with North London TEC and the **Team Loan Scheme** is to help small companies raise loans (for information about these contact **Business Link London North,** ☎ 0208-447 9422). The **North London Business Development Agency** (☎ 0207-359 7405) provides support and advice to businesses run by members of ethnic minority groups.

South: The **South Central Business Advice Service** in Brixton (☎ 0207-924 9078) was created to support and advise businesses with fewer than ten employees, while the **Wandle Valley Partnership** (☎ 0208-874 3561, ✉ enterprisehse@swrp.org.uk) fosters economic development in the boroughs of Croydon, Merton, Sutton and Wandsworth through training, courses, consultations and a recruitment service.

South-East: The **Business Information Service** (☎ 0208-290 0145) serves Bromley and south-east London, providing information to help businesses with planning and marketing, although this isn't a free service.

South-West: Point Digital (☎ 0208-541 5614/5, 💻 www.pointdigital. com) provides impartial advice and help with all Internet-related matters, while **Search Careers** (☎ 0208-296 1020) is a small company based in south-west London offering careers information and guidance to people of all ages with centres in Battersea (Wandsworth), New Malden (Kingston) and Wimbledon (Merton).

West: West London Leadership (☎ 0208-453 0910) covers the boroughs of Brent, Ealing, Hammersmith, Hillingdon and Hounslow. It promotes the development of new technologies and works for the economic prosperity of the area by promoting initiatives such as the Park Royal Partnership and the CrossRail project. **West London Inward** (☎ 0208-814 0842) provides information about business premises.

Boroughs

London's boroughs compete vigorously for business investment and most have an **Economic Development Unit** (or something similar) that can provide local demographic and other statistical information and an industrial profile of the borough, including local market information and wage rates. It can also provide information about the local property market, house prices and availability; vacant office and industrial premises, development sites and managed workspaces; information about renting council premises; help in identifying local suppliers; recruitment advice; a list of key local contacts and business support services; details of grants, loans and funds for which you may be eligible; and information about the regulations concerning your business. Borough councils also issue licences for certain types of businesses. Your local Chamber of Commerce may organise free, impartial business advice sessions, such as explaining the loans and grants available.

Most councils have established **Local Business Partnerships** (e.g. with Chambers of Commerce and local businesses) to enable new businesses and local authorities to work together to streamline the various regulatory processes (e.g. consumer, health and safety, and standards). The aim is to make it easier for businesses to understand and comply with regulations, and consequently save money and become more competitive. Councils provide information about legal requirements and good business practice, inform you how to apply for registration or approval, and act as the co-ordinator with the relevant regulatory bodies to smooth your path. Councils may also have a **Business Support Unit** that will put you in touch with people and organisations who can provide the help and advice you need, and a **Business Network** providing links between businesses.

There are also numerous local organisations offering help and information, some of which are listed below:

Bromley: The **Bromley Business Partnership** (☎ 0208-315 6740) is a members' organisation that includes representatives of Bromley Council, SOLOTEC, Business Link London South, the Bromley Enterprise Agency Trust and local businesses, with the aim of providing networking opportunities and representing local business interests. The **Bromley Business Relocation Help Line** (☎ 0208-313 4100) helps businesses wanting to move to the borough by providing details of vacant commercial property and relevant local business support services. The **Bromley Enterprise Agency Trust** (☎ 0208-290 6568) provides a free and confidential service promoting the establishment of new businesses with up to five employees.

Camden: The **Camden Training Centre** (☎ 0207-482 2101) offers courses in trades which include construction, catering, childcare and horticulture, with subsidised travel and child care for trainees.

Greenwich: The **Greenwich Business Support Service** (☎ 0208-309 8059) maintains a database of available commercial property, information on grants and other forms of financial assistance, and links to business support agencies in the borough including **Greenwich Local Labour and Business**.

Hackney: Hackney Business Venture (☎ 0207-254 9595) aims to improve local business skills and opportunities, particularly for those under 25 and **Hackney Co-operation Developments** (☎ 0207-254 4829) is a non-profit organisation that helps women and people from ethnic minority groups to establish businesses and co-operatives. **Social & Environment Analysis** (☎ 0207-923 9230) provides business start-up and self-employment training.

Hammersmith & Fulham: BETA 2000 (☎ 0208-740 6262) is a 'one-stop shop' for support services, while the **Business Enterprise Centre** (☎ 0208-746 0355) is a resource centre for companies of all sizes. The **Community & Enterprise Opportunities Centre** (☎ 0208-746 2120) concentrates on projects in media and IT. The **Park Royal Partnership** (☎ 0208-961 9696) provides advice and assistance for local businesses.

Haringey: The **Haringey Business Development Agency** (☎ 0208-880 4250) assists in the creation of new businesses and helps existing businesses to survive and expand. It also manages a loan fund. **Haringey Business Support Services** operates within Business Link London North (☎ 0208-880 4475) and provides a Small Firms Loan Guarantee Scheme. The

Haringey Business Technology Centre (☎ 0208-880 4475) aims to increase the competitiveness of small and medium size enterprises by providing access to computerised and on-line services, while the **Haringey Education Business Partnership** (☎ 0208-880 4460) provides work experience and training.

The **Lea (or Lee) Valley Clothing Industry Business and Design Centre** in Haringey co-ordinates services relating to the clothing industry (☎ 0208-808 6712). The **Lea Valley Technopark** provides business start-up units (☎ 0208-880 3636) and the **London Lea Valley Business Innovation Centre** (☎ 0208-350 1350), one of 100 BICs across Europe representing the skills and needs of its region through the European Business Innovation Centre Network, focuses on technology and supports technological innovation by sourcing available grants and expertise. **Middlesex University Services Ltd**. (☎ 0208-362 5734–7), based at the Lea Valley Technopark, provides local businesses expertise ranging across the arts and sciences.

Islington: The **Islington Enterprise Agency** (☎ 0207-226 2783) provides training and small business support and encourages management development and the setting-up of co-operatives.

Merton: The **Merton Enterprise Agency** (☎ 0208-545 3067) gives support to businesses in the borough.

Sutton: Sutton's **Business Mentoring** project (☎ 0208-770 4641) brings senior managers from large local firms to small local businesses to help them exploit new opportunities. The **Sutton Regeneration Partnership** (☎ 0208-770 4620/4630) encourages self-employment and helps existing businesses to expand and develop, and has set up the **Sutton Business Federation** (☎ 0208-642 9193), which provides support and advice to small and medium size enterprises. Sutton also operates a **Growth Sector Support** project (☎ 0208-770 4623) that provides grants to small and medium size enterprises for purchasing new equipment, developing new products and exploiting new markets.

Wandsworth: The **Wandsworth Business Advice Centre** (☎ 0208-871 5247–9) is a division of Greater London Enterprise funded by Wandsworth Borough Council, providing free help and advice to new and established businesses in Wandsworth including loans, grants, training and finding vacant commercial property. Wandsworth's **Economic Development Office** (☎ 0208-871 8037) provides grants and interest-free loans of up to 20 per cent to companies setting up in Wandsworth through its Business Development Scheme.

Westminster: Westminster Council provides an **Economic Enabling Unit** (☎ 0207-641 2750) to promote business and employment growth in the borough. The EEU provide a wide range of services in partnership with a number of central London business support organisations.

The Internet

The following websites are just a few of those providing help and advice to people planning to establish a business in London:

- www.brint.com/interest.html (provides the text of business management and IT journals)

- http://bubl.ac.uk/uk/england/london.htm (has links to all borough sites, many of which have search pages where you can look up businesses of a particular type in the area)

- www.businesslink.co.uk (the site of Business Link London – see page 143)

- www.croydon.gov.uk/index-working.htm (provides lists of premises in Croydon)

- www.dis.strath.ac.uk/business (a guide to business information sites including a range of useful statistics and information)

- www.enterprisezone.org.uk (Enterprise Zone, the DTI site for small businesses, providing links to the most relevant information on the net)

- www.govgrants.com (site of the private Enterprise Advisory Service for information on financial support available from the UK government and the EU)

- www.martex.co.uk/taf (the Trade Association Forum, with links to more than 650 trade organisations and thousands of companies in the UK)

- www.netaccountants.com (provides accounting and tax information for small and medium size businesses)

- www.inlandrevenue.gov.uk/home.htm (the Inland Revenue's site containing information on self-assessment, etc.)

- www.pikeperry.co.uk (the Pikeperry Company's site, providing links for small and medium size enterprises and information on business development)

- www.reedinfo.co.uk (a database of more than 12,000 companies)

- www.tec.co.uk (the national website for Training & Enterprise Councils)

- http://seirc.org.uk (site of the south-east England Innovation Relay Centre, serving small and medium size businesses by helping them find European partners)

- www.u-net.com/bureau (the site of Business Bureau UK for small businesses looking for useful websites)

- www.yahoo.com/business/small_business_information (information and services for businesses with a useful A-Z list of other sites)

REGENERATION

Many parts of London are either undergoing or are planned for regeneration, thanks to large injections of government, local council or private money. The most high-profile scheme is the transformation of London's former docks into the now thriving business area known as Docklands. Whether you're thinking of setting up your own business or looking for a position as an employee, there are many projects worth investigating, some of which are listed below:

- **Bankside** (Southwark) is now emerging as new cultural quarter.

- Brent's successful **City Challenge** bid will bring £37.5 million of government funds into the borough over the five years to 2004, principally to regenerate the Park Royal (see below), Harlseden and Stonebridge areas.

- Cityside (the area bordering the City and Tower Hamlets) is being revitalised through the **Cityside Regeneration Company**, which has won £11.5 million of government funding. Major office developments are scheduled for Aldgate and Spitalfields.

- Cray Valley in the eastern part of Bromley is in line for regeneration.

- The **Crystal Palace Partnership** (☎ 0208-313 4303) is responsible for implementing a £150 million regeneration scheme for Crystal Palace Park and the surrounding area, including almost 50 separate projects designed to create new jobs for the area.

- East Battersea (Wandsworth) has received £2.6 million from the government to transform the former **Battersea Power Station** into a leisure facility.

- **Haringey** has a total of 31 development sites centred on Tottenham and Wood Green. Grants are available for the Tottenham High Road shop premises improvement scheme and Tottenham High Road corridor improvement scheme.

- Kensington & Chelsea has a **Unitary Development Plan** run by Employment Projects (☎ 0207-361 2071) listing the best property investment opportunities and offering incentives, particularly in North Kensington.

- The **Lea (or Lee) Bridge Gateway Partnership** (☎ 0208-556 3644) is operating a five-year 'business enhancement' project due to end in 2001, centred on Leyton Industrial Village (Waltham Forest).

- The **Leaside (or Leeside) Regeneration Company** (☎ 0207-364 4639) has £7.5 million to spend on developing 46.5 hectares of land on the eastern edge of Tower Hamlets.

- The **London Lea Valley Partnership** (☎ 0207-247 5556) is promoting the River Lea area in Tower Hamlets. Businesses locating to this area may be eligible for grants and assistance under various schemes: Regional Selective Assistance (mainly for manufacturing companies) through Business Link London North; SMART Awards (for development of new products or processes); Support for Products under Research (also for new product/process development, but for small and medium size businesses); Regional Enterprise Grant for Innovation (for small companies); infrastructure grants; redundant building grants; and other grants for export development under the EUREKA and Export Marketing Research Schemes and the DTI Consultancy service.

- Another regeneration company is being established for the **Lower Lee Valley**, aiming to make it a 'high profile, dynamic business location' by 2006.

- The **Park Royal Partnership** (☎ 0208-961 9696) aims to create an additional 20,000 jobs within the Park Royal Industrial Estate in Brent. Around 30,000 people are currently employed on the estate, where there are more than 800 small and medium size companies as well as large enterprises such as Guinness.

- **Peckham** (Southwark) is the site of a £250 million regeneration scheme. Other nearby areas due for redevelopment are the Elephant & Castle, Old Kent Road and Burgess Park.

- The **Thames Gateway London Partnership** (☎ 0208-221 2880) has been dubbed 'the largest and most important development project to be undertaken in this country'. The area comprises 2,000 hectares of development land, mostly zoned for employment use. Government support is available in the form of grants through the Single Regeneration Budget, Regional Selective Assistance and English Partnerships.

- The **Upper Lea Valley Partnership** (☎ 0208-880 4666) is one of the largest partnerships in Britain, investing £120 million over seven years.

- The **Wandsworth Challenge Partnership** has £20 million from the government to develop Wandsworth town centre including the Arndale Shopping Centre and Estate.

- The **White City** development scheme plans to develop a 40-acre site into a vast shopping and leisure centre.

5.

BACK TO SCHOOL

Like all major capital cities, London represents a wide social, economic and cultural mix which is reflected in its education system. In few other places in the world can you find such a diversity of educational options at all levels, from pre-school to university postgraduate. Most establishments cater for overseas students, many of whom are attracted by London's reputation as a centre of educational excellence.

However, the range of choices may not be quite as wide as it appears at first glance. Some of the best establishments may be closed to you because they are either too expensive, too exclusive, too popular, cater for a religious group or nationality to which you don't belong, or you cannot meet the entry criteria. Although London has some of the best schools in the country, within both the state and private (fee-paying) sectors, it also has some of the worst. These include a number of relatively poor independent schools that do little to justify their fees and many under-performing state schools, some of which have failed official inspections and face closure if their standards don't improve.

Information: The weekly *Times Educational Supplement* (available from newsagents) contains up-to-the-minute news and opinion about education and schools in England, including management, governors, research and teaching posts. There are numerous books for parents faced with choosing a suitable state or private school including the Daily Telegraph *Schools Guide* and the *Good Schools Guide*. You can also consult an independent adviser such as **Gabbitas Educational Consultants** Ltd. (126-130 Regent Street, London W1R 6EE, ☎ 0207-734 0161, 🖳 www.gabbitas.co.uk), who can provide advice and information on any aspect of education in Britain. The official annual guide to full-time courses in Greater London, *Full-Time Floodlight*, is published by Floodlight Publishing and available direct from them (🖳 www.floodlight.co.uk) or from bookshops in London.

In addition to **Floodlight** there are many other useful education-related websites including **Schoolsnet** (www.schoolsnet.com), 'the UK's No1 education website; the **National Grid for Learning** (www.ngfl.gov.uk); **BBC Education** (www.bbc.co.uk/education); **Eduweb** (www.eduweb.co. uk); and **Learnfree** (www.learnfree.co.uk). The **Department for Education and Employment (DfEE)** has a 'learning direct' telephone helpline for learning and career queries (☎ 0800-100900).

PRE-SCHOOL

Pre-school is for children aged two to five and takes place in nursery schools or nursery classes attached to a primary school, and may be private or state-maintained. In practice, however, there's little state provision for pre-school education in London (or, indeed, in the UK as a whole). Workplace nurseries and crèches are often greatly over-subscribed, private nannies are expensive and places at private nurseries, pre-preps and prep schools in inner London are so rare that many people register their children at birth. Finding reliable childcare for babies and toddlers under the age of four can be one of the biggest headaches for working parents. However, the present government is now offering four-year-olds a free place in a private or community nursery school, playgroup, or special nursery class, and it has also begun to extend the provision to three-year-olds. Before that comes about – unless you're lucky – you'll have to pay.

There are too many nursery schools in London to list here, but there are some useful resources to help you find those in your area. The **British Association for Early Childhood Education** (111 City View House, 463 Bethnal Green Road, London E2 9QY, ☎ 0207-739 7594) concentrates on quality childcare and education for under eight-year-olds. The **Pre-School Learning Alliance** (Holly Building, Holly Street, Sheffield S1 2GT, ☎ 0114-273 1007) was established in 1963 when parents, frustrated by the lack of nursery provision, decided to take matters into their own hands and created their own self-help nursery schools. Today it's a registered charity and the single largest provider of education and care for under-fives in England.

PRIMARY & SECONDARY SCHOOLS

Competition for places at the best and most popular London schools – whether fee-paying or state-funded – is fierce. In many areas, getting your children into the a particular state school may be dependent on how close you live to it, so before buying or renting a home check the current position as regards school catchment areas. If you go for that terrific house at 14 Acacia Drive, what's your choice of schools going to be like? How good are they and what are their reputations locally? More importantly, what chance do you stand of getting your children accepted? How easy would it be for your children to get there every day, e.g. a ten-minute walk or two rush-hour buses? Don't rely on what an estate or letting agent tells you – he's only concerned with getting his commission – but ask local people their opinions before plumping for an area.

Take care not to rely on out-of-date information – London is in a constant state of flux and an area that was firmly downmarket five years ago when you were last in London may have suddenly become fashionable, driving up house prices and over-subscribing the local state schools. An inspired new head teacher and a glowing report from Ofsted (the Office for Standards in Education) – the official UK school inspectorate – can have much the same effect.

Read the latest 'good school' guides, scrutinise the latest exam results published in the Department of Education's annual league tables (🖳 www. dfee.gov.uk/perform.htm) and the official Ofsted school inspection reports (🖳 www.ofsted.gov.uk). Obtain local authority information leaflets, and most importantly, whether you opt for an independent or a state school, visit and talk to the teachers to form your own impression of a school's atmosphere and the staff's attitude. How big are class sizes? How well qualified and experienced are the teaching staff? Are there regular parents' evenings and opportunities for consultation? Are there problems with maintaining discipline or with drugs? Is there a uniform? What extracurricular activities are offered, such as sports and after-school clubs and societies? Talk to playgroup leaders, nursery teachers, school secretaries or parent governors, all of whom can keep you up-to-date and pass on the kind of information the school may not care to reveal.

Because of the lottery in state education, many people believe that state schools should be privatised in order to provide a more equitable system, a thesis that's outlined in an interesting book, *Reclaiming Education*, by Professor James Tooley (Continuum).

STATE SCHOOLS

State schools don't charge fees and are run by the 32 London Local Education Authorities (LEAs). They are broadly divided into primary and secondary establishments, except for two boroughs, Harrow and Merton, which have a three-tier school structure with primary, middle and high schools. The **National Curriculum** is compulsory in all state schools in England and affects most pupils between the ages of 5 and 16. It's designed to ensure that all children have a broad and balanced education up to the age of 16, as well as standardising education in state schools throughout the country. So if you decide at a later date to move from London to Manchester or Bristol, the disruption to your child's education should be minimal. Bear in mind though, that Scotland operates an entirely different educational system.

The National Curriculum determines what children must study and what they are expected to know at different stages of their school career. Four 'Key Stages' broadly relate to pupils' ages: KS1 from 5 to 7, KS2 from 7 to 11, KS3 from 11 to 14 and KS4 from 14 to 16. National tests are set to check whether children are meeting these targets. By 2002, the government expects 80 per cent of 11-year-olds in England to meet the standards expected for their age in English and 75 per cent of 11-year-olds to match the standards required in maths. In 1998, the equivalent figures were 65 and 59 per cent.

The 'core subjects' of the national curriculum are English, maths and science. Layered on top of these basics are so-called 'foundation' subjects which include technology (incorporating design and technology as well as computer-based information technology), history, geography, music, art, physical education and, in secondary schools, a modern foreign language. Religious and sex education must also be provided, but parents have a right to withdraw children from these subjects if they wish.

The government plans to amend the curriculum in England in the year 2000. The biggest change will be the addition of 'citizenship' as a foundation subject, which will, however, be delayed until 2002 – perhaps to give people time to work out exactly what on earth it is!

Primary Schools

State primary schools are obliged to take local children from the term in which their fifth birthday falls, although some will accept younger children into nursery or reception classes. Many schools admit new pupils at just one point in the year, which means they will take children who will be five within the coming school year (September to August). Therefore, children born in summer start school in the autumn, not long after their fourth birthdays, which is an advantage or a disadvantage depending how you view it. Primary schools consist mainly of infant departments for children aged 5 to 7 and junior departments for those aged 7 to 11. Primary schools tend to operate their admissions policies purely on catchment area, unless they're voluntary aided and stipulate parental religious observance.

Secondary Schools

Most children transfer from primary schools to secondary schools at the age of 11 in the state sector. Most secondary schools (almost 90 per cent of English children attend them) are comprehensives, which cater for children of all abilities, but there are still some selective or 'grammar' schools, mainly in the wealthier suburbs in south London, which are always vastly oversubscribed. These schools select pupils on the basis of academic attainment. The government has pledged that there will be no new grammar schools but will allow existing schools to continue, providing they have the support of local parents. Opinion polls have indicated that there's strong parental support for selection by ability, so their future – although by no means certain – seems relatively safe for now.

Single-sex schools are also increasingly popular within the state system, particularly for girls. Many parents believe girls do better without boys around to distract them and there are several good girls' schools in the capital. However, bear in mind that if there are a lot of girls' schools in a particular area, then local mixed schools can become very male-dominated.

Generally, schools in the 23 inner London authorities achieve worse results than those in the outer boroughs, although there are notable exceptions. Pupils living in inner London boroughs such as Lambeth, Southwark, Hackney or Tower Hamlets frequently come from poorer families where the parents may be unemployed and living in poor housing. There's also a much higher percentage of children who don't speak English as their first language. Because of the difficulties associated with teaching children in these areas, there's often a high turnover of teaching staff and a consequent lack of commitment and continuity.

Ofsted reports have spotlighted low teacher expectations in some inner London schools and poor teaching of basic literacy and numeracy skills at the primary school level. The London borough of Hackney recently became the first education authority to be stripped of its powers by the government, which plans to put education services in the area out to private tender. Islington and Southwark are also under threat of similar treatment. Those who can afford to pay their way out of this situation do so and the professional middle classes in inner London have largely deserted the state sector, most parents preferring to pay for independent education.

The present government has implemented several new measures to help improve standards in the worst inner London state schools, encouraging them to form 'Education Action Zones' run by partnerships of local authorities, private businesses and community groups. If you're going to be living in a 'bad' London borough (education-wise) then the best thing to do is to try to live near the border so that you can try to get your child into a school in the neighbouring borough. It's illegal for a state school to select a resident child for a place over a non-resident child if the non-resident actually lives nearer. Most migrations are from inner to outer London, but not always, for example, many families living in Islington try to get their children into a Camden school, replacing the children who scramble over the border from Camden into Westminster!

School league tables are produced annually by the government according to pupils' exam performance. The table opposite shows the position of each borough out of the 150 local authority areas in England in the 1998 league tables. The best overall performers are listed first, the worst last. (But keep an eye on the latest tables as the position can change from year to year.)

State School Performance Table:

BOROUGH	PRIMARY	SECONDARY
City of London*	2nd	N/A
Kingston	6th	3rd
Barnet	17th	7th
Bromley	15th	9th
Richmond	3rd	29th
Harrow#	16th	20th
Havering	24th	31st
Sutton	52nd	4th
Redbridge	48th	10th
Bexley	65th	42nd
Kensington & Chelsea	51st	58th
Hillingdon	39th	71st
Hounslow	82nd	50th
Camden	80th	54th
Brent	70th	65th
Ealing	73rd	66th
Westminster	43rd	120th
Croydon	76th	92nd
Enfield	89th	84th
Hammersmith & Fulham	101st	77th
Merton#	86th	101st
Wandsworth	93rd	115th
Waltham Forest	120th	102nd
Barking & Dagenham	106th	131st
Lewisham	126th	128th
Lambeth	120th	139th
Greenwich	143rd	127th
Newham	149th	123rd
Islington	131st	147th
Southwark	142nd	137th
Haringey	138th	144th
Tower Hamlets	148th	142nd
Hackney	146th	145th

*   There's only one state primary school and no state secondary schools in the City of London.

\#   Harrow and Merton have a primary/middle/high system.

INDEPENDENT SCHOOLS

Parents seeking private (fee-paying) education for their children will find many excellent independent schools in London (over 400). Most independent secondary schools are single-sex, at least up until the sixth form, and most are day rather than boarding schools. Almost all of them are located in north, west and south London, rather than in the east. The best schools are very expensive and exclusive with long waiting lists, although it's generally easier to find places at short notice in outer London independent schools. It's also worth bearing in mind that, although you may be living and working in London, your children can be educated further afield. This may allow you to spread your net wider in search of the right school; for example, if you wish your child to attend a special school due to your religious beliefs or because they have a particular gift that you wish to foster. Fees for independent schools vary from about £4,000 per annum in the least expensive day schools up to £14,000 or more for a boarding school place.

Children pass through several stages within the independent school system. Preparatory schools take pupils from as young as two if they have a nursery or pre-prep department, or more usually from six or seven up to the age of fourteen. After prep school they progress to a senior school (sometimes confusingly called a 'public' school) where they take GCSE examinations at the age of around 16 and A-levels two years later, going to university at the age of 17 or 18. Entry to some independent schools involves a tough selection process, whereas others achieve good results from a wider ability range. Most day schools still use the '11 Plus' examination as an academic filter, while senior boarding schools tend to favour the Common Entrance Examination (CEE), usually taken two years later at the age of 13. Details and past papers are available from the Independent Schools Examinations Board, Jordan House, Christchurch Road, New Milton, Hampshire BH25 6QJ (☎ 01425-621111).

Many independent senior schools have associated junior, preparatory, pre-prep or even nursery schools. If you're likely to be staying in London for the majority of your child's education, this is a good way of ensuring confidence-building continuity as they grow up.

The Internet is a valuable resource when researching independent schools in London, where the website (www.johncatt.com) of publisher **John Catt Educational** is an excellent starting point. It provides a free search facility via e-mail where you enter details about your child and your requirements for their education and they will search their database and suggest suitable schools. If you already have some idea of possible schools, you can search yourself on the related **Schoolsearch** site (www.school search.co.uk) which has links to schools' own websites. Most independent (and many state) schools also have their own websites which should be examined in conjunction with their printed prospectuses.

John Catt's annual book, *Which London School?*, available via their website (see above), is also an invaluable source of information. Other useful resources for those interested in independent education include the following:

- The **Independent Schools Council/ISC** (Grosvenor Gardens House, 35-37 Grosvenor Gardens, London SW1W 0BS, ☎ 0207-630 0144, ✉ bc@online.rednet.co.uk) is the central body that co-ordinates and represents the interests of the various organisations concerned with independent education in the UK, the most significant of which are listed below. Some 80 per cent of independently-educated children in the UK attend ISC schools.

- The **Independent Schools Information Service/ISIS** (56 Buckingham Gate, London SW1E 6AG, ☎ 0207-630 8793, 💻 www.isis.org.uk) is an offshoot of the ISC (above) and provides invaluable material to parents and other interested parties.

- The **Girls' Schools Association/GSA** (130 Regent Road, Leicester LE1 7PG, ☎ 0116-254 1619) represents around 220 independent girls' schools throughout the UK. Focusing exclusively on girls' achievement, the GSA believes that girls benefit most from a single-sex environment until university.

- The **Girls' Day School Trust** (100 Rochester Row, London SW1P 1JP, ☎ 0207-393 6666) was founded in 1872 and was the original pioneer of quality education for girls.

- The **Headmasters' & Headmistresses' Conference/HMC** (130 Regent Road, Leicester LE1 7PG, ☎ 0116-285 4810, ✉ mc@webleicester.co.uk) represents a membership of 250 heads of boys' and co-educational independent schools. The HMC is proud of the fact that their pupils come from a wide variety of backgrounds and that, although the assisted places scheme (whereby pupils receive government grants to attend independent schools) is now being phased out, many schools still provide bursaries and scholarships for over a third of their pupils. Over 90 per cent of pupils go on to higher education.

- The **Independent Association Of Preparatory Schools/IAPS** (11 Waterloo Place, Leamington Spa, Warwickshire CV32 5LA, ☎ 01926-887833) is a professional body representing prep school heads throughout the UK and overseas. As well as completely independent prep schools, the association also represents schools affiliated to senior schools. These range from rural to urban, single-sex to co-ed, and offers day, boarding and, in some cases, flexible (e.g. weekday) boarding places.

- The **Independent Schools Association/ISA**, (Boys' British School, East Street, Saffron Walden, Essex CB10 1LS, ☎ 01799-523619) has a membership of 300 schools covering a wide variety of establishments including nursery, prep, junior, senior, single-sex, co-ed, day and boarding schools. Their main criterion (apart from academic excellence) is that schools shouldn't be directly controlled by the Department of Education & Employment.

- The **Society of Heads of Independent Schools/SHIS** (Celdeston, Rhosesmor Road, Halkyn, Holywell CH8 8DL, ☎ 01352-781102) represents a range of smaller independent schools which include those catering for pupils with a specific religious orientation, pupils gifted in one of the performing arts and those with special needs. Most schools have around 300 pupils or less and are co-educational.

RELIGIOUS SCHOOLS

Schools linked to a particular church or religion include both state (e.g. many voluntary-aided schools) and independent schools. The former often have wider catchment areas than other state schools, taking pupils from all over London who satisfy their entry requirements and whose families are devout. These include the Roman Catholic London Oratory School (favoured by the current Prime Minister) and Sacred Heart High School (both in Hammersmith), the Anglican girls' comprehensive Lady Margaret in Parson's Green and Hasmonean in Hendon which serves the Jewish community.

Many independent schools cater for particular religious beliefs. If you're looking for a fee-paying school with a particular religious affiliation, you should contact one of the organisations listed below:

- The **Agency for Jewish Education** (Education Resource Centre, Schaller House, Albert Road, London NW4 2SJ, ☎ 0208-457 9700, 🖳 www. brijnet.org/aje) provides training for teachers, runs an educational resource centre and acts as a liaison between secular institutions and the Anglo-Jewish community. It also acts as the examination board and internal inspectorate for Jewish educational institutions.

- The **Catholic Education Service for England & Wales** (39 Eccleston Square, London SW1V 1BX, ☎ 0207-828 7604, 🖳 www.tasc.ac.uk/cc/ agen/agen01.htm) represents Catholic interests in education with government and national agencies, advises teachers and supports the work of Catholic schools and colleges.

- The **British Sikh Education Council**, (10 Featherstone Road, Southall, Middlesex UB2 4AA, ☎ 0208-574 1902) supports the religious and educational needs of Sikhs in Britain and assists parents, teachers and LEAs.

- The **Methodist** Colleges **and Schools Organisation** (25 Marylebone Road, London, ☎ 0207-935 3723) takes administrative responsibility for Methodist colleges and schools and provides advice to the church on the formulation of educational policy.

- The **Muslim** Educational **Trust/MET** (130 Stroud Green Road, London N4 3RZ, ☎ 0207-272 8502) is Britain's oldest national Muslim educational organisation dealing with the concerns of Muslim parents and children. The MET arranges for teachers to give lessons in Islamic Studies in English to Muslim children in state schools and publishes a range of internationally-orientated books and posters on Islam for use by pupils and teachers.

SPECIALIST SCHOOLS

Specialist schools within the state system in England are those that develop particular skills, e.g. in technology, languages, sports or the arts. They also include schools that provide for special educational needs such as pupils with a condition that hinders or prevents them from making use of the facilities provided for pupils of their age at mainstream schools or those who need extra tuition of some kind. There are almost 2,000 special schools (both day and boarding) in the UK for pupils with special educational needs, some of which are contained within hospitals. The typical pupil-teacher ratio in special schools is around 6:1 compared to 20:1 in mainstream state schools. However, the government wishes to see more special needs children entering mainstream schools. In 1997, almost 60 per cent of special needs pupils were in maintained mainstream schools, 4 per cent were in special schools and 3 per cent in independent schools.

All state secondary schools are eligible to apply for specialist school status if they can raise at least £100,000 in private sector sponsorship, prepare a three-year development plan and demonstrate provision to involve other schools and the wider community. If they succeed they receive an annual government grant of £100,000, plus £100 per pupil (up to a maximum of £100,000 a year) for three years.

Some independent schools provide education wholly or mainly for children with special educational needs or learning difficulties such as dyslexia. They're required to meet similar standards to those for maintained special schools and their pupils should have access to as much of the national curriculum (see page 156) as possible. The **Dyslexia Institute** (133 Gresham Road, Staines TW18 2AJ, ☎ 01784-463851) is a charitable body that has been responsible for setting up a range of institutes providing instruction and support for pupils and teachers dealing with dyslexia.

Other independent schools exist to provide a special education for gifted or talented children, such as choir or cathedral schools. For information contact the **Choir Schools' Association** (The Minster School, Deangate, York YO1 7JA, ☎ 01904-624900) which represents all cathedral and chorister schools in England. If your son or daughter is blessed with angelic vocal chords, entering them for voice trials can be a wonderful way of ensuring they receive a superior education for which you're usually required to pay only a portion of the full fees. There isn't always a stipulation regarding religion and musical talent is generally deemed more important than religious beliefs.

The world-famous, Italian teaching system, **Montessori**, is also popular in London, mainly in the pre-school age range. Information is available from the **Maria Montessori Training Organisation** (26 Lyndhurst Gardens, Hampstead London NW3 5NW, ☎ 0207-435 3646).

INTERNATIONAL SCHOOLS

International schools teach foreign pupils in their home languages, but are also used by native Londoners who have family or working links with other countries or who simply want their children to be bilingual. London has six international schools in addition to around a dozen schools following the curriculum of particular countries. Some examples are the **King Fahad Academy** (Bromyard Ave, Acton, London W3 7HD, ☎ 0208-743 0131) which serves the Arab community; the **Hellenic College of London** (67 Pont Street, London SW1X 0BD, ☎ 0207-581 5044) serving the Greek community; the **Lycée Français Charles de Gaulle** (35 Cromwell Road, London SW7 2DG, ☎ 0207-584 6322, ⌨ http://easyweb.easynet.co.uk/~lyceefrlondres); and the **International School of London** (139 Gunnersbury Ave, London W3 8LG, ☎ 0208-992 5823) catering for all nationalities. London also boasts German, Japanese, Norwegian and Swedish schools.

American schools in the London area include the **American College in London** (110 Marylebone High Street, London W1M 5FP, ☎ 0207-486 1772), the **American School in London** (2-8 Loudoun Road, London NW8 ONP, ☎ 0207-449 1200) and the three **American Community Schools** just outside London in Uxbridge (☎ 01895-259771), Cobham (☎ 01932-869744) and Egham (☎ 01784-430611).

For further information about schools teaching in a specific language contact your country's embassy in London (see **Appendix A**).

UNIVERSITIES & COLLEGES

Statistically, London has the largest student population of any city in the world, totalling some 250,000 students, many of whom are from overseas. EEA nationals can freely enter the UK but if you're a non-EEA national it's important to check whether you need a student visa. If you require a visa, you'll need to prove that you have been accepted for a full-time course of study, that you can meet the cost of your fees and maintenance (plus any dependants you bring with you) without recourse to public funds, and that you intend to leave the UK at the end of your course.

An invaluable organisation for overseas students is the **UK Council for Overseas Student Affairs** (UKCOSA, 9-17 St Alban's Place, London N1 0NX, ☎ 0207-354 5210, ⌨ www.ukcosa.org.uk). UKCOSA is a registered charity established in 1968 to promote the interests and meet the needs of overseas students in Britain and those working with them as teachers, advisors or in other capacities. Another important organisation is the **British Council** (10 Spring Gardens, London SW1A 2BN, ☎ 0207-389 4383, 💻 www.britishcouncil.org) which has over 250 offices in some 110 countries and provides foreign students with information concerning all aspects of education in Britain.

Note that universities insist that students possess a reasonable command of English, which may be tested, before they are enrolled on a course. If your mother-tongue isn't English you should check a college's prospectus or website for specific requirements.

Universities in London

London has 14 universities and 11 colleges of higher education – the **University of London** itself comprises 34 colleges scattered throughout the city. The university's heart is in Bloomsbury but the institution was allowed to grow in such a haphazard way that the area lacks any of the cohesion or focus of a traditional university campus. Each college has its own individual strengths and weaknesses and publishes its own prospectus, so write or phone for your copy or check out their websites before making a choice. Listed below are some of the best known colleges, although it isn't an exhaustive list:

- **Courtauld Institute of Art**, Somerset House, Strand WC2R ORN (☎ 0207-872 0220, 💻 www.courtauld.ac.uk, Temple tube). One of the best centres for the study of the history of art in the world.

- **Goldsmiths' College**, Lewisham Way SE14 (☎ university 0207-919 7171, students union 0208-692 1406, 💻 www.goldsmiths.ac.uk/gcexp/ overseas.html, New Cross tube or New Cross Gate rail). Goldsmiths' College has been running English for academic purposes programmes for overseas students since 1987. The English Language Unit, established in 1993, offers a number of different English language programmes for non-native speakers of English.

- **Imperial College of Science, Technology and Medicine**, Exhibition Road, London SW7 2AZ (☎ university 0207-589 5111, students union 0207-594 8060, 💻 www.ic.ac.uk, South Kensington tube). Situated in South Kensington's scientific heartland, the Imperial College (founded 1907) was formed from the merger of the Royal College of Science, the City and Guilds College and the Royal School of Mines.

- **King's College**, Strand, WC2 (☎ university 0207-836 5454, students union 0207-836 7132, 💻 www.kcl.ac.uk, Temple tube). King's College London was established in 1829 and was one of the founding colleges of the University of London. It now has over 16,000 students and one of the best reputations in the UK for teaching and research.

- **London School of Economics and Political Science**, Page Building, Houghton Street WC2 (☎ university 0207-405 7686, students union 0207-955 7158, 💻 www.lse.ac.uk, Holborn tube). The LSE accepts around 3,000 overseas students annually from over 140 countries.

- **Queen Mary & Westfield College**, Mile End Road, E1 (☎ university 0207-975 5555, students union 0207-975 5390, 💻 www.qmw.ac.uk, Mile End or Stepney Green tube). The College is situated in the heart of London's East End – a wholly different and often more vibrant experience of London from that of the average student. Some 20 per cent of students here are from overseas.

- **Royal Acadamy of Dramatic Art (RADA)**, 18-22 Chenies Street, WC1 (☎ 0207-636 7076, 💻 www.rada.org, Goodge St tube). RADA is one of the world's leading colleges for budding actors and actresses.

- **Royal College of Art (RCA)**, Kensington Gore, SW7 (☎ 0207-590 4444, 💻 www.rca.ac.uk, Kensington tube), London's foremost art school.

- **Royal College of Music (RCM)**, Prince Consort Road, SW7 (☎ 0207-589 3643, 💻 www.rcm.ac.uk, South Kensington tube). Along with the Royal Academy and Trinity School of Music, the RCM is one of the foremost colleges for classical musicians in the UK.

- **The Slade School of Fine Art**, University College, Gower Street WC1 (☎ university 0207-504 2313, 💻 www.ucl.ac.uk/slade, Euston, Warren Street or Goodge St tube). The Slade is a department of University College and one of London's premier art schools.

- **University College**, Gower Street WC1 (☎ university 0207-387 7050, students union 0207-387 3611, 💻 www.ucl.ac.uk, Euston, Warren St or Goodge St tube). UCL was founded on unusually radical principles and still has a reputation for unorthodox approaches to research.

Other Universities in the London area include:

- **Brunel University**, Clevedon Road, Uxbridge, Middlesex (☎ university 01895-274000, students union 01895-462200, 💻 www.brunel.ac.uk, Uxbridge tube).

- **City University**, Northampton Square, EC1 (☎ university 0207-477 8000, students union 0207-505 5600, 💻 www.city.ac.uk/international, Barbican or Angel tube). City has its own e-zine written by international students.

- **Guildhall University**, 2 Goulston Street, E1 (☎ university 0207-320 1000, students union 0207-247 1441, 💻 www.lgu.ac.uk, Aldgate East tube).

- **South Bank University**, Borough Road, SE1 (☎ university 0207-928 8989, students union 0207-815 6060, 💻 www.southbank-university.ac. uk, Elephant & Castle tube).

- **University of East London**, Stratford Campus, Romford Road E15 (☎ university 0208-590 7722, students union 0208-590 7722 ext. 4210, Stratford tube).

- **University of Greenwich**, Wellington Street SE18 (☎ university 0208-331 8000, students union 0208-331 8268, 💻 www.greenwich.ac.uk, Woolwich Arsenal rail).

- **University of Kingston**, Penrhyn Road, Kingston, Surrey (☎ university 0208-547 2000, students union 0208-255 2222, 💻 www.kingston.ac.uk, Kingston rail).

- **University of Middlesex**, Trent Park, Bramley Road N14 (☎ university 0208-362 5000, students union 0208-362 6450, 💻 www.mdx.ac.uk, Oakwood or Cockfosters tube).

- **University of North London**, 166-220 Holloway Road, N7 (☎ university 0207-607 2789, students union 0207-753 3361, 💻 www.unl. ac.uk, Holloway Rd tube).

- **University of Westminster**, 309 Regent Street, W1 (☎ university 0207-911 5000, 💻 www.wmin.ac.uk, Oxford Circus tube).

There are also two American universities in the capital: the **American International University in Richmond** (Queens Road, Richmond TW10, ☎ 0208-332 9000, 💻 www.richmond.ac.uk) and **Huron University USA** (58 Princes Gate, Exhibition Road, London SW7 2PG, ☎ 0207-584 9696, 💻 www.huron.ac.uk).

Courses

Britain offers the widest choice of university courses in Europe with a mind-boggling over 40,000 subjects available! The main categories of courses are as follows:

- Three or four-year degree courses leading to qualifications such as Bachelor of Arts (BA) and Bachelor of Science (BSc). These tend to be taken by those who want a recognised academic qualification in a specific subject area, although there's scope to combine different subjects in a modular degree (see below).

- Two-year Higher National Diploma (HND) or Diploma of Higher Education (DHE) courses. These vocational courses are generally related to particular career areas such as Agriculture, Art and Design, Business Studies, and Hotel and Catering. HNDs are made up of units of study and are usually taken over two years on a full-time basis. Courses may be longer if they include work experience or are taken part-time. HND students can sometimes subsequently transfer to the second (or occasionally third) year of a degree course, although the HND qualification is fully recognised by employers in its own right.

- The Higher National Certificate (HNC) is usually taken part-time by those in employment.

Part-time degree courses are normally taken over a longer period which may vary according to the individual institution. As a general rule, you should allow at least five years from beginning to completion of a part-time degree course. The distinction between part and full-time study is becoming increasingly blurred and some institutions offer flexible arrangements to suit individual needs.

Many higher education establishments have adopted a modular structure for their courses which allows students to build a personalised degree by choosing modules or units of study from different subject areas. Modularity provides a high degree of flexibility and enables students to design personalised programmes to match their needs.

Tuition Fees

Students ordinarily resident in the UK or another EU country qualify as 'home' students. Overseas students ordinarily resident in the UK for a period of three years immediately prior to the start of a course are also treated as 'home' students, except where residence was wholly or mainly for educational purposes.

UK and EU students enrolled on undergraduate courses must pay up to £1,025 per year. The exact amount payable is means-tested and dependent upon parental or individual income. Overseas undergraduate students should expect to pay up to £7,000 per year for an arts course, with annual fees increasing to £7,500 for engineering, £8,500 for computing and £9,000 for optometry. Overseas postgraduates fees range from £6,000 to £15,000. All fees are payable at the time of registration.

EU Students are normally eligible to apply to the **Department for Education and Employment** for help with the payment of tuition fees. Further details can be obtained from the Department for Education & Employment, European Team, Student Support Division 1, 2F Area B Mowden Hall, Staindrop Road, Darlington DL3 9BG (☎ 01325-391199).

Living Expenses

As a student in London you will obviously need sufficient funds money to support yourself on a day-to-day basis including accommodation, food, clothing, travel, equipment, books and other incidental expenses. Under immigration regulations, you aren't usually permitted to work and study at the same time, so you cannot rely on topping up your wallet with casual wages from temporary work such as waiting tables or bartending. As a guide, you should have an income of around £7,000 to £9,000 per year if you're single and some £11,000 per year if you're married. You should also bear in mind that you could incur extra expenses when you first arrive in the UK, such as temporary hotel accommodation.

As detailed elsewhere in this book (see **Cost of Living** on page 265), London can be expensive, although many shops and companies provide student concessions. In order to qualify for them you must obtain a National Union of Students (NUS) card or an International Student Identity Card (ISIC), available from student union offices. Discounts are often available by showing your student card at theatres, cinemas, travel bureaux, driving schools, clothes shops and so on. Information about the discounts obtainable in London with an NUS Card are available on the Internet (www.nuscard. com) and students' unions also have information about the local discounts available.

Accommodation

General information about student accommodation is provided in university and college prospectuses. If you're a mature student or will have a family living with you, you will need to check the facilities offered and whether family accommodation is available. Many institutions have halls of residence, with or without catering facilities, some single-sex and some mixed. While a number of educational establishments guarantee accommodation for the first year, it's common for students in later years to rent accommodation in the private sector. The staff at university accommodation offices can advise you about the costs and availability and may be able to help you find accommodation.

An increasing number of universities and colleges make specific housing provision for mature students and their families. You should, however, make enquiries with accommodation offices well in advance, particularly if you require family accommodation. The availability and cost of childcare facilities is also an important factor for families. If you're going to need support of this kind, you should contact the student services office of your chosen institution as far in advance as possible to check what childcare provision is available, what it costs and whether it will allow you sufficient time to study. Facilities vary considerably and there's stiff competition for places at a nursery or crèche; therefore, it's advisable to apply as early as possible. Facilities and costs vary considerably from one institution to another, which may be a key factor in determining where you study. Unless you're in a favourable financial position, you'll probably have to make sacrifices as a student and shouldn't expect your accommodation and general standard of living to match what you've been used to.

The **International Students House/ISH** (229 Great Portland Street W1, ☎ 0207-631 8300 ext. 744, ✉ accom@ish.org.uk, Great Portland St tube) is a useful meeting place where foreign students can compare notes and share impressions of the life and studying in London. It also has single, twin and dormitory rooms available for visiting students as well as sports facilities, a bar and restaurant. ISH also operates an excellent travel club with cheap rates for students.

Student Entertainment

London provides a wealth of entertainment for the young (see **Chapter 8**), in addition to which most universities have student unions which are a valuable source of local information and support. Unions also provide excellent entertainment such as live music, often featuring world-class bands. Because student bars and entertainment are subsidised, most student unions admit only those with a student ID, so make sure that you have your NUS or ISIC card with you (see page 169). The best student unions in London include the following:

- **University of London Students Union** (Malet Street WC1, ☎ 0207-664 2000, Russell Square/Goodge St tube), affectionately known as ULU. With two bars, this is probably London's trendiest student union, frequently offering the hottest up-and-coming bands. See them here first!

- **King's College Students Union** (Macadam Building, Surrey Street WC2, ☎ 0207-836 7132, Temple tube) vies with the ULU as the best student union in town. Following recent renovation it now boasts a great venue for live music as well as bar and food.

- **University of Westminster Students Union** (35 Marylebone Road W1, ☎ 0207-911 5000, Baker St tube), as you might expect given its location, is quite the swankiest union in town.

- **Imperial College Students Union** (Beit Quad, Prince Consort Road SW7, ☎ 0207-589 5111, South Kensington tube) is big, basic and friendly with cheap beer.

Useful Resources

All applicants for entry to full-time, first degree (undergraduate) courses at British universities must be made to the Universities and Colleges Admissions Services (UCAS, Fulton House, Jessop Avenue, Cheltenham GL50 3SH, ☎ 01242-222444, 🖥 www.ucas.co.uk). UCAS publish the *UCAS University and College Entrance Official Guide* and *The Parent's Guide to Higher Education*, both of which are available free from UCAS, while a more detailed book, *The Complete Parent's Guide to Higher Education* (UCAS/Trotman and Co Ltd.), is available from bookshops. The **British Council** (see page 165) publishes *Access to British Higher Education Institutions 1998-200, your route to a British degree*, which details the overseas qualifications necessary for acceptance on courses at UK colleges and universities.

Information about universities and colleges is available on the Internet (www.scit.wlv.ac.uk/ukinfo/alpha.html), with links to college websites. The NUS website (www.nus.org.uk) is an invaluable source of information and advice on the courses available, your rights and what you can expect as a student in London. The free fortnightly newspaper, *London Student*, available in most student unions, is a mine of local information and the weekly *Time Out* entertainment magazine publishes a student listings section and also publishes an annual *Student Guide*.

VOCATIONAL COURSES

In addition to establishments offering traditional academic courses, London also offers a wealth of vocational courses in fields such as childcare, cooking, beauty therapy, English-language classes, and a wide range of evening classes and distance learning.

Childcare

If you're seeking a childcare qualification in preparation for working as a nanny or a nursery nurse, you'll need to find a college providing training for a recognised childcare qualification. The National Nursery Examination Board's (NNEB) diploma is the best known and most universally recognised qualification in this field, covering care of children from birth to eight years of age. The NNEB is a full-time, two-year course comprising around 60 per cent theory and 40 per cent work experience on placements with families, nursery schools and hospital maternity units. If required, there's usually an opportunity for students to undertake a placement within a special needs environment.

The Business and Technical Education Council (BTEC) National Diploma (Diplomas in Nursery Nursing/Childcare and Education) course covers many practical placements and can involve care of those in early education as well as very young children. The course covers care of sick children, growth and development, and community assignments. This is often a more flexible option but involves up to 800 hours work experience. Alternatively, you can undertake the National Association of Maternal and Child Welfare (NAMCW) diploma, which also lasts two years and involves both practical experience and attendance at college, or the shorter one-year NAMCW certificate course. However, the NAMCW alone isn't generally recognised as a suitable qualification for a position in a day nursery and if you're planning to work in this field the NNEB or BTEC are preferable.

For more information about qualifications in childcare contact the **Council for Awards in Children's Care and Education** (CACHE, 8 Chequer Street, St Albans, Herts, AL1 3XZ, ☎ 01727-810818, ✉ cache @compuserve.com).

Cookery

Many planning to enter the restaurant trade or train as chefs do so by taking catering courses at higher education establishments or by training 'on-the-job' as assistants or sous-chefs at one of London's better restaurants. However, **Leith's School of Food and Wine** (21 St Alban's Grove, London W8 5BP, ☎ 0207-229 0177, ▭ www.leiths.co.uk, High St Kensington or Gloucester Rd tube) is one of several establishments in the capital offering professional training for career cooks and qualification for those wishing to enter the highly competitive food and wine business. Leith's also provides short courses and evening classes for 'amateurs'.

Beauty Therapy

Beauty therapists' courses are popular in London and if you want to follow this path you should write to the **Independent Beauty Schools' Association** (PO Box 781, London SW3 2PN) for their *Guide to Training in Beauty Therapy* and a list of members in the London area.

English-Language Schools

Teaching English as a second language is big business in the UK, particularly in London, where there are dozens of English-language schools. However, the cost and quality of teaching can vary considerably and it's advisable to enrol with a reputable school such as those that are members of the **Association of Recognised English Language Schools (ARELS)** which has around 90 schools in the capital, a few of which are listed below. For further details of these and other schools contact ARELS (56 Buckingham Gate, London SW1E 6AG, ☎ 0207-802 9200, ▭ www.arels. org.uk).

- **Shane English School**, 59 South Molton Street, London W1Y 1HH (☎ 0207-499 8533, ▭ www.shane-english.co.uk, Bond St tube).

- **Regent London School**, 12 Buckingham Street, London WC2N 6DF (☎ 0207-872 6620, ▭ www.regent.org.uk, Charing Cross tube).

- **International Community School**, 4 York Terrace East, Regent's Park, London NW1 4PT (☎ 0207-935 1206, ▭ www.skola.co.uk, Regent's Park tube).

- **Saint Patrick's International College**, 24 Great Chapel Street, Soho, London W1V 3AF (☎ 0207-734-2156, ▭ www.st-patricks.org.uk, Tootenham Court Rd tube).

- **Central School of English**, 1 Tottenham Court Road, London W1P 9DA (☎ 0207-580 2863, ▭ www.centralschool.co.uk, Tottenham Court Rd tube).

- **SELS College London**, 64/65 Long Acre, Covent Garden, London WC2E 9JH (☎ 0207-240 2581, 💻 www.sels.co.uk, Covent Garden tube).

Evening Classes & Distance Learning

Evening classes in London range from spare-time interests such as flower-arranging and painting to academic and vocational courses leading to recognised qualifications in subjects such as information technology and accounting. Classes are usually provided by individual boroughs and you should contact the local education authority for details. The bible for part-time courses in London is *Floodlight Part-Time*, a guide to part-time day and evening classes, and *Summertime Floodlight*, a guide to summertime courses in Greater London. Both are published by Floodlight Publishing and available direct from them (💻 www.floodlight.co.uk) or bookshops and newsagents in London.

Those who need (or prefer) to study at home or whose job frequently takes them away from home can enrol in a distance learning course. The **Open University** (OU), established in 1969, is the best-known provider of such courses and offers everything from vocational qualifications to undergraduate and research degrees. Although jokes are often made about course programmes going out on TV at 5am, the widespread ownership of video recorders means that programmes can be viewed at a more 'civilised' hour. There are also courses that can be done online via the Internet. For information contact the London branch of the OU at Parsifal College (527 Finchley Road, London NW3 7BG, ☎ 0207-431 3215, 💻 www.open.ac.uk/near-you/in-london).

The UK's largest provider of distance learning courses, the **National Extension College**, offers written home study courses and, depending on circumstances, the support of a local college should you need it. Qualifications offered primarily focus on GCSEs, A-levels and National Vocational Qualifications (NVQs). For information contact the National Extension College (18 Brooklands Avenue, Cambridge CB2 2HN, ☎ 01223-316644, 💻 www.nec.ac.uk).

The **London School of Journalism** (22 Upbrook Mews, London W2 3HG, ☎ 0207-706 3536, 💻 www.octacon.co.uk/ext/ociplc/lsj.htm) is the longest-established writing school in Europe (founded in 1920) and runs summer schools for prospective journalists and writers as well as offering correspondence courses.

6.

STAYING HEALTHY

One of the most important aspects of living in London (or anywhere else for that matter) is maintaining good health. Britain is famous for its National Health Service (NHS), which provides 'free' health care to all British citizens and most foreign residents. The standard of training, dedication and medical skills of British doctors and nursing staff is among the highest in the world, and British medical science is in the vanguard of many of the world's major medical advances (many pioneering operations are performed in Britain). Many foreigners visit Britain for private medical treatment, and Harley Street (London) is internationally recognised as having some of the world's pre-eminent (and most expensive) specialists, encompassing every conceivable ailment. .

If you don't qualify for health care under the public health service, it's essential to have private health insurance (in fact, you may not qualify for a residence permit without it). This is often advisable in any case if you can afford it, due to the inadequacy of public health services in many areas and long waiting lists for specialist appointments and non-urgent operations. Visitors to Britain should have holiday health insurance if they aren't covered by a reciprocal arrangement.

If you're taking regular medication, you should bear in mind that the brand names of drugs and medicines vary from country to country, and should ask your doctor for the generic name. If you wish to match medication prescribed abroad, you will need a prescription with the medication's trade name, the manufacturer's name, the chemical name and the dosage. Most drugs have an equivalent in other countries, although particular brands may be difficult or impossible to obtain in Britain. It's also advisable to take some of your favourite non-prescription drugs (e.g. aspirins, cold and flu remedies, lotions, etc.) with you, as they may be difficult to find or may be much more expensive. If applicable, you should also take a spare pair of spectacles, contact lenses, dentures or a hearing aid.

If you're planning to take up residence in London, even for part of the year only, you may wish to have a health check (medical or screening, eyes, teeth, etc.) before your arrival, particularly if you have a record of poor health or are elderly. There are no special health risks in Britain and no immunisations are required unless you arrive from an area infected with yellow fever. You can safely drink the water (unless there's a sign to the contrary), although it sometimes tastes awful, and many people prefer bottled water (when not drinking wine and various other alcoholic beverages!).

EMERGENCIES

If you're unlucky enough to be involved in an accident or suffer a sudden serious illness in Britain, you'll be pleased to know that emergency transport by ambulance and treatment at a hospital Accident & Emergency (A&E) department is free to everyone. In a medical emergency, simply dial 999 from any telephone (calls are free) and ask for the ambulance service. State your name and location and describe your injuries or symptoms (or those of the patient) and an ambulance with paramedics will be despatched immediately to take you to hospital (the actual wait will depend on your location and how busy the ambulance service is at that time). **Note that calls to 999 must be made in emergencies only and health authorities can levy a fee if an emergency ambulance is called unnecessarily.** Britain doesn't have a national air ambulance service, although there are emergency helicopter services in London for critical cases.

In minor emergencies or for medical advice, you should phone your family doctor (see page 185) if you have one. Failing this you can ask the operator (100) for the telephone number of a local doctor or hospital (or consult your phone book). Police stations keep a list of doctors' and chemists' private telephone numbers, in case of emergency. There are private, 24-hour, doctor and dental services in London that make house calls, but check the cost before using them (see the Yellow Pages).

If you're physically capable, you can go to the Accident, Casualty or Emergency department of an NHS general hospital, many of which provide a 24-hour service (see below). Check in advance which local hospitals are equipped to deal with emergencies and the fastest route from your home. This information may be of vital importance in the event of an emergency, when a delay could mean the difference between life and death. Not all London hospitals have Accident & Emergency (A&E) departments and of those that do, not all are open round the clock. Hospitals in inner London (there are more in the outer suburbs) with 24-hour emergency facilities include the following:

- **Central:** St Mary's Hospital, Praed Street, W2 (☎ 0207-886 6666, Paddington tube) and University College Hospital, Grafton Way, WC1 (☎ 0207-387 9300, Euston Sq/Warren St tube).

- **West:** Charing Cross Hospital, Fulham Palace Road, London, W6 (☎ 0208-746 5555, Barons Court/Hammersmith tube) and Chelsea & Westminster Hospital, 369 Fulham Road, SW10 (☎ 0208-746 8000, bus Nos 14, 73, 211).

- **East:** Hackney & Homerton Hospital, Homerton Row, E9 (☎ 0208-510 5555, Homerton rail) and Royal London Hospital, Whitechapel Road, E1 (☎ 0207-377 7000, Whitechapel tube).

- **North:** Royal Free Hospital, Pond Street, NW3 (☎ 0207-794 0500, Belsize Park tube) and Whittington Hospital, St Mary's Wing, Highgate Hill, N19 (☎ 0207-272 3070, Archway tube).

- **South:** St Thomas's Hospital, Lambeth Palace Road, SE1 (☎ 0207-928 9292, Waterloo/Westminster tube), Guy's Hospital, St Thomas Street, SE1 (☎ 0207-955 5500, London Bridge tube) and St George's Hospital, Blackshaw Road, SW17 (☎ 0208-672 1255, Tooting Broadway tube).

If you have a rare blood group or a medical problem that cannot easily be seen or recognised, e.g. a heart condition, diabetes, epilepsy, haemophilia or a severe allergy, you should join **Medic-Alert**. Medic-Alert members wear a necklace or bracelet containing an internationally-recognised symbol and engraved with their medical problem, membership number and a telephone number. When you're unable to speak for yourself, doctors, police or anyone providing aid can immediately obtain vital medical information from anywhere in the world by phoning a 24-hour emergency number. Medic-Alert is a non-profit registered charity and life membership is included in the cost of the bracelet or necklace (costing from £19.95) plus an annual £10 fee. For more information contact the Medic-Alert Foundation, 1 Bridge Wharf, 156 Caledonian Road, London N1 9UU (☎ 0207-833 3034).

It's advisable to keep a record of the telephone numbers of your doctor, local hospitals and clinics, ambulance service, first aid, poison control, dentist, and other emergency services next to your telephone.

NATIONAL HEALTH SERVICE (NHS)

The National Health Service (NHS) was established in 1948 to ensure that everyone had equal access to medical care. NHS services include family doctors, specialists, hospitals, dentists, chemists, opticians, community health services (e.g. the district nursing and health visitor services), the ambulance service, and maternity and child health care. Originally, all NHS medical treatment was free, the service being funded entirely from general taxation and National Insurance contributions.

However, as the cost of treatment and medicines have increased, part of the cost has been passed onto patients via supplementary charges. While hospital treatment, the ambulance service, and consultations with doctors remain free, many patients must now pay fixed charges for prescriptions, dental treatment, sight tests and NHS glasses, although charges are usually well below the actual cost. Family doctors, called General Practitioners (GPs), still make free house calls and community health workers and district nurses visit people at home who are convalescent, bedridden, or have new-born babies.

The NHS is run by Regional Health Authorities, District Health Authorities (corresponding roughly to local authority boundaries), Family Practitioner Committees and Special Health Authorities. If you want to find the name of your District Health Authority, inquire at your local library or ask any doctor's receptionist. Often health service boundaries aren't the same as the local council area or borough in London. For information about how to register with an NHS family doctor (GP), see **Doctors** on page 185. The quality of service you receive from the NHS depends very much on where you live, as waiting lists for specialist appointments and hospital beds vary from area to area. Patients of fundholding GPs (see page 186) often have shorter waits, as GPs can shop around for the shortest queues. In fact, even the treatment you receive varies depending on you local health authority, some of which don't provide certain expensive treatment (e.g. for cancer) as they simply cannot afford it.

The NHS provides free or subsidised medical treatment to all British nationals and foreigners with the right of abode in Britain and to anyone who, at the time of treatment, has been a resident for the previous year. Exceptions to the one-year qualifying rule include European Union (EU) nationals (with a form E111); refugees or those with 'exceptional leave to remain' in Britain; students on a course of over six months; foreign nationals coming to take up permanent residence in Britain; certain groups of sailors or off-shore workers; non-EU recipients of British war disablement pensions; overseas crown servants; British pensioners living abroad; NATO personnel stationed in Britain; prisoners; anyone with a permit to work in Britain; and the spouse and children of the above.

Nationals of countries with reciprocal health agreements with Britain also receive free or subsidised medical treatment, including all EU nationals and citizens of Anguilla, Australia, Barbados, British Virgin Islands, Bulgaria, Channel Islands, Czech Republic, Falkland Islands, Gibraltar, Hong Kong, Hungary, Iceland, Isle of Man, Malta, Montserrat, New Zealand, Norway, Poland, Romania, Russia (and other former Soviet states excluding Latvia, Lithuania and Estonia), Slovak Republic, St Helena, Turks & Caicos Islands, and states comprising the former Yugoslavia. Exemption from charges for nationals of the above countries is generally limited to emergency or urgent treatment (e.g. for a communicable disease) required during a visit to Britain.

Anyone who doesn't qualify under one of the above categories must pay for all medical treatment received, although minor medical and dental emergencies may be treated free of charge, e.g. emergency treatment at a hospital 'out patients' department as a result of an accident (or patients admitted to hospital for no longer than one night).

The NHS Today

In the last few decades, there have been sweeping NHS reforms, which have included self-governing hospitals, practise and prescribing budgets for GPs, funding and contracts for hospital services, and the creation of an NHS internal market. The NHS has traditionally been a political football and some of these reforms are now being reversed by the current Labour government. The services provided by the NHS have come under increasing pressure in recent years, largely as a result of a lack of funding by central government and the increasing demands on the NHS from an ageing population.

One of the most serious problems facing the NHS is a chronic shortage of staff, particularly nurses (especially specialist-trained nurses), midwives, and health visitors who have been leaving the NHS at a rate of up to 50,000 a year. The main problem is low salaries (one in five nurses is forced to take a second job to survive), although poor working conditions, long hours (the hours worked by junior doctors in NHS hospitals is a national scandal), a lack of resources and stress also take their toll. Some of London's best hospitals such as the Royal Marsden and St Bartholomew's (Bart's) have been closed in recent years, and it's undeniable that NHS health services aren't as universally available as they once were. The best doctors (general practitioners) and dentists in London have patient lists that are full to capacity.

A lack of doctors has meant that many hospitals and deputising services are forced to recruit an increasing number of doctors from abroad. Foreign doctors have flooded into Britain in recent years (5,500 were registered in 1997 – one-third more than the number trained in Britain), most from EU countries. Although Britain doesn't train sufficient doctors, it also loses many doctors to other countries. One-fifth of all GPs practising in Britain are from overseas, some of whom speak poor English or lack sufficient experience. The bulk of supply or locum doctors (who fill shortages when doctors are on holiday or sick) are also foreign.

Lack of funds have resulted in hospital ward closures, long waiting lists for specialist appointments and hospital beds (patients are often left on trolleys in hospital corridors because no beds are available), cancelled operations, and long queues in doctors' surgeries and hospital waiting rooms. Although funding has been increasing (in real terms) for a number of years, demand is rising at an ever-faster rate. Lack of resources have meant that NHS health services are having to be rationed and decided on the basis of a patient's chances of recovery or life expectancy. This means the elderly, heavy smokers, alcoholics and those who are seriously obese have little chance of receiving expensive life-saving operations such as heart surgery and transplants on the NHS. There are long waiting lists for non-vital procedures such as hip replacements, varicose vein surgery, hernia operations and even sterilisation. The number of people on NHS surgery waiting lists was over one million in 1999, with many waiting a year or longer for treatment.

The present government is attempting to address the NHS problems by injecting extra funds and resources, although it will take many years to resolve the problems of under-staffing and eradicate the waiting lists (if it's ever possible). Another problem that requires addressing is how to tackle the long-term needs of an ageing population. Many people believe that more resources should be channelled into preventive medicine rather than cure, in particular the promotion of regular exercise and a healthy diet.

PRIVATE HEALTH INSURANCE

If you won't be covered by the NHS you should take out private health insurance, as medical treatment in Britain can be very expensive with the cost of an operation and hospitalisation running into £thousands. The number of people with private health insurance in Britain increased from around 1.5 million in 1966 to some 6.5 million in 1998 (around 12 per cent of the population), half of whose premiums are paid by their employers. The remainder are spilt between those who pay their own premiums and those who share them with their employers. Private health care is restricted mainly to the middle to upper income brackets. The best advertisement for private health insurance is the eternal NHS waiting lists for non-emergency operations. One five operations in Britain is performed privately.

Most patients who receive private health treatment in Britain are insured with provident associations such as BUPA and PPP, which pay for specialist and hospital treatment only, and don't include routine visits to doctors and dentists (which are covered by the NHS). Private patients are also free to choose their own specialists and hospitals, and are usually accommodated in a private, hotel-style room with a radio, telephone, colour TV, en suite bathroom and room service. Although some health checks and scans are available on demand under the NHS or with private health insurance, many aren't (including the most expensive). They don't, for example, include a comprehensive health check-up or screening, which can be performed at private clinics throughout Britain for around £200 to £300.

Private health insurance isn't usually intended to replace NHS treatment, but to complement it. Most health insurance policies fall into two main categories: those providing immediate private specialist or hospital treatment (e.g. BUPA, PPP and WPA) and so-called 'budget' or 'waiting-list' policies, where you're treated as a private patient only when waiting lists exceed a certain period. Under waiting-list policies, if you cannot obtain an appointment with an NHS specialist or an NHS hospital admission within a certain period (e.g. six weeks), you can do so as a private patient.

The cost of private health insurance depends on your age and the state of your health. There are maximum age limits for taking out health insurance with some insurers, e.g. 65 for BUPA, although age limits may be higher if you're willing to accept some restrictions. Some companies have special policies for those aged over 50 or 55. There are generally no restrictions on continuing membership, irrespective of age. Treatment of any medical condition for which you have already received medical attention or were aware existed in the five years prior to the start date of the policy may not be covered. However, existing health problems are usually covered after two years membership, providing that no further medical attention has been necessary during this period. Some group policies do, however, include cover for existing or previous health problems. Other exclusions are listed in the policy rules.

Standard policies may offer three scales (usually designated A, B and C) of hospital treatment which may include London NHS teaching hospitals (A, high scale), provincial NHS teaching hospitals (B, medium scale) and provincial non-teaching hospitals (C, low scale). Accommodation is usually in a private room, but in some hospitals it may be in a twin or four-bedded ward. Premiums range from a few pounds a week for a budget plan offering limited benefits (e.g. HSA) up to £hundreds a month for a comprehensive policy with a major insurance company. Comprehensive, top-of-the-range cover costs from £40 a month for a single person and from around £100 for a family (some companies offer lower premiums but have a compulsory annual excess of £500 or £1,000).

When deciding on the type and extent of health insurance, make sure that it covers *all* your family's present and future health requirements in Britain before you receive a large bill. A health insurance policy should cover you for essential health care required as a result of accidents (e.g. sports accidents) and injuries, whether they occur in your home, at your place of work or when travelling. Don't take anything for granted, but check in advance that you're covered. Long-stay visitors should have travel or long-stay health insurance or an international health policy. If your stay in London is limited, you may be covered by a reciprocal agreement between your home country and the UK.

If you need private treatment in the UK you may be required to pay in advance and reclaim the cost from your insurance company later, although some foreign insurers will pay bills directly (although your choice of hospital may be limited). If you must pay up front, you will need to ensure that you have sufficient funds available to pay for medical care while you're in the UK and that you understand how to make claims.

PRIVATE HEALTH TREATMENT

If you aren't entitled to treatment under the NHS you will be treated as a private patient by a doctor or hospital (except in emergencies) and the cost will be borne by you or your health insurance company. Private hospital care in the UK is provided in private clinics and hospitals, which are completely independent of the NHS, and in private wings or wards of large NHS hospitals. Private patients can choose to pay for treatment in most NHS hospitals and NHS consultants also treat private patients.

In addition to specialist appointments and hospital treatment, people commonly use private health treatment to obtain second opinions, for private health checks and screening, complementary medicine and cosmetic surgery. Over six million people have private health insurance of some kind in Britain and around a quarter of all operations are performed privately. If you need to see a GP or specialist privately, you (or your insurance company) must pay the full fee, which is usually left to the doctor's discretion. You should expect to pay around £30 or more for a routine visit to a GP.

Harley Street is the most famous address for private medicine in the UK (and possibly the world), where leading practitioners are skilled in virtually every medical discipline, from cardiac surgery to liposuction. It has the single greatest concentration of medical expertise anywhere in the world, with over 1,400 specialist medical and dental consultants and practitioners in 'residence'. If money's no object and you're seeking the best treatment that money can buy, your first stop should be the website of **The Harley Street Bureau** (www.harleystreetmedical.com/bureau.htm), which is a non-profit organisation that provides a free service to patients seeking specialist private medical services. Simply fill in the online questionnaire and the bureau will provide details regarding the availability of treatment in the area.

Always make sure that a 'doctor' or medical practitioner is qualified to provide the treatment you require, as (surprisingly) anyone can call himself a doctor in Britain. When selecting a private specialist or clinic, you should be extremely cautious and only choose someone who has been recommended by a doctor or organisation that you can trust. It's sometimes advisable to obtain a second opinion, particularly if you're diagnosed as having a serious illness or require a major operation (but don't expect your doctor or specialist to approve). According to some reports, unnecessary operations are becoming increasingly common in Britain. Private patients don't have the same protection as NHS patients, although complaints about treatment paid for by a private health insurance policy may be taken up by your insurance company. As a last resort you can complain to the General Medical Council, providing a medical practitioner is a qualified doctor.

Note that the quality of private treatment isn't necessarily superior to that provided by the NHS and you shouldn't assume that because a doctor (or any other medical practitioner) is in private practise, he's more competent than his NHS counterpart. In fact, often you will see the same specialist or be treated by the same surgeon on the NHS and privately. If you see a private physician his offices will be plush and welcoming, you will be greeted courteously by his receptionist, he'll have more time to lavish on you and his bedside manner will be impeccable. However, he won't necessarily be a better doctor than the one in the high street community clinic.

Drop-In Medicentres: A new innovation in recent years has been the introduction of private drop-in medicentres (☎ 0870-600 0870, 💻 www.medicentre.com) where doctors and nurses are on hand for consultations and to perform tests, screening, health checks, vaccinations and minor treatment. Medicentre is a walk-in service designed to fit around your schedule – there's no need to be registered and you don't require an appointment. Medicentres are located in the high street, e.g. in branches of Boots the chemist, and in shopping centres. Patients pay around £36 for a consultation and package deals are available from insurers such as Norwich Union (☎ 0800-056 2591). **Medical Express**, 117a Harley Street, W1 (☎ 0800-980 0700, Mon-Fri 9am to 6pm, 9.30am to 2.30pm Sat) operates a walk-in casualty clinic and health screening service in central London.

Complementary Medicine

Complementary (or alternative) medicine is popular in Britain and is chosen by some five million patients a year, although with the exception of certain fields such as acupuncture, chiropractic, homeopathy and osteopathy, it isn't usually covered by the NHS or private health insurance in Britain. To find a homeopath or homeopathic pharmacist (such as Ainsworth's, 38 New Cavandish Street, W1, ☎ 0207-935 5330) in your area contact the **British Homeopathic Association**, 27A Devonshire Street, W1 (☎ 0207-935 2163). London is also the base for Europe's largest provider of complementary medicine, the **Royal London Homeopathic Hospital NHS Trust**, which is the only independent public sector hospital in Europe dedicated to complementary medicine.

If you're seeking a chiropractor, contact the **British Chiropractic Association**, Blagrave House, 17 Blagrave Street, Reading, Berkshire RG1 1QB (☎ 0118-950 5950, ✉ www.chiropractic-uk.co.uk). To find a doctor practising acupuncture, contact the **British Acupuncture Council**, Park House, 206 Latimer Road, W10 (☎ 0208-964 0222) and for a holistic practitioner contact the **British Holistic Medical Association**, 59 Lansdowne Place, Hove, East Sussex BN3 1FL (☎ 01273-725951). If you're interested in Reflexology, the specialist foot massage therapy, contact the **Association of Reflexologists**, 27 Old Gloucester Street, W1 (☎ 0870-5673320, ✉ www.reflexology.org/aor) to find a therapist in your area.

A list of professional bodies governing alternative medical practitioners is contained in the *Time Out Guide to Shopping & Services Guide in London*.

Cosmetic Surgery

A glance through the advertisements in any women's, and increasingly, men's magazines will give you some indication of just how big (and lucrative) a business cosmetic surgery has become in London, although plastic surgeons are still relatively rare in the UK as a whole. If your nose, ears or derrière are too big, or you would love to fill a full C cup, just pop down to your local plastic surgeon who will remove those unwanted bits (or make others more prominent) as fast as you can say £2,000. If you're contemplating cosmetic surgery, you would be well advised to contact one of the professional associations listed below for advice before parting with any money. They also provide informative websites with search facilities for surgeons in a particular speciality, and the BAPS site also contains a handy glossary of esoteric medical terms.

The most respected professional associations include the **British Association of Plastic Surgeons (BAPS)**, The Royal College of Surgeons of England, 35-43 Lincoln's Inn Fields, London WC2A 3PN (☎ 0207-831-5161/2, ✉ www.baps.co.uk); the **British Association of Aesthetic Plastic Surgeons (BAAPS)**, The Royal College of Surgeons of England, 35-43

Lincoln's Inn Fields, London WC2A 3PN (☎ 0207-405-2234, ⌨ www. baaps.org.uk) and the **Breast Implant Information Society (BIIS)**, PO Box 1084, Mitcham, Surrey CR4 4ZU (☎ 0208-640 8040, helpline 0208-640 5040, ⌨ http://wkweb4.cableinet.co.uk/heasman/home.htm).

A few of the best-known clinics specialising in plastic surgery in and around London are the **Pountney Clinic** (☎ 0208-570 9658, www. pountneyclinic.co.uk) near Heathrow Airport, which performs the whole range of cosmetic surgery for face and body; the **Cosmetic Surgery Clinic, 100 Harley Street, W1** (☎ 0207-486 5111, ⌨ www.cosmeticsurgeryclinic. co.uk) that specialises in breast enhancement; and **Guy's Nuffield House** (☎ 0207-955 4761) which is attached to Guy's Hospital and emphasises extensive consultation and counselling before surgery.

DOCTORS

There are excellent family doctors, generally referred to as General Practitioners (GPs), in all areas of London. The best way to find a doctor, whether as an NHS or a private patient, is to ask your (healthy?) colleagues, friends or neighbours if they can recommend someone. Alternatively, you can consult a list of GPs for your Health District in your Community Health Council (CHC) office or contact your local Family Health Services Authority (FHSA). FHSAs publish lists of doctors, dentists, chemists and opticians in their area, which are available at libraries, post offices, tourist information offices, police stations and Citizens Advice Bureaux. If you're a student, some colleges have their own student health centre where you should register. GPs or family doctors are also listed under 'Doctors (Medical Practitioners)' in the Yellow Pages.

Surgery hours vary, but are typically from 8.30am until 6 or 7pm, Mon-Fri, with early closing one day a week, e.g. 5 or 5.30pm on Fridays (evening surgeries may also be held on one or two evenings a week). Emergency surgeries may be held on Saturday mornings, e.g. from 8.30 until 11.30am or noon. Most doctors' surgeries have answering machines outside surgery (office) hours, when a recorded message informs you of the name of the doctor on call (or deputising service) and his telephone number.

NHS Doctors: NHS doctors have a contract with their local FHSAs to look after a number of patients (average around 2,000) who make up their list. Doctors are paid by the NHS according to the number of patients on their list and an NHS doctor can refuse to register you as a patient if he has no vacancies. If you're looking for an NHS doctor, you must live within his catchment area from where he's permitted to draw his patients. If you have trouble getting onto an NHS doctor's list contact your local FHSA, who have a duty to find you a doctor. If you're living in a district for less than three months or have no permanent home, you can apply to any doctor in the district to be accepted as a temporary resident for three months. After this period you must register with the doctor as a permanent patient or you may register with another doctor. An NHS doctor must give 'immediate necessary treatment' for up to 14 days to anyone without a doctor living in his area, until the patient has been accepted by a doctor as a permanent or temporary resident. The NHS operates a walk-in surgery for those without a doctor at the **Great Chapel Street Medical Centre**, 13 Great Chapel Street, W1 (☎ 0207-437 9360, Tottenham Court Rd tube).

Fundholding GPs: Under the NHS reforms instituted in 1991, the government created fundholding GPs, where GPs manage their own budgets and can shop around and buy services for their patients direct from hospitals and other health service providers. Over 40 per cent of doctors are GP fundholders. Non-fundholding GPs must rely on their district health authority (DHA) for health services and cannot refer patients to hospitals of their choice. Fundholding GPs usually provide a wider range of services and their patients experience shorter waits to see specialists and for hospital beds, as GPs can shop around for the shortest queues. This has created a two-tier health system with patients of non-fundholders being disadvantaged. However, because fundholding GPs tend to spend more time managing their funds, they spend less time with their patients than non-fundholding GPs. Generally, you're much better off with a fundholding GP.

Group Practices: Around 80 per cent of GPs work in a partnership or group practise, around 25 per cent of whom practise in health centres, providing a range of medical and nursing services. Health centres may have facilities for immunisation, cervical smears, health education (e.g. a well person clinic), family planning, speech therapy, chiropody, hearing tests, physiotherapy and remedial exercises. Many also include dental, ophthalmic, hospital out-patient and social work support. Most health centres or large surgeries have district nurses, health visitors, midwives and clinical psychologists in attendance at fixed times. Bear in mind that if your doctor is part of a partnership or group practise, when he's absent you'll automatically be treated by a partner or another doctor (unless you wish to wait until your doctor returns).

NHS GPs must produce practise guides for patients containing the names of doctors, times of surgeries and any special services they provide, such as ante-natal, family planning, well woman/man, or diabetic clinics. It's often advisable to meet a prospective doctor before deciding whether to register with him. When you have found a suitable NHS doctor who'll accept you, you must register with him by completing part A of your medical card and giving it to his receptionist. If you don't have an NHS medical card, you must complete a form provided by the GP which he will send to the local FHSA (who will send you a medical card within a few weeks of registration).

Appointments & House Calls: Note that most doctors operate an appointment system, where you must make an appointment in advance. You cannot just turn up during surgery hours and expect to be seen. If you're an urgent case (but not an emergency), your doctor will usually see you immediately, but you should still phone in advance. Note, however, that surgeries are often overrun and you may have to wait well past your appointment time to see a doctor. NHS doctors make free house calls and emergency visits outside surgery hours (at their discretion) when patients are bedridden or unable to visit the surgery. In Britain, a doctor is responsible for his patients 24 hours a day and when he's unavailable he must make alternative arrangements, either through his partners in a group practise, a voluntary roster between individual doctors or a commercial deputising service. When you call your GP outside normal hours he's unlikely to attend you personally at home. Most GPs use an outside medical service which exists to provide house calls and an 'after hours' service.

DRUGS & MEDICINES

Medicines and drugs are obtained from a chemist (pharmacy) in Britain, most of which provide free advice regarding minor ailments and suggest appropriate medicines. There are three categories of drugs and medicines in Britain: those that can be prescribed only by a doctor (via an official form called a prescription) and purchased from a chemist, medicines that can be sold only under the supervision of a pharmacist, and general-sale list medicines (such as aspirin and paracetamol) that can be sold in outlets such as petrol stations and supermarkets.

Most chemists are open during normal shopping hours and at least one chemist is open in most towns during evenings and on Sundays for the emergency dispensing of medicines and drugs. A rota is posted on the doors of chemists and published in local newspapers and guides (information is also available from police stations). If you need medicines after normal hours there are a number of chemists that regularly open late in central London including **Bliss** (5-6 Marble Arch, W1, ☎ 0207-723 6116) which is open from 9am until midnight daily, and **Boots** (75 Queensway, W2, ☎ 0207-229 9266), open from 9am to 10pm Mon-Sat and from 5 to 10pm on Sundays. If you require medicine urgently when all chemists are closed, you should contact your GP or local police station.

To obtain medicines prescribed by a doctor, simply take your prescription form to any chemist. Your prescription may be filled immediately if it's available off the shelf or you may be asked to wait or come back later. NHS prescriptions for medicines are charged at a fixed rate of £5.90 (they cost just 20p in 1979!) per item, although four out of five prescriptions are free. Although the average cost of prescription drugs would be around £10 if they were bought over the counter, many drugs would cost less than the prescription charge if they were available over the counter. Those with comprehensive private (e.g. foreign) health insurance may be able to reclaim the cost of prescriptions from their insurance company.

The Consumers' Association (see page 298) publish a booklet entitled *Cheaper than a prescription*, listing medicines that you can buy over the counter and prescription-only drugs costing less than a prescription (which your GP may prescribe privately). Some medicines prescribed by a doctor (e.g. certain pain killers) can be replaced by substitute medicines that can be purchased over the counter for less than the prescription charge. Boots, Britain's largest chain of chemists with over 1,300 stores, is often the cheapest place to buy non-prescription drugs (many own brands).

Many people qualify for free prescriptions (e.g. prescriptions for hospital out-patients and day patients) including children under 16; students under 19 in full-time education; pensioners (men over 65, women over 60); expectant mothers and those who have had a baby in the last year; those with certain medical conditions, e.g. diabetes or epilepsy, or a permanent disability which prevents them getting around without help; and people on low incomes receiving state benefits. With the exception of children under 16 and pensioners, all those entitled to free prescriptions must apply for an exemption certificate or a refund.

Always use, store and dispose of unwanted medicines and poisons safely, e.g. by returning them to a pharmacist or dispensing doctor, and never leave them where children can get their hands on them.

HOSPITALS & CLINICS

All London boroughs owns have one or more NHS hospitals or clinics, indicated by the international hospital sign of a white 'H' on a blue background. There are many kinds of hospitals in London, including community hospitals, district hospitals, teaching hospitals and cottage hospitals. Major hospitals are called general hospitals and provide treatment and diagnosis for in-patients, day-patients and out-patients. Most have a maternity department, infectious diseases unit, psychiatric and geriatric facilities, rehabilitation and convalescent units, and cater for all forms of specialised treatment.

Some general hospitals are designated teaching hospitals which combine treatment with medical training and research work. In addition to general hospitals, there are also specialist hospitals for children, the mentally ill and handicapped, the elderly and infirm, and for the treatment of specific complaints or illnesses. There are also dental hospitals. Only major hospitals have an Accident & Emergency (A&E) department. Many NHS hospitals have sports injury clinics, although you must usually be referred by your GP, and some have minor injuries units. In many areas there are NHS Well Woman Clinics, where women can obtain medical check-ups and cervical smear tests, and NHS Family Planning Clinics. You can be referred to these clinics by your GP or can refer yourself. You can also refer yourself to an NHS Sexually Transmitted Diseases (STD) or VD clinic for an examination.

Choice of Hospital: Except for emergencies, you may be admitted or referred to an NHS hospital or clinic for treatment only after consultation with a GP or a consultant (or from an NHS clinic such as a family planning or well woman clinic). Patients with private health insurance may be treated at the hospital of their choice, depending on their insurance cover. NHS patients can ask to be treated at a particular hospital or to be referred to a particular consultant, but have no right to have their request met. If your GP isn't an NHS fundholder (see page 186), you're admitted to a hospital under the control of your local health authority, unless special surgery or treatment is necessary that's unavailable locally. Patients of fundholding GPs may be admitted to any NHS hospital. In an emergency you will be treated at the nearest hospital.

Accommodation: NHS hospital accommodation is in wards of various sizes, e.g. 12-beds, some of which are mixed. Many NHS hospitals have private rooms (known as 'pay beds') and under NHS reforms, they're permitted to charge for extras such as a single room with a telephone, a TV or a wider choice of meals. In most NHS hospitals, you choose the meals you would like the day before and provision is made for vegetarian and other diets. Some wards have dining rooms for those sufficiently mobile and most have day rooms for mobile patients. The service, facilities and standards of NHS hospitals vary considerably depending on the area, the best of which compare favourably with private hospitals (apart from a possible lack of modern conveniences). On the other hand, some NHS hospitals are dingy and depressing and are perhaps the last place on earth you would wish to be when you're ill. However, there's some consolation to being in an NHS general ward – just think how lonely and bored those poor private patients must be, ensconced in their luxury rooms with nobody to talk to all day!

Private Hospitals & Clinics

In addition to NHS hospitals, there are around 50 private hospitals and clinics in London, many of which are owned by provident associations such as BUPA and PPP and other health insurers. The most striking difference between NHS and private hospitals is in the standard of accommodation. Instead of being housed in a public ward with other patients, you'll have a private room equipped with all the comforts of home, including a radio, TV, telephone, en suite bathroom and room service (a visitor can usually enjoy a meal with a patient in the privacy of his room). The corridors will be carpeted, the food will be edible and there will be frills and extras galore – which may even include interpreters and special diets for overseas patients – and the nurses and other staff will wait on you hand and foot.

If you don't have health insurance or are a visitor to Britain, you may be asked to pay a (large) deposit in advance, particularly if there's any doubt that you will survive the ordeal (private hospitals usually accept credit cards). Many private hospitals also provide fixed-price surgery, subject to an examination by a consultant surgeon. Some hospitals offer interest-free loans to pay hospital bills (e.g. a 10 per cent deposit with the rest payable over 12 months). This is one solution for those who cannot afford health insurance and don't want to wait for an operation. However, make sure that you aren't being overcharged as you can often have an operation cheaper elsewhere in Britain or even abroad (e.g. in France) and possibly save thousands of pounds.

According to Action for Victims of Medical Accidents (AVMA), there are higher health risks in private hospitals than in NHS hospitals, and there may be less emergency equipment and fewer experienced staff. You have almost no protection under the law when you're treated at a private clinic or hospital compared with your rights as an NHS hospital patient, and when things go wrong (as they occasionally do) you're usually better off in an NHS hospital. Many experts believe that the best solution is a private ward in an NHS teaching hospital, where, if anything goes wrong and your life's on the line, you're far better off than you are in a small private clinic. Private Hospitals and Clinics in London include the following:

The Clementine Churchill Hospital, Sudbury Hill, Harrow HA1 3RX (☎ 0207-872 3872, 🖳 www.clemchur-bmihealth.co.uk, Harrow-on-the Hill tube or rail) provides sophisticated diagnostic services, including a new imaging centre and comprehensive health screening.

The Cromwell Hospital, Cromwell Road, SW5 (☎ 0207-460 2000, 🖳 www.cromwell-hospital.co.uk, Earls Court/Gloucester Road/High St Kensington tube) is one of the major private hospitals in the capital. Its specialities include cancer treatment, liver disease and transplants, pancreas and kidney transplants, neurosurgery, spinal surgery, heart surgery, gamma knife surgery (radiosurgery) and IVF.

The Devonshire Hospital, 29-31 Devonshire Street, W1 (☎ 0207-486 7131, 🖳 www.stmartins-healthcare.co.uk/dvnshr/index.htm, Baker St tube) specialises in the rehabilitation of those suffering from neurological conditions such as head and spinal cord injuries and strokes.

The Harley Street Clinic, 35 Weymouth Street. W19 (☎ 0207-935 7700, 🖳 www.columbiahealthcare.co.uk/hsc, Regents Park tube) is an acute care hospital with the accent on cardiology and cancer treatment.

The Lister Hospital, Chelsea Bridge Road, SW1 (☎ 0207-730 3417, 🖳 www.stmartins-healthcare.co.uk/lister, Sloane Sq/Victoria tube) has a wide range of specialities including assisted conception and skin lasers.

The London Bridge Hospital, 27 Tooley Street, SE1 (☎ 0207-407 3100, 🖳 www.stmartins-healthcare.co.uk/lndnbrdg, London Bridge tube) specialises in breast care, physiotherapy, cardiology and sports medicine.

The London Clinic, 20 Devonshire Place, W1 (☎ 0207-935 4444, 🖳 www.lonclin.co.uk, Regent's Park tube) caters particularly to overseas patients, particularly (rich) Arabs and Greeks. It provides a wide range of diagnostic services and treatment options.

The Portland Hospital for Women and Children, 205-209 Great Portland Street, W19 (☎ 0207-580 4400, 🖳 www.columbiahealthcare.co. uk/phwc, Great Portland St/Regent's Park tube) is the only private London hospital entirely dedicated to caring for women and children. It specialises in obstetrics, gynaecology and paediatrics.

The Princess Grace Hospital, 42-52 Nottingham Place, W1 (☎ 0207-486 1234, 🖳 www.columbiahealthcare.co.uk/pgh, Baker St/Regents Park tube) is another acute unit specialising in many disciplines. It also has a sleep apnoea (excessive snoring) clinic and is a major centre for the diagnosis and treatment of all forms of hepatitis.

The Wellington Hospital, Wellington Place, St Johns Wood Road, NW8 (☎ 0207-586 5959, 🖳 www.columbiahealthcare.co.uk/wellington, St John's Wood tube) is one of the largest, purpose-built, private hospitals in the UK offering all the resources of a first class general hospital. It also has a major sport injuries clinic.

The Wellman Clinic, 32 Weymouth Street, W1 (☎ 0207-6372018, 🖳 www.freepages.co.uk/wellman, Regent's Park/Gt Portland St tube) is a preventative healthcare centre designed exclusively for men. Treatments offered include prostate cancer treatment, impotence treatment and testosterone replacement therapy, as well as treatment for sports injuries and general health screening.

CHILDBIRTH

Childbirth in Britain usually takes place in a hospital, where a stay of a few days is usual. If you wish to have a child at home, you must find a doctor or midwife (see below) who's willing to attend you, although it's generally impossible for the birth of a first child. Some doctors are opposed to home births, particularly in cases where there could be complications and when specialists and special facilities (e.g. incubators) may be required. You can also choose to hire a private midwife (a nurse specialising in delivering babies), who'll attend you at home throughout and after your pregnancy.

For hospital births, you can usually decide (with the help of your GP or midwife) the hospital where you wish to have your baby. You aren't required to use the hospital suggested by your GP, but should book a hospital bed as early as possible. Your GP will also refer you to an obstetrician. Find out as much as possible about local hospital methods and policies on childbirth, either directly or from friends or neighbours, before booking a bed. The policy regarding a father's attendance at a birth varies depending on the hospital. A husband doesn't have the right to be present with his wife during labour or childbirth (which is at the consultant's discretion), although some doctors expect fathers to attend. If the presence of your husband is important to you, you should check that it's permitted at the hospital where you plan to have your baby and any other rules that may be in force.

In Britain, midwives are responsible for educating and supporting women and their families during the childbearing period. Midwives can advise women before they become pregnant, in addition to providing moral, physical and emotional support throughout a pregnancy and after the birth. Your midwife may also advise on parent education and ante-natal classes for mothers. After giving birth, mothers are attended at home by their midwife for the first ten days or so, after which they see a health visitor and their GP to monitor their child's health and development.

Family Planning Services

Family planning services such as contraceptives (including the morning-after pill), advice on how to use them and if necessary, abortions, are free to foreign nationals living and working in Britain. For information visit your doctor or a family planning clinic. To find the nearest clinic to your home contact the **Family Planning Association**, 2-12 Pentonville Road, N1 (☎ 0207-837 5432, contraceptive education helpline 0207-837 4044, Angel tube). The **International Planned Parenthood Federation** (☎ 0207-487 7900, ☐ www.ippf.org) provides general information on contraception, condoms and abortion, while the **National Childbirth Trust** (☎ 0208-992 8637, 9.30am to 4,30pm Mon-Fri) provides information and support to women during pregnancy, childbirth and early parenthood.

If you want an abortion, you will need to satisfy two UK doctors that the operation is justified under British law. Information about contraception, pregnancy and abortion is available from a number of organisations including the **British Pregnancy Advisory Service**, 7 Belgrave Road, SW1 (☎ 0207-828 2484, Victoria tube), the **Brook Advisory Centre**, 233 Tottenham Court Road, W1 (☎ 0207-323 1522, 24-hour helpline 0207-617 8000, Tottenham Court Rd tube) and **Marie Stopes House**, Family Planning Clinic, 108 Whitfield Street, W1 (☎ 0207-388 0662, Warren St tube). If you're pregnant and don't want to consider an abortion, contact **LIFE** (☎ 01926-311511, ☐ www.lifeuk.org) for practical help and support, counselling and advice.

DENTISTS

Britain's annual consumption of over 750,000 tonnes of sweets (over 13kg per person) ensures that dentists (and sweet manufacturers) remain financially healthy, although despite the efforts of dentists to promote preventive dentistry, many Britons never go near a dentist (mostly out of fear) unless they are dying from toothache. Fortunately, when you need help there are excellent dentists in all areas. The best way to find a good dentist, whether as an NHS or a private patient, is to ask your colleagues, friends or neighbours (particularly those with perfect teeth) if they can recommend someone.

Dentists are listed under 'Dental Surgeons' in the Yellow Pages and are permitted to advertise any special services they provide such as private and NHS patients, emergency or 24-hour answering service, dental hygienist, and evening or weekend surgeries. The **British Dental Association** (64

Wimpole Street, London W1M 8AL, ☎ 0207-935 0875) can also provide a list of dentists in your area. In some areas, community dental clinics or health centres provide a dental service for children, expectant and nursing mothers, and handicapped adults.

The cost of dental treatment has risen considerably in recent years and it will pay you to keep your mouth shut during dental check-ups, which are recommended every six months in Britain. However, dental care isn't particularly expensive in Britain compared with many other western countries, although fees vary depending on the area and the particular dentist, e.g. from £10 to £35 for a check-up, from £15 to £30 for scaling and polishing, and from £20 to £35 for an X-ray and a small (amalgam) filling.

NHS Treatment: Dental care is covered by the NHS but is only completely free to those under the age of 18 (19 if in full-time education), pregnant women, mothers with a baby under one year of age and those who are receiving state benefits (Income Support, Jobseeker's Allowance, Family Credit or Disability Working Allowance). Other patients must pay a proportion of their treatment costs, which is currently around £5 for a check-up, plus the cost of any work carried out.

Dentists are over-stretched in London and many are unwilling to accept new NHS patients onto their lists if their quotas are already full, although a dentist may offer to treat you as a private patient. If applicable, and to avoid misunderstandings, you should ensure that the dentist knows you expect NHS treatment when you register and that you remain entitled to NHS-subsidised treatment by attending regular check-ups – otherwise you may find yourself dropped from the dentist's NHS list. Private dentistry usually involves less waiting and treatment may be of a better quality (e.g. you can decide the quality of fillings, etc.), but it's much more expensive.

Many dentists operate an emergency service and in some areas an emergency dental service is operated by the local health authority. (Note, however, that a dentist isn't obliged to treat someone who isn't a patient of his, even in an emergency.) If you're suffering from agonising toothache, you can try the **Dental Emergency Care Service** (☎ 0207-955 2186, 08.45am to 3.30pm Mon-Fri), which will refer you to a dental surgery. Alternatively, **Guy's Hospital Dental School** Guy's Tower, St Thomas Street, SE1 (☎ 0207-955 4317, London Bridge tube) provides a free emergency dental service from 9.30am to 4pm Mon-Fri, as does the **Eastman Dental Hospital**, 256 Gray's Inn Road, WC1 (☎ 0207-837 3646, Chancery Lane/King's Cross tube) from 8.30am until 5.30pm weekdays.

OPTICIANS

As with dentists, there's no need to register with an optician. You simply go to the one of your choice, although it's advisable to ask your colleagues, friends or neighbours if they can recommend someone. Opticians are listed under 'Opticians-dispensing' or 'Opticians-ophthalmic (optometrists)' in the

Yellow Pages and may advertise their services such as contact lenses or an emergency repair service. Opticians (like spectacles) come in many shapes and sizes.

Your sight can be tested only by a registered ophthalmic optician (or optometrist) or an ophthalmic medical practitioner. Most 'high street' opticians are both dispensing opticians (who make up spectacles) and ophthalmic opticians, who test eyesight, prescribe glasses and diagnose eye diseases. An eye specialist may be an ophthalmic medical practitioner (a doctor who treats eye diseases and also tests eyesight and prescribes lenses), an ophthalmologist (a senior specialist or eye surgeon) or an orthoptist (an ophthalmologist who treats children's eye problems). If you need to see an eye specialist, you must usually be referred by your GP. The **Eye Care Information Bureau** (☎ 0207-928 9435) can provide advice and direct you to an appropriate eye specialist.

The optometrist business is competitive in Britain and unless someone is highly recommended, you should shop around for the best deal. Recent years have seen a flood of 'chain store' opticians such as Vision Express (and those in Boots stores) opening in high streets and shopping centres. Prices for both spectacles and contact lenses vary considerably, so it's wise to compare costs (although make sure you're comparing like with like) before committing yourself to a large bill, particularly for contact lenses. The prices charged for most services (spectacle frames, lenses, hard and soft contact lenses) are often cheaper in Britain than elsewhere in Europe, although higher than North America.

Sight Tests: If you aren't entitled to a free sight test under the NHS, you must have the test as a private patient which usually costs between £15 and £20. Some opticians offer a special low price (or even free tests) for pensioners. Sight tests are valid for two years, although you should be aware that your eyesight can change considerably during this time. You don't need to buy your spectacles (lenses or frames) or contact lenses from the optician who tests your sight, irrespective of whether you're an NHS or private patient, and you have the right to a copy of any prescription resulting from an NHS or private sight test.

Certain people receive free sight tests under the NHS including children under 16; full-time students under 19; the registered blind or partially sighted; diagnosed diabetic or glaucoma sufferers; and people on low incomes receiving state benefits. NHS leaflet G11, *NHS sight tests and vouchers for glasses*, explains who's entitled to free sight tests and NHS vouchers for glasses, and is available from social security offices, NHS family doctors and opticians.

SEXUALLY-TRANSMITTED DISEASES

Many hospitals have clinics for sexually transmitted diseases such as HIV/AIDS, syphilis or gonorrhoea, or you can go to a Sexually Transmitted

Diseases (STD) or VD clinic . Both provide free tests, treatment and advice. You can also obtain free confidential advice, diagnosis and treatment at the **Centre for Sexual Health**, Genito-Urinary Clinic, Jefferiss Wing, St Mary's Hospital, Praed Street, W2 (☎ 0207-886 1697), which will also help with non sexually-transmitted diseases such as cystitis and thrush.

Like most western countries, Britain has its fair share of sexually-transmitted diseases, including the deadly Acquired Immune Deficiency Syndrome (AIDS). The furore over AIDS has died down in the past few years, which many fear may cause those most at risk to be lulled into a false sense of security. The explosion of AIDS predicted by many 'experts' hasn't materialised, particularly among the heterosexual population. **AIDS is always fatal (over 10,000 people have died from it in the UK) and to date there's no cure.**

The spread of AIDS is accelerated by the sharing of syringes by drug addicts, among whom AIDS is rampant (many of Britain's heroin addicts are infected with the HIV virus). In an effort to reduce syringe sharing among HIV positive drug addicts, syringe exchange centres have been set up throughout England (☎ 0800-567123, 24-hours), and free syringe vending machines have been provided. The spread of AIDS is also accelerated by prostitutes, many of whom are also drug addicts, which is an increasing international problem. Prostitution is illegal in Britain, therefore it's impossible to effect any control over the spread of sexually-transmitted diseases by prostitutes. The best protection against AIDS is for men to wear a condom, although they're not foolproof (either against AIDS or pregnancy) and the only real protection is abstinence. Condoms are on sale at chemists, some supermarkets, men's hairdressers, and vending machines in public toilets in pubs and other places. They are also available free from family planning clinics.

If you would like to talk to someone in confidence about AIDS, there are many organisations and self-help groups providing information, advice and help in all areas. These include the **National AIDS Helpline** (☎ 0800-567123, 24 hours) which has counsellors who speak around ten languages. Those who have been diagnosed with AIDS can obtain help and advice from the **Terrence Higgins Trust** (☎ 0207-242 1010) or **Body Positive** (☎ 0800-616212). All cases of AIDS and HIV-positive blood tests in Britain must be reported to the local health authorities (patients' names remain anonymous).

HEALTH INFORMATION

For a quick and confidential answer to health problems, you could try calling one of the many helplines that have sprung up in recent years, which provide recorded information on a wide variety of topics. These include the **Healthline** (☎ 0345-678444, 10am to 5pm Mon-Fri) which provides pre-recorded advice and information on a range of 400 health problems. The

College of Health publishes a *Consumers' Guide to Health* and the Health Education Authority (Trevelyn House, 30 Great Peter Street, London SW1P 2HW, ☎ 0207-222 5300) publishes information on a wide range of health topics (a catalogue is available), many of which are available free from chemists, clinics and doctors' surgeries.

Useful Websites on UK Health Issues include **Your NHS**, the official NHS website (www.nhs50.nhs.uk); **Healthgate UK** (www.healthgate.co.uk) where you can read *Healthy Living* magazine with its explanations of diagnostic procedures and articles on wellness topics and search its MEDLINE database; **BBC Health News** (http://news2.thls.bbc.co.uk/hi/english/health/default.htm) which is part of the encyclopaedic BBC Online site; **Handbag Health and Beauty** (www.handbag.com/health), containing health resources and up-to-date news stories; **Wired For Health** (www.wiredforhealth.gov.uk), which contains health information for young people; and **Healthworks** (www.healthworks.co.uk).

Note that information obtained from recorded telephone helplines, websites and books, although usually recorded, written or approved by medical experts, must be used with caution and shouldn't be used as a substitute for consulting your family doctor.

Health Helplines

There are many health helplines in London covering a broad range of medical and related problems, many operated by volunteers. Some helplines provide a 24-hour service, although most have limited 'business' hours, so if you don't receive a reply the first time, try again later. Bear in mind that the advice you receive shouldn't replace that of a doctor, but supplement it. Some of the most useful helplines are listed below:

- **Alcoholics Anonymous** (☎ 0207-352 3001, 10am to 10pm daily) is the number to ring if you want help with an alcohol-related problem. They organise meetings where alcoholics support each other in their efforts to kick the habit and will even send someone to go with you and offer support when you attend your first meeting.

- The **Capital Radio Healthline** (☎ 0207-484 4000, 10am to 10pm Mon-Fri, 10am to 4pm Sat), run in conjunction with Capital Radio, answers queries about virtually anything and if they cannot help you they will put you in touch with someone who can.

- **Childline** (Freepost 111, London N1 0BR, ☎ 0800-1111 or 0207-239 1000) provides a free, confidential, 24-hour national helpline for children and young people in danger or trouble.

- **Just Ask** (☎ 0207-628 3380, 10am to 6pm Mon-Thu, 10am to 5pm Fri) specialises in providing counselling for young people aged under 35 who are homeless, unemployed or on a low income, although advice is given to anyone with a personal problem.

- The **London Rape Crisis Centre** (☎ 0207-837 1600) and the **Rape & Sexual Abuse Centre** (☎ 0208-239 1122) help with counselling and advice if you have been raped or sexually abused.

- The **Medical Advisory Service** (☎ 0208-994 9874, 5 to 10pm Mon-Fri) can offer you help on almost any health-related problem.

- **Narcotics Anonymous** (☎ 0207-730 0009, 10am to 10pm daily) provides the same sort of services for drug addicts as Alcoholics Anonymous does for those with an alcohol problem.

- The **National Health Information Service** (☎ 0800-665544) provides factual information about waiting lists within the NHS and on immunisation schemes.

- **NHS Direct** (☎ 0845-4647) is a new helpline currently in the testing phase. South London is one of the areas covered by the pilot scheme and the government expects the service to be extended nation-wide by the middle of the year 2000. It's designed to supplement the work of doctors by offering advice about everyday worries such as crying babies, minor injuries and routine health concerns.

- The **Samaritans** (☎ 0207-734 2800, 24-hours) will help anyone talk through emotional problems and it isn't, as many believe, purely for those contemplating suicide.

7.

SPEND, SPEND, SPEND

London is one of the world's great shopping cities, catering for all tastes and pockets. It has an abundance of smart department stores and designer shops, the equal of any European or American city, although the prices aren't always as keen – avoid stores that don't display their prices as, if you need to ask, it usually means you cannot afford it (without a platinum credit card or two)! However, whilst it's true that London's most exclusive shops are ruinously expensive, there's also much to offer the budget shopper including a wealth of discount stores, street markets and out-of-the-way shops to reward the diligent bargain seeker.

Opening hours for shops in central London are usually from between 9 and 10am until 5.30 or 6pm, Mon-Sat. Shops don't shut for lunch and some stay open later until between 7 and 8pm, especially on 'late night shopping day' (usually Wednesday or Thursday) and in the run-up to Christmas. Stores are permitted to open on Sundays between the hours of 10am and 6pm and many major stores open from noon until 6pm, although you should check in advance if you're planning to visit a particular store.

In most shops you have a choice of payment methods: cash, cheques (with a guarantee card), debit cards and major credit cards are almost universally accepted, although some stores won't accept them for purchases under £5. Most of the larger department stores and chains also issue their own store cards. However, traveller's cheques and foreign currency are rarely accepted. It's worth noting that if you're a foreign national living outside the European Union you can apply for reimbursement of British value added tax (17.5 per cent) on purchases. Stores will give you a form to complete which you must have stamped by customs when you leave the country with the goods.

British law allows you to return goods that prove to be faulty for a full refund or a replacement, but make sure you keep your receipt as proof of purchase. If you simply change your mind about something you've bought or discover it doesn't fit, a shop isn't obliged to change it for another item or refund your money. However, many chain stores (such as Marks & Spencer) will make cash refunds for any reason and most will give you a credit note if a purchase is returned in mint condition.

Most London stores hold at least two sales a year – in January and July – when you can buy branded goods at greatly reduced prices. Old stock and ends of lines are sometimes marked down by 50 per cent or more, so it's worthwhile earmarking some money from your Christmas and holiday budgets to spend in the sales. Other 'minor' sales may be held throughout the year. Many stores will post or deliver goods to you if you order by phone and pay by credit or debit card. Many large stores make free home deliveries within a certain radius and many also despatch items by mail to anywhere in the country (and abroad). Major stores have a long tradition of making home deliveries and for over a century Britain's wealthy shoppers have been able to order goods from their favourite London stores while spending time by the sea or looking after affairs at their country estates.

Shopping from home has recently taken a giant leap forward with the advent of the Internet (see page 215), although Londoners tend not to be dedicated Internet shoppers as they have virtually everything they need on their doorstep. However, most major supermarket chains now offer home shopping and delivery via the Internet if you live within a certain distance of a participating store. Although little more than a pilot scheme a year ago, this service has now spread throughout London – if you're interested try Sainsburys (www.sainsburys.co.uk/orderline), Tesco (www.tescodirect.com/default.asp) or Waitrose (www.waitrosedirect.co.uk). Those with Sky digital television (see page 286) can use the recently launched interactive shopping service, **Open**, to order goods from a growing number of stores including groceries from Somerfield, CDs from Woolworths and books from WH Smith (but check to see whether your area qualifies for home delivery).

Although central London's crowded streets can present difficult terrain for wheelchair users, some shops and malls operate 'shop mobility' schemes. Access to London's shops for disabled people is detailed on a useful website (www.disabilitynet.co.uk/info/access/guides/london/shops.html) and in a book entitled *Access in London* by Gordon Couch, William Forrester and Justin Irwin (Quiller Press).

Britain officially converted to metrication on 1st October 1995 and all retailers must now price goods in kilogrammes, litres and metres, despite the fact that many Britons haven't got a clue whether a pound (454 grammes) weighs more or less than a kilogramme (1,000 grammes). However, British measures such as pounds, pints and feet can be used alongside metrication and many stores display conversion tables. For those who aren't used to buying goods with British measures and sizes, a list of comparative weights and measures are provided in **Appendix C**.

It's often said that London isn't so much a city as a collection of villages (from which it grew) – and nowhere is this more evident than when shopping. The cheap tourist 'trinkets' on sale in the eastern half of Oxford Street has little in common with the exotic fare of Soho or the exclusive goods to be found in Old Bond Street, yet these areas are little more than a mile apart. In every suburb of the metropolis you'll find branches of supermarkets and chain stores that have spread throughout the UK, which makes one city shopping street seem much like any other.

These include the mid-range fashion stores Accessorize, French Connection, Gap, Laura Ashley, Monsoon, Next, Oasis and Warehouse; cheap-and-cheerful budget fashion stores BHS, H&M, Miss Selfridge, New Look and Top Shop/Top Man; toiletries giants The Body Shop, Boots and Superdrug; record stores HMV, Our Price and Virgin; book chains Books Etc, Dillons, Waterstones and WH Smith; and supermarkets Co-op, Safeway, Sainsburys, Tesco and Waitrose – not to mention stalwarts such as Marks & Spencer and the budget-conscious Woolworths. These stores are so commonplace that, apart from a few flagship branches that are special cases, there's little point in describing them in detail here. If you want to get a feel for what they offer, just stroll inside and browse.

To make the most of shopping in London you need to know where the really interesting independent shops are; where you can buy a chic pair of shoes or an organic sausage, and how to find industrial work-wear or a left-hand potato peeler. Below is a region by region 'tour' of some of the best and most fascinating stores London has to offer. For further information, obtain a copy of the annual *Time Out Guide to Shopping & Services in London* listing over 2,000 shops, *The Serious Shoppers' Guide to London* by Beth Reiber (Prentice Hall Press), *Frommer's Born to Shop London* by Suzy Gershman (IDG Books) or *The Markets of London* by Alec Forshaw & Theo Bergström (Penguin). If you're looking for second-hand bargains try *Exchange & Mart* or *Loot* or any local newspaper.

WEST END

Let's start our shopping tour where everyone begins: in the central area of the capital known as the West End, where **Oxford Street** represents the heart of London's West End shopping and is Britain's busiest street (although it's increasingly under threat from vast out-of-town shopping centres). At peak shopping times the pavements are almost gridlocked and it isn't uncommon for workers to be late back to their offices after a lunchtime shopping dash, having got stuck in a 'people-jam' of purchase-laden pedestrians. In addition, around nine million foreign tourists trudge up and down the street each year, accounting for some 20 per cent of its income.

Until the '60s, Oxford Street was a smart place to shop with Edwardian department stores Selfridges, Debenham & Freebody and Waring & Gillow dominating its length. Only Selfridges (see below) remains now in anything like its original form, and much of Oxford Street, particularly the eastern half, is now dominated by tatty tourist souvenir shops, jeans emporia, record stores, snack bars and employment agencies. However, its Christmas lights still draw the crowds, and the police and the Oxford Street Association (a trader's organisation) between them do their best to control shoplifting and pickpockets through all-seeing CCTV cameras. Don't pick your nose or scratch your backside here – you're on candid camera!

Despite the crowds, crime and the tatty souvenirs, the pick of Oxford Street is well worth visiting. In the part of the street west of the central crossroads known as Oxford Circus, the mighty department store **Selfridges** (☎ 0207-629 1234, 💻 www.selfridges.co.uk) at 400 Oxford Street (Bond St/Marble Arch tube) has recently undergone a major refit to drag it kicking and screaming into the 21st century. It's still a delightfully eccentric and sprawling place to go browsing, with the largest cosmetics department in the whole of Europe and a wide range of fashion clothing, although some departments are strangely disappointing.

Close to Selfridges at 458 Oxford Street (Bond St/Marble Arch tube) is the flagship branch of national chain **Marks & Spencers** (☎ 0207-935 7954, 💻 www.marks-and-spencer.com). A long-term British institution,

M&S has been having problems in recent years which have been blamed on its unexciting fashion ranges. The stores specialise in sensible, classic clothes for both sexes – and are the chief purveyors of comfortable and reasonably-priced underwear to the nation! This enormous store has the best choice of any branch in London, although you can find them in any high street, and there's a second branch at 173 Oxford Street, near Oxford Circus. Further east towards Oxford Circus at 278-306 Oxford Street (Oxford Circus tube) is the **John Lewis** (☎ 0207-629 7711, 💻 www.johnlewis.co.uk) department store, which is also part of a national chain. Once again, this is their flagship store and it tends to concentrate on goods that the other stores don't stock. The furniture department is excellent and in recent years has imported all kinds of exotica from India and other Asian countries, and there's a terrific haberdashery department for all those bits and pieces you need to complete an outfit.

Another department store, **D H Evans** (☎ 0207-834 1234), can be found at 318 Oxford Street at the more downmarket, eastern end of the street. Together with **Debenhams** (☎ 0207-580 3000) at 334-338 Oxford Street (Oxford Circus/Tottenham Court Rd tube) it handles the mid-range goods available in almost any urban shopping centre. Like all London shopping streets, Oxford Street is also dotted with branches of run-of-the-mill chain stores. Of these, probably the best examples are the flagship branches of **Top Shop** and **H&M** at Oxford Circus, and **Miss Selfridge** at 40 Duke Street, just round the corner from its parent Selfridges store. **HMV** has stores selling CDs, videos, computer games and entertainment-linked merchandise at 150 and 363 Oxford Street and its main rival, the enormous **Virgin Megastore,** is at 14 and 527 Oxford Street.

Oxford Street also features two noteworthy shopping malls; **The Plaza** at 120 Oxford Street (☎ 0207-637 8811) is a recent development at the eastern end (Tottenham Court Rd tube), while the smarter **West One** shopping centre within the Bond Street underground station complex is at the western half of the street.

Running at right angles to Oxford Street is the crescent-shaped thoroughfare **Regent Street**, once a gloriously upmarket area now looking more down-at-heel with the influx of a plethora of travel agencies and chain stores. One of the best places to visit here is **Liberty** (☎ 0207-734 1234) at 214-220 Regent Street (Oxford Circus tube). Home of the original Liberty print fabrics, this rambling mock-Tudor department store has a decidedly late 19th century Arts and Crafts feel to it and stocks some wonderfully original women's fashion and jewellery. A stone's throw away from Liberty is **Dickins & Jones** (☎ 0207-734 7070) at 224-244 Regent Street (Oxford Circus tube), part of the House of Fraser group, and devoted to fashion and beauty items with a particularly strong line in accessories. Classic English outdoor fashion for weekends in the country can be found at **Burberry's** (☎ 0207-734 5928) at 165 Regent Street (Piccadilly Circus tube), while a classic of a different cut can be found at the **Levi's** store at 174-176 Regent Street (Oxford Circus tube).

If you have children or grandchildren, don't miss **Hamleys** (☎ 0207-734 3161) at 188-196 Regent Street (Oxford Circus tube). Although it isn't cheap, it has a greater range of toys than you're liable to see anywhere outside an out-of-town branch of Toys 'Я' Us. There are five floors in all and the largest selection of board games anywhere in London. At Christmas time it's a war zone!

At the extreme eastern end of Oxford Street is **Tottenham Court Road**, running north to south. It's best known for its 'electronics' shops, selling hi-fi, computers and cameras, and for its furnishing and interior design stores. **Gultronics** (☎ 0207-637 1619) at 223 and 217 Tottenham Court Road (Tottenham Court Rd/Goodge St tube) stocks a wide range of computer hardware but specialises in laptops. You can pick up second-hand equipment at **Computer Exchange** (☎ 0207-916 3110) at 219 (Goodge St tube). For hi-fi, head for **Hi-Fi Experience** (☎ 0207-580 3535) at 227 (Tottenham Court Rd tube) or the oddly named **Cornflake Shop** (☎ 0207-631 0472) round the corner at 37 Windmill Street (Goodge St tube). **Jessops** (☎ 0207-240 6077), another national chain, has one of the world's largest camera shops at 63-69 New Oxford Street. Competition in Tottenham Court Road is fierce and most shops will match or beat any advertised price, so this is the place to buy the latest electronic gizmos. If you're looking for some new furniture, scout around stylish **Heal's** (☎ 0207-636 1666) at 196 (Goodge St tube), the adjacent branch of **Habitat** (☎ 0207-631 3880) or **Purves & Purves** at 80-83 (Goodge St/Warren St tube).

There are many worthwhile shops in the area around Oxford Street and Regent Street. For many years the pedestrianised **Carnaby Street** and its satellites survived on the myth of a glorious past in the swinging '60s, but lately the shabby souvenir shops and jeans chains have begun to give way to more interesting fare once again. Carnaby Street proper is still dominated by tatty fashion boutiques and **Soccer Scene** (☎ 0207-439 0778), 'Europe's leading soccer store', on the corner with Great Marlborough Street (Oxford Circus tube). At 29 Foubert Place there's **Yesterday's Bread** (☎ 0207-287 1929), selling second-hand period clothing, and the designer menswear shop **Fletcher** in Newburgh Street, while at 22a Conduit Street (Oxford Circus tube) there's **Rigby & Peller** (☎ 0207-491 2200), corsetières to the Queen. If you're tired of making do with badly-fitting off-the-peg underwear, splash out here, where your 'protruding bits' can be expertly corralled into shape by friendly, understanding assistants.

Old Bond Street and **New Bond Street** and their tributaries make up much of the **Mayfair** district. This is the province of the seriously rich and almost every major designer name has a foothold here. If your credit cards will take it, visit **Gucci** (☎ 0207-499 1080) at 32-33 Old Bond Street, **Nicole Farhi** (☎ 0207-499 8368) at 158 New Bond Street, **Donna Karan** (☎ 0207-493 3100) at 19 New Bond Street (its sister store **DKNY** – ☎ 0207-499 8089 – selling younger and slightly cheaper clothes, is at 27 Old Bond Street, both Bond St/Green Park tube), **Comme des Garçons** (☎ 0207-493 1258) at 59 Brook Street (Bond St tube), **Joseph** (☎ 0207-629

3713) at 23 Old Bond Street or **Vivienne Westwood** (☎ 0207-629 3757) at 6 Davies Street (Bond St tube).

Fenwick (☎ 0207-629 9161) at 63 New Bond Street (Bond St tube) and **Browns** (☎ 0207-491 7833) at 23-27 South Molton Street (Bond St tube) stock a range of designer names and **Watches of Switzerland** (☎ 0207-493 5916) at 16 New Bond Street (Green Park tube) is worth a visit if you wish to purchase an elegant and expensive timepiece. If you're after fine jewellery or silverware, try **Asprey & Garrard** (☎ 0207-734 7020), the royal jewellers, who have their base at 167 New Bond Street (Green Park tube), or you can choose **Tiffany & Co** (☎ 0207-409 2790) at 25 Old Bond Street (Green Park/Piccadilly Circus tube) or **Cartier** (☎ 0207-408 5700) at 175-176 New Bond Street. Slightly less atmospherically-priced jewellery can be found at the **Electrum Gallery** (☎ 0207-629 6325) at 21 South Molton Street (Bond St tube), where over 100 designers sell their wares. **Mulberry** (☎ 0207-493 2546) at 11-12 Gees Court (Bond St tube) is the place to go for expensive leather bags and accessories, or try the hand made leather goods at **Osprey** in St Christopher's Place (Bond St tube). **Sotheby's** (☎ 0207-493 8080), the auction house, can also be found here at 34 New Bond Street (Green Park tube).

Piccadilly could be said to be part of **Mayfair**, although it's at the rather less salubrious end. The gaudy neon signs of Piccadilly Circus have, surprisingly, been around since Edwardian times – the drug addicts and rent-boys who cluster round the statue of Eros not quite so long. Piccadilly itself is home to several notable stores. The ground floor of **Fortnum & Mason** is London's food store *par excellence*, a cornucopia of yummy goodies from around the world, from truffles to pickled walnuts. Their food hampers are internationally famous and are despatched around the globe. Fashion clothes can be found upstairs. **Hatchards** at 187 Piccadilly has been a bookshop since 1797 but has now become the flagship branch of the **Dillons** chain, while at number 203-206 the former Simpsons store has become **Waterstone's** new flagship outlet and the biggest bookshop in Europe.

Near Piccadilly Circus at 24-36 Lower Regent Street, **Lillywhites** (☎ 0207-930 3181) has six floors of sportswear and equipment; whatever you're into, it's here. There's also the quirky Victorian survival the **Burlington Arcade**, a Grade II listed arcade built in 1819 with a glass canopy and shops with Regency styled mahogany fronts. Patrolled by 'beadles' in period costume, it's famous for quality leather goods, bespoke shoes, antique and contemporary jewellery, cashmere and perfumes.

The **Trocadero** is about as far from the period charm of the Burlington Arcade as it's possible to get. It's a horribly tacky place – a kind of hi-tech amusement arcade with overpriced rides including those at **Segaworld**, where there are also six floors of video games to browse (heaven for kids!). Elsewhere in the mall you'll find more eager branches of those same old chain stores. Another shrine to modern consumerism can be found at **Tower Records** (☎ 0207-439 2500) at 1 Piccadilly Circus, which has possibly the best all-round selection of modern music in the capital including exhaustive rock and indie sections.

Venture south of Piccadilly and you enter the time warp area known as **St James's**. It's a world of gentleman's clubs, bespoke tailoring shops and strange little places dedicated to traditional male grooming. If this is your thing, you can order a bespoke (made-to-measure) tailored suit for a modest £2,000 from a tailor such as **Gieves & Hawke** (☎ 0207-434 2001) at 1 Savile Row (Piccadilly Circus tube). Bespoke shirts are available from **Turnbull & Asser** (☎ 0207-808 3000) at 23 Bury Street (Green Park tube) and you can complete your outfit with a hat from **James Lock** (☎ 0207-930 5849) at 6 St James's Street and luxurious, made-to-measure shoes from **John Lobb** (☎ 0207-930 3664) at 9 (Green Park tube). While you're there, you may wish to have an old-fashioned shave, with a cut-throat razor, and a high-class haircut at **G F Trumper** (☎ 0207-499 1850) at 9 Curzon Street (Green Park tube) or buy gentleman's cologne (and perhaps a floral scent for a special lady) at **Floris** (☎ 0207-930 2885) at 89 Jermyn Street (Green Park/Piccadilly Circus tube).

At the other extreme from the elegant retro of St James's and smart and expensive Mayfair is **Soho**, which together with its neighbouring district of **Covent Garden**, houses many of the more interesting shops to be found in central London including grocers and delicatessens to delight any gourmet's taste buds.

Soho is the area cornered by the four tube stations: Tottenham Court Road, Leicester Square, Piccadilly Circus, and Oxford Circus. Soho and Covent Garden are divided by Charing Cross Road, which is the focus for the London book trade; numerous bookstores can be found here selling both new and second-hand/antiquarian titles (the latter also buy books from the public). Their future is less certain since the scrapping of the Net Book Agreement in 1995, as major booksellers can now discount books and there are fears they could price the smaller independent shops out of the market. Take a break from the superstores and try **Blackwell's** (☎ 0207-292 5100) at 100 Charing Cross Road (Tottenham Court Rd tube) or the endearingly chaotic **Foyles** (☎ 0207-437 5660) at 119 Charing Cross Road (Tottenham Court Rd tube), staffed by eccentric assistants who arrange books by publisher rather than author or subject and make you queue up twice to buy a book.

If it's second-hand books you're after, try the excellent **Henry Pordes** (☎ 0207-836 9031) at 58-60 Charing Cross Road and **Quinto** (☎ 0207-379 7669) at 48a (Leicester Sq. tube). Specialist bookshops in this quarter include **Grant & Cutler** (☎ 0207-734 2012) at 55-57 Great Marlborough Street (Oxford Circus tube), the best bookshop in London for foreign-language books; **Murder One** (☎ 0207-734 3485) at 71-73 Charing Cross Road (Leicester Sq. tube), which specialises in genre books (not just 'whodunnits' but science fiction, fantasy, horror and romance as well); **Forbidden Planet** (☎ 0207-836 4179) at 71 New Oxford Street (Tottenham Court Rd tube), which carries a vast range of adult comic books and magazines; and **Edward Stanford** (☎ 0207-836 1915), the map and travel book specialists at 12-14 Long Acre (Covent Garden/Leicester Sq tube).

Soho proper – or rather improper – is known first and foremost as the capital of London's sex industry, with public call boxes littered with prostitutes' business cards and walk-up flats advertising the attractions of 'new young models'. There are also sex shows, hostess bars, triple-X cinemas and sex shops aplenty, mostly around the area west of Wardour Street, home of London's movie and advertising industries. There's also a thriving gay scene here, based around the pubs and bars of Old Compton Street which has some fine, long-established specialist shops.

Stop off at the **Algerian Coffee Store** (☎ 0207-437 2480) at 52 Old Compton Street (Leicester Sq/Piccadilly Circus tube) and sample a choice of over 40 different coffees from one of London's oldest wholesale merchants, or if you're after something stronger, try **The Vintage House** off-licence which stocks literally hundreds of malt whiskies. Italian salami, pasta and oils are on sale at **I. Camisa & Son** (☎ 0207-437 7610) at 6 (Leicester Sq/Piccadilly Circus tube) and particularly mouth-watering Parisian cakes and croissants can be had at the **Patisserie Valerie** (☎ 0207-437 3466) at 44 (Leicester Sq tube). There's also plenty of interesting fashion on offer – try **American Retro** (☎ 0207-734 3477) at 35 Old Compton Street for themed fashion and witty bits and pieces, or **Paradiso** (☎ 0207-287 6913) at 41 for fetish-wear in PVC, rubber and leather. The **Prowler Superstore** (☎ 0207-734 4000, 🖳 www.prowler.co.uk) at 3-7 Brewer Street is a 'gay lifestyle' shop selling everything from clothes to books and videos. It even has its own travel agency! **Janet Fitch** (☎ 0207-287 3789) at 25a Old Compton Street sells beautiful jewellery and accessories and there's another branch at 37a Neal Street (☎ 0207-240 6332) in Covent Garden (Covent Garden tube).

Interesting little shops abound in Brewer Street, such as **Anything Left-handed** (☎ 0208-770 3722) which sells everything from scissors and knives to pens and potato peelers in left-handed versions. **Tinks** at 53 Brewer Street is one of Soho's best delicatessens, specialising in additive-free foods including unpasteurised cheeses and ham on the bone. The **Vintage Magazine Company** (☎ 0207-439 8525) at 29-43 Brewer Street sells magazines, collectables and memorabilia relating to the movies and theatre. **Chinatown** is the area around Gerrard Street, where you can find some of the best Chinese food shops and restaurants in London. Two of the best food stores in which to buy your exotic ingredients are **Loon Fung** (☎ 0207-437 7332) at 41-42 Gerrard Street and **New Loon Moon** (☎ 0207-734 3887) at 9a (Piccadilly Circus tube).

Recording studios, music stores and rehearsal spaces are concentrated in Denmark Street, where the biggest and most important shop is **World of Music** (☎ 0207-240 7696) with branches at 8, 20 and 21-24 Denmark Street (Tottenham Court Rd tube). Here you can buy almost anything connected with music – pianos, guitars, drums, amps, recording equipment and sheet music. If you're a guitarist you cannot afford not to know about **Andy's Guitar Centre** and **Workshop** at 27 Denmark Street (Tottenham Court Rd tube) which specialises in electric and acoustic guitars and also does repairs. Round the corner at 144 Shaftesbury Avenue (Leicester Sq/Tottenham Court Rd tube) is **Bill Lewington** (☎ 0207-240 0584), sellers of brass instruments, while **Soundhouse/Turnkey** (☎ 0207-379 5148) at 114 Charing Cross Road (Tottenham Court Rd tube) stocks studio gear and computer-based musical equipment.

Soho also has a vast concentration of independent record stores, so if you're tired of the stranglehold exerted by the mainstream giants, HMV, Our Price and Virgin, head over here. There are far too many to list individually, but some of the best are **Daddy Kool** (☎ 0207-437 3535) at 12 Berwick Street (Piccadilly Circus tube) for ska and reggae, **Ray's Jazz Shop** (☎ 0207-240 3969) at 180 Shaftesbury Avenue, **Black Market** (☎ 0207-437 0478) at 25 D'Arblay Street (Tottenham Court Rd tube) for hip-hop and rap, **Sister Ray** (☎ 0207-287 8385) at 94 Berwick Street for indie, or cross into Covent Garden to **Rough Trade** (☎ 0207-240 0105) at 16 Neal's Yard (Covent Garden tube).

Soho also has its own fruit and vegetable market in Berwick Street (Leicester Sq/Tottenham Court Rd tube) offering some of the lowest prices in central London. You can also get good fish, cheeses, herbs and spices here, where **Simply Sausages** (☎ 0207-287 3482) at 93 are purveyors of superior bangers to go with your mash. On the other side of Charing Cross Road, **Covent Garden**, and to some extent Soho as well, has become the centre of London's small, idiosyncratic shops, although the mainstream is beginning to make itself felt here as everywhere else. **The Piazza**, the pedestrianised site of the old fruit and vegetable market near the Opera House, is the place to go if you're looking for upmarket souvenirs, superior toiletries or designer nick-nacks. You can also browse through the interesting **Apple Market** in the disused market halls for crafts and clothes, or the **Jubilee Market** containing cheaper goods aimed mainly at tourists. Both markets change on Mondays, when the stalls are given over to antiques and collectables.

Also pedestrianised, the Neal Street area is the place for anything 'alternative' such as whole-food shops, arts and crafts, esoterica and so on. **Neal Street East** (☎ 0207-240 0135) sells a range of eastern artefacts, books and toys, while **Ortak** design and make modern gold and silver jewellery, specialising in art nouveau, Celtic, Charles Rennie Mackintosh and related styles. The midnight blue-fronted **Astrology Shop** (☎ 0207-497 1001) at 78 has plenty for the fans of esoterica, as does **Mysteries** (☎ 0207-240 3688), one of the best new age shops in the capital on the other side of **Seven Dials** at 11 Monmouth Street. Clubbers can pick up new clobber at **Red or Dead** at 43 (Covent Garden tube). Kids will love **Benjamin Pollock's Toy Shop** (☎ 0207-379 7866) at 44 The Market, which is full of traditional toys, and outdoor types can visit the **Kite Store** (☎ 0207-836 1666) which sells frisbees and rockets as well as kites.

If you're into conservation, head for the **Natural Shoe Store** (☎ 0207-836 5254) at 21 where everything has been produced without cruelty to animals or environmental damage. If you don't mind wearing leather, you can do a lot worse than the **Dr Marten** Department Store at 1-4 King Street, which sells clothes as well as every available model of Doc Martens on five floors. Long Acre is largely designer fashion, including **Emporio Armani** (☎ 0207-917 6882) at 57 and the minimalist Japanese store **Muji** (☎ 0207-379 0820) at 135, but is otherwise packed with chain stores and other uninteresting stuff. For some unknown reason, Southampton Street leading to the Strand has several camping and outdoor shops; while, more predictably, Floral Street is full of interesting fashion retailers selling the kind of clothes you would wear to enjoy the local nightlife – try **Robot** (☎ 0207-836 6156) at 37 and **Agnes B** (☎ 0207-379 1992) at 35 (Covent Garden tube – for all the above).

Fine foods and natural remedies are also available in Covent Garden; **Carluccio's** at 28a Neal Street has a stunning selection of Italian groceries and **Neal's Yard Dairy** (☎ 0207-379 7646) at 17 Shorts Gardens sells mature farmhouse cheeses, chutneys and breads. If you need some extra pots and pans to cook all your goodies, look no further than the **Elizabeth David Cookshop** at 3a North Row. **Neal's Yard Remedies** (☎ 0207-379 7922) at 15 Neal's Yard stocks medicinal herbs, oils and potions, and **Lush** (☎ 0207-240 4570) on the Piazza has environmentally friendly cosmetics and soaps (Covent Garden tube – for all the above).

WEST LONDON

The West End or central area really ends at Marble Arch, where Hyde Park begins. South of here you enter an area between the park and the river including the fashionable shopping centres of **Knightsbridge**, **Kensington** and **Chelsea**, know as West London. Like Mayfair, Knightsbridge is an upper-crust (i.e. expensive) area servicing the rich of Belgravia to the immediate west of the capital's centre.

It's here that you'll find the 'world's most famous department store' **Harrods** (☎ 0207-730 1234, 💻 www.harrods.co.uk) at 87 Brompton Road (Knightsbridge tube). Harrods started life as a humble family grocer in the 19th century and 150 years later is rated the third most popular 'tourist attraction' in London. It has been owned for some years by Mohammed Al Fayed, whose son perished in the same car crash as the Princess of Wales and who reputedly rules the store with a rod of iron, turning away customers whose costume is deemed too revealing (don't wear shorts or crop-tops!). Harrods has a reputation as the 'top people's store', where you can buy all the world's best brand names under one roof and they claim to be able to obtain virtually anything.

Almost as interesting as Harrods is **Harvey Nichols** (☎ 0207-235 5000) at 109-125 Knightsbridge (Knightsbridge tube). This is another decidedly upmarket department store, concentrating on designer fashion and food, although the fifth floor bar is known to be something of a posh pickup joint. Like Mayfair, Knightsbridge also boasts some of London's smartest fashion boutiques. As it shades west towards Kensington you'll find all the designer names that you didn't find in Bond Street in Sloane Street, Beauchamp Place and Brompton Road. Check out **Jean-Paul Gaultier** (☎ 0207-584 4648) at 171-175 Draycott Avenue, **Issey Miyake** (☎ 0207-581 3760) at 270 Brompton Road (South Kensington), **MaxMara** (☎ 0207-235 7941) at 32 Sloane St (Knightsbridge tube) and **Betty Jackson** (☎ 0207-589 7884) at 311 Brompton Road (South Kensington tube). For beautiful Chinese and Indian designs, visit **Egg** (☎ 0207-235 9315) at 36 Kinnerston St (Knightsbridge tube). If you're after exotic underwear that flatters (rather than flattens) a good figure, you need **Janet Reger** (☎ 0207-584 9360) at 2 Beauchamp Place or **Agent Provocateur** (☎ 0207-235 0229) at 16 Pont Street (both Knightsbridge tube). If you're a well-built chap, either unusually tall or 'well rounded', you can find clothes to fit at **High & Mighty** (☎ 0207-589 7454) at 81-83 Knightsbridge (Knightsbridge tube).

In **Kensington** there's plenty for shopaholics of all persuasions. Kensington High Street features the usual parade of designer shops including **Kookai** and **Hype DF** (☎ 0207-938 3801) at 48-52 and the **Urban Outfitters** (☎ 0207-761 1001) at 36-38 (High St Kensington tube). The Edwardian department store **Barkers of Kensington** is also worth a visit. Next door, the old Derry & Toms department store (later Biba) is now closed but you can still gain access (from Derry St) to its spectacular roof garden and gaze out over the city. Don't leave the street without a visit to the indoor **Kensington Market** – a rabbit warren of bohemian shops and stalls offering unusual clothes and accessories. Some of the upper levels have lost their pizzazz in recent years but if you're of the Gothic persuasion, venture into the basement – you'll think you've died and gone to heaven (or is it hell?). Round the corner at 1-22 Kensington Church Street (High Street Kensington tube), visit **Amazon**. No, it isn't a real-world outpost of the famous Internet bookstore but sells designer clothes at cut-to-the-bone prices. There's no phone, so you have to turn up in person if you want to know what's on offer.

In **Chelsea**, the Kings Road, like Carnaby Street, owes much of its cachet to the '60s and '70s. However, unlike the pedestrianised West End streets it's still a living part of London and fashion victims still prance and preen here on Saturdays. When the swingers and hippies departed, the peacock punks moved in and, like long-surviving pop stars Bowie and Madonna, the street has succeeded in repeatedly reinventing itself to move with the times. Kings Road stretches from the upmarket Sloane Square at one end, down to the World's End pub at the other before becoming New King's Road and continuing on to Putney Bridge.

At the posh end visit the department store **Peter Jones**, or if you have fashion-conscious youngsters, call in at **Trotters** (☎ 0207-259 9620) at 34 King's Road, which even has a children's library. At 121 King's Road try the **CM Store** (☎ 0207-351 9361) for trendy club-wear or **Steinberg &**

Tolkien (☎ 0207-376 3660) at 193 King's Road for quality second-hand designer wear. If it's antiques you're after, there's plenty of choice such as **Antiquarius** at 131-141 King's Road. Further down you can visit **World's End** at 430 King's Road, once the notorious punk emporium **Sex** where Vivienne Westwood's outrage gear sold by the truckload in the mid-'70s. Despite her latter day elevation to *haute couture*, she still sells some of her designer clobber from this address. At 49-51 Old Church Street (Sloane Sq tube, then take a cab or catch an 11, 19 or 22 bus) you'll find the most marvellous shoes in the world at **Manolo Blahnik** (☎ 0207-352 3863).

Even further into west London at 42 Westbourne Grove (Bayswater/ Queensway tube) you can find **Planet Organic** (☎ 0207-221 7171), one of London's best organic supermarkets with a butcher's, fresh fish counter, juice bar, and 'miles' of fresh produce and groceries, all produced without the aid of nasty chemicals. **Notting Hill** is famous for its **Portobello Road Market** (🖳 www.portobelloroad.co.uk or www.london-calling.co.uk) which has expanded and flourished in recent years, now catering for both the affluent 'trustafarians' of the area (rich kids living off their trust funds) and the genuinely impecunious. Portobello is really several markets rolled into one; at the top end it sells antiques, bygones and collectibles, including quality antiques at prices which are almost modest compared with the fancy antique emporiums in other parts of London.

Further down the road there's a fruit and veg (produce) market and at the end (which disappears under the Westway) you'll find clothes, jewellery, books and music. The market starts slowly at about 5.30am each morning, although at this ungodly hour it's mainly professional antique dealers trading among themselves. Most traders arrive between 6.30 and 8.30am and by 10am the street is bustling. Some traders disappear after lunch but many stay until late afternoon. If you're after some cutting-edge fashion, try **The Dispensary** (☎ 0207-221 9290) at 25 Pembridge Road (Notting Hill Gate tube) and **Souled Out** (☎ 0208-964 1121) in the Portobello Green Arcade at 281 Portobello Road (Ladbroke Grove/ Westbourne Park tube).

EAST LONDON

City of London shopping tends to be geared to the bright, moneyed yuppies heading for burnout on the trading floors and in the merchant banks of the financial quarter. Here there's an abundance of fancy shops selling silk ties, flashy accessories, classy smokes and luxury chocolates for the girlfriend. However, there's also more down-to-earth shopping to be found and the redeveloped **Liverpool Street Station**, with its quality chain stores and food outlets, is a good place to start while you're waiting for your train home. If you're choosier, spend your lunch hour at **Spitalfields Market** in Brushfield Street (Liverpool St tube) where organic foods are on sale alongside jewellery and clothes.

On Sundays (9am to 2pm), **Petticoat Lane Market** in Middlesex Street (Aldgate/Aldgate East tube) is more of a tourist attraction, but still worth a look, while if you're after good household goods go on a weekday pilgrimage to **Leather Lane Market** (Chancery Lane tube). One noteworthy independent in the area is **The Hat Shop** (☎ 0207-247 1120) at 14 Lamb Street, Spitalfields (Liverpool St/Aldgate East tube), which has every style of hat you could possibly desire, or for a more fashionable approach to headgear, try **Fred Bare** (☎ 0207-729 6962) at 118 Columbia Road (Old St tube). If you're looking for unusual and irreplaceable jewellery try **Beau Gems** (☎ 0207-623 7634) at 26 Royal Exchange, Threadneedle Street (Bank tube), which sells antique pieces.

Further into the wilds of the East End, try **Brick Lane Market** (Aldgate East/Shoreditch tube), which sells fruit and veg as well as cheap clothes and household goods (8am to 1pm). The further east you go from Brick Lane into Cheshire Street, the tattier the market becomes – although if it's East End authenticity you're seeking, you'll certainly find it here. Another East End market worthy of mention is **Walthamstow Market** (Walthamstow Central tube), Europe's longest daily street market (Mon-Sat 8am to 6pm) with some 300 shops and 450 stalls.

NORTH LONDON

North London has an atmosphere quite unlike the sophistication and glitz of much of the West End. **Bloomsbury** stands at the border between central and northern London and has a tradition of being a centre for academic and specialist shops, perhaps because of the presence of the British Museum and much of London University. However, it becomes increasingly rundown and ugly as it shades northwards into the rough, red-light area of **King's Cross** where cheap prostitutes and drug dealers ply their trades after dark. Nevertheless, Bloomsbury contains many fascinating little specialist bookshops, including **Bookmarks** (☎ 0207-637 1848) at 1 Bloomsbury Street (Tottenham Court Rd tube), which specialises in left-wing literature; the excellent **Belmont Travel Books** (☎ 0207-637 5862) at 31 & 40 Museum Street (Tottenham Court Rd tube), which also keeps a good selection of modern first editions; **Gay's The Word** (☎ 0207-278 7654) at 66 Marchmont Street (Russell Sq tube); and **Unsworth, Rice and Coe** (☎ 0207-436 9836) at 12 Bloomsbury Street (Tottenham Court Rd tube), which is good on arts subjects.

The **Tibet Shop** (☎ 0207-405 5284) at 10 Bloomsbury Way (Holborn tube) sells goods made or donated by Tibetan exiles, with all profits going to the Tibetan Foundation. Towards Euston, army surplus and militaria can be found at the chaotic **Lawrence Corner** (☎ 0207-813 1010) at 62-64 Hampstead Road (Warren St tube) and devotees of African music are sure to find what they're looking for at **Stern's African Record Centre** (☎ 0207-387 5550) at 293 Euston Road (Warren St tube).

Further north, **Camden Town** is a bustling Bohemian area full of aspiring actors, musicians, artists and misfits, though lacking the sex industry that gives Soho its seedy, inner-city character. **Camden Market** stretches from Camden High Street to Chalk Farm Road (Camden Town tube). The covered section (Thu-Sun only) is where you'll find rare records and interesting clothes, while the fruit and veg market in Inverness Street is open daily except Sundays. At **Camden Lock** there are arts and crafts, jewellery and clothes, although not all shops and stalls are open or even there during the early part of the week – go between Wednesdays and Sundays for the best choice. In **The Stables** is the flea market with the cheapest stalls of all, where the Electric Ballroom opens its doors to a jewellery and alternative clothing market on Sundays. **Compendium** (☎ 0207-485 8944) at 234 Camden High Street (Camden Town/Chalk Farm tube) is the place for a wide range of alternative literature, including cutting-edge fiction, anarchist newspapers and magazines on body piercing.

If you're a British size 16 or over, don't limit yourself to the unimaginative clobber to be found at high street chains such as **Evans**, but pop along to oversize comedienne Dawn French's shop, **Sixteen 47** (☎ 0207-483 4174) at 69 Gloucester Avenue (Camden Town tube). It's named after the 47 per cent of British women who take larger sizes, yet aren't catered for in most of London's fashionable stores, and features comfortable yet imaginative clothes from designer Helen Teague who co-owns the store. Feeling stressed? Learn to keep all those balls in the air at the **Oddball Juggling Company** (☎ 0207-284 4488) at Camden Lock (Camden tube), or get rid of some energy on a skateboard after a trip to **Skate Attack** (☎ 0207-485 0007) at 95 Highgate Road (Kentish Town tube), the largest skateboarding shop in Europe.

Along with Hampstead, **Islington** is one of the habitats of the 'chattering classes': middle-class, well-educated and possessed of too much money. Consequently, many of the shops in the area cater to refined or specialist tastes. If you're fed up with the kind of plastic 'junk' that you find at high street toy shops, **Donay Antiques** (☎ 0207-359 1880) at 35 Camden Passage (Angel tube) stock antique and early 20th century toys and games, although the prices will probably mean your children don't get to play with them. If your sartorial tastes veer some way from the mainstream, **Regulation** (☎ 0207-226 0665) at 17a St Albans Place (Angel tube) is reputedly one of the capital's foremost suppliers of fetish-wear and industrial clothing. Or, if you're searching for an unusual gift, try **Get Stuffed** (☎ 0207-226 1364) at 105 Essex Road (Angel tube), where stuffed wildlife of every description can be found.

Hampstead is another sophisticated, well-heeled, north London quarter just north of Camden, where the natives are largely middle-class intelligentsia. When you aren't walking on the still-charming heath, browse along the high street with its arty little eateries – try the **Louis Patisserie** at No. 32 where they sell fabulously sticky cakes – and fashion boutiques. In neighbouring **Highgate**, stock up on intellectual property at **Fisher & Sperr**, a great second-hand bookshop specialising in books about London.

SOUTH LONDON

South London is often portrayed as a cultural and shopping desert, but although its outer suburbs such as **Croydon** are dull and ordinary, there are some treasures to be found in among the suburban dross. Immediately south of the river, the **South Bank** area has much to recommend it shopping-wise. The **Oxo Tower** (☎ 0207-401 2255) in Bargehouse Street is a complex of retail studios selling 'the best in UK contemporary design' from Tuesdays to Sundays (Blackfriars/Waterloo tube). **Gabriel's Wharf** is also good for designer crafts; check out **Ganesha** (☎ 0207-928 3444) at No. 3 which sells vibrant, hand-crafted, Indian textiles and crafts, including tiger rugs and hand-stitched wall-hangings.

In the wilds of Waterloo at 87 Lower Marsh you can find **Radio Days** (☎ 0207-928 0800) with its stock of '50s memorabilia, collectables, books, magazines and posters. At the rear of the store is **Masquerade**, a store within a store selling second-hand retro clothing. After a good browse there you can fortify yourself with some delicious continental foods – Italian panettone, cheeses, charcuterie, honey, jams, olives and delicious sandwiches – from delicatessen **Delirium** (☎ 0207-928 4700) at 19 Lower Marsh (Waterloo tube). In the **One World Shop** (☎ 0207-401 8909) at St John's Church, Waterloo Road, you can buy goods from the developing world including Tanzanian honey, Central American coffee, Lombok pottery tableware and Indonesian silver jewellery, plus craft toys, T-shirts and Christmas cards.

Greenwich has much more than the Dome and the Observatory and there's a tangle of markets to tempt the shopper including a good antiques market on Thursdays in Greenwich High Road, a central covered market selling handmade crafts (Fri-Sun), and a Sunday flea market on Thames Street (Greenwich rail).

Further south, **Brixton Market** in Electric Avenue (Brixton tube) is loved by outsiders, but many local residents reckon it's overrated. A large West Indian community is based here and the goods on offer, such as plantain, breadfruit, strange varieties of fish, exotic herbs and incense, reflect this. There are some second-hand clothes and bric-a-brac stalls to explore at the east of the market proper and some interesting shops – try **Pendragon Records** (☎ 0207-733 3450) at 424 Coldharbour Lane, who, despite their new age name, actually specialise in hard house, trance and techno. If you like deliberately gaudy decor, you'll adore **The Kitsch & Co Shop** (☎ 0207-622 4252, 🖳 www.kitsch.co.uk) at 82 Clapham Park Road, where you'll find lava lamps, glitter balls, movie star cufflinks and a host of other items of dubious taste (Clapham Common tube).

INTERNET SHOPPING

Shopping via the Internet is the fastest-growing form of retailing and, although it's still in its infancy, UK sales are forecast to be over £3 billion a year by 2003. Shopping on the Internet is generally secure (secure servers, with addresses beginning https:// rather than http://, are almost impossible to crack) and in most cases safer than shopping by phone or mail-order. **However, it isn't foolproof and credit card fraud is a growing problem.** There are literally thousands of shopping sites on the Internet including **Taxi** (www.mytaxi.co.uk), containing the Internet addresses of 2,500 world-wide retail and information sites; www.abargain.co.uk; www.buy.co.uk; www. shopsmart.com; www.iwanttoshop.com; www.amazingemporium.co.uk; and www.virgin.net/shopping/index.html.

You can buy almost anything via the Internet and save money. For example, **Chateauonline** (www.chateauonline.so.uk) and **Orgasmicwines** (www.orgasmicwines.com) claim they can save you up to 30 per cent on UK wine prices; you can save up to 50 per cent on selected books from www.amazon.co.uk, www.bookshop.co.uk and www.uk.bol.com; and **Value Direct** (www.value-direct.co.uk/wol) and **Home Electrical Direct** (www.hed.co.uk) claim to offer the lowest prices in Britain on household goods. Many websites offer online auctions such as www.qxl.com, www.ebay.co.uk, www.auctions.yahoo.com and www.loot. com. A new innovation from Scandinavia is **Letsbuyit** (www.letsbuyit. com), which offers huge savings by grouping bands of customers together to buy direct from manufacturers over the Internet (click on the Union Jack in the top right-hand corner for the English version).

With Internet shopping the world is literally your oyster and savings can be made on a wide range of goods including CDs, clothes, sports equipment, electronic gadgets, jewellery, books, CDs, wine and computer software, and services such as insurance, pensions and mortgages. Huge savings can also be made on holidays and travel. Small, high-price, high-tech items (e.g. cameras, watches and portable and hand-held computers) can usually be purchased cheaper somewhere in Europe or (particularly) in the USA, with delivery by courier within a few days.

Buying Overseas: When buying goods overseas ensure that you're dealing with a bona fide company and that the goods will work in Britain (if applicable). If possible, *always* pay by credit card when buying by mail-order or over the Internet, as when you buy goods costing between £100 and £30,000 the credit card issuer is jointly liable with the supplier. Note, however, that many card companies claim that the law doesn't cover overseas purchases, although many issuers will consider claims up to the value of the goods purchased (and they *could* also be liable in law for consequential loss). When you buy expensive goods abroad you should have them insured for their full value.

8.

TIME OFF

Whether your idea of pleasure is a quiet stroll round an art gallery or a night out at one of the capital's hottest night-spots, London is one of the best places in the world to enjoy yourself. It doesn't matter whether you're nineteen or ninety, a drinker or a thinker, gay bachelor or a mother of four, whether it's night or day, there's something here for you. The variety of leisure opportunities in London is enormous and it provides more cultural activities than any other city in the world, including over 1,500 events per week and some 60,000 seats at cultural events each night. Whatever your favourite leisure pursuits, you'll find them in abundance in London, including art galleries, museums, cinemas, theatres, dance, music, gambling, pubs and restaurants, gardens, stately homes, zoos, theme parks, sports facilities and sporting events, children's entertainment and much more.

This chapter provides just a taste of what London has to offer – further information is available from a multitude of tourist guides, newspapers (many of which publish free weekly entertainment guides) and magazines, including London's weekly *Time Out* and *What's On* leisure guides. *Time Out* also publishes a number of excellent annual guides for visitors and residents alike, including the essential *London Visitors' Guide*. The latest tourist information is available from the London Tourist Board, who provide a recorded information service (☎ 0207-971 0026) and a **visitorcall** service (☎ 0839-123456) with details of events and entertainment. For Internet fans there's a wealth of excellent websites including www.londontown.com (London Tourist Board), www.thisislondon.com (*Evening Standard*), www. timeout.com (*Time Out*), www.ukguide.org/london.html, www.londonnet. co.uk, www.sorted.org/london, www.uktravel.com/london.htm, and www. virgin.net.

There are numerous organisations in London working for the disabled, many of which help the disabled gain access to the arts and entertainment in London such as **Artsline** (☎ 0207-388 2227) – a number of others are listed on the *Time Out* website (www.timeout.com/london/esinf/disabled_london. html).

LONDON BY DAY

Art Galleries

London has an international reputation for its art galleries and boasts some of the world's finest collections of art and antiquities. Many galleries don't charge for admission and you can wander in and out as you please, making it worthwhile browsing even if you've only an hour or two to spare. However, opening hours vary, so you should check before making a special journey.

London's flagship art gallery is the **National Gallery** (☎ 0207-839 3321, 💻 www.nationalgallery.org.uk) in Trafalgar Square (Leicester Square/Charing Cross tube) where you can see over 2,000 priceless paintings dating from the 13th to 20th centuries, including masterpieces such as Constable's *The Hay Wain* and Van Gogh's *Sunflowers*. Admission is free, an audio guide can be rented at the entrance and you can even lounge on leather sofas when you get tired or are all cultured out. Don't miss a visit to the Micro Gallery, where you can display any of the gallery's paintings on a screen and print a reproduction.

The **National Portrait Gallery** (☎ 0207-306 0055, 🖳 www.npg.org.uk) is close to the National Gallery in St Martin's Place (Leicester Square/Charing Cross tube) and, as the name suggests, it specialises in portraits of famous people through the ages. Here you can look into the eyes of William Shakespeare or Diana, Princess of Wales, plus a host of kings, queens and political figures from the past. Admission is free and the gallery also stages regular themed exhibitions. The **Tate Gallery** (☎ 0207-887 8000, 🖳 www.tate.org.uk) at Millbank (Pimlico tube) takes over where the National Gallery ends, specialising in 20th century art. However, it also houses some fine works from earlier periods including a fabulous collection of works by the famous English impressionist Turner. Admission is free. In May 2000, a new **Tate Gallery of Modern Art** is scheduled to open at the transformed Bankside Power Station, leaving the Millbank gallery free to concentrate on British art.

The **Courtauld Institute** (☎ 0207-873 2526) at Somerset House in the Strand (Covent Garden tube) usually charges £4 (£2 concession) for admission, although it provides free admission from 10am to 2pm on Mondays. Recently restored, the building houses some wonderful paintings by impressionists and post-impressionist artists such as Degas, Cezanne, Monet, Renoir, Gauguin and Toulouse-Lautrec, as well as works by Botticelli, Breughel and Rubens.

The **Hayward Gallery** (☎ 0207-928 3144, 🖳 www.hayward-gallery.org.uk) is part of the South Bank Centre by the river (Embankment/Waterloo tube) which also houses the National Theatre and Royal Festival Hall complex. It has no permanent collection of its own, but is one of the best venues in London to see temporary exhibitions, although admission charges can be high depending in the particular exhibition. The **Royal Academy of Arts** (☎ 0207-300 8000, 🖳 www.royalacademy.org. uk) in Piccadilly (Piccadilly Circus/Green Park tube) is famous for its annual Summer Exhibition, as well as for a range of themed arts events. The **Institute of Contemporary Arts** (☎ 0207-930 3647, 🖳 www.ica.org.uk) in the Mall (Piccadilly Circus/Charing Cross tube) is celebrated for its exhibitions of challenging avant-garde work.

Two notable smaller galleries outside the central area include the **Dulwich Picture Gallery** (☎ 0208-693 5254) at Dulwich (North Dulwich/ West Dulwich rail), famous for its 17th and 18th century European painting, and the **Queen's Gallery** (☎ 0207-930 4832) at Buckingham Palace (St James's Park/Victoria tube) which houses selected works from the Queen's own vast private collection (both unfortunately closed for refurbishment at the time of writing).

Museums

London has some 300 museums, many containing world-renowned collections and covering a wide range of subjects. Although some national museums introduced entrance fees in the last decade due to a new government policy, most will gradually return to being free in the next year or so (i.e. for children in 1999, pensioners in 2000 and for all by 2001). Other private London museums and art galleries charge an admission fee, although students, the unemployed, the disabled, carers and pensioners often receive a reduction (or 'concession') on production of an identity card, and are sometimes admitted free. Museum fans can buy a 'white card' (☎ 0207-923 0807, 🖳 www.london-gosee.com), a three or seven-day pass for 16 museums and galleries in London, costing around £16 for three days or £25 for seven days (to make it pay you need to visit four museums in three days or six in seven days). Some museums also offer annual family season tickets. Many museums allow free entrance for the last hour or two of the day, and most have special access for the disabled or provide wheelchairs.

The Victorian method of displaying artefacts in dusty wooden cabinets within silent, cavernous halls has largely been consigned to history's dustbin. Nowadays, many of London's museums have replaced static displays with bright new interactive models and themed multimedia exhibitions that appeal to everyone – not just scholars and enthusiasts.

Probably the best place to start is the **British Museum** (☎ 0207-636 1555, 🖳 www.british-museum.ac.uk) in Bloomsbury (Holborn/Russell Square/ Tottenham Court Rd tube). Although the **British Library** has now moved to new premises at St Pancras and the site is currently being redeveloped to mark its 250th anniversary, the British Museum is still one of the wonders of the capital and its number one tourist attraction, attracting six million visitors a year. It's also free! It takes days to see the whole museum and many treasures are tucked away, but venture if you can into the eerie Clocks Room and don't miss the unrivalled collection of Egyptology, the Anglo-Saxon Sutton Hoo Ship Burial artefacts and the famous Elgin Marbles (still the subject of a vociferous ownership wrangle between Britain and Greece).

You'll find the greatest concentration of museums in South Kensington. Here you can spend several days exploring the delights of the **Natural History Museum** (☎ 0207-938 9123, 🖳 www.nhm.ac.uk) in Cromwell Road (South Kensington tube). The museum has changed out of all recognition in the past decade, although the famous dinosaur skeletons remain (and have been joined recently by a robotic T Rex), and it's worth visiting for the extraordinary Victorian architecture alone. However, the fusty displays have given way to the interactive 'Life Galleries' featuring a wonderful section of 'creepy crawlies', including a giant animatronic scorpion and the 'Earth Galleries', which replaced the old Geological Museum. This is as much fun as any theme park and educational to boot.

Here you can ride a vast escalator through the centre of a rotating globe, experience an earthquake and marvel at real moon rocks.

The **Science Museum** (☎ 0207-938 8000, 🖳 www.nmsi.ac.uk) in Exhibition Road (South Kensington tube) contains a wealth of historical technological wonders from Stephenson's Rocket to the command module of Apollo 10. In the Flight Lab you can take the controls inside a full-size aeroplane cockpit and kids can experiment with a range of interactive machines at the Launch Pad. There's even a special hands-on area for 3 to 6-year-olds in the basement, called 'The Garden' and another for 7 to 11-year-olds called simply 'Things'. A new, ultra-modern 'Wellcome Wing', heralded as the 'world's leading centre for the presentation of contemporary science and technology', is due to open in the summer of 2000.

The **Victoria & Albert (V&A) Museum** (☎ 0207-938 8500, 🖳 www.vam.ac.uk) in Cromwell Road (South Kensington tube) houses unrivalled collections of sculpture, historical costumes and examples of the applied and decorative arts, from Korean ceramics and Lalique glassware to famous Raphael cartoons, an unparalleled jewellery collection, historical musical instruments and a whole gallery devoted to Frank Lloyd Wright (one of Britain's foremost architects).

The **Imperial War Museum** (☎ 0207-416 5000, 🖳 www.southwark.gov.uk/tourism/attractions/imperial_war_museum) is situated south of the river in the Lambeth Road (Lambeth North/Waterloo tube). Nearly 200 years ago the building housed the infamous 'Bedlam' lunatic asylum, but it's now a grim reminder of the horror and heroism of warfare. In addition to static exhibits of the machinery of war, including a Spitfire, Sopwith Camel and V2 rocket, it also features multimedia 'experiences' which bring to life the First World War trenches and London's Blitz in World War II.

The **National Maritime Museum** (☎ 0208-858 4422, 🖳 www.nmm.ac.uk) is located at Greenwich (Greenwich/Maze Hill rail or Islands Gardens DLR). When the Millennium Dome begins to pall (or is sold off), here's where you can appreciate Britain's historic role as a great sea-going power. There's an interactive gallery called 'All Hands' where you can send a signal in Morse Code or with flags, or, more poignantly, view the uniform in which Admiral Nelson died at the Battle of Trafalgar.

The **Horniman Museum** (☎ 0208-699 1872, 🖳 www.horniman.demon.co.uk) is an odd little place in the south London suburbs (Forest Hill rail), but well worth the trip from the centre. Founded by 19th century tea merchant Frederick Horniman, it boasts a marvellous gallery of African art and culture, an underwater aquarium (Living Waters), and the eco-friendly 'Centre for Understanding the Environment'. A great day out for families, it even boasts a small menagerie of farmyard animals.

Madame Tussauds (☎ 0207-935 6861) is a traditional waxworks museum that continues to draw the crowds, despite its rather static displays and lack of interactive fun. Here you can see disturbingly life-like models of historical and modern-day figures, from kings and queens to Hollywood stars – there's even an infamous Chamber of Horrors with its roster of serial

killers and criminals. You can buy a joint ticket for Tussauds and the adjacent **London Planetarium** (☎ 0207-935 6861), where you sit in comfort and view the night sky projected onto the domed roof and enjoy a 30-minute show about the cosmos enhanced by modern computer graphics.

If you enjoyed the Chamber of Horrors, you might like to pay a visit to the even grislier **London Dungeon** (☎ 0207-403 0606) in Tooley Street (London Bridge tube). Not one for young children (or squeamish parents) who might be terrified by the graphic scenes of torture and death or by the costumed actors who 'enliven' the experience. The **Museum of London**, (☎ 0207-600 3699, 🖥 www.museum-london.org.uk) on London Wall near the Barbican Centre (Barbican/Moorgate tube) presents the capital's history from prehistoric times to the present day. Don't miss the Roman London gallery which uses thousands of original Roman objects, including recent archaeological discoveries, to recreate the life of Londinium's Roman culture.

Finally, the **Millennium Dome**, which officially opens on New Year's eve 31st December 1999. Although not strictly a museum, it promises to combine elements of theme park, funfair, gallery and museum in fourteen huge 'zones' each featuring a different aspect of mankind at the turn of the millennium. Costing in excess of £750 million to build, it's the biggest structure of its kind in the world. The Dome has been dogged by controversy since its inception, just as the Great Exhibition of 1851 and the Festival of Britain in 1951 were in their time, both of which were subsequently huge triumphs!

Parks

If a visit to a museum isn't for you, why not try a relaxing stroll through one of London's many parks – few cities in the world are better endowed with public parks and open spaces and almost 30 per cent of London is comprised of green space. Although surrounded on all sides by some of the busiest roads in the world, it's surprising how peaceful these oases of calm are, even when packed with sandwich-toting office workers at lunchtime, boisterous schoolchildren and tourists.

Hyde Park, **Kensington Gardens**, **Green Park** and **St James's Park** are all part of a huge green area in central London, although bisected by the hurly-burly of Hyde Park Corner and the grandeur of Buckingham Palace, the main London residence of the British Royal Family. You could almost say St James' Park is the Queen's front garden, but you can rest assured that she has ample private grounds to the rear of her palace! Further north is **Regent's Park** (and London Zoo) and the kite-flyers' Mecca, **Primrose Hill**, not forgetting the dog-walker's 900-acre paradise of **Hampstead Heath**. These parks have for centuries been the scene of many urban children's first outings with mummy or nanny, an almost infinite number of lover's trysts and numerous peaceful afternoon naps. There's plenty to see, too: palaces, villas, gardens, statuary and water features fill the parks, and are there to be enjoyed by all, mostly free of charge.

In **Hyde Park** you can see Rotten Row, where the fashionable members of society used to parade on horseback. Near Long Water in **Kensington Gardens** keep an eye out for two beautiful Edwardian statues; George Frampton's 'Peter Pan' by the Long Water and George Frederick Watt's bronze statue of 'Physical Energy' before marvelling at that Victorian monument to 'bad taste', the Albert Memorial, which stands opposite the Royal Albert Hall. Alternatively, you can make a 'pilgrimage' to Kensington Palace, another royal residence and the home of the late Diana, Princess of Wales. In **Hyde Park** you can swim at the Serpentine's open-air Lido (☎ 0207-298 2100) during the summer months.

Regent's Park has a boating lake fed by an underground river, a bandstand, a ravishing rose garden and a magical open-air theatre where Shakespearean productions are performed in summer in an enchanting evening atmosphere – providing it doesn't rain! Non-Moslems are also sometimes allowed to visit the London Central Mosque at the park's western edge. Further from the centre, you might consider a visit to **Victoria Park** in the east, **Finsbury Park** in the north, **Battersea Park** to the south, and **Richmond Park,** and **Kew Gardens** (London's celebrated botanical gardens) to the west.

London for Children

London can sometimes seem an unfriendly place to bring up a family, mainly due to the lingering English attitude that children should be seen and not heard. Kids aren't made welcome in many restaurants and pubs, unless they're the kind that serve plastic burgers, chips and chicken nuggets and have a multicoloured squashy play centre in the corner. Still, there are the parks (see above), the largely child-friendly museums (see page 220) and a wealth of shows, special events and workshops, particularly during the school holidays.

London also provides plenty of attractions for days out with the children. **London Zoo** (☎ 0207-722 3333, 🖳 www.londonzoo.co.uk) is situated in the north-eastern corner of Regent's Park (Camden Town tube). It's great fun for kids (there's even a petting zoo where they can touch and handle the animals), although older animal-lovers may find it vaguely depressing. The zoo does its level best to make the enclosures humane and, along with its out-of-town partner at **Whipsnade** in Bedfordshire, carries out valuable work in saving endangered species. Don't miss the '30s spiral penguin pool or the Lord Snowdon-designed aviary resembling a huge aluminium tent.

Children also adore the **London Aquarium** (☎ 0207-967 8000, ⌨ www.londonaquarium.co.uk) in County Hall, Westminster Bridge Road (Westminster/Waterloo tube). It's a wonderful display of aquatic life on three levels, with scary sharks and friendly rays which you can even touch. **Battersea Park** (☎ 0208-871 7540) in Albert Bridge Road, SW11 (Battersea Park rail/Queenstown tube) has a small children's zoo plus an adventure playground. Admission is £1.20 (60p for kids), although the playground is free and you can also visit the Buddhist Peace Pagoda in the park. In August the park is the venue for a huge Teddy Bear's Picnic.

London is also home to many 'city farms' where children can get a feel for rural life without leaving the city. One of the best is **Mudchute City Farm** (☎ 0207-515 5901) in Pier Street, E14 (Mudchute/Island Gardens DLR) which, at 35 acres, is London's largest city farm. As well as farmyard animals, it has llamas, a pet's corner and a study centre. **College Farm** (☎ 0208-349 0690) in Fitzalan Road, Finchley (Finchley Central tube) is a former dairy farm where you can see horses, donkeys, pigs, highland cattle and rabbits. To the south of the city, **Crystal Palace Farm** (☎ 0208-778 4487) is also well worth a visit (Crystal Palace rail), boasting some rare farm animals and birds. Finally, right in the centre of town in Guildford Street, WC1 (Russell Sq tube) lie **Coram's Fields** (☎ 0207-837 6138) on the site of the old Foundling Hospital where illegitimate and abandoned children were once cared for. The grounds are closed to adults unless accompanied by a child and there's a large free playground plus farmyard animals and birds.

If the weather is bad (as it so often is, even in summer), then London has a wide variety of indoor play centres for children of all ages. Try the **Discovery Zone** (☎ 0207-223 1717) at Clapham's Junction shopping centre which has many activities for 2 to 12-year-olds. At Ladbroke Grove there's **Bramley's Big Adventure** (☎ 0208-960 1515) in Bramley Road (Ladbroke Grove/Latimer Rd tube) with a wide range of activities for all ages and an adult crèche where kids can park their parents to read in peace!

If your children aren't the active type, many local London cinemas hold Saturday morning or afternoon shows especially for kids. One of the best events in the centre is the **Barbican Children's Cinema Club** (☎ 0207-382 7000) on a Saturday afternoon at the city's cavernous Barbican Centre (Barbican/Moorgate tube). For a £4 annual membership, children can bring up to three guests with them. Alternatively, the **National Film Theatre** (☎ 0207-928 3232) on the south bank (Waterloo tube) holds regular Junior NFT matinees on Saturday and Sunday afternoons (adults £4.75, children £3.35).

London boasts several dedicated children's theatres. The **Unicorn Arts Theatre** (☎ 0207-836 3334) in Great Newport Street, WC2 (Leicester Sq tube) is the oldest professional children's theatre in London and stages plays, mimes and puppet shows at weekends and during school holidays.

Islington's **Little Angel Theatre** (☎ 0207-226 1787) in Dagmar Passage, N1 (Angel/ Highbury & Islington tube) is a permanent puppet theatre and has shows for three to six-year-olds on weekend mornings and for older children in the afternoons. The **Bull Theatre** (☎ 0208-449 0048) in High Street Barnet (High Barnet tube) to the north of the city has also gained a reputation for good shows in recent years. Many of London's smaller, independent theatres cater for children with special shows at weekends including the **Lyric Theatre** (☎ 0208-741 2311) in Hammersmith (Hammersmith tube) and the **Tricycle Theatre** (☎ 0207-328 1000) in Kilburn High Road (Kilburn tube), which also runs courses and workshops for budding junior actors.

There are a number of books dedicated to entertaining children in London including *Children's London* (Nicholson) and *Evening Standard Children's London* by Linda Conway (Prentice Hall). See also **Days Out** on page 242.

Sport Facilities & Clubs

Sport is a major leisure pursuit for most Britons, although many are more interested in watching it on TV than (horror of horrors) actually taking any exercise themselves. However, in recent years health and fitness awareness has increased, along with the demand for accessible and affordable sports facilities.

Gyms, Swimming Pools and Fitness Centres: London has facilities to suit every pocket, from exclusive members-only clubs to inexpensive council-run gyms and sports halls, many of which have swimming pools and also offer aerobics, step, dance, squash and badminton. There are far too many to list here, but you can obtain details from your London Business phone book or call Sportsline (☎ 0207-222 8000) for information. Remember to book ahead if you're after a squash court or wish to join a class. Some of the most popular central facilities include the following:

The **Jubilee Hall Leisure Centre** (☎ 0207-836 4835) in the Covent Garden piazza (Covent Garden tube) is enormous, well-equipped, and provides a vast selection of free weights in its cavernous gym, plus aerobics, step and martial arts classes. The **Seymour Leisure Centre** in Seymour Place, W1 (Edgware Rd/Marble Arch tube) is another centrally located fitness centre with a sports hall and cardiovascular suite as well as the usual steam room, sauna and Jacuzzi. It also offers classes in aerobics, step and body conditioning. The **Michael Sobell Leisure Centre** (☎ 0207-609 2166) at Hornsey Road, N7 (Finsbury Park/Holloway Rd tube) is another enormous centre boasting a climbing wall, trampolining and a gym. The **Queen Mother Sports Centre** (☎ 0207-630 5522) in Vauxhall Bridge Road, SW1 (Victoria tube) has not only a gym, but two dance studios, a sauna and steam room, martial arts, aerobics and a swimming pool. **Swiss Cottage Sport Centre** (☎ 0207-413 6490) in Winchester Road, NW3 (Swiss Cottage tube) has two pools, a gym, squash courts and a sports hall.

For women only there's **The Sanctuary** (☎ 0207-420 5151) in Floral Street, WC2 (Covent Garden tube). It's ruinously expensive at almost £50 for a day ticket (£30 for an evening), but it's worth it just to luxuriate in the tropical plant-filled interior or swim naked in the wonderful pool. Your admission fee also includes unlimited use of the sauna, Jacuzzi and steam room, and there's a range of beauty treatments on sale if you have any money left.

Tennis: Everyone's heard of Wimbledon and Queens, but you don't need to join a fancy club to play in London – in any case, the most prestigious clubs have long waiting lists that reflect their lofty status. Many of London's parks provide tennis courts, most for little or no fee, but you must make a reservation. Courts are available at Hyde Park (☎ 0207-298 2100), Regent's Park (☎ 0207-486 7905), Victoria Park (☎ 0208-533 2057), Hampstead Heath (☎ 0207-485 3873) and Battersea Park (☎ 0208-871 7530). Alternatively, there's the fashionable (and more expensive) Islington Tennis Centre (☎ 0207-700 1370) in Market Road, N7 (Caledonian Rd tube) which has three floodlit outdoor and three indoor courts and also provides coaching. For further information write to the **Lawn Tennis Association Trust** (Queen's Club, West Kensington, London W14 9EG, ☎ 0207-381 7000) for a copy of their leaflet, *Where to Play Tennis in London.*

Horse Riding: Once again, the parks turn up trumps. Hyde Park Stables in Bathurst Mews, W2 (Lancaster Gate tube) is one of the nicest places to ride in London; you can trek through the park for a flat fee of £25 (children £23), although lessons are considerably more expensive. Further out, try Belmont Riding Centre (☎ 0208-906 1255) in The Ridgeway, NW7 (Mill Hill East tube), which has a full-scale indoor school, a cross-country course on 160 acres, and provides tuition for all ages and levels from beginner to advanced. Wimbledon Village Stables (☎ 0208-946 8579) in High Street, SW19 (Wimbledon tube) is a smaller operation, offering a range of classes and riding in Richmond Park or on Wimbledon Common (but watch out for the Wombles!).

Ice Skating: If you're looking for something central, try Leisurebox (☎ 0207-229 0172) in Queensway, W2 (Bayswater/Queensway tube) which offers general and family sessions and trains young skaters after school. Friday and Saturday night are disco nights! In the City area you'll find the UK's only outdoor ice rink. Broadgate Ice Rink (☎ 0207-505 4068) at Broadgate Circus, EC2 (Liverpool St tube) is a friendly and fun place to visit and is famous for a bizarre game called 'broomball', played on Monday to Wednesday evenings. Out in the suburbs you can visit Streatham Ice Rink (☎ 0208-769 7771) in Streatham High Road, SW16 (Streatham rail) or Lee Valley Ice Centre (☎ 0208-533 3154) in Lea Bridge Road, E10 (Blackhorse Rd tube).

Watersports: This is where London's River Thames comes into its own. The Docklands boast three separate clubs. If it's sailing that you're after, try the Docklands Sailing and Watersports Club at Millwall Dock E14 which provides a variety of courses. At King George V Dock (Gallions Reach DLR/North Woolwich rail) you can learn to jet-ski at the Docklands Watersports Club (☎ 0207-511 7000) or water-ski at the Royal Docks Waterski Club (☎ 0207-511 2000) inside London City Airport. If you would rather learn to row, try the Capital Rowing Centre (☎ 0208-395 2190) in Ibis Lane, W4 (Chiswick rail) which has beginner's courses starting at £4 for an hour and a half. If you would rather go it alone, you can rent a rowing boat in Hyde Park, Regent's Park or Battersea Park.

Cycling: If you aren't exhausted from trying to commute across town using pedal power, you can let off steam at the Lee Valley Cycle Circuit (☎ 0208-534 6085) at Temple Mills Lane, E15 (Leyton tube). You can also hire a bike here and take part in BMX, time-trialling, road racing and cyclo-cross.

Golf: Yes, you can play golf in the big city! If it's tuition you want, contact the English Golf Union (☎ 01526-354500) for details. You may like to start with Regent's Park Golf School (☎ 0207-724 0643), Outer Circle, Regent's Park (Baker St tube). If you just fancy a quick round, there are 18-hole public courses throughout the suburbs as well as more exclusive clubs, although none are on the tube network. Try one of the two courses at Richmond Park (☎ 0208-876 3205) or Chingford Golf Course at Bury Road, E4 (☎ 0208-529 5708).

Bungee Jumping: If you fancy a thrill, try a bungee jump from Adrenalin Village (☎ 0207-720 9496) in Queenstown Road, SW8 (Sloane Sq tube). It'll cost you in the region of £50 to jump from the 300ft (92m) Chelsea Bridge tower, which has a cage ride to the top so your friends can see you off!

Rugby: There are two kinds of rugby football played in Britain: 15-a-side rugby union, the code most common in London, and 13-a-side rugby league, which is played mainly in the north of the country. London has two major local rugby union teams: the Harlequins, based at Stoop Memorial Ground (☎ 0208-892 0822) in Twickenham (Twickenham rail) and the Wasps whose home is at the Rangers Stadium (☎ 0208-743 0262), South Africa Road, W12 (White City tube). However, there are a number of other teams, including London Scottish, London Irish and the London Broncos. The headquarters of rugby union is Twickenham Stadium, Whitton Road (Twickenham rail) which stages international matches and the highlight of the club season, the Pilkington Cup Final in April.

Soccer: Not surprisingly, as the capital of a soccer-mad nation, soccer clubs abound in London. The season runs from late August to early May and there are four league divisions, headed by the Premier League (the FA Carling Premiership) and three less exalted divisions. London's premiership clubs are Arsenal (Highbury Stadium, ☎ 0207-704 4000, Arsenal tube), Chelsea (Stamford Bridge, ☎ 0207-385 5545, Fulham Broadway tube), Tottenham Hotspur (White Hart Lane Stadium, ☎ 0208-356 5000, White Hart Lane rail), Watford (Vicarage Road Stadium, ☎ 0891-400401, Watford rail), West Ham United (Upton Park, ☎ 0208-548 2748, Upton

Park tube/Stratford rail) and Wimbledon, which shares a stadium with division one team Crystal Palace at Selhurst Park (☎ 0208-771 2233, Selhurst rail). You can obtain more information about these clubs and their fixtures from the premiership's official website (www.fa-premier.com). Other London clubs include Charlton Athletic, Fulham and Queens Park Rangers (league division 1), Brentford and Millwall (league division 2), and Barnet and Leyton Orient (league division 3).

British soccer fans have a terrible reputation for drunkenness and violence abroad, although it's generally safe for women and children to attend a major premier league match. Stadiums are now all-seat and much of the old violence and hooliganism has disappeared along with the terraces, although the experience certainly isn't what you could call 'refined;. Don't go if you have a sensitive nature and are shocked by bad language! Tickets for big matches are difficult to obtain; try the club ticket office first and if they cannot help, seats are sometimes available from the main London ticket agencies. The biggest club soccer match is the FA Cup Final at Wembley Stadium (☎ 0208-900 1234, 💻 www.wembleynationalstadium.co.uk) in May, for which tickets are almost impossible to obtain (unless you're wealthy and can afford to buy them on the black market). If you fancy a game, amateur clubs abound throughout London.

Cricket: If cricket's more your thing, the season runs from April to September. Although the English invented cricket, they are regularly beaten nowadays by their ex-colonies, including Australia, India, New Zealand, Pakistan, South Africa and the West Indies. The big events of the London season are the two five-day test matches, played at **Lord's** (☎ 0207-289 1611, 💻 www.lords.org, St John's Wood tube) and **The Oval** (☎ 0207-582 6660, Oval tube). Touring sides also play at least two, one-day international games in London at the aforementioned grounds. You can also see top county cricket played at the Oval (Surrey) and Lord's (Middlesex).

Tennis: If you're a tennis fan, chances are you'll be keen to attend **Wimbledon** where the Grand Slam championship is played in the last week of June and the first week of July on the hallowed lawns of the All England Lawn Tennis and Croquet Club, Church Road, Wimbledon (☎ 0208-946 2244, 💻 www.wimbledon.org, Southfields/Wimbledon Park tube). If you want a ticket for centre or number one court and aren't connected with a club member or corporate sponsor, you must first obtain an application form. You need to apply by post between 1st September and 31st December of the previous year, enclosing a stamped addressed envelope. You'll then go into a ballot and will be informed later whether you've been successful, although there's nothing to stop you queuing for hours each day during the championships for a ticket to the outside courts. You need to arrive before 9am for a realistic chance of getting in when play starts at noon, or even earlier if you wish to have a chance at the tiny number of centre and number one court tickets sold on match days.

You can also see top-class men's tennis at the **Queen's Club** tournament (☎ 0207-385 3421) in Palliser Road, W14 (Baron's Court tube) which is the main curtain-raiser to Wimbledon. Once again, application forms must be obtained the previous year and returned by 30th September in order to go into the ballot for tickets, although returns are for sale on match days.

LONDON BY NIGHT

Clubs

When the sun goes down in London, the city really comes alive and the sheer diversity of entertainment on offer can bewilder even the most dedicated night owls. During the last decade the accent has shifted from pubs and discos to a well-established club culture – no other European city offers such a variety and choice of constantly changing venues. The secret of the club scene's success is its mutability; it's in a constant state of flux, reacting swiftly to the latest developments in style and underground dance music.

Most clubs open between 10pm and midnight and don't close until after dawn. The majority of clubs are open every night, others at weekends only, while some are strictly 'one-nighters' hosted by an umbrella venue that features a different attraction each night of the week. It would be impossible to list every club on offer and such information would, in any case, swiftly become out-of-date, but listed below are some of the more established club venues.

Before making plans, phone or check their websites, or obtain up-to-date information from a weekly listings magazine such as *Time Out* (🖳 www.timeout.com). If you want the latest information on music, opening times and door policy, ask around, as the 'bouncers' (doormen) won't let you in if your face or outfit doesn't fit. Find out the best times to arrive and the appropriate clothes to wear if you want to avoid disappointment, and remember that virtually no place will let you in wearing jeans and trainers or a business suit. As for music venues – it's no longer just house music – you'll find clubs playing techno, hard house, hardcore, deep house, garage, drum 'n' bass, jungle and speed garage, as well as the older hybrids acid-jazz and swing/hip-hop.

The **Ministry of Sound**, 103 Gaunt Street, SE1 (☎ 0207-378 6528, 🖳 www.ministryofsound.co.uk, Elephant & Castle tube) is London's most famous dance club and still one of the trendiest, despite its downmarket setting in one of the poorest parts of town. It has an exceptional sound system and attracts some of the biggest name DJs from the USA as well as home-grown talent. **The Fridge**, Brixton Hill, SW2 (☎ 0207-326 5100, 🖳 www.fridge.co.uk, Brixton tube) is south London's biggest night out. It hosts occasional club nights like Saturday's gay Love Muscle and Friday's trance/psychedelic night Escape from Samsara, but musical policy runs the gamut from funk to techno and garage. In the City, **Turnmills**, 63 Clerkenwell Road, EC1 (☎ 0207-250 3409, 🖳 www.turnmills.co.uk/

turnmills, Farringdon tube) is host to three popular one-nighters – The Gallery house party on Fridays, Heavenly Jukebox on Saturdays, which morphs into gay marathon Trade (💻 www.dircon.co.uk/trade) from 4am until Sunday afternoon.

Heaven (☎ 0207-930 2020) in Villiers Street, WC2 (Embankment/ Charing Cross tube) was the most famous gay club in the capital, but became a victim of its own success. These days only Saturday nights are strictly for gays, and nowadays more and more straight clubbers and tourists are diluting the original recipe. Since a recent refit, you can get to new underground techno club **The Soundshaft** (☎ 0207-287 9608) from Heaven on Saturdays and Sundays, and the original venue still has three floors playing different music. **The End**, 18 West Central Street, WC1 (☎ 0207-419 9199) is owned by Mr. C of The Shamen, who you'll have heard of if you're up on dance music history. It's spacious, minimalist chrome and plays a wide range of music. **Hanover Grand**, Hanover Street, W1 (☎ 0207-499 7977, Tottenham Court Rd tube) is a super-cool club catering to the top-notch glitterati. It has a balconied dance floor upstairs, an incredible light show and some serious 'style-police' on the door at weekends. Midweek, it's home to Fresh 'n' Funky playing R&B and hip-hop.

The Cross (☎ 0207-837 0828) under the arches in Goods Way Depot, off York Street, N1 (King's Cross tube) has a marvellous garden as well as a rave reputation for garage and hard-house music. **Subterania** (☎ 0208-960 4590) under the Westway at 12 Acklam Road, W10 (Ladbroke Grove tube) attracts a trendy west London crowd and is hugely popular for Friday's Rotation and Saturday's Soulsonic, which is a very dressy event. Islington's **The Complex** (☎ 0207-288 1986) in Parkfield Street, N1 (Angel tube) is a fashionable club as far as music goes and plays a wide variety of radical sounds. It has four floors, including the Love Lounge where you can chill out and get friendly in a restful rosy glow. Catch its Camouflage night on Saturdays for excellent funk, swing and US garage.

The latest development in club culture is a new club/pub hybrid called, unsurprisingly, the Club Bar. These are bars that stay open later than standard pub closing time of 11pm (although they charge for admission after a certain time) and have in-house DJs playing club-style music. Although drinks tend to be expensive, food is usually on offer and you can sit around and hold conversations more easily than in a club, while still enjoying the music. Now becoming popular with the in-crowd, club bars fill the void between traditional London pubs and full-scale night-spots, and can be great places for a late night out. Here are some good examples from around the capital.

Dogstar (☎ 0207-733 7515) is at 389 Coldharbour Lane, Brixton (Brixton tube). A converted pub, it's almost a club in its own right at weekends playing techno, house and disco, but also staging comedy improvisation from the Top Dog Players on Thursdays. **The Embassy Bar** (☎ 0207-226 9849) at 119 Essex Road, Islington (Angel tube) is a retro-styled, suave joint with a sweeping chrome bar and a fashionable and diverse music policy. **Jerusalem** (☎ 0207-255 1120) at 33-34 Rathbone Place, W1 (Tottenham Court Rd tube) is stratospherically trendy, with velvet drapes and chandeliers, giving it an air of *fin de siècle* decadence; it plays *all* kinds of music.

The Pharmacy (☎ 0207-221 2442) in Notting Hill Gate, W11 (Notting Hill Gate tube) is co-owned by the controversial artist Damien Hirst and looks exactly like it sounds. If you're into hanging out in chemist's shops, come here. **Alphabet** (☎ 0207-439 2190) in the heart of the West End at 61-63 Beak Street, W1 (Oxford Circus tube) serves gorgeous food – try the upstairs lounge with its luxurious leather sofas. **Village Soho** (☎ 0207-434 2124) at 81 Wardour Street, W1 is a gay club bar with two separate entrances leading to its cafe and very busy bar. **A.K.A.** (☎ 0207-836 0110) in West Central Street, WC1 (Tottenham Court Rd tube) is a chrome-infested minimalist bar next door to The End (see clubs) and shares its design philosophy.

If all this is a little cutting-edge for you and all you want is a good old-fashioned night-club or disco, there's still plenty of choice. Many places cater for the more mature, conservative crowd, so don't feel you have to stay in with your pipe and slippers if you're over 40. Here are some alternatives to the fashionable club scene, ranging from smart and exclusive night-clubs to mass-market discos and haunts for tired businessmen.

The **Equinox** (☎ 0207-437 1446) in Leicester Square (Leicester Sq tube) is a typical cavernous West End disco with lots of lights and lasers where you can dance to mainstream 'commercial' music. The **Hippodrome** (☎ 0207-437 4311) round the corner in Charing Cross Road, WC2 (Leicester Sq tube) is another monster disco that attracts tourists, albeit of the smarter variety, by the coach load. It's clad in retro chrome, but watch out for the trapeze artists who swing dangerously back and forth over your head. **Stringfellows** is run by and named after the ageing 'king of clubs', Peter Stringfellow, and attracts a clientele of besuited businessmen and trendies in pursuit of pleasure. It features table-dancing from Mondays to Thursdays, filling the gap between a disco and strip joint. At weekends it fills up with a more straight-ahead disco crowd. There's a restaurant if you're hungry.

If you're after something smarter and want to try a bit of celeb-spotting, try **Browns** at 4 Great Queen Street, WC2 (Holborn tube). Lots of celebrity parties are held in this two-floor, very chic night-spot. Alternatively, you could pop along to **The Emporium** at 62 Kingly Street, W1 (Oxford Circus tube) which is a busy club popular with the rich and famous. Another chic night-spot is the recently refurbished **Café de Paris** (☎ 0207-734 7700) at 3 Coventry Street, W1 (Leicester Sq/Piccadilly Circus tube); a classic '20s ballroom beautifully restored to its original elegance with a balcony from where you can watch the dancing, and an excellent restaurant.

London, particularly Soho, positively pulsates with seedier places to spend your leisure time, from strip bars and lap-dancing joints to so-called 'gentlemen's clubs'. If this is your thing, information is readily available on the Internet and there's a forthright and amusing book, *The Good Striptease Guide to London,* which you can order direct from the publishers (Tredegar Press, Dept IN/CO, PO Box 4830, London SW11 4XQ, 💻 www.stripguide. co.uk).

Pubs & Bars

Setting aside the new 'club bar' hybrids described above, most London pubs (short for public houses) – and there are literally hundreds – are an institution. Many began life as coaching inns in the days long before motor travel and served as the focal point for local communities in much the same way as a church or village hall. The best traditional pubs serve good, unpretentious food, as well as a range of traditional 'real ales' and have a buzzy, convivial atmosphere. The worst pubs cut corners, serving poor food, fizzy lager and flat, warm beer to tourists in depressing surroundings. The only way to find a really good one which suits you is to try as many as you can: it's a tough job, but someone's got to do it.

A few London pubs still cling to the old division between 'public' and 'saloon' (or lounge) bars. The former is a 'rough-and-ready' room for men in working clothes to unwind after their labours, while the latter is a more comfortable place for the well-dressed and where young men can take their girlfriends for a quiet drink. You'll tend to find the snooker and pool tables, dartboards, jukeboxes and gambling machines in the public bar, and the nice upholstery and buffet in the saloon.

Nowadays, however, many pubs have undergone a transformation and shed their old class-consciousness and have just one huge 'lounge' bar. Many welcome allcomers to all areas and some even have special areas for families with children or gardens where the young ones can play. Children aren't supposed to sit in a bar until they're 14 years old and cannot drink alcohol until they're 18, but are allowed entry to a restaurant area, family room or outdoor area. Don't expect many non-smoking pubs, however, as breweries and landlords have rather dug their heels in when it comes to smoking. If you want fresh air, if such a thing exists anywhere in London, sit outside or find a non-smoking table in a restaurant.

Although Britain is supposed to have gone metric, you'll be hard-pressed to find a pub that sells beer by the litre – you can have a pint or half-pint. If you have the option you should try a 'real ale', which is brewed from fresh barley, hops and oats – it's superior to most other beers and a truly traditional British drink. Avoid anything that comes out of an electric pump if you want real ale, which is pumped by hand from a barrel; it's also perishable (unlike modern pasteurised brews), so go somewhere with a high turnover. If you don't know what to look for, ask the bar staff or seek out London pubs owned by Fullers or Youngs.

If you visit a 'free house', i.e. a pub that isn't tied to a specific brewery for its supplies, you'll be able to sample a range of real ales from around Britain from companies such as Greene King, Flower's or smaller independents. Another option is draught Guinness, the rich black Irish 'stout' that's pumped electrically but is far superior to pasteurised beers. It now has UK competitors such as Beamish and Murphy's (also from Ireland) to keep it on its toes, although any Irishman will tell you the stuff they sell in Dublin is entirely different and much better! There's also a wide range of bottled beers available from good brewers throughout Britain and farther afield, many of which are excellent. If you want to learn more about good British ale, buy a copy of the CAMRA (Campaign for Real Ale) *Good Beer Guide* edited by Jeff Evans. *The Good Pub Guide* (Ebury Press) edited by Alisdair Aird is also worth a read.

Spirits such as whisky, vodka, gin and rum are sold in measures of 24ml, (although you can order a 'double', also called a 'large', or even a 'triple' measure if your 'thirsty' or have had a hard day at the office!). Mixers and soft drinks are where publicans make most of their money, so don't expect a non-alcoholic option to be cheaper than the hard stuff (which is a sore point among teetotallers). Wine is simply sold by the glass (size unspecified), which gives publicans a lot of leeway! Most wine sold in traditional pubs is of poor quality and you may get a choice of 'red' or 'white' only (it saves having to remember all those fancy names). Go to a wine bar if you want some decent stuff, although dedicated wine bars were rather an '80s fashion and aren't as common now as they were.

Many pubs feature entertainment such as live music or stand-up comedy, while others have karaoke or single-sex nights featuring male or female strippers. Some are gay or lesbian haunts and some attract ethnic minorities of one kind or another, for example Irish pubs in predominantly Irish areas such as Kilburn. London's licensing laws allow pubs to open from 11am until 11pm, Mondays to Saturdays, and from noon until 10.30pm on Sundays. On public holidays such as Christmas Day, Boxing Day and New Year's Eve, pubs are usually allowed to stay open until midnight or even 1am. Drink-driving laws are sensibly strict in Britain and strictly enforced by London's police, but the densely-populated city is a great place for a pub crawl on foot or by tube or taxi. Just make sure you don't get too drunk to find your way home!

Hotel bars are another option if you have someone to meet and fancy a quiet drink before a show or a night-club. All the larger, ritzier hotels (mostly in the Mayfair area) open their bars to non-residents, although drinks (particularly those extravagant cocktails) are *very* expensive and the dress code is usually a jacket and tie for men. Outside normal pub opening hours they may insist you buy food before serving you with alcohol. Some hotel bars are also unofficial pickup joints where high-class hookers hang out, but whisper it quietly – many hotels turn a blind eye to the practice and don't wish to be reminded. Pick of the hotel bars has to be **Claridge's** (☎ 0207-629 8860) in Brook St, W1 (Bond St tube), which serves marvellous cocktails at stratospheric prices, is furnished in Art Deco style and staffed by waiters who have stepped straight from a P.G. Wodehouse (Jeeves) novel.

In Park Lane (Hyde Park Corner tube) you'll find the **Dorchester** (☎ 0207-629 8888), owned by the Sultan of Brunei and recently refurbished in fantastic style to his specifications. The **Langham Hilton** (☎ 0207-636 1000) in Portland Place (Oxford Circus tube) is frequented by BBC staff from Broadcasting House over the road and serves a ridiculous number of different vodkas in its Tsar Bar. Don't confuse it with the **London Hilton** (☎ 0207-493 8000) in Park Lane (Hyde Park Corner tube), where Trader Vic's bar resembles a tacky film set complete with costumed waitresses. The **Waldorf** (☎ 0207-836 2400) in Aldwych (Covent Garden tube) has a wonderfully relaxed Palm Court bar where you don't need to wear a tie and a pianist entertains during the evenings.

For more information consult the *Evening Standard London Pub and Bar Guide* by Edward Sullivan (Simon & Schuster) or the *Time Out Eating and Drinking Guide*.

Restaurants

Most foreigners are familiar with the infamous (and previously well-deserved) image of a London full of 'greasy spoon' establishments specialising in fried food, burnt meat and overcooked vegetables. However, those who think that a period spent in London means bringing your own food supply or facing starvation or death by food poisoning are in for a pleasant surprise. There has been a revolution in London restaurants in the last few decades and it now provides a wealth of excellent eateries offering a quality and variety of culinary delights rivalling those of Paris (the only city in the world with more Michelin-starred restaurants). You need only open the pages of the latest restaurant guide to realise that British food doesn't always live up (or down) to its dreadful reputation, and London is now at the cutting edge of food fashion. On the negative side, prices for good food are often astronomical (wine is also *very* expensive) and even modest food can be costly.

It's a cliché that Britain has no recognisable cuisine of its own, although with the renaissance of traditional English cooking in recent years, this is no longer true. However, you're unlikely to come across much English cuisine in London's ubiquitous foreign restaurants and could be forgiven for thinking that Britain's national dish is curry! London has a huge variety of ethnic restaurants (respresenting some 70 countries) and some of the best Chinese and Indian restaurants outside Asia (it's said that the British founded an Empire so they could get some decent food!), and numerous establishments serving admirable French, Italian and international cuisine. The best bet for those wishing to eat well and cheaply are ethnic restaurants, where the standard of food is invariably high and a filling meal can be had for around £10 to £15 a head (without wine).

Always phone ahead to check opening hours and ask whether you need to book a table. Most restaurants stop serving early, e.g. between 10.30 and 11.30pm, so it's usually best to eat before going to a show, pub or club.

There are, however, a number of notable exceptions, mainly in the traditionally nocturnal Soho area. Indian restaurant **Soho Spice** (see below) takes last orders at 2.30am, Chinese restaurant **Mr Kong** at 3am and if you're gay you might like to drop in at the 24-hour **Old Compton Cafe** in Old Compton Street. Most restaurants accept all major credit cards and are licensed to serve alcohol. Tipping is discretionary, but check whether a service charge is added to your bill before leaving a tip, as there's no need to pay twice no matter how sorry you feel for the impecunious waiting staff. If you're American, be warned; British appetites aren't as large as on the other side of the pond and you may be disappointed by the portion size until your stomach acclimatises!

Many of London's best restaurants are concentrated near the centre around Soho, where they outnumber the ubiquitous peep shows and sex shops, and include some of the best eateries in London such as the many Chinese restaurants in the 'Chinatown' district south of Shaftesbury Avenue. For Cantonese cuisine try **Chuen Cheng Fu** (☎ 0207-437 1398) at 17 Wardour Street (Leicester Sq). It's an enormous and wholly authentic Hong Kong-style restaurant serving real dim sum as well as a huge range of dishes from the menu. If sushi's more to your taste, avoid the trendier media spots and go to **Kulu Kulu** (☎ 0207-734 7316) at 76 Brewer Street (Piccadilly Circus tube), which is a friendly and compact restaurant with the accent on excellent food rather than expensive decor. For European food try **Andrew Edmunds** (☎ 0207-437 5708) at 46 Lexington Street (Oxford Circus/Piccadilly Circus tube), which is a tiny but very popular bistro.

Covent Garden is another hotspot for restaurants, although there are some terrible tourist traps serving overpriced burgers and other 'fast' foods. For superb French food at an affordable price look no further than **Mon Plaisir** (☎ 0207-836 7243) at 21 Monmouth Street (Covent Garden/ Leicester Sq tube). If you're starving, **Café Pacifico** (☎ 0207-379 7728) serves enormous portions of superior Mexican food at 5 Langley Street (Covent Garden tube) or **Stephen Bull** (☎ 0207-379 7811) at 12 Upper St Martin's Lane (Leicester Sq tube) is one of those new wave of restaurants serving 'modern British food'; its fish and puddings are highly recommended and good value.

Bloomsbury and Fitzrovia traditionally make up London's intellectual quarter, although based on the number of good restaurants, one could be forgiven for thinking its inhabitants are keener on feeding their stomachs than their minds. The **Diwana Bhel Poori House** (☎ 0207-387 5556) in the oriental quarter of Drummond Street (Euston tube) serves vegetarian southern Indian food and is a great place for a weekday lunch. **Interlude** is an unpretentious French restaurant in Charlotte Street (Goodge St/Tottenham Court Rd tube), and at 67a Tottenham Court Road (Goodge St tube) you'll find **Ikkyu** (☎ 0207-636 9280), which serves authentic Japanese cuisine. For something different, try **R.K. Stanley** (☎ 0207-662 0099) which specialises in sausages from all over the world.

St James's and Mayfair are home to the 'poshest' of haute cuisine restaurants with strictly formal dress codes (e.g. jacket and tie for men). Try the celebrated Marco Pierre White's **Criterion** (☎ 0207-930 0488) at 224 Piccadilly (Piccadilly Circus tube) or the elegant but not too expensive **Mirabelle** in Curzon Street (Green Park tube). Terence Conran's **Quaglino's** (☎ 0207-930 6767) at 16 Bury Street (Green Park tube) was one of the most fashionable places in London a couple of years ago, but now the beautiful people have largely moved on to be replaced by tourists who gawp at its splendid converted ballroom ambience. If you must be informal, try the ultra-hip **Momo** (☎ 0207-434 4040) in Heddon Street (Piccadilly Circus tube), where the Moroccan food is so good you need to book three weeks in advance.

Stylish European restaurants abound in Kensington and Chelsea. Try ultra-smart Polish restaurant **Wodka** (☎ 0207-937 6513) at 12 St Albans Grove, W8 (Gloucester Rd/High St Kensington tube), named after its extensive range of flavoured iced vodkas, or the noisy and popular Portuguese eaterie **O Fado** (☎ 0207-589 3002) in Beauchamp Place (Knightsbridge tube). For well-cooked Italian fare try **Zafferano** (☎ 0207-235 5800) at 15 Lowndes Street (Knightsbridge tube), which gets booked out very early, or head over to **Boisdale** (☎ 0207-730 6922) at 15 Ecclestone Street (Victoria tube), owned by a latter-day clan chief, for gamey Scottish haute cuisine.

The business and financial quarter of the City isn't exactly packed with fine restaurants but you could do worse than **Singapura** (☎ 0207-329 1133) in Limeburner Lane off Ludgate Hill (St Paul's/Blackfriars tube) which serves a strange hybrid of Chinese and Malay food from Singapore. Rampant carnivores might like to brave the portals of **St John** (☎ 0207-251 0848) near Smithfield meat market at 26 St John Street (Farringdon tube), a vegetarian's nightmare specialising in offal dishes including unusual dishes made from brains and bones. The East End boasts some fine Asian restaurants such as **Cafe Spice Namaste** (☎ 0207-488 9242) at 16 Prescott Street (Tower Hill tube) serving Kashmiri and Goan delicacies, or the cheap but authentic Pakistani restaurant **Lahore Kebab House** (☎ 0207-481 9737) which has stewed sheep's feet on the menu along with more mainstream fare. There's also a splendid Vietnamese restaurant beyond the reach of the tube in Shoreditch called the **Viet Hoa** (☎ 0207-729 8293) at 70-72 Kingland Street, E2. Catch a No. 67, 242 or 149 bus to get there or push the boat out and get a taxi.

Further out in arty, middle-class Hampstead and Camden, go for cheerful African eaterie **Wazobia** (☎ 0207-284 1059) at 257 Royal College Street (Camden Town tube) which serves Nigerian and West African dishes. If you fancy Russian cuisine, head for Primrose Hill and book a table at **Trojka** (☎ 0207-483 3765) in Regent's Park Road (Chalk Farm tube). **Solly's** (☎ 0208-455 2121) is a popular kosher restaurant in Golders Green Road (Golders Green tube) and excellent Greek food can be found at the popular **Lemonia** (☎ 0207-586 7454) in Regent's Park Road (Chalk Farm tube). In the Marylebone/Bayswater/Notting Hill area, try classy Sudanese restaurant **The Mandola** (☎ 0207-229 4734) at 139 Westbourne Grove – the spiced coffee comes highly recommended – while nearby at 21-23 Westbourne Grove is **The Standard**, serving some of the most delicious (and best value) Indian food in London. Brazilian restaurant **Rodrizio Rico** (☎ 0207-792 4035) in Westbourne Grove (Notting Hill Gate/Queensway tube) specialises in grilled meats; and if you want good English fish and chips there are few better places than **Sea-Shell** (☎ 0207-723 8703) in Lisson Grove (Marylebone tube).

South of the river, try Brixton's 'global' eaterie **Helter Skelter** (☎ 0207-274 8600) at 50 Atlantic Road (Brixton tube), the welcoming Gujerati restaurant and takeaway **Hot Stuff** (☎ 0207-720 1480) at 19 Wilcox Road (Vauxhall tube) or **Fina Estampa** (☎ 0207-403 1342) at 150 Tooley Street, London's only Peruvian restaurant with lots of yummy seafood.

If you want to check out these or any other restaurants further before paying them a visit, get yourself a copy of a good restaurant guide such as the *Time Out Eating and Drinking Guide*, listing over 1,300 restaurants, cafés and bars, the *Evening Standard London Restaurant Guide* by Nick Foulkes (Simon & Schuster) or *London Restaurants: The Rough Guide* by Charles Campion (Rough Guides). If you love eating out but cannot afford the wine, obtain a copy of *Capital BYOs: A Guide to London's Bring Your Own Wine Restaurants* by Victoria Alers (Hankey VBAH). If you prefer Internet reviews, try the excellent **Restaurant & Food Guide** (www. thisislondon.com), which contains reviews of over 800 restaurants, or **Eat London** (www.londontown.com).

Cyber Cafes

Cyber (or Internet) cafes have proliferated in London in recent years in order to meet the demand for Internet access from those who aren't on-line at home and don't have access at their workplace or college. Londoners tend not to be so hot on the 'net as those living in rural or remote areas for obvious reasons; so much is happening on the spot that they don't have the same need for its information or communication facilities. Most London cyber-cafes also serve drinks and food, and a few even offer free websurfing, although most charge around £5 an hour.

Cyberia in Whitfield Street (☎ 0207-681 4200, 🖳 www. cyberiacafe.net) is the one that started it all (Goodge St tube), while **Room Service @ the Vibe Bar** (☎ 0207-247 3479, 🖳 www.vibe-bar.co.uk) in the Truman Brewery, Brick Lane doesn't charge for net access but has only four terminals (Aldgate East tube). The **Global Cafe** (☎ 0207-287 2242, 🖳 http://gold.globalcafe.co.uk) in Golden Square (Oxford Circus/ Piccadilly Circus tube) serves great food and the **Buzz Bar** (☎ 0207-460 4906, 🖳 www.portobellogold.com) in Portobello Road (Notting Hill Gate/Ladbroke Grove tube) is one of the friendliest places to surf the web in London.

Live Music

Classical: As far as classical music goes, London is one of the great music capitals of the world. It has five major orchestras: the London Symphony Orchestra or LSO (🖳 www.lso.co.uk), the London Philharmonic, the Royal Philharmonic (🖳 www.rpo.co.uk), the Philharmonia and the BBC Symphony Orchestra, plus many excellent smaller ensembles such as the English Chamber Orchestra and the Academy of St Martin-in-the-Fields.

London also has a wealth of excellent music venues. The major classical venues include **The Barbican Centre** (☎ 0207-638 8891, 🖳 www. barbican.org.uk) in the City's Silk Street (Barbican/Moorgate tube) which is an enormous, confusing concrete jungle on several levels containing theatres, libraries and galleries as well as a concert hall. The **South Bank Centre** (☎ 0207-960 4242, 🖳 www.sbc.org.uk) at Waterloo (Waterloo tube) incorporates the Royal Festival Hall, the smaller Queen Elizabeth Hall and the intimate chamber music venue, the Purcell Room. Other chamber music venues include **St John's** (☎ 0207-222 1061), a deconsecrated church in Smith Square (Westminster tube), **Wigmore Hall** (☎ 0207-935 2141) in Wigmore Street (Bond St tube) and **Blackheath Concert Hall** (☎ 0208-463 0100) in Lee Road, SE3 (Blackheath rail).

As well as secular venues, many central London churches provide live music, particularly free lunchtime recitals which are popular with workers. Drop in at **St Bride's** (☎ 0207-353 1301 in Fleet Street (Blackfriars tube), **St James's** (☎ 0207-381 0441) in Piccadilly (Piccadilly Circus tube) or best of all, **St Martin-in-the-Fields** (☎ 0207-839 8362) in Trafalgar Square (Charing Cross tube), which also stages 'ticketed' concerts in the evenings featuring its own top-class classical ensemble. You can also catch free lunchtime concerts by the students at the **Royal Academy of Music** (☎ 0207-873 7373, 🖳 www.ram.ac.uk) in Marylebone Road (Regent's Park/Baker St tube) or the **Royal College of Music** (☎ 0207-589 3643, 🖳 www.rcm.ac.uk) in Prince Consort Road, Kensington (South Kensington tube).

One of the great joys of London is its summer music festivals. One of the most famous classical music seasons anywhere in the world is the **Proms** (promenade concerts), or to give them their full name, the BBC Sir Henry Wood Promenade Concerts. They're performed between July and September at the **Royal Albert Hall** (☎ 0207-589 8212) in Kensington (South Kensington tube). This budget-price season – if you're prepared to queue for promenade (standing) tickets costing just £3 – combines musical favourites with cutting-edge works and culminates in the celebrated 'Last Night of the Proms' concert for which tickets are allocated by ballot. Maybe it's jingoistic, but it's also huge, good-natured fun as the audience, many knowledgeable music students, wave flags and outsize mascots as they sing Rule Britannia and Land of Hope and Glory at the concert's climax. Details are available from the annual *Proms* guide, published in May, or on the Internet (www.bbc.co.uk/proms).

Other festivals include the **City of London Festival** (🖳 www.city-of-london-festival.org.uk) that's held at the Barbican Centre and other city venues during June and July; **Meltdown** at the South Bank Arts Centre in June/July featuring avant-garde music; and the **Kenwood Lakeside Concerts**, which are outdoor events featuring classical favourites (and often firework displays) held on Saturday evenings from June to September outside Kenwood House (☎ 0207-973 3427) in Hampstead (shuttle bus from East Finchley tube).

Rock/Pop: The main venues for big rock and pop concerts are divided between the mega-stadiums and the smaller concert halls and clubs. Stadium gigs can be spectacular, but what you gain on the lasers and inflatables you often lose on the human scale – the performers are likely to be dots in the distance or blown-up images on a huge screen above the stage. Unless you're down the front, you're often better off buying the tour video. Nevertheless, you can see the big bands on tour at the soulless **Earl's Court** exhibition hall (☎ 0207-385 1200, Earl's Court tube), the huge **London Arena** in the Isle of Dogs (DLR) the indoor **Wembley Arena** (☎ 0208-902 0902, Wembley Park/Wembley Central tube) and at the granddaddy of all British stadiums, **Wembley Stadium** itself (☎ 0208-902 0902, 🖳 www. wembleynationalstadium.co.uk) where you can sit on the hallowed turf of the home of English football (Wembley Park/Wembley Central tube).

Better places to see live bands are the concert hall venues, most of which are seated venues where you can buy drinks only before the show or in the interval, theatre-style. Usually there's a support band whose thankless task is to warm up the audience before the main attraction, although in practice, most people forego the experience for an extra half-hour in the bar. **Labatt's Apollo** (☎ 0207-416 6080) in Queen Caroline Street (Hammersmith tube), the former Hammersmith Odeon, is the largest of these. The **Brixton Academy** (☎ 0207-924 9999) in Stockwell Road (Brixton tube) is a converted Victorian hall that welcomes medium-league bands rather than the really big names. The **Forum** (☎ 0207-344 0044) in Highgate Road (Kentish Town tube) was once called the Town and Country Club and is possibly the best place to see live bands in London. Finally, there's the **Astoria** (☎ 0207-434 0403) in Charing Cross Road (Tottenham Court Rd tube), another converted theatre that welcomes bands during the week and hosts club nights at weekends, and the grand old **London Palladium** (☎ 0207-494 5020) in Argyll Street (Oxford Circus tube), which stages all kinds of music and theatre, occasionally featuring something of interest to rock or pop fans.

Bottom of the pecking order are the clubs – the places where all live bands begin their apprenticeships, desperately angling for a following while their debut single languishes in the shops or their demo tapes do the rounds of record companies. Like dance clubs, these come and go, but some of the best and most established are **The Borderline** (☎ 0207-734 2095) in Orange Yard, W1 (Tottenham Court Rd tube) which sometimes features 'secret' gigs by mega-bands playing under pseudonyms, the **Mean Fiddler**

(☎ 0208-961 5490) in Harlesden High Street (Willesden Junction tube) and pub venues such as the **Dublin Castle** (☎ 0207-485 1773) in Parkway (Camden Town tube) and the **Half Moon** (☎ 0208-780 9383) in Lower Richmond Road (Putney Bridge tube). More obscure bands, some playing their first live gig, can be seen at talent scout haunts such as the **Rock Garden** (☎ 0207-240 6001) in Covent Garden's piazza (Covent Garden tube), the **Bull & Gate** (☎ 0207-485 5358) in Kentish Town Road (Kentish Town tube) and the **Hope & Anchor** (☎ 0207-354 1312) in Upper Street (Angel tube).

Jazz: The most famous jazz club in London is the poky and smoky **Ronnie Scott's** (☎ 0207-439 0747) in Frith Street (Leicester Sq tube) where you can book a table or stand at the back. Big jazz names play here. The **100 Club** (☎ 0207-636 0933) in Oxford Street (Tottenham Court Rd tube) used to be a punk club in the late '70s, but has now reverted to its original purpose as a jazz venue. Other worthwhile central places to hear good jazz are Chelsea's **606 Club** in Lots Road off the King's Road (Fulham Broadway tube) and the **Jazz Cafe** in Parkway (Camden Town tube), which has a broad definition of what passes for 'jazz'. If you don't mind heading out of town a bit, visit the excellent **Vortex** in Stoke Newington Church Street (Stoke Newington rail) or the **Bull's Head** on Barnes Bridge (Hammersmith tube then the No. 9 bus or Barnes rail) which attracts some big national names.

Theatres

London is renowned for the quality, quantity and variety of its theatre, which is the most vibrant in the world. There are over 150 commercial and subsidised theatres in London (50 in the West End) producing up to 25 new productions every week. Theatre entertainment includes modern drama; classical plays; comedy; modern and traditional musicals; revue and variety; children's shows and pantomime; opera and operetta; and ballet and dance. The theatre is widely patronised throughout the country and is one of the delights of living in London. Fringe theatre is both lively and extensive, and provides an excellent training ground for new playwrights and companies. Many London and provincial theatres support youth theatres (e.g. 14 to 21) and people of all ages who see themselves as budding Lawrence Oliviers or Katherine Hepburns can audition for local amateur dramatic societies.

The cost of tickets for most London musicals and plays range from around £5 to £35. When buying tickets for any event, whether theatre, cinema, opera or a concert, it's advisable to purchase them direct from the venue. If you're in central London and wish to buy tickets for a West End show, it's usually convenient to buy tickets in person from a theatre box office, most of which are open from around 10am daily on performance days. Tickets can also be purchased from most box offices by mail, simply by writing and requesting tickets for a particular performance (give alternatives if possible). However, it's advisable to telephone in advance and make a reservation. Tickets must either be collected in person or payment sent, usually within three days. Telephone credit card bookings can also be made, usually by telephoning a special number.

Tickets can also be purchased from ticket agencies, who charge a booking fee anywhere from 15 to 25 per cent of the face value of the ticket (similar to ticket touts). Before buying tickets from any source other than from a theatre, you should check the official box office price first (printed on the ticket) so that you know exactly how much commission you're being asked to pay. Most ticket agencies don't actually have any tickets but simply ring the box office, which you can do yourself. If you desperately want to see a show and cannot wait, you may be able to buy tickets from ticket touts, although you may be asked two or three times a ticket's face value.

Theatre listing are provided in newspapers and magazines, including London's weekly *Time Out* and *What's On* guides, and information is also available (and booking can also be made) via the Internet (www. officiallondontheatre.co.uk and www.whatsonstage.com).

Cinemas

London's cinemas are divided into mainstream commercial cinema, usually catered for by large central London cinemas mostly in and around Leicester Square, and by suburban multiplexes with several screens showing different current movies. There are also arthouse cinemas showing fringe movies and foreign films, usually with subtitles. Films on general release are classified by the British Board of Film Censors according to their suitability for a given audience, as shown below:

Classification	Age Restrictions
U	no restrictions;
PG	parental guidance advised (not mandatory);
12	no-one under age 12 admitted;
15	no-one under age 15 admitted;
18	no-one under age 18 admitted.

In practice, most 'U' and 'PG' films are family movies or summer blockbusters, while 12, 15 and 18 rated movies have increasingly more adult content – either 'bad' language or scenes of a violent or sexual nature. At the two extremes, George Lucas's *Star Wars* prequel, *The Phantom Menace,* received a U certificate, which is crucial for the sales of associated toys and other merchandise, while Stanley Kubrick's sexually-explicit last movie, *Eyes Wide Shut*, was rated 18.

The best places to see the new blockbusters and summer hits are the **Odeon Leicester Square** and the **Empire 1** which face each other across Leicester Square. Both these huge cinemas stage star-studded premieres, are the first to get the new releases, and have huge screens and excellent sound systems. Most suburban high streets have a local cinema or two, many owned by the ABC, Odeon, Virgin or Warner chains. These chains offer passes for participating cinemas that are good value for film buffs. Notable independent art house cinemas in London include the **National Film Theatre** (☎ 0207-928 3232, 💻 www.bfi.org.uk) on the South Bank (Waterloo tube), the **Lux Cinema** (☎ 0207-684 0201) in Hoxton Square (Old St tube) and the **Everyman Cinema** in Hollybush Vale (Hampstead tube). You can see German films at the **Goethe Institut** (☎ 0207-411 3400, 💻 www.goethe.de/london) in Princes Gate (South Kensington tube) and French films at the **Ciné Lumière** (☎ 0207-838 2144) at the Institut Français in Queensberry Place (South Kensington tube).

You can find reviews and details about films old and new, plus details of where they're currently showing, in *Time Out* magazine (who also publish an annual *Film Guide*), *What's On in London* magazine, the *Evening Standard* and other local newspapers, and on the **Internet Movie Database** (www.uk.imdb.com).

DAYS OUT

If you want a change from the big city, there are many interesting places and attractions to visit within a few hours of London. Many historic cities and towns are within easy reach of the capital by train or road, including the world-renowned university cities of Oxford and Cambridge plus many fine cathedrals, castles and stately homes.

The ancient university city of **Cambridge** is just 50 minutes from King's Cross or you can drive there on the M11 (exit at junction 11 or 12). The oldest college buildings (at Peterhouse in Trumpington Street) date from the 13th century and Corpus Christi in the same street was built in the 14th century. Most famous of all, though, is the Gothic King's College Chapel, home to the world-famous boys' choir that sings at evensong each afternoon during term time. Check out the university's main website (www.cam.ac.uk), which has links to the colleges and their attractions. You can picnic on the grassy area called the Backs behind the main parade of colleges or hire a punt on the river Cam and lie back lazily as you drift along, propelled by one of the professional boatmen (or by a friend if you choose to do-it-yourself). While you're in the city don't miss the marvellous **Fitzwilliam Museum** in Trumpington Street which has a collection as grand as many London museums and galleries. There are also excellent second-hand bookshops and a bustling open-air market in the central square. The Tourist Information Centre (☎ 01223-322640) is in Wheeler Street.

Oxford, Britain's other world-famous university city, is an hour from London by train from Paddington or by road via the M40 (junction 8) and the A40. Its oldest college buildings are at University College (13th century), but the finest architecture is to be seen at Christ Church with its wonderful chapel and Magdalen with its unparalleled grounds. Information is available on the university website (www.ox.ac.uk). You can punt on both the Isis, a tributary of the River Thames, and the Cherwell. Oxford also has an excellent **Museum of Modern Art** (☎ 01865-722733) in Pembroke Street and the **Pitt Rivers Museum of Archaeology and Anthropology** (☎ 01865-270949) has an amazing collection of ethnic art. There's a covered market dating from 1774 and a huge range of antique shops in Park End Street. The Tourist Information Centre (☎ 01865-726871) is at Gloucester Green.

Windsor Castle (☎ 01753-831118, 🖳 www.windsorcastle.com), standing on a steep chalk bluff overlooking the River Thames, is the world's largest inhabited castle. It's one of Britain's premier tourist attractions and has been a home to British royalty (from which the family took its name) continuously for over 900 years, having been originally built by William the Conquerer in 1070. The castle is open to the public from 10am to 5.30pm from 13th March to October 31st and closes an hour earlier during the rest of the year. Highlights include the State Apartments (badly damaged in a horrendous fire in 1992, but now restored to their former glory), St George's Chapel and Queen Mary's Dolls' House. If you have any energy left afterwards you may wish to take a stroll in **Windsor Great Park**, from where there are marvellous views of the castle. Nearby **Eton College** (☎ 01753-671177, 2 to 4.30pm during term time, from 10.30am to 4.30pm during Easter and summer holidays) dates from the 15th century (founded in 1440) and is Britain's most exclusive public school (where the royal princes are educated). Windsor is just 20mi (32km)) from central London taking 50 minutes by train from Waterloo (direct) to Windsor & Eaton Riverside station or 35 minutes from Paddington to Windsor & Eaton Central station (change at Slough), or around the same time by car (via the M4).

Brighton, 50 minutes from London (Victoria) by train, is in many ways an outpost of London by the sea. Its bright, breezy, and incorrigibly trendy with a liberal, slightly eccentric atmosphere, due in part to its large student population and thriving gay community. It also has much that has survived from the forgotten age of British seaside towns and has now acquired its own delightfully camp charm. Don't fail to visit the gaudy **Palace Pier** – where fish and chip shops and candy-floss vendors rub shoulders with slot machines and a summer funfair. The outrageous **Royal Pavilion** bears an uncanny resemblance to the Kremlin and was built by Nash in 1823 for the Prince Regent. Children love the **Sea Life Centre** (☎ 01273-604234) with its huge glass tanks housing enormous aquatic life-forms and you can spend your life savings shopping for antiques and nick-nacks in **The Lanes**, with its maze of specialist shops, pubs and cafes. As for nightlife, it's worth staying late to sample places such as the **Zap Club** (☎ 01273-202407) and **Honey** (☎ 01273-202807). There's also a fine art house cinema in the **Duke of York's** (☎ 01273-626261) in Preston Circus.

Stratford-upon-Avon is, of course, Shakespeare's birthplace, and not surprisingly one of Britain's most visited towns. It's a relatively long haul from London, taking 2 hours 10 minutes from Paddington by train or you can drive via the M40 (junction 15) and the A46. The literary tourist trail takes in Shakespeare's birthplace (☎ 01789-204016), his wife Anne Hathaway's cottage (☎ 01789-292100) and his mother Mary Arden's childhood home (☎ 01789-293455). Round off your 'day' with a trip to the Royal Shakespeare Theatre (☎ 01789-295623 – be sure to book well in advance), home of the world-famous **Royal Shakespeare Company** (RSC). When you've had your fill of Shakespeare, you can admire the brightly-painted narrow boats on the River Avon and Stratford Canal.

Theme Parks: If you've children to amuse, you might prefer a trip to an out-of-town theme park. The most accessible from London is **Chessington World of Adventures** (☎ 01372-729560) in Surrey, just 30 minutes by train from Waterloo to Chessington South or by car via the M25 (junction 9). It's expensive and perhaps a little tacky, but kids love the terrifying white-knuckle rides – don't miss Rameses' Revenge and the new Samurai ride. There's also a zoo, so arrive early! **Thorpe Park** (☎ 01932-569393, 💻 www.thorpepark.co.uk) is a larger, more modern theme park 45 minutes from Victoria by train (change at Clapham Junction for Staines, then catch a shuttle bus), or by car via the M25 (junction 11 or 13). It's a 500-acre park with all the usual Disneyland-style rides and shows (including new ride 'No Way Out'), as well as a real working farm.

Legoland (☎ 0990-040404, 💻 www.legoland.co.uk) just outside Windsor (train as above for **Windsor** or by car via the M25, junction 13). As its name suggests, it promotes the perennial building toy and includes not only incredibly complex miniature copies of cities from around the world, but inventive and original theme park rides for all ages, including some beautifully gentle ones for tiny tots and grannies, and a chance to pan for gold (children get a medal when they've found enough) in the Wild Woods. The accent is on originality and good design rather than thrills and nausea, but food and drink is expensive and the park is so popular that the time spent queuing for the main attractions can eat into your fun-time to an alarming degree.

If your kids prefer animals to rides, take a trip to **Whipsnade Wild Animal Park** in Dunstable (☎ 01582-872171, 💻 www.londonzoo.co.uk/whipsnade), set in 600 acres of parkland. It's around 30 minutes from King's Cross to Luton followed by a bus ride or by car via the M1 (junction 9), A5 and B4540. As well as doing valuable work in the conservation of endangered species – you'll see elephants, hippos, wallabies and Chinese water deer – it features a children's farm, miniature railway and a great play area. Not far from Whipsnade is **Woburn Abbey** (☎ 01525-290666, 💻 www.camelotintl.com/heritage/house/woburn.html), which is 30 minutes from Euston to Bletchley by train or by car via the M1 (junction 13) and the A4012. Woburn Abbey is an 18th century stately home built on the foundations of a 12th century monastery. Children love it, not least due to the **Safari Park** (💻 www.woburnsafari.co.uk) in the grounds where you can see lions, tigers and bears. There are also five adventure playgrounds, including one for under-fives.

If you're looking for historic sites, the **National Trust (NT)** should be your first point of reference. It's a privately funded charity that looks after historic buildings, gardens and parks throughout Britain. Membership gives you free access to all NT properties and you receive a free *Family Handbook* packed with ideas for family day trips. Contact the National Trust, Membership Department, Freepost MB1438, Bromley, Kent BR1 3XL (☎ 0208-315 1111, 💻 www.nationaltrust.org.uk) or you can join at any NT property. You can also join **English Heritage** which provides free admission to over 350 properties and special events. For information contact English Heritage (Membership Department, PO Box 1BB, London W1A 1BB, ☎ 0207-973 3434, 💻 www.english-heritage.org.uk). If you're keen on gardens, you may wish to join the **Royal Horticultural Society** (Membership Department, 80 Vincent Square, London SW1P 2PE, ☎ 0207-821 3000), in return for which you receive free entry to beautiful gardens throughout the country.

For further information consult a guidebook such as *The Heinz Guide to Days Out with Kids: South East* by Janet Bonthron (Bon Bon) or consult the Internet **Days Out Guide** (www.thisislondon.com).

9.

ARRIVAL &
SETTLING IN

If you're coming to London from overseas, your first task on arrival in Britain will be to negotiate immigration and customs, which fortunately present no problems for most people. Non-EEA nationals must complete a landing card on arrival, which are distributed on international flights and available from the information or purser's office on ferries. British customs and immigration officials are usually polite and efficient, although they may occasionally be a 'trifle overzealous' in their attempts to deter smugglers and illegal immigrants.

Britain isn't a signatory to the Schengen agreement (named after a Luxembourg village on the Moselle River where the agreement was signed), which was fully implemented on 1st July 1995 and introduced an open-border policy between certain member countries. These now comprise Austria, Belgium, France, Germany, Greece, Italy, Luxembourg, the Netherlands, Portugal and Spain. The Scandinavian countries of Denmark, Finland, Iceland, Norway and Sweden have observer status. Britain isn't a member and has no plans to join, ostensibly because of fears of increased illegal immigration and cross-border crime such as drug smuggling. Therefore anyone arriving in Britain from a 'Schengen' country must go through the normal passport and immigration controls, both on arrival in the UK and when entering a Schengen country from the UK.

In addition to information about immigration and customs, this chapter contains checklists of tasks to be completed before or soon after arrival in Britain and when moving house, plus suggestions for finding local help and information.

IMMIGRATION

When you arrive in Britain, the first thing you must do is go through Passport Control which is usually divided into two areas: 'EU/EEA Nationals' and 'All Other Passports'. Make sure you join the right queue! Passport control is staffed by immigration officers who have the task of deciding whether you're subject to immigration control, and if so, whether or not you're entitled to enter Britain. You must satisfy the immigration officer that you're entitled to enter Britain under whatever category of the rules you're applying to enter.

The immigration officer may also decide to send you for a routine (and random) health check, before allowing you to enter the country. Britain has strict regulations regarding the entry of foreigners whose reason for seeking entry may be other than those stated. Generally, the onus is on anyone visiting Britain to *prove* that he's a genuine visitor and won't infringe the immigration laws. The immigration authorities aren't required to establish that you will violate the immigration laws and can refuse your entry on the grounds of suspicion only.

EEA nationals are given a form IS120 by the immigration officer on arrival, which must be produced if they remain in Britain longer than six months. If you're entering Britain from a country other than an EEA member state, you may be required to have immunisation certificates. Check the requirements in advance at a British Diplomatic Post abroad before arriving in Britain.

CUSTOMS

When you enter Britain to take up temporary or permanent residence, you can usually import your personal belongings duty and tax free. Any duty or tax due depends on where you came from, where you purchased the goods, how long you have owned them, and whether duty and tax has already been paid in another country. Note that there are no restrictions on the importation of goods purchased with tax and duty paid in another European Union country, although there are limits for certain goods, e.g. alcohol and tobacco products.

All ports and airports in Britain use a system of red and green 'channels'. Red means you have something to declare and green means that you have nothing to declare, i.e. no more than the customs allowances, no goods to sell and no prohibited or restricted goods. **If you're <u>certain</u> that you have nothing to declare, go through the green channel, otherwise go through the red channel.** Customs officers make random checks on people going through the green channel and there are stiff penalties for smuggling. If you're arriving by ferry with a motor vehicle, you can affix a green or red windscreen sticker to your windscreen, which helps customs officers direct you through customs.

A list of all items you're importing is useful, although the customs officer may still want to examine your belongings. If you need to pay duty or tax, it must be paid at the time the goods are brought into the country. Customs accept cash (sterling only), sterling travellers' cheques, personal cheques and eurocheques supported by a cheque guarantee card, Mastercard and Visa, and some ports and airports also accept debit cards. If you're unable to pay on the spot, customs will keep your belongings until you pay the sum due, which must be paid within the period noted on the back of your receipt. Postage or freight charges must be paid if you want the goods sent on to you. Your belongings may be imported up to six months prior to your arrival in Britain, but no more than one year after your arrival. They mustn't be sold, lent, hired out or otherwise disposed of in Britain within one year of their importation or of your arrival (whichever is later), without obtaining customs authorisation.

If you're shipping your personal belongings (which includes anything for your family's personal use such as clothing, cameras, TV and stereo, furniture and other household goods) unaccompanied to Britain, you *must* complete (and sign) customs form C3, available from your shipping agent or HM Customs and Excise (Excise and Inland Customs Advice Centre, Southbank, Dorset House, Stamford Street, London SE1 9PY, ☎ 0207-928

3344) and attach a detailed packing list. If you employ an international removal company, they will handle the customs clearance and associated paperwork for you. Any items obtained in Britain or within the EU can be brought into Britain free of customs and excise duty or VAT, provided:

- any customs duty, excise duty or VAT was paid and not refunded when they were exported from Britain (or the EU in the case of customs duty);
- they were in your private possession and use in Britain before they were exported;
- they haven't been altered abroad, other than necessary repairs.

The personal belongings you're allowed to bring into Britain duty and tax free depend on your status, as shown below.

Visitors or Students Resident Abroad

If you're a **visitor**, you can bring your belongings to Britain free of duty and tax without declaring them to customs providing:

- all belongings are brought in with you and are for your use alone;
- they are kept in Britain for no longer than six months in a 12-month period;
- you don't sell, lend, hire out or otherwise dispose of them in Britain;
- they're exported either when you leave Britain or before they have been in Britain for more than six months, whichever occurs first.

If you're unable to export your belongings when you leave Britain you must apply to the nearest Customs and Excise Advice Centre for an extension.

People Moving or Returning to Britain

If you're moving or returning to Britain (including British subjects) from a country outside the European Union (EU), you can import your belongings free of duty and tax, provided you have lived at least 12 months outside the EU. Your possessions must have been used for at least six months outside the EU before being imported. Tax and duty must have been paid on all items being imported, with the exception of those belonging to diplomats, members of officially recognised international organisations, members of NATO or British forces, and any civilian staff accompanying them. Articles must be for your personal use, must be declared to customs, and you mustn't sell, lend, hire out or otherwise dispose of them in Britain within 12 months without customs authorisation.

People with Secondary Homes in Britain

If you're setting up a secondary home in Britain, you can bring normal household furnishings and equipment with you free of duty and tax if you usually live in another EU country. If you give up a secondary home outside the EU, there's no special relief from tax and duty for importing belongings from that home. If you have lived outside the EU for at least 12 months you can import household furnishings and equipment for setting up a secondary home free of duty, **but not free of VAT, which is levied at 17.5 per cent.**

To qualify, you must either own or be renting a home in Britain for a minimum of two years and your household furnishings and equipment must have been owned and used for at least six months. Articles must be for your personal use, must be declared to customs, and you mustn't sell, lend, hire out or otherwise dispose of them in Britain within 24 months without customs authorisation. If goods are imported separately, a customs form C33 must be completed.

POLICE REGISTRATION

Foreigners over 16 may be required to register at their local police station within seven days of arrival if they:

- are non-EEA and non-Commonwealth nationals;
- have limited permission to enter Britain;
- have been granted an extension of stay by the Home Office;
- have been allowed to work in Britain for more than three months;
- have been given leave to remain in Britain for longer than six months.

Registration also applies to the dependants aged over 16 of anyone required to register, including those who turn 16 while living in Britain. **When required, registration is indicated by the immigration stamp in your passport**. You must report to the police station nearest to where you're staying within seven days, even when you're staying in temporary accommodation. You will require your passport, two passport-size photographs (black and white or colour) and the fee.

You're required to carry your police registration certificate with you at all times, but not your passport. It's also advisable to take your police registration certificate with you when travelling abroad, as this will make re-entry into Britain easier, although it should be surrendered to the immigration officer if you're travelling abroad for longer than two months. Note that unlike many other Europeans, Britons aren't legally required to prove their identity on demand by a police officer or other official.

COUNCIL TAX REGISTRATION

All residents or temporary residents of Britain are required to register with their local authority or council for council tax purposes soon after their arrival in Britain or after moving to a new home, either in the same council area or a new area. For information see page 131.

FINDING HELP

One of the biggest difficulties facing new arrivals in Britain is how and where to obtain help with essential everyday tasks such as buying a car, obtaining medical help and insurance requirements. How successful you are at finding help will depend on your employer (if applicable), the town or area of London where you live, your nationality and your English proficiency. Obtaining information isn't a problem, as there's a wealth of data available in Britain on every conceivable subject. The problem is sorting the truth from the half-truths, comparing the options available and making the right decisions. Much information naturally isn't intended for foreigners and their particular needs. You may find that your friends, colleagues and acquaintances can help, as they are often able to proffer advice based on their own experiences and mistakes. **But beware!** Although they mean well, you're likely to receive as much false and conflicting information as you are accurate (not always wrong, but possibly invalid for your particular area or situation).

Your local council offices, library, tourist information centre and Citizens Advice Bureau are excellent sources of reliable information on almost any subject. Libraries in particular are an excellent local community resource. There are expatriate clubs and organisations in most areas, many of which provide detailed local information regarding all aspects of living in Britain, including housing costs, schools, names of doctors and dentists, shopping and much more. Clubs often produce data sheets, booklets and newsletters, and organise a variety of social events that may include day and evening classes ranging from cooking to English-language classes. One of the best ways to get to know local people is to join a social club, of which there are hundreds throughout London (look under 'Clubs and Associations' in your local Yellow Pages).

Embassies and consulates (see **Appendix A**) may provide information bulletin boards (jobs, accommodation, travel) and keep lists of social clubs for their nationals and many businesses (e.g. banks and building societies) produce books and leaflets containing valuable information for newcomers. Libraries and bookshops usually have books about local areas.

CHECKLISTS

Before Arrival

The checklists on the following pages list tasks that you need (or may need) to complete before and after arrival in Britain, and when moving your home permanently to Britain.

- Check that your and your family's passports are valid!

- Obtain a visa, if necessary, for all your family members. Obviously this *must* be done before arrival in Britain.

- Arrange health and travel insurance for yourself and your family. This is essential if you aren't covered by an international health insurance policy and won't be covered by the National Health Service (NHS).

- If you don't already have one, it's advisable to obtain an international credit or charge card (or two), which will prove invaluable in Britain.

- If necessary, obtain an international driver's licence.

- Open a bank account in Britain (see page 262) and transfer funds. You can open an account with many British banks while abroad, although it's best done in person in Britain.

- It's advisable to obtain some pounds sterling before arriving in Britain, which will save you having to queue to change money on arrival (and you may receive a better exchange rate).

- If you plan to become a permanent resident you may also need to do the following:

  - Arrange schooling for your children.

  - Organise the shipment of your personal and household effects.

  - Obtain as many credit references as possible, for example from banks, mortgage companies, credit card companies, credit agencies, companies with which you have had accounts, and references from professionals such as lawyers and accountants. These will help you establish a credit rating in Britain.

If you're planning to become a permanent resident, you should take all your family's official documents with you. These include birth certificates; driving licences; marriage certificate, divorce papers or death certificate (if you're a widow or widower); educational diplomas and professional certificates; employment references and curriculum vitaes; school records and student ID cards; medical and dental records; bank account and credit card details; insurance policies (plus records of no-claims' allowances); and receipts for any valuables. You also need the documents necessary to obtain a residence permit plus certified copies, official translations and numerous passport-size photographs (students should have at least a dozen).

After Arrival

The following checklist contains a summary of the tasks to be completed after arrival in Britain (if not done before arrival):

- On arrival at a British airport, port or border post, have your visa cancelled and your passport stamped, as applicable.

- If you aren't taking a car with you, you may wish to rent or buy one locally. Note that it's difficult to get around outside London without a car.

- Open a bank account (see page 271) at a local bank and give the details to your employer and any companies that you plan to pay by direct debit or standing order (such as utility and property management companies).

- Arrange whatever insurance is necessary such as health, car and home.

- Contact offices and organisations to obtain local information (see page 252).

- It's worthwhile making courtesy calls on your neighbours within a few weeks of your arrival.

- If you plan to become a permanent resident in Britain, you may need to do the following soon after your arrival (if not done beforehand):
  - apply for a residence permit;
  - apply for a National Health Service card from your local health authority;
  - apply for a British driving licence;
  - register with a local doctor and dentist;
  - arrange schooling for your children.

Moving House

When moving permanently to Britain there are many things to be considered and a 'million' people to be informed. Even if you plan to spend just a few months a year in Britain, it may still be necessary to inform a number of people and companies in your home country. The checklists below are designed to make the task easier and help prevent an ulcer or a nervous breakdown (providing of course you don't leave everything to the last minute).

- If you live in rented accommodation you will need to give your landlord notice (check your contract).

- If you own your home, arrange to sell or let it (if applicable) well in advance of your move to Britain.
- Inform the following:
  - Your employer, e.g. give notice or arrange leave of absence.
  - Your local town hall or municipality. You may be entitled to a refund of your local taxes.
  - If it was necessary to register with the police in your home country, you should inform them that you're moving abroad.
  - Your electricity, gas, water and telephone companies. Contact companies well in advance, particularly if you need to have a deposit refunded.
  - Your insurance companies (for example, health, car, home contents and private pension); banks, post office (if you have a post office account), stockbroker and other financial institutions; credit card, charge card and hire purchase companies; lawyer and accountant; and local businesses where you have accounts.
  - Your family doctor, dentist and other health practitioners. Health records should be transferred to your new doctor and dentist in Britain.
  - Your children's schools. Try to give a term's notice and obtain a copy of any relevant school reports or records from your children's schools.
  - All regular correspondents, subscriptions, social and sports clubs, professional and trade journals, and friends and relatives. Give them your new address and telephone number and arrange to have your mail redirected by the post office or a friend.
  - If you have a driving licence or a car that you're taking to Britain, you will need to give the local vehicle registration office your new address abroad and, in some countries, return your car's registration plates. If you're exporting a car to Britain permanently, you will need to complete the relevant paperwork in your home country and re-register it in Britain after your arrival. Contact the DVLC, Swansea SA99 1AR (☎ 01792-772134) for information.
- Return any library books or anything borrowed.
- Arrange shipment of your furniture and belongings by booking a shipping company well in advance. International shipping companies usually provide a wealth of information and can advise on a wide range of matters concerning an international relocation. Find out the procedure for shipping your belongings to Britain from a British embassy or consulate.
- Arrange to sell anything you aren't taking with you (e.g. house, car and furniture). If you're selling a home or business, you should obtain expert legal advice as you may be able to save tax by establishing a trust or other legal vehicle. Note that if you own more than one property, you

may need to pay capital gains tax on any profits from the sale of second and subsequent homes.

- Arrange inoculations, shipment and quarantine (if applicable) for any pets that you're bringing with you (see page 271).

- You may qualify for a rebate on your tax and social security contributions. If you're leaving a country permanently and have been a member of a company or state pension scheme, you may be entitled to a refund or may be able to continue payments to qualify for a full (or larger) pension when you retire. Contact your company personnel office, local tax office or pension company for information.

- It's advisable to arrange health, dental and optical check-ups for your family before leaving your home country. Obtain a copy of all your health records and a statement from your private health insurance company stating your present level of cover.

- Terminate any outstanding loan, lease or hire purchase contracts and pay all bills (allow plenty of time as some companies may be slow to respond).

- Check whether you're entitled to a rebate on your road tax, car and other insurance. Obtain a letter from your motor insurance company stating your no-claims' discount.

- Check whether you need an international driving licence or a translation of your foreign driving licence(s) for Britain. Note that some foreign residents are required to take a driving test in order to drive in Britain.

- Give friends and business associates an address and telephone number where you can be contacted in Britain.

- If you will be living in Britain for an extended period (but not permanently), you may wish to give someone 'power of attorney' over your financial affairs in your home country so that they can act for you in your absence. This can be for a fixed period or open-ended and can be for a specific purpose only. **Note, however, that you should take expert legal advice before doing this!**

- Allow plenty of time to get to the airport, register your luggage, and clear security and immigration.

Have a nice journey!

10.

ODDS & ENDS

This chapter contains miscellaneous information of interest to anyone planning to live or work in London. Subjects covered include banks, building societies, climate, cost of living, crime, insurance, permits and visas, pets, post office services, retirement, telephone, and television and radio.

BANKS

The major British banks with branches in London and towns throughout Britain (termed 'high street' banks) include the Abbey National, Barclays, HSBC (formerly Midland), Lloyds TSB and National Westminster. Other major banks with branches in London and large towns are the Bank of Scotland, the Royal Bank of Scotland and the Co-operative Bank. There are also telephone banks (including First Direct and Girobank) that don't have branches and are 'open' 24-hours a day. For the wealthy there are many private banks (mainly portfolio management) and foreign banks, of which there are over 500 in the City of London alone. Most banks have Internet websites and many offer online banking, although it's in its infancy with less than a million customers in late 1999. In recent years there has been a flood of new-style 'banks' such as Virgin Direct, supermarkets and stores such as Marks and Spencer, which have shaken up traditional high street banks with their innovative accounts and services.

British banks provide free banking for personal customers who remain in credit, pay nominal interest on account balances and offer a range of financial services (although they usually *aren't* the best place to buy insurance or pensions). If you do a lot of travelling abroad, you may find the comprehensive range of services offered by high street banks advantageous. In a small country town or village there's usually a post office, but not usually a bank. Note that many services provided by British banks are also provided by building societies (see below).

The relationship between the major banks and their customers has deteriorated in the last decade (particularly during the recession), during which banks dramatically increased their charges to personal and business customers to recoup their losses on bad loans to developing countries. Few people in Britain have a good word to say about their banks, which are widely regarded as profit-hungry, impersonal and definitely not customer-friendly (complaints have risen dramatically in recent years). British banks have made record profits (running into £billions) in the '90s, which has served only to further antagonise their customers (who think their banks are ripping them off). Note that often the worst place to buy financial products is from a major high street bank, and building societies usually offer better deals.

Not surprisingly, banks aren't exactly happy about their poor public image (on a par with that of used car salesmen and politicians) and most have been busy trying to improve customer relations by introducing codes of conduct and payments for mistakes or poor service. Many people could save money by changing their accounts or banks.

Deposit Protection: All banks, including branches and subsidiaries of foreign banks accepting sterling deposits in Britain, must be licensed by the Bank of England and contribute to the Deposit Protection Fund (DPF), which guarantees that 90 per cent of deposits up to £20,000 will be repaid if a bank goes bust.

Complaints: British banks are very (very) slow to rectify mistakes or to resolve disputes and rarely accept responsibility, even when clearly in the wrong. It has been estimated (based on actual proven cases) that banks routinely overcharge small business customers by hundreds of £millions a year. If your bank makes a mess of your account and causes you to lose money and spend time putting it right, you're quite within your rights to claim financial compensation for your time and trouble in addition to any financial loss. Note, however, that banks typically stall complaints for up to six years and use their financial muscle to wear down customers (some banks fight every case with litigation). If you have a complaint against a British bank and have exhausted the bank's complaints' procedure, you can apply for 'independent' arbitration to the Office of the Banking Ombudsman (70 Grays Inn Road, London WC1X 8NB, ☎ 0207-404 9944), although your chances of success are slim.

BUILDING SOCIETIES

Building societies date back to 1775 and were originally established to cater for people saving to buy a home. Savers saved a deposit of 5 or 10 per cent of the cost of a home with the building society, who then lent them the balance – they would rarely lend to anyone who wasn't a regular saver, although this changed many years ago. In 1987, the regulations governing institutions offering financial services were changed and as a result banks and building societies now compete head-on for customers. There have been a wave of mergers and take-overs in recent years and in the past decade the number of societies has fallen dramatically. Many building societies have converted to banks (called demutualisation) in recent years, earning £millions for account holders and many people (known as carpetbaggers) have taken advantage by opening accounts at a number of building societies.

Nowadays building societies offer practically all the services provided by banks, including current and savings accounts; cheque guarantee cards; cash, debit and credit cards; personal loans; insurance; and travel services. In an attempt to woo customers away from banks, many building societies produce special brochures and 'transfer packs' (even containing pre-printed 'letters') detailing exactly how to transfer your account. Building societies don't all offer the same services, types of accounts or rates of interest, and those offering the best interest rates are often the smaller societies. If you're looking for a long-term investment, the number of branches may not be of importance, and members of all building societies can use cash dispensers at other banks and building society branches via the Link system.

Complaints: If you have a complaint against a building society and have exhausted its complaints' procedure, you can apply for independent arbitration to the Office of the Building Societies' Ombudsman, Millbank Tower, Millbank, London SW1P 4XS (☎ 0207-931 0044). Deposits in British building society accounts are protected by a similar compensation scheme to banks, under which you're guaranteed to receive 90 per cent of your investment (up to a maximum of £20,000) if it goes bust.

Business Hours

Normal bank opening hours are from 9 or 9.30am until 3.30 or 4pm (some are open until 5.30pm) Mondays to Fridays, with no shutdown over the lunch period in cities and most towns. Most branches are open late one day a week until between 5.30 or 6pm (it varies depending on the bank and its location) and many open on Saturdays, e.g. from 9.30am until 12.30pm (some are open until 3.30pm). Building societies are generally open from 9am to 5pm, Mondays to Fridays, and from 9am to noon on Saturdays.

Bureaux de change have longer opening hours, including Saturdays and Sundays in London, but they should be used in dire circumstances only (e.g. the taxi meter is running and the driver is threatening your life if you don't pay him!) due to their high commission and/or poor exchange rates. When banks are closed you can change money at post offices, which are usually open from 9am to 5.30pm Mon-Fri and from 9am to 12.30pm on Saturdays. All banks are closed on public holidays, which, in Britain, are also called bank holidays (no prize for guessing why!).

Banks at major airports are open from 6.30 or 7am until 11 or 11.30pm seven days a week and some airports, e.g. London's Gatwick and Heathrow airports, have 24-hour banks. Some banks at London railway stations also have extended opening hours (e.g. Victoria). Most banks, building societies and main post offices in Britain have 24-hour cash machines (officially called Automatic Teller Machines/ATMs) at branches for cash withdrawals, deposits and checking account balances. Cash machines are also located in some supermarkets and large stores.

Opening an Account

If you're planning to work in Britain and will be paid monthly, one of your first acts should be to open a current (or cheque) account with a bank or building society. Your salary will usually be paid directly into your account by your employer and your salary statement will be either sent to your home address or given to you at work. Employees who are paid weekly are often paid in cash, in which case it's up to you whether you open a bank or building society account (although it's difficult to survive without one nowadays).

Many people have at least two accounts; a current account for their out-of-pocket expenses and day-to-day transactions, and a savings account for long-term savings (or money put aside for a rainy day – which is every other day in Britain). Many people have both bank and building society accounts. Before opening an account, compare bank charges, interest rates (e.g. on credit cards) and other services offered by a number of banks. **If you're planning to buy a home with a mortgage, one of the best accounts is an all-in-one account or mortgage current account (see page 129).**

To open an account, you simply go to the bank or building society of your choice and tell them you wish to open an account. You will be asked for proof of identity, e.g. usually a passport or driving licence, plus proof of your address in the form of a utility bill. Foreign residents may be required to provide a reference from their employer or a foreign bank. Many banks provide new account holders with a free cash card wallet, a cheque book cover and a statement file. After opening an account, don't forget to give the details to your employer (if you want to get paid). The facilities you should expect from a current account include a cheque book; a paying-in book; a cheque guarantee card (preferably for £100 or £250); interest paid on credit balances; no charges or fees when in credit; a free cash/debit card and lots of local cash machines; monthly statements; an automatic authorised overdraft facility; and the availability of credit cards. Most of these are standard.

With a current account you receive a cheque book (usually containing 30 cheques) and a cash card. A cheque guarantee card is usually provided on request and guarantees cheques up to £50, £100 or £250. Note that when using a cheque guarantee card, the card number must be written on the back of the cheque. Most businesses won't accept a cheque without a guarantee card. A cheque book usually also contains paying-in slips (at the back), with which you can make payments into your account, although you will also receive a separate paying-in book.

Most people pay their bills from their current account, either by standing order or by cheque. Bank statements are usually issued monthly (optionally quarterly), interest may be paid on deposits (usually quarterly) and an overdraft facility may be provided. Most banks don't levy any charges on a current account, providing you stay in credit. However, if you overdraw your account without a prior arrangement with your bank, you may be billed for bank charges on all transactions for the accounting period (usually three months).

High-Interest Cheque Accounts: Most banks and building societies offer high-interest cheque accounts for customers who maintain a minimum balance, e.g. £1,000. These accounts offer a range of benefits, including a cheap overdraft facility and a £250 cheque guarantee card. Some current accounts pay variable rates of interest depending on the account balance. Interest on high-interest accounts may be paid monthly and there's usually no transaction or monthly fees. However, if you don't need instant access to large sums of cash, you're better off with a savings account than a high-interest cheque account. **It isn't advisable to keep a lot of cash in an account with a cash card, as fraudulent withdrawals aren't unknown!**

It would appear that many people in Britain have money to throw away, as they keep quite large sums in accounts that pay no interest or minimal interest only, e.g. 0.5 per cent. Naturally, banks don't go out of their way to explain to customers the most advantageous accounts for their money – some banks even discourage staff from advising customers about accounts paying higher interest – or even explain about account fees or charges (which helps boosts profits by £millions each year). Even modest balances in an interest-earning account can earn enough to ward off inflation. If you never overdraw on your current account and aren't being paid interest, you're making a free loan to your bank (something they most certainly *won't* do for you).

CLIMATE

London has a relatively mild and temperate climate, although it's extremely changeable and usually damp at any time. The least hospitable months are November to February when it's often very cold and the days are short; March and October are slightly better but can still be quite cold. December and February are traditionally the severest months, when it's often cold, wet and windy. Although temperatures drop below freezing in winter, particularly at night, it's rarely below freezing during the day, although the average temperature is a cold 4°C (39°F). The most unpleasant features of British winters are freezing fog and black ice, which make driving hazardous. However, the 'pea-soup' fog that was usually the result of smog and pollution, and which many foreigners still associate with London, is thankfully a thing of the past. Rain is fairly evenly distributed throughout the year (many Londoners carry an umbrella at all times), although the wettest month is usually November. Average rainfall is January 54mm, April 37mm, July 59mm and October 57mm.

April to September are the best months, with July and August the warmest. Spring is generally the most pleasant time of year, although early spring is often very wet. Summer temperatures are often around 26°C (75°F) and occasionally rise above 30°C (86°F), although the average temperature is 15° to 18°C (60° to 65°F). Average high and low temperatures are: January 6/2°C (43/36°F), April 13/6°C (55/43°F), July 22/14°C (72/57°F) and October 14/8°C (57/46°F).

The worst aspect of British weather is the frequent drizzle (light rain) and grey skies, particularly in winter. This has given rise to a condition known as seasonal affective disorder (SAD), which is brought on by the dark, dull days of winter and causes lethargy, fatigue and low spirits. However, there's some good news – British winters are becoming milder and in recent years have been nothing like as severe as in earlier decades, although whether this is a permanent change is unclear. In fact, British weather is becoming warmer all round, with recent years experiencing some of the driest summers since records began in 1659.

To add a little spice to the usual diet of cold and rain, in the last decade Britain has been afflicted with gales and torrential rain (including the infamous storms of 1987 and 1990), which have caused severe damage and flooding in many areas. Tornadoes also occur in Britain, but are extremely rare. There's considerable debate among weather experts and scientists as to whether the climatic changes (not just in Britain, but world-wide) are a result of global warming or just a temporary change. If present trends continue, some scientists predict that temperatures will increase considerably in the next century and the south of England could become frost-free.

Weather forecasts are available via TV teletext services, in daily newspapers, via premium rate telephone services, on the Internet, and on TV and radio (usually after the news). Warnings of dangerous weather conditions affecting motoring, e.g. fog and ice, are broadcast regularly on all BBC national and local radio stations. The most detailed weather forecasts are broadcast on BBC Radio 2 and BBC Radio 4, which also broadcasts weather forecasts for shipping. During the early summer, when pollens are released in large quantities, the pollen count is given on radio and TV weather forecasts and in daily newspapers. In summer, the maximum exposure time for the fair-skinned is also included in TV weather forecasts on hot days.

COST OF LIVING

No doubt you would like to know how far your pounds will stretch and how much money (if any) you will have left after paying your bills. In common with most capital cities, the cost of living in London is high and prices (particularly property) are the highest in Britain, although higher salaries compensate to some extent. Britain generally has high indirect taxes and rates of duty on everything from petrol to tobacco and alcohol to cars, making it one of the most expensive places to live. In fact, London's one of the world's most expensive cities with a higher cost of living than Amsterdam, Berlin, Luxembourg, Montreal, Munich, New York and Sydney.

Britain's inflation rate is based on the Retail Prices Index (RPI), which gives an indication of how prices have risen (or fallen) over the past year. The prices of around 600 'indicator' items are collected on a single day in the middle of the month (a total of around 130,000 prices are collected for the 600 items in the RPI basket). Britain's inflation rate in 1999 was around 2.5 per cent.

On the plus side, Britain's standard of living has soared in recent years and compared with most other European Union countries, British workers take home a larger proportion of their pay after tax and social security.

There's a huge gap between the wealthy south of England and the poor north of England, Scotland and Northern Ireland, and it's increasing. The gap between rich and poor in Britain is the largest since records began in 1886, and state pensioners are often unable to afford basic comforts such as a healthy diet, a car and an annual holiday. In contrast, the middle classes have never been better off than in recent years and the super rich go on spending sprees buying holiday homes, cruises, yachts, power boats, luxury cars and private aircraft.

It's difficult to calculate an average cost of living as it depends on each individual's particular circumstances and lifestyle. What is important to most people is how much money they can save (or spend) each month. Your food bill will naturally depend on what you eat and is usually around 50 per cent higher than in the USA, and up to 25 per cent higher than in other western European countries. Approximately £200 should be sufficient to feed two adults for a month in most areas (excluding alcohol, fillet steak and caviar). However, the cost of living needn't be astronomical. If you shop wisely, compare prices and services before buying and don't live too extravagantly, you may be pleasantly surprised at how little you can live on. Note that it's also possible to save a considerable sum by shopping for alcohol and other products in France, buying your car in Europe, and shopping overseas by mail and via the Internet (see page 215).

CRIME

Overall, the number of reported crimes (apart from violent crimes) has fallen in the last decade, although some sceptics believe it's because people are simply reporting less crime because they consider it a waste of time (in some areas 95 per cent of crimes are unsolved). The number of violent crimes has increased in the last decade, although they're still relatively low compared with many other countries – the risk of being a victim of crime is around the European average. There are around 500 murders a year in Britain, which is less than in most other European countries, and you're more likely to choke to death on your food than you are to meet a violent death.

The level of street crime (where men under 30 are most at risk) is higher than official figures suggest and the actual number of crimes is reckoned to be around four times the number recorded by the police. However, muggings and crimes of violence are still rare in most areas of London, where you can safely walk in most places day or night, although the police warn people (particularly young women) against walking alone in dark and deserted areas late at night. Many crimes are drug-related and due to the huge quantity of drugs flooding into Britain in recent years. The use of hard drugs (particularly cocaine and crack) is a major problem in London, where gangs increasingly use guns to settle their differences.

Crime is a major concern for residents of some London suburbs, where elderly people are often afraid to leave the relative safety of their homes at any time of day or night. The increase in crime is attributed by psychologists to poverty, the breakdown of traditional family life, the loss of community and social values in society, and a growing lack of parental responsibility and skills. The failure to deal with juvenile crime is one of the biggest threats facing Britain and many children are totally out of control by the age of ten or even younger.

Crimes against property are escalating, particularly burglary and housebreaking, car thefts and thefts from vehicles. In London, where around 20 per cent of all crime takes place, professional thieves even steal antique paving stones, railings and antique doors and door casings. Fraud or so-called 'white-collar' crime (which includes credit card fraud, income tax evasion and VAT fraud), costs £billions a year and accounts for larger sums than the total of all other robberies, burglaries and thefts added together.

Although the foregoing catalogue of crime may paint a depressing picture, London is a generally safe place to live. In comparison with many other countries, including most European countries, Britain's crime rate isn't high and the incidence of violent crime is low. If you take care of your property and take precautions against crime, your chances of becoming a victim are small. Note, however, that the crime rate varies considerably from area to area, and anyone planning on living in London should avoid high crime areas if at all possible.

The Metropolitan Police publishes a crime rate (shown in the table overleaf) for each borough which indicates the number of crimes committed each year per 1,000 population. There are no comparable statistics for the City of London, which has its own police force.

Crime Rates:

BOROUGH	CRIME RATE
Barnet	75
Havering	78
Harrow	79
Bexley	79
Sutton	81
Richmond	81
Bromley	81
Redbridge	81
Kingston	95
Enfield	96
Merton	96
Hillingdon	103
Croydon	103
Barking & Dagenham	113
Brent	113
Waltham Forest	115
Ealing	118
Wandsworth	121
Lewisham	122
Hounslow	126
Greenwich	139
Haringey	140
Newham	148
Hammersmith & Fulham	163
Tower Hamlets	170
Islington	176
Hackney	179
Lambeth	180
Kensington & Chelsea	181#
Southwark	181
Camden	221#
Westminster	384#

\#   Figures in these areas are distorted by non-resident visitors, e.g. temporary workers and tourists.

INSURANCE

In Britain you can insure practically anything from your car to your camera, the loss of your livelihood to your life. You can also insure against most eventualities, such as rain on your parade or village fete, or the possibility of twins (or sextuplets) or missing your holiday. For particularly unusual requests you may be required to obtain a quote from Lloyd's of London, the last resort for unusual insurance needs (not only within Britain, but also internationally). If you earn your livelihood courtesy of a particular part of your anatomy, e.g. your voice, legs, teeth or posterior, you can also insure it against damage or decline. Note, however, that if an insurance requirement is particularly unusual or risky, you may find the premiums prohibitively high and restrictions may be placed on what you can and cannot do.

Britain is renowned as a nation of gamblers, which is reflected in the relatively low level of insurance, not only for such basic requirements as loss of income or life insurance, but also insurance for homes and their contents. After serious flooding caused £millions of damage in recent years, it was revealed that up to half of all households in some areas had no building or home contents insurance or were under-insured. Many people tend to rely on state 'insurance' benefits, which come under the heading of 'social security'. These include sickness and unemployment pay, income support (for families on low incomes) and state pensions. Note, however, that social security usually provides for the most basic needs only and those who are reduced to relying on it often exist below the poverty line.

It isn't necessary to spend half your income insuring yourself against every eventuality from the common cold to a day off work, but it's important to be covered against any event which could precipitate a major financial disaster (like telling your boss what you think of him when you've had a few drinks too many). **As with everything to do with finance, it's important to shop around when buying insurance. It bears repeating – always shop around when buying or renewing insurance!** Simply picking up a few brochures from insurance brokers or making a few phone calls can save you a lot of money (enough to pay for this book many times over).

If you're coming to Britain from abroad, you would be wise to ensure that your family has full health insurance during the period between leaving your last country of residence until your arrival in Britain. This is particularly important if you're covered by a company health insurance policy terminating on the day you leave your present employment. If possible, it's better to continue with your present health insurance policy, particularly if you have existing health problems that may not be covered by a new policy. If you aren't covered by the National Health Service it's important to have private health insurance.

There are just two cases in Britain when insurance for individuals is compulsory: buildings insurance if you have a mortgage (because your lender will insist on it) and third party motor insurance, which is required by law. You may also need compulsory third party and accident insurance for high-risk sports. Voluntary insurance includes pensions, accident, income protection, health, home contents, personal liability, legal expenses, dental, travel, motor breakdown and life insurance. If you want to make a claim against a third party or a third party is claiming against you, you would be wise to seek legal advice for anything other than a minor claim. Note that British law is likely to be different from that in your home country or your previous country of residence and you should never assume that it's the same.

PERMITS & VISAS

Before making any plans to live or work in Britain, you *must* ensure that you have the appropriate entry clearance (e.g. a visa) and permission, because without the correct documentation you will be refused permission to enter the country. If you were born in a European Economic Area (EEA) country (Austria, Belgium, Denmark, Finland, France, Germany, Greece, Iceland, Ireland, Italy, Liechtenstein, Luxembourg, Netherlands, Norway, Portugal, Spain, Sweden and the UK) or can show that at least one of your parents or grandparents was born in Britain, you're free to live in Britain without restrictions, providing you're able to support yourself (and any dependants) without state assistance.

If you're a national of a non-EEA country, you may need to obtain *entry clearance*, e.g. persons intending to stay permanently, coming to work or who are visa nationals. **If you're in any doubt as to whether you require clearance to enter Britain, enquire at a British Embassy, High Commission or other British Diplomatic Mission (collectively known as British Diplomatic Posts) overseas before making plans to travel to Britain.** Note that in some countries, entry clearance can take some time to be granted due to the high number of applications to be processed.

Nationals of some non-Commonwealth and non-EEA countries who have been given permission to remain in Britain for more than six months or who have been allowed to work for more than three months, are required to register with the police (see page 251). When applicable, this condition is stamped in your passport, either on entry or by the Immigration and Nationality Directorate (IND) of the Home Office when granting an extension of stay. The Home Office (called the Interior Ministry in many countries) has the final decision on all matters relating to immigration.

The latest information about immigration, permits and visas can be obtained from the **Immigration and Nationality Department**, which publishes leaflets and booklets regarding all immigration categories, local law centres, Citizens Advice Bureaux and community relations councils. At the time of writing, the immigration service had introduced a new Integrated Casework Directorate and a restricted service was being operated by the Public Enquiry Office in London. All applications for permits or visas should be sent to the Immigration and Nationality Directorate (IND), Block

C, Whitgift Centre, Croydon CR9 2AR (⌨ www.homeoffice.gov.uk/ind/hpg.htm). The appropriate telephone number depends on the type of enquiry: general enquiries about immigration rules and procedures (☎ 0870-606 7766); requests for immigration application forms (☎ 0870-241 0645); and enquires about individual cases already under consideration (☎ 0870-608 1592).

Information about work permits is also available on the **Overseas Labour Service** website (www.dfee.gov.uk/ols).

PETS

Britain is a nation of animal lovers and has some 14 million pet owners (including seven million dog owners). This is supported by the number of bequests received by the Royal Society for the Prevention of Cruelty to Animals (RSPCA), which far exceed the amount left to the Royal Society for the Prevention of Cruelty to Children (RSPCC). The British are almost uniquely sentimental about animals, even those reared for food, and protests over the exports of calves for veal (which are raised in small crates) and other livestock have caused headline news in recent years. Britons are also prominent in international animal protection organisations that attempt to ban cruel sports and practices in which animals are mistreated (such as bullfighting).

Quarantine: Britain has some of the toughest quarantine regulations in the world in order to guard against the importation of rabies and other animal diseases (we have enough problems with 'mad cow disease' and crazy politicians). Britain has been virtually free of rabies for over 60 years. **However, there's good news for those who cannot bear to be parted from their pets, as Britain plans to introduce a new system without quarantine in the year 2000 (see below) on a trial basis.** Under the quarantine laws all mammals other than specific breeds of horses and livestock must spend a period of six months in quarantine in an approved kennel to ensure that they are free of rabies and Newcastle disease. Rabies is a serious hazard throughout the world, including many parts of Europe. You can catch this disease if you're bitten, scratched, or even licked by an infected dog, cat, fox, monkey, bat or other animal.

Quarantine in Britain applies to all cats and dogs, including guide dogs for the blind. If you're coming to Britain for a limited period only, it may not be worth the trouble and expense of bringing your pet with you and you may prefer to leave it with friends or relatives during your stay. Before deciding to import an animal, contact the Ministry of Agriculture, Fisheries and Food, Hook Rise South, Tolworth, Surbiton, Surrey KT6 7NF (☎ 0208-330 8174, ⌨ www.maff.gov.uk) for the latest regulations, application forms, and a list of approved quarantine kennels and catteries (the ministry also publishes a number of free brochures about rabies).

Applications for the importation of dogs, cats and other mammals should be made at least eight weeks prior to the proposed date of importation. To obtain a licence to import your pet you must have a confirmed booking at an approved kennel (it's possible to change kennels after arrival), enlist the services of an authorised shipper to transport your pet from the port to the quarantine kennels, and your pet must arrive at an approved port or airport. Animals must be transported in approved containers, available from air transport companies and pet shops, and must be shipped within six months of the date specified by the licence.

The cost of quarantine for six months is from £75 to £150 per month for a dog depending on its size (and what it eats), and about £50 per month for a cat. You must also pay for any vaccinations and veterinary costs incurred during your pet's quarantine period. You're permitted, in fact encouraged, to visit your pet in quarantine, but won't be able to take it out for exercise. There are different regulations for some animals – birds, for example, serve a shorter quarantine time than other animals, until it's established that there's no danger of psittacosis. Pet rabbits must be inoculated against rabies and cannot be imported from the USA. There's no quarantine for cold-blooded animals such as fish and reptiles. Around 5,000 dogs and 3,000 cats are quarantined annually in Britain.

New Regulations: A new pilot 'Pet Travel Scheme (PETS)' will replace quarantine for qualifying cats and dogs from April 2000. Under the scheme, pets must be microchipped (they have a microchip inserted in their neck), vaccinated against rabies, undergo a blood test (**six months prior to travelling!**) and be issued with a 'health certificate' ('passport'). The scheme will be restricted to animals imported from rabies-free countries and countries where rabies is under control (initially Western Europe and possibly including North America later), but the current quarantine law will remain in place for pets coming from Eastern Europe, Africa, Asia and South America. The new regulations are expected to cost pet owners around £100 (for a microchip, rabies vaccination and blood test) plus £60 a year for annual booster vaccinations and around £20 for a border check. Shop around and compare fees from a number of veterinary surgeons. To qualify, pets must travel by sea via Dover or Portsmouth, by train via the Channel Tunnel or via Heathrow airport (only certain carriers will be licensed to transport animals). More information is available from the Ministry of Agriculture, Fisheries and Food (☎ 0208-330 6835, ✉ pets@ahvg.maff.gov.uk).

An import licence and a veterinary examination is required for some domestic animals, e.g. horses, of which only certain breeds are kept in quarantine. Dangerous animals require a special import licence and you also require a licence from your local council to keep a poisonous snake or other dangerous wild animal, which must be properly caged with an adequate exercise area and must pose no risk to public health and safety. **It's a criminal offence to attempt to smuggle animals into Britain and it's almost always discovered.** Illegally imported animals are either 'deported' immediately or destroyed and the owners are prosecuted. Owners face (and invariably receive) a heavy fine of up to £1,000 or an unlimited fine and up to a year's imprisonment for serious offences. There's no VAT or duty on animals brought into Britain as part of your 'personal belongings', although if you import an animal after your arrival, VAT and duty may need to be paid on its value.

There isn't a dog registration or licence scheme in England, which was abandoned some years ago. Attempts to introduce a dog registration scheme have been defeated by the government, much to the dismay of veterinary surgeons and the RSPCA, who have mounted a campaign to reintroduce dog registration (which has the support of the vast majority of people).

Before buying a home in a community development such as an apartment block, townhouse development or a development within its own private grounds, you should check whether there are any restrictions regarding pets. Some apartment developments ban dogs and many London developments with private gardens have restrictions on the walking of dogs and may not allow it at all (when it's allowed, you must usually pay for the privilege of using the gardens and dogs may need to be kept on a lead).

POST OFFICE SERVICES

There's a post office in most London suburbs and towns in Britain, providing over 100 different services, which (in addition to the usual post office services provided in most countries) include a number of unique services. The term 'post office' is used in Britain as a general term for three separate businesses: the Royal Mail, Post Office Counters Limited and Parcelforce (formerly Royal Mail Parcels). Girobank plc, the former post office banking division, still operates from post offices, but is now owned by Alliance & Leicester.

Inland mail refers to all mail to addresses in Great Britain, Northern Ireland, the Channel Islands and the Isle of Man. Of some 19,000 post offices in Britain, only around 600 are operated directly by the post office. The remainder are franchise offices or sub post offices which don't offer all the services provided by a main post office and they are operated on an agency basis by sub-postmasters. There are plans to partly privatise the post office – the government has already been accused of back-door privatisation with the transfer of many post offices from the high street to supermarkets, stationery stores, newsagents and other shops.

In addition to postal services, the post office also acts as an agent for a number of government departments and local authorities (councils), for example, the sale of TV licences (exclusive to post offices), national insurance stamps and road tax. You can also pay many bills at a post office including electricity, gas, water, telephone, cable, store cards, mail-order bills, council tax, rent payments and housing association rents. The post office is also the largest chain of outlets for the national lottery and a distribution centre for social security leaflets. It provides bureaux de change facilities in main branches (although you may need to order foreign currency) and provides an expensive international money transfer service in conjunction with Western Union International.

The post office (founded in 1635) is the last bastion of the old state sector and like all nationalised companies it's over-staffed and inefficient in some areas. Despite this, it provides one of the best postal services in the world, delivering some 75 million letters and packets every day to around 26 million addresses. Services have improved considerably in recent years and it's now one of the world's most modern and automated post offices, offering a vast range of services compared with most foreign post offices. The Royal Mail even has an office in New York (offering a cheaper and faster international service than the US postal service) from where it ships mail in bulk to London and forwards it to other international destinations. However, overseas rivals are also muscling in on Royal Mail services and a number of overseas groups also handle mail in Britain.

Post office business hours in Britain are usually from 9am to 5.30pm, Mondays to Fridays, and from 9am to 12.30pm on Saturdays. In small towns and villages there are sub post offices (usually part of a general store) that provide many of the services provided by a main post office. Sub post offices usually close for an hour at lunchtime, e.g. 1 to 2pm, Mondays to Fridays, and may also close one afternoon a week, usually Wednesday. Main post offices in major towns don't close at lunchtime.

There are post offices at major international airports, some of which are open on Sundays and public holidays, and in major cities some post offices have extended opening hours, e.g. the Trafalgar Square post office (24-28 William IV Street, WC2, ☎ 0207-930 9580, Charing Cross tube) is open from 8am to 8pm Mon-Thu and Saturdays, and from 8.30am to 8pm on Fridays. If you want to receive mail in London and don't have a permanent address, you can use the *poste restante* service and have mail sent to: Poste Restante, Post Office, 24-28 William IV Street, London WC2N 4DL. Mail is kept for one month and an identity card or passport is required to collect it.

Letter Post: The post office provides a choice of first and second class domestic mail delivery (further evidence of the British preoccupation with class). The target for the delivery of first class mail is the next working day after collection and the third working day after collection for second class. Some 95 per cent of first class mail is delivered the next day, although some letters fail to arrive until weeks after posting (probably those that are delivered by rail). It's unnecessary to mark mail as first or second class, as any item that's posted with less than first class postage is automatically sent second class.

Airmail letters to Europe take an average of from two to three days to Denmark, Norway and Switzerland and up to seven days to Italy and some other countries (which provides a good indication of the relative efficiency or otherwise of European postal services). Airmail to other destinations usually takes four to seven days. Surface mail takes up to two weeks to Europe and up to 12 weeks outside Europe. Underpaid airmail items may be sent by surface mail or will incur a surcharge. Leaflets are published in September, listing the latest mail posting dates for Christmas for international mail.

International letters, small packets and printed papers (both airmail and surface) are limited to a maximum of 2kg and up to 5kg for books and pamphlets. Second class mail mustn't exceed 750g (£1.45), although there's no limit for first class mail. This means that parcels weighing between 750g and 1kg must be sent by first class mail. Parcel mail standard service costs £2.70 for up 1kg, which is more expensive than first class mail (£2.50 for 1kg). Inland postage rates have been frozen for three years and the cost of sending a 2nd class letter was actually reduced from 20p to 19p in April 1999 (a 1st class letter costs 26p). To ensure delivery the next day, first class mail should be posted by 5pm for the local area (e.g. a letter posted in the south-east of England to any address in the same region) or by 1pm for other parts of Britain, excluding Northern Scotland.

Private sector couriers are able to handle only time-sensitive and valuable mail, subject to a minimum fee of £1. The courier industry, particularly in London and other major cities, is growing by some 20 per cent a year and Britain is a major centre for international air courier traffic. Major companies include Federal Express, DHL, UPS and TNT, plus the post office Parcelforce service. The post office produces a wealth of brochures about postal rates and special services, including a *Mini Mailguide* containing information about all Royal Mail products and services. It also has a telephone helpline (☎ 0345-223344) and a website (www.royalmail.co.uk).

RETIREMENT

Pensioners who are EEA nationals have the right of residence in any EEA country, providing they can prove they have sufficient income so as not to become a burden on the host country and have private health insurance (if they're ineligible for cover under the National Health Service). An application for a residence permit must be made before an EEA national has spent six months in Britain. Non-EEA nationals who wish to live but not work in Britain require entry clearance in the form of a Letter of Consent before arrival in Britain. To qualify you must be aged at least 60 and have under your control and disposal in the UK an income of not less than £25,000 a year. You must also be able to show that you're able to support and accommodate yourself and your dependants indefinitely without working and without recourse to public funds. Your presence must be in the best interests of Britain (whatever that means) or you must have close ties with Britain, e.g. close relatives, children attending school there or periods of previous residence in Britain. If you're prohibited from working in

Britain, this also applies to members of your family and any dependants. Persons of independent means are usually admitted for an initial period of one year and qualify for settlement (permanent residence) after four years continuous residence.

TELEPHONE

The telephone system in Britain is dominated by British Telecom (BT), created with a 25-year licence (to print money) in 1984 when the state-owned telephone system was privatised. In 1991, the government ended the duopoly of BT and Mercury and opened up the telecommunications market to national and international competition (although BT still has a monopoly on local calls in most areas). Britain is at the forefront of telecommunications technology and other European countries lag behind when it comes to telecoms liberalisation (although most countries have now privatised their former public monopolies). Over 100 companies are licensed to operate telecoms services in Britain and the market is very competitive for most services, therefore it's important to shop around and compare rates in order to save money.

Users can choose between BT, cable companies, radio-based networks and a large number of indirect operators. In recent years, cable (TV and phone) companies have proliferated and now cover some 11 million homes. To find out which cable phone company operates in your area ☎ 0990-111777. Radio-based companies include Ionica, Atlantic Telecom and Scottish Telecom, which operate in restricted areas but are planning to increase their coverage. With indirect companies you need to dial a code before each number you call or call a free number to obtain a dialling code.

The major telephone companies include ACC Telecom*, AT&T*, Atlantic Telecom, BT*, Cable & Wireless*, The Cable Corporation, CableTel, ComTel, Eurobell, First Telecom*, Ionica, Kingston, Scottish Telecom, Telewest and Yorkshire Cable (* = national operators). In 1998, Ionica, Eurobell and Kingston offered the largest savings for most users, but are available in certain parts of the country only. ACC Telecom is among the cheapest national indirect companies and Scottish Telecom provides the cheapest direct service. The savings depend on how large your monthly bill is, when you make most calls and what sort of calls you make (e.g. local, national or international). Connection costs range from free up to around £30. Also shop around the Internet, e.g. www.toll.co.uk, which provides tariff calculators for both terrestrial and mobile phone services.

Installation: Before moving into a new home, check whether there's a telephone line and that the number of lines or telephone points is adequate (most new homes already have phone lines and points in a number of rooms). If a property has a cable system or other phone network (see above), you could decide not to have a BT phone line installed. If you move into an old house or apartment (where you aren't the first resident), a telephone line will probably already be installed, although there won't be a phone. If you're moving into a house or apartment without a phone line, e.g. a new house, you may need to apply to BT for a line to be installed.

BT's target for residential line installation is four working days, depending on the area and the particular exchange. The installation of a new line (to an address where there wasn't previously a service) is £99 and to take over an existing line costs £9.99 or is free of charge if you move house and take over a working phone line on the *same day* as the existing customer moves out. If a property has an old-style phone point (which cannot be unplugged), it should be replaced with a new-style linebox or master socket. This can be done by BT only and it's illegal to do it yourself or get anyone other than a BT engineer to do it. Once you have a BT linebox or master socket, you can install as many additional sockets as you like, but you shouldn't connect more than four telephones to one telephone line. You can install additional sockets yourself by buying DIY kits from BT or a DIY shop, or BT can install them for you (although their labour charges are astronomical). BT sell a wide range of extension kits, sockets and cords.

Using the Telephone: Using the telephone in Britain is much the same as in any other country, with a few British eccentricities thrown in for good measure. When dialling a number within your own exchange area, dial the number only, e.g. if you live in Toy Town and wish to dial another subscriber in Toy Town. When dialling anywhere else, the area code must be dialled before the subscriber's number. When telephone numbers are printed, they may be shown as any of the following: Toy Town 1234, 01567-1234 or Toy Town (01567) 1234, the recommended method. One problem when the area name isn't shown is that you may not know whether a number is in the local area or at the other end of Britain (although you can ask the operator). When dialling a number in Britain from overseas, you dial the international access code of the country from which you're calling (e.g. 00), followed by Britain's international code (44), the area code *without* the first 0 (e.g. 1567 for Toy Town) and the subscriber's number. For Toy Town 1234, you would dial 00-44-1567-1234.

London telephone codes changed on 1st June 1999, just four years after the last shake-up, although the old codes can continue to be used until 22nd April 2000. The 0171 code (inner London) has changed to 0207 and the 0181 code (outer London) became 0208. Note that not all the outer boroughs have 0208 codes.

Freefone (or toll-free) numbers have a prefix of 0800 (BT), 0500 (Mercury) or 0321 (Vodaphone). They are usually provided by businesses who are trying to sell you something, or having sold you something, provide a free telephone support service. Numbers with the prefix 0345 (BT), 0645 (Mercury) and 0845 (various operators) are termed **Lo**-call numbers and are charged at the local rate, irrespective of where you're calling from. Numbers with the prefix 0990 (BT), 05415 (Mercury) and 0870 (various operators) are charged at the national rate, even when you're calling locally. At the moment it's difficult to know what kind of phone (or even a pager) you're calling and what it's costing. In future, a number's prefix will tell you what type of number it is; for example 00 (international dialling), 01/02 (national area codes), 03 to 06 (these are reserved for future use), 07 (mobiles, pagers and personal numbers), 08 (free or toll-free and special rate services) and 09 (premium-rate services).

The use of premium-rate information and entertainment numbers has increased considerably in recent years and includes numbers with the prefixes 03311, 03313, 03314, 0336, 0338, 0880, 08364, 0839, 0881, 0891, 08941, 08942, 08943, 08944, 0895, 0897, 08975, 0898, 09301, 09305, 09309 and 0991. The rate for premium-rate numbers, which must be shown when they are listed or quoted, is a minimum of 39p at cheap rate and 49p at all other times, e.g. 0839 numbers. Calls to 0897 numbers cost £1.49 per minute at all times. Call rates for numbers with the above prefixes are listed in a BT leaflet *UK call prices*. They are huge money-spinners for the companies and are beloved by TV and radio competitions, and an increasing number of companies (such as banks) now use 0870 (national rate) numbers for their customer lines, when you're often left listening to expensive music. **If you use these numbers frequently you can go bankrupt!**

Standard telephone tones (the strange noises phones make when they aren't connected to a subscriber) are provided to indicate the progress of calls. Note that tones in Britain may be completely different from those used in other countries. There's sometimes a pause before you hear a tone, so you should wait a few seconds to allow the equipment time to connect your call. To listen to typical examples of tones ☎ 0800-789456. In Britain you dial 100 for the operator, 155 for the international operator, 192 for domestic directory enquiries (fee 40p – or you can call Talking Pages free ☎ 0800-600900) and 153 for international directory enquiries. The emergency number is 999.

Extra Services: BT network or select services are available to subscribers with a tone phone connected to a digital exchange, which includes most BT customers. If you subscribe to Mercury or Energis you can still use most network services and most cable companies offer similar services. Network services include call barring, caller display, call diversion, call minder, call return, call waiting, reminder call, ring back, ring me free and three-way calling. Services can be ordered individually or as part of a package and cost from around £3 to £7 a quarter or, in some cases, you can choose to pay on a 'per call' basis. For more information or to order network services ☎ 0800-334422.

Costs: BT remains by far the largest telephone company in Britain and therefore its call rates are listed here for comparison purposes. They are **NOT** meant as an endorsement of BT, which charges some of the highest rates in Britain. BT charges for all calls, including local calls, for which there's no standard flat-rate charge or a number of free calls. For their standard service, BT levy a quarterly line rental fee of £27.77 for a residential line including three hour per quarter of free local calls at the weekend rate. VAT (at 17.5 per cent) is levied on line rental and all calls, and is included in all rates shown unless otherwise noted. For a large percentage of BT's customers, the line rental fee accounts for over half their bill.

BT have three charge rates for self-dialled, domestic calls from ordinary lines (not payphones or mobile phones), depending on the time and day. **Daytime Rate** is in operation from 8am to 6pm, Mon-Fri; **Evening and Nightime Rate** is from 6pm to 8am, Mon-Fri; and **Weekend Rate** from midnight Friday until midnight Sunday. Note, however, that BT charges a minimum of 5p for all calls, therefore your cheap weekend local call will need to be at least five minutes in length to take advantage of the 1p a minute rate. Some companies (e.g. AXS Telecom and One.Tel) offer national calls for 2p or 2½p per minute at all times and are therefore cheaper for daytime calls and evening/night national calls.

Tariff/Cost Per Minute (1999)

Type of Call#	Daytime	Evening/Night	Weekend
Local	4p	1.5p	1p
National	8p	3.95p	2p

\# Local calls are calls made within your local call area and all other calls are national calls.

BT (and some other telephone companies) offer a confusing (deliberate?) range of tariffs and discount schemes, which make it difficult to compare their relative value for money, although most 'discount' schemes offer relatively small savings. Calls to mobile phones are more expensive and range from a maximum of around 25p per minute during the day to as little as 2p per minute at weekends, depending on the network.

International Calls: BT charges for dialled international calls from ordinary lines are based on charge bands (1 to 16), which are shown in phone books with international dialling information. In 1999, BT's lowest weekend rates were 39.11p per minute to Australia, 23.12p to France and Germany, 17.76p to Ireland, 54.29p to Japan, 67.47p to South Africa, and 20.86p to the USA and Canada. These can be reduced by 25 per cent with BT's Friends & Family option using a BT Chargecard, which costs an additional £24 a year. International charges are listed in a BT leaflet entitled *International Call Prices.* **Note that rates are much higher during the daytime from Mondays to Fridays. Using an alternative company to BT, e.g. an indirect access company (see below), can result in HUGE savings.**

Indirect Access Companies: The cheapest companies for international calls are usually indirect access companies (previously termed 'callback' companies as you needed to ring a number and receive a call back to obtain a line). Nowadays you simply dial a toll-free number to connect to the company's own lines or dial a code before dialling a number. They may offer low rates for national long-distance and international calls. Some charge a subscription fee. Calls are charged at a flat rate 24 hours a day, seven days a week. Some companies allow you to make calls from any tone phone (even abroad), while others restrict you to a single (e.g. home or office) number. Calls may be paid for with a credit card, either in advance when you must buy a number of units, or by direct debit each month. Alternatively, you may be billed monthly in arrears.

Low cost companies have drastically reduced BT's share of the international market in recent years, particularly in transatlantic calls, which isn't surprising when you consider the savings that can be made. For example in mid-1999, One.Tel (☎ 0800-634 1860) charged a flat rate of 3p per minute to the USA, 5p to Australia and Canada, 6p to Ireland and New Zealand, 7p to France and Germany, 8p to Japan and 18p to South Africa (these rates aren't applicable to mobile phones or payphones). **Compare these rates with BT's above – isn't competition wonderful!** Most other indirect access companies such as Alpha Telecom (☎ 0800-279 0000), AXS Telecom (☎ 0800-954 2223), Callmate (☎ 0800-376 3000), First Telecom (☎ 0800-782 2000), Planet Talk (☎ 0800-036 2106), Primus (☎ 0800-036 0003) and Swiftcall (☎ 0800-769 0200) have similar rates to One.Tel. It's possible to buy a box that you connect between your phone and wall socket which automatically routes long-distance and international calls via the cheapest carrier.

Home Country Direct: Many European countries subscribe to a Home Country Direct service that allows you to call a special number giving you direct and free access to an operator in the country you're calling. The operator will connect you to the number required and will also accept credit card and reverse charge calls. The number to dial is shown in phone books in the International code section. **You should avoid making international reverse charge calls to Britain using BT's UK Direct scheme, which will cost you from £5.89 to £13.12 for a three-minute call!** For information about countries served by the Home Country Direct service, call international directory enquiries on 153.

Bills: You're billed for each quarter (three months) by BT for your line rental, phone rental (if applicable) and calls, when you're sent a blue *Telephone Account* plus a 'Statement'. If applicable, the telephone connection fee is included in your first bill. BT provides free itemised bills to all customers on demand which include the number called, the date and time, the duration and the call cost. Customers can choose to have all calls itemised or some only. BT bills can be paid via a budget account (to spread bills evenly over 12 months); quarterly direct debit; by post using the envelope provided; at your bank (complete the form provided) or a post office; and at BT phone shops. The best way for most people to pay their phone bill is monthly via a budget account or quarterly from an interest-bearing bank or building society account. With quarterly direct debit, your account is debited 14 days after you receive the bill. Other phone companies may bill you monthly, bimonthly or quarterly.

Payphones: Most payphones (public telephones) permit International Direct Dialling (IDD) and international calls can also be made via the operator. Payphones in Britain were traditionally located in the famous red telephone boxes, which have been replaced in the last few decades by sterile, 'vandal-proof', steel and glass booths containing push-button payphones. Many payphones aren't enclosed and some offer little protection from the elements and surrounding noise (although if they remain in working order, most people will be happy). New payphones are easier to use than the old ones; for example, handsets are set at a lower, more convenient height for those in wheelchairs and they're fitted with an 'inductive coupler' for wearers of post-aural hearing aids. They also have a wider entrance to provide access for wheelchair users. There are also private 'call shops' in major cities where you can buy a pre-paid calling card and make calls in comfort.

Payphones in Britain are operated by British Telecom (with a green Phoncard symbol) and IPM and accept coins (BT only), Phonecards (BT and IPM) and credit cards (BT and IPM). Cards are replacing cash in payphones and various new payment cards have been introduced in recent years. Since installing new payphones in the last decade, BT claims that over 95 per cent (almost 100,000) are in working order at any one time. Public payphones are widely available in all cities and towns in Britain: in public streets, inside and outside post offices and railway stations, and in hotels, pubs, restaurants, shops and other private and public buildings.

Charges for dialled inland calls from payphones are calculated in units of 10p, which is the minimum charge. This means the cost of a call from a payphone is double the minimum cost (5p) from a private phone using BT. Operator connected calls from payphones are roughly double the cost of dialled calls and should be avoided if at all possible. Most payphones are push-button operated and accept all coins except for 1p and 5p (i.e. 10p to £2). You'll need at least £1 to make an international call or a Phonecard with at least ten units left on it. Note, however, that payphones should be avoided at all costs when making international calls, as the rates are prohibitively high, although they are cheaper with an international pre-paid phonecard (sold at newsagents and convenience stores).

Mobile Phones: Britain has among the highest number of mobile phone users in Europe, over ten million in 1999, which is expected to double by 2006. In addition to being a necessity for travelling business people, a mobile phone is a vital status symbol for yuppies and the young. Some car manufacturers fit phones in their cars as standard equipment, particularly to attract women drivers (a mobile phone is useful in an emergency). On the negative side, mobile phones are now so widespread that many businesses (e.g. restaurants, cinemas, theatres, concert halls, etc.) ban them and some even use mobile phone jammers that can detect and jam every handset within 100m. In recent years there has been widespread publicity about a possible health risk to users from the microwave radiation emitted by mobile phones (research is continuing).

There are four digital mobile phone companies in Britain: Cellnet, Vodafone, One-2-One and Orange, all with their own networks covering most of Britain (maps showing the areas covered are available). There's little difference between the two major companies, Cellnet and Vodafone, although you should check out the reception in your local area, particularly if you live or work in a remote rural area. Some companies (particularly Vodafone) have been criticised for their poor reception in many areas of the country (and even worse customer service). Subscribers can buy a GSM phone that can be used in many countries world-wide including most of western Europe, Australia, Hong Kong, South Africa and parts of the Middle East. You must have a contract with a 'roaming' agreement if you wish to use your mobile phone abroad and should check the countries your service provider has contracts with.

TELEVISION & RADIO

Television

Watching television (TV), referred to colloquially as the 'box' or 'telly', is Britain's most popular pastime (or a national epidemic, depending on how you view it). This unsocial disease has all but replaced all those boring things like talking, listening to music, exercise, visiting people (particularly people without TVs), or generally doing anything which might exercise the brain or the body (perish the thought!). Most British homes have at least one TV and over 60 per cent have more than one (25 per cent have three or more) and 80 per cent also have a video recorder.

Many families have a TV in each room except the toilet, particularly in children's rooms where TVs (and computers) serve as tranquillisers for overactive kids, i.e. anytime when they're awake. In households where TV reigns supreme, the box is far more influential with children than parents. However, although TV may have killed off conversation in many homes, in deprived households with only one TV it does wonders for arguments (about which programme to watch). The average Briton is glued to the box for over 15 hours a week or 33 (24-hour) days a year, although homes with cable and satellite TV surprisingly watch little more than those receiving terrestrial TV only. Interactive TV services are the latest offering for couch potatoes and include home shopping and banking, educational programmes, computer games and videos on demand.

While still producing a surfeit of nonsense (e.g. inane quiz shows and soaps, otherwise known as 'tabloid' TV) to cater for TV junkies, British TV (and British produced TV programmes) is generally recognised as the best (or least worst) in the world. British TV companies produce many excellent programmes including documentaries, wildlife and nature programmes, serialised adaptations of novels, TV films, situation comedy, and variety shows, which are sold throughout the world. Other excellent programmes include current affairs, serious music, chat shows and sports events. Some three-quarters of Britons receive their main information about the world from TV News, although the presentation is becoming more showbiz (newscasters are often stars in their own right). Some critics complain that there's too little live TV, where comedians fluff their lines, jugglers drop their balls and dancers fall about (although there are plenty of live chat shows). Explicit sex is becoming commonplace and has led to the Broadcasting Standards Council trying to ban gratuitous sex scenes.

Standards: The standards for TV reception in Britain aren't the same as in many other countries. TVs and video recorders manufactured for use in the USA (NTSC Standard) and continental Europe won't function in Britain due to different transmission standards. Most European countries use the PAL B/G standard except for, you guessed it – France – which has its own standard called SECAM. All British channels broadcast on 625 lines ultra-high frequency (UHF) and around 99 per cent of the population live within the transmission range. The British standard is a modified PAL-I system in which the audio signal is shifted to avoid the buzz plaguing the conventional PAL system when, for example, transmitting subtitles or other white areas.

If you bring a TV to Britain from the USA or the continent, you will get either a picture or sound, **but not both.** A TV can be converted to work in Britain, but it isn't usually worth the trouble and expense. If you want a TV and video recorder (VCR) that will work in Britain and other European countries (including France) and/or the USA, you must buy a multi-standard model. Some multi-standard TVs also handle the North American NTSC standard and have an NTSC-in jack plug connection allowing you to play American videos.

Digital TV: All major terrestrial stations are now broadcast in both digital and analogue format and in late 1999 around 90 per cent of viewers could receive digital TV. However, in order to receive digital terrestrial or satellite TV you need a separate aerial and decoder or an integrated TV with a built-in decoder. In addition to providing a superior picture, better (CD) quality sound and wide-screen cinema format with a digital TV, digital TV also allows for interactive services, digital text and interactive TV (see also **Digital Satellite TV** on page 286).

Stations: In most city and rural areas, five TV stations can be received: BBC1, BBC2, ITV3 (independent television), Channel 4 and Channel 5. In areas where two ITV3 stations overlap, viewers can usually receive both stations. Under the Broadcasting Act 1990, the ITV channel was officially renamed Channel 3, shown as ITV3 in this book, thus allowing all channels to be referred to by a number (although to most people it will always be simply 'ITV'). London has two ITV3 stations: Carlton, which broadcasts from Mondays to Fridays, and London Weekend Television (LWT) which covers the weekend.

The BBC channels carry no advertising and are publicly funded through an annual TV licence (see below), the sale of the *Radio Times*, and the trading activities of BBC Enterprises. With the exception of Wales, where many Welsh-language programmes are broadcast, and regional news broadcasts, BBC programmes are the same throughout Britain. All terrestrial TV stations broadcast for 24 hours a day, as do many satellite and cable stations. Programmes on BBC begin at odd times (e.g. 6.20, 8.05), depending on the length of programmes, as they aren't subject to commercial breaks. ITV programmes usually start on the hour or half hour. The terrestrial TV audience in Britain is fairly evenly divided between BBC and ITV.

TV Licence: An annual TV licence (£101 for colour, £32.50 for black and white) is required by all TV owners in Britain. Registered blind people are generously offered a reduction of £1.25 on production of the local authority's certificate for the blind. The fee is linked to the cost of living and is subject to a five-year agreement under the BBC's charter. The fee is set to increase in the next few years to pay for digital broadcasts, although a special 'digital levy' has been axed. TV licences must be renewed annually and can be purchased from post offices or from TV Licensing, Freepost (BS6689), Bristol BS98 1TL (☎ 0990-226666). A 'Television Licence Application' form must be completed. The licence fee can also be paid by direct debit from a bank or building society account in one payment or in quarterly or monthly payments (which include a small premium). The post office operates a TV licence saving scheme for philatelists, through the purchase of £1 TV licence stamps. If you're leaving Britain, you can obtain a refund on any unexpired three-month period of a TV licence by applying in writing to Customer Services, TV Licensing, Freepost (BS6689), Bristol BS98 1TL.

Cable TV: Cable television in Britain was originally confined to areas of poor reception (e.g. due to natural geographical features or high-rise buildings) or where external aerials weren't permitted. However, there has been an explosion in cable TV in the last decade and it's the fastest growing sector of the TV industry. Over ten million homes can now receive cable TV and there are around three million subscribers (although Britain still has a long way to go to match European countries such as Belgium, the Netherlands and Switzerland, where up to 90 per cent of the population has access to cable TV).

The new broadband cable systems can carry up to 30 channels including terrestrial broadcasts, satellite TV, channels delivered by videotape and local services. Most cable TV companies provide all the stations offered by satellite TV plus a few others, a total of up to 40 (possibly including local cable TV companies). There's an initial connection fee of around £25 for cable TV and a subscription of around £15 a month for the basic package or up to £35 a month for a package including all the premium channels. One of the main advantages is that most cable companies offer inexpensive telephone services, possibly including free local off-peak calls, which can save you enough on your phone bill to pay for your cable TV. Digital TV was introduced in 1999 and is cheaper than satellite digital TV. Companies may also offer pay-per-view broadcasts, movies on demand, home shopping and access to the Internet.

Satellite TV: Although many people complain endlessly about the poor quality of TV in their home countries, many find they cannot live without it when abroad. Fortunately the advent of satellite TV in the last few decades means that most people can enjoy TV programmes in English and a variety of other languages almost anywhere in the world. Britain is well served by satellite TV, where a number of satellites are positioned carrying over 200 stations broadcasting in a variety of languages.

Astra: Although it wasn't the first in Europe (which was Eutelsat), the European satellite revolution really took off with the launch of the Astra 1A satellite in 1988 (operated by the Luxembourg-based *Société Européenne des Satellites* or SES), positioned 22,300mi (36,000km) above the earth. TV addicts (easily recognised by their antennae and square eyes) are offered a huge choice of English and foreign-language stations which can be received throughout most of Britain with a 60cm (or smaller) dish and receiver. Since 1988 a number of additional Astra satellites have been launched, increasing the number of available channels to 64 (or over 200 with digital TV). An added bonus is the availability of radio stations via satellite including all the national BBC stations (see **Satellite Radio** on page 289).

Among the many English-language stations available on Astra are Sky One, Movimax, Sky Premier, Sky Cinema, Film Four, Sky News, Sky Sports (three channels), UK Gold, Channel 5, Granada Plus, TNT, Eurosport, CNN, CNBC Europe, UK Style, UK Horizons, the Disney Channel and the Discovery Channel. Other stations broadcast in Dutch, German, Japanese, Swedish and various Indian languages. The signal from many stations is scrambled (the decoder is usually built into the receiver) and viewers must pay a monthly subscription fee to receive programmes. You can buy pirate decoders for some channels. The best served by clear (unscrambled) stations are German-speakers (most German stations on Astra are clear).

BSkyB Television: You must buy a Videocrypt decoder, an integral part of the receiver in the latest models, and pay a monthly subscription to receive all BSkyB or Sky stations except Sky News (which isn't scrambled). Various packages are available costing from around £12 to £30 a month for the premium package offering all movie channels plus Sky Sports. Subscribers are sent a coded 'smart' card (similar to a credit card) which must be inserted in the decoder to switch it on (cards are frequently changed to thwart counterfeiters). Sky subscribers receive a free copy of *SkyTVguide* monthly.

Digital Satellite TV: Digital TV was launched on 1st October 1998 by Sky Television (☎ 08702-404080, 🖳 www.sky.co.uk) in the UK. To watch digital TV you require a set-top box and a digital dish, which in 1999 were being offered free to new customers by both Sky and ONdigital (see below). You must pay for installation (Sky charges £40 or £100 without a subscription) and sign up for a 12-month subscription. In addition to the usual analogue channels (see above), Sky digital TV offers BBC1 & 2 and Channels 4 and 5 (but not ITV3), plus many new digital channels (a total of 200 with up to 500 possible later). Sky digital TV also offers an interactive shopping service, called **Open.** ONdigital (☎ 0808-100 0101, 🖳 www. ondigital.co.uk) launched a rival digital service on 15th November 1998 which, although it's cheaper than Sky digital, provides a total of 30 channels only (15 free and 15 subscription) including BBC1 & 2, ITV3, Channel 4 and Channel 5. Digital TV is also available via cable and terrestrial aerials. Contact your local TV store for further information and installation.

Eutelsat: Eutelsat (owned by a consortium of national telephone operators) was the first company to introduce satellite TV to Europe (in 1983) and it now runs a fleet of communications satellites carrying TV stations to over 50 million homes. Until 1995 they had broadcast primarily advertising-based, clear-access cable channels. Following the launch in March 1995 of their Hot Bird satellite, Eutelsat hoped to become a major competitor to Astra, although its channels are mostly non-English. The English-language stations on Eutelsat include Eurosport, BBC World and CNBC Europe. Other channels broadcast in Arabic, French, German, Hungarian, Italian, Polish, Portuguese, Spanish and Turkish.

BBC World-wide Television: Although intended for an international audience, it's possible to receive the BBC World-wide TV stations, BBC Prime (general entertainment) and BBC World (24-hour news and information) in Britain, via the Intelsat VI and Eutelsat II F1 satellites respectively. BBC Prime is encrypted and requires a D2 Mac decoder and a smartcard (around £75 plus VAT per year). BBC World is clear (unencrypted) and is financed by advertising revenue. For more information and a programming guide contact BBC World-wide Television, Woodlands, 80 Wood Lane, London W12 0TT, UK (☎ UK 0208-576 2555). The BBC publishes a monthly magazine, *BBC On Air*, giving comprehensive information about BBC World-wide Television programmes. A programme guide is also listed on the Internet (www.bbc.co.uk/schedules) and both BBC World and BBC Prime have their own websites (www.bbcworld.com and www.bbcprime.com). When accessing them, you need to enter the name of the country so that schedules are displayed in local time.

Equipment: A satellite receiver should have a built-in Videocrypt decoder (and others such as Eurocrypt, Syster or SECAM, if required) and be capable of receiving satellite stereo radio. A 60cm dish (to receive Astra stations) costs from around £150 plus the cost of installation (which may be included in the price). Larger (from 90cm) motorised dishes cost from £600 to over £1,000. Shop around as prices vary enormously. Systems can also be rented, although renting isn't good value for money. You can also buy a 1.2 or 1.5 metre dish and receive hundreds of stations in a multitude of languages from around the world. If you wish to receive satellite TV on two or more TVs, you can buy a system with two or more receptors. To receive stations from two or more satellites simultaneously, you need a motorised dish or a dish with a double feed (dual LNBs) antenna. **When buying a system, ensure that it can receive programmes from all existing and planned satellites.**

Location: To receive programmes from any satellite, there must be no obstacles between the satellite and your dish, i.e. no trees, buildings or mountains (or anything else) must obstruct the signal, so check before renting or buying a home. Under current planning regulations most householders are permitted to erect one satellite dish aerial without planning permission, provided it's no bigger than 90cm. Dishes can be mounted in a variety of unobtrusive positions. Apartment blocks usually have cable TV or communal aerials. You may need planning permission to install a satellite dish or antenna on a house depending on its size, height, position, the location of the property, and whether or not a dish is already installed. If in doubt contact your local council's planning department. Note that those living in conservation areas and in listed buildings are banned from erecting aerials on buildings (or may be required to mount them so they cannot be seen from public roads). In strong signal areas it's possible to mount a dish indoors, providing there's a direct line to the satellite through a window or skylight.

Programme Guides: Many satellite stations provide teletext information, which include programme schedules. Satellite programmes are also listed in most local and national daily newspapers, general TV magazines and satellite TV magazines such as *What Satellite*, *Satellite Times* and *Satellite TV* (the best), available from newsagents or on subscription. The annual *World Radio and TV Handbook* (Billboard) contains over 600 pages of information and the frequencies of all radio and TV stations world-wide.

Radio

Radio reception in Britain is excellent in most parts of the country, including stereo reception, which is clear in all but the most mountainous areas (although FM reception isn't always good in cars). To further improve the sound and reception, digital radio was launched on 15th November 1999 covering some 70 per cent of the country (a special digital radio is required). The radio audience in Britain is almost equally split between the British Broadcasting Corporation (BBC) and commercial radio stations (although the BBC has been losing listeners to commercial stations at an alarming rate in recent years). Community and ethnic radio is also popular in many areas and a number of universities operate their own radio stations. In addition to the FM or VHF stereo wave band, medium wave (MW or AM) and long wave (LW) bands are in wide use throughout Britain. Shortwave (SW) band is useful for receiving foreign radio stations. London's music radio stations are classified by the kind of music they play such as middle-of-the-road (MOR), adult-oriented-rock (AOR), rock, pop, classical, Indie, country, jazz or blues.

BBC Radio: The BBC operates five network radio stations with easy to remember (if unimaginative) names: BBC Radio 1 (contemporary music, 98.8 FM), BBC Radio 2, dubbed 'the opium of the people', (entertainment, culture and music, 89.1 FM), BBC Radio 3 (classical music, jazz, drama, discussions, documentaries and poetry, FM 91.3 FM), BBC Radio 4 (conversation, comedy, drama, documentaries, magazine programmes, news, 198/720 LW, 93.5 FM), BBC Radio 5 Live (news, current affairs and sports, 693/909 MW) and around 40 English BBC local radio stations with some ten million listeners. The BBC World Service (mixed) is available in London on 648 MW. There's no advertising on BBC radio stations, although it's the main source of income for commercial radio stations (the other is selling T-shirts). BBC radio is financed by the government and the revenue from TV licence fees, as no radio licence is necessary in Britain.

BBC radio programmes are published in local and national newspapers and Radios 1, 3 and 4 are broadcast both in stereo on FM and in mono on AM. BBC radio programmes are also listed on the BBC TV teletext information service. If you have any difficulty locating the BBC's stations, send a stamped, self-addressed envelope to the BBC, Listener Correspondence, Broadcasting House, Portland Place, London W1A 1AA (☎ 0207-580 4468).

Commercial Radio: Commercial radio is hugely popular in Britain and is Britain's fastest growing entertainment medium, although there are only a few hundred commercial radio stations in the whole of Britain, compared with around 1,000 in France and Italy, and over 9,000 in the USA. There are around 20 commercial stations in London include Capital FM (pop, 95.8 FM), Capital Gold (oldies, 1548 MW), Choice (soul, 96.9 FM), Classic (classical, 100.9 FM), Country (country, 1035 AM), GLR (AOR/talk, 94.9 FM), Heart (AOR, 106.2 FM), Jazz (jazz/blues, 102.2 FM), Kiss (dance, 100 FM), LBC/London Newstalk (talk, 1152 AM), Liberty (music/chat 963/972 MW), Magic (MOR, 105.4 FM), Millennium (music/talk, 103.8 FM), News Direct (news, 97.3 FM), Premier Radio (Christian, 1305/1332 AM), Spectrum (558/990 AM), Talk Radio (phone-ins, 1089/1053 AM), Virgin (AOR, 105.8 FM, 1215 AM) and XFM (Indie, 104.9 FM). London also has a number of foreign radio stations including Greek (ethnic, 103.3), LTR (Turkish, 1584 AM), Spectrum (ethnic, 558 AM) and Sunrise (Asian, 1458 AM).

Daily programmes are listed in the London *Evening Standard* newspaper. Britain also has three national commercial radio stations: Classic

FM (classical music), Virgin Radio (popular music) and Talk Radio, Britain's first 24-hour, national, speech-only commercial station. Britain's most popular commercial radio station is Capital Radio, which has stations in Birmingham, Kent, Hampshire and Sussex in addition to London and is the world's largest metropolitan radio station with over three million listeners.

The British are keen radio listeners and the majority of people listen to the radio for 20 hours or more each week. Commercial radio is reported to have some 36 million listeners or almost 80 per cent of all adults. Stations vary from large national stations with vast budgets and millions of listeners to tiny local stations run by volunteers with just a few thousand listeners. They provide a comprehensive service of local news and information, music and other entertainment, education, consumer advice, traffic information and local events, and provide listeners with the chance to air their views, often through phone-in programmes (talkzak). Advertising on commercial radio is limited to nine minutes an hour, but is usually less (although it sometimes appears to be endless, particularly on Capital FM).

Satellite Radio: If you have satellite TV you can also receive radio stations via your satellite link. For example, BBC Radio 1, 2, 3, 4 and 5, BBC World Service, Sky Radio (a popular music station *without DJs*), Virgin 1215 and many foreign (i.e. non-English) stations are broadcast via the Astra satellites. Satellite radio stations are listed in British satellite TV magazines such as the ***Satellite Times***. If you're interested in receiving radio stations from further afield you should obtain a copy of the ***World Radio TV Handbook*** (Billboard). Readers may also be interested in the **World Radio Network** (www.wrn.org).

APPENDICES

APPENDIX A: USEFUL ADDRESSES

London Embassies and Consulates

A selection of foreign embassies and High Commissions (Commonwealth countries) in London are listed below. Many countries also have consulates in other cities e.g. Belfast, Birmingham, Cardiff, Edinburgh, Glasgow and Manchester), which are listed in phone books. All London embassies are listed in *The London Diplomatic List* (The Stationery Office).

Argentina: 65 Brook Street, London W1M 5LD (☎ 0207-486 7073).

Australia: Australia House, Strand, London WC2B 4LA (☎ 0207-379 4334).

Austria: 18 Belgrave Mews West, London SW1X 8HU (☎ 0207-235 3731).

Bahamas: 10 Chesterfield Street, London W1X 8AH (☎ 0207-408 4488).

Bangladesh: 28 Queen's Gate, London SW7 5JA (☎ 0207-584 0081).

Barbados: 1 Great Russell Street, WC1B 3JY (☎ 0207-631 4975).

Belgium: 103-105 Eaton Square, London SW1W 9AB (☎ 0207-470 3700).

Belize: 22 Harcourt House, 19 Cavendish Square, London W1M 9AD (☎ 0207-499 9728).

Bolivia: 106 Eaton Square, London SW1W 9AD (☎ 0207- 235 4248).

Bosnia & Herzegovina: 4th Floor, Morley House, 320 Regent Street, London W1R 5AB (☎ 0207-255 3758).

Brazil: 32 Green Street, Mayfair, London W1Y 4AT (☎ 0207-499 0877).

Brunei: 19/20 Belgrave Square, London SW1X 8PG (☎ 0207-581 0521).

Bulgaria: 186-188 Queen's Gate, London SW7 5HL (☎ 0207-584 9400).

Cameroon: 84 Holland Park, London W11 3SB (☎ 0207-727 0771).

Canada: Macdonald House, 1 Grosvenor Square, London W1X 0AB (☎ 0207-258 6600).

Chile: 12 Devonshire Street, London W1N 2DS (☎ 0207-580 6392).

China: 49-51 Portland Place, London W1N 4JL (☎ 0207-636 9375).

Colombia: Flat 3a, 3 Hans Crescent, London SW1X 0LN (☎ 0207-589 9177).

Croatia: 21 Conway Street, London W1P 5HL (☎ 0207-387 2022).

Cuba: 167 High Holborn, London WC1 6PA (☎ 0207-240 2488).

Cyprus: 93 Park Street, London W1Y 4ET (☎ 0207-499 8272).

Czech Republic: 26-30 Kensington Palace Gardens, London W8 4QY (☎ 0207-243-1115).

Denmark: 55 Sloane Street, London SW1X 9SR (☎ 0207-333 0200).

Dominica: 1 Collingham Gardens, South Kensington, London SW5 0HW (☎ 0207-370 5194).

Ecuador: Flat 3b, Hans Crescent, Knightsbridge, London SW1X 0LS (☎ 0207-584 2648).

Egypt: 12 Curzon Street, London W1Y 7FJ (☎ 0207-499 2401).

El Salvador: Tennyson House, 159 Great Portland Street, London W1N 5FD (☎ 0207-436 8282).

Fiji: 34 Hyde Park Gate, London SW7 5DN (☎ 0207-584 3661).

Finland: 32 Chesham Place, London SW1X 8HW (☎ 0207-838 6200).

France: 58 Knightsbridge, London SW1X 7JT (☎ 0207-201 1000).

The Gambia: 57 Kensington Court, Kensington, London W8 5DG (☎ 0207-937 9095).

Germany: 23 Belgrave Square, 1 Chesham Place, London SW1X 8PZ (☎ 0207-824 1300).

Ghana: 13 Belgrave Square, London SW1X 8PN (☎ 0207-235 4142).

Greece: 1A Holland Park, London W11 3TP (☎ 0207-229 3850).

Grenada: 1 Collingham Gardens, Earls Court, London SW5 0HW (☎ 0207-373 7809).

Guatemala: 13 Fawcett Street, London SW10 9HN (☎ 0207-351 3042).

Guyana: 3 Palace Court, Bayswater Road, London W2 4LP (☎ 0207-229 7684).

Holy See: Apostolic Nunciature, 54 Parkside, London SW19 5NF (☎ 0208-946 1410).

Honduras: 115 Gloucester Place, London W1H 3PJ (☎ 0207-486 4880).

Hungary: 35 Eaton Place, London SW1X 8BY (☎ 0207-235 5218).

Iceland: 1 Eaton Terrace, London SW1W 8EY (☎ 0207-590 1100).

India: India House, Aldwych, London WC2B 4NA (☎ 0207-836 8484).

Indonesia: 38 Grosvenor Square, London W1X 9AD (☎ 0207-499 7661).

Iran: 16 Prince's Gate, London SW7 1PT (☎ 0207-225 3000).

Ireland: 17 Grosvenor Place, London SW1X 7HR (☎ 0207-235 2171).

Israel: 2 Palace Green, Kensington, London W8 4QB (☎ 0207-957 9500).

Italy: 14 Three Kings Yard, Davies Street, London W1Y 2EH (☎ 0207-312 2200).

Jamaica: 1-2 Prince Consort Road, London SW7 2BZ (☎ 0207-823 9911).

Japan: 101-104 Piccadilly, London W1V 9FN (☎ 0207-465 6500).

Jordan: 6 Upper Phillimore Gardens, Kensington, London W8 7HB (☎ 0207-937 3685).

Kenya: 45 Portland Place, London W1N 4AS (☎ 0207-636 2371).

Korea: 60 Buckingham Gate, London SW1E 6AJ (☎ 0207-227 5500).

Kuwait: 2 Albert Gate, London SW1X 7JU (☎ 0207-590 3400).

Lebanon: 21 Kensington Palace Gardens, London W8 4QM (☎ 0207-229 7265).

Lesotho: 7 Chesham Place, Belgravia, London SW1 8HN (☎ 0207-235 5686).

Luxembourg: 27 Wilton Crescent, London SW1X 8SD (☎ 0207-235 6961).

Malawi: 33 Grosvenor Street, London W1X 0DE (☎ 0207-491 4172).

Malaysia: 45 Belgrave Square, London SW1X 8QT (☎ 0207-235 8033).

Malta: Malta House, 36-38 Piccadilly, London W1V 0PQ (☎ 0207-292 4800).

Mauritius: 32/33 Elvaston Place, London SW7 5NW (☎ 0207-581 0294).

Mexico: 42 Hertford Street, Mayfair, London W1Y 7TF (☎ 0207-499 8586).

Morocco: 49 Queen's Gate Gardens, London SW7 5NE (☎ 0207-581 5001).

Mozambique: 21 Fitzroy Square, London W1P 5HJ (☎ 0207-383 3800).

Namibia: 6 Chandos Street, London W1M 0LQ (☎ 0207-636 6244).

Nepal: 12a Kensington Palace Gardens, London W8 4QU (☎ 0207-229 1594).

Netherlands: 38 Hyde Park Gate, London SW7 5DP (☎ 0207-590 3200).

New Zealand: New Zealand House, Haymarket, London SW1Y 4TQ (☎ 0207-930 8422).

Nigeria: Nigeria House, 9 Northumberland Avenue, London WC2 5BX (☎ 0207-839 1244).

Norway: 25 Belgrave Square, London SW1X 8QD (☎ 0207-591 5500).

Oman: 167 Queen's Gate, London SW7 5HE (☎ 0207-225 0001).

Pakistan: 35-36 Lowndes Square, London SW1X 9JN (☎ 0207-664 9200).

Papua New Guinea: 3rd Floor, 14 Waterloo Place, London SW1R 4AR (☎ 0207-930 0922).

Paraguay: Braemar Lodge, Cornwall Gardens, London SW7 4AQ (☎ 0207-937 1253).

Peru: 52 Sloane Street, London SW1X 9SP (☎ 0207-235 1917).

Philippines: 9a Palace Green, London W8 4QE (☎ 0207-937 1600).

Poland: 47 Portland Place, London W1N 3AG (☎ 0207-580 4324).

Portugal: 11 Belgrave Square, London SW1X 8PP (☎ 0207-235 5331).

Qatar: 1 South Audley Street, London W1Y 5DQ (☎ 0207-493 2200).

Romania: Arundel House, 4 Palace Green, London W8 4QD (☎ 0207-937 9666).

Russia: 13 Kensington Palace Gardens, London W8 4QX (☎ 0207-229 2666).

Saudi Arabia: 30 Charles Street, Mayfair, London W1X 7PM (☎ 0207-917 3000).

Sierra Leone: 33 Portland Place, London W1N 3AG (☎ 0207-636 6483).

Singapore: 9 Wilton Crescent, London SW1X 8RW (☎ 0207-235 8315).

Slovak Republic: 25 Kensington Palace Gardens, London W8 4QY (☎ 0207-243 0803).

Slovenia: 11-15 Wigmore Street, London W1H 9LA (☎ 0207-495 7775).

South Africa: South Africa House, Trafalgar Square, London WC2N 5DP (☎ 0207-451 7299).

Spain: 39 Chesham Place, London SW1X 8SB (☎ 0207-235 5555).

Sri Lanka: 13 Hyde Park Gardens, London W2 2LU (☎ 0207-262 1841).

Swaziland: 20 Buckingham Gate, London SW1E 6LB (☎ 0207-630 6611).

Sweden: 11 Montagu Place, London W1H 2AL (☎ 0207-917 6400).

Switzerland: 16-18 Montagu Place, London W1H 2BQ (☎ 0207-616 6000).

Syria: 8 Belgrave Square, London SW1X 8PH (☎ 0207-245 9012).

Tanzania: 43 Hertford Street, London W1Y 8DB (☎ 0207-499 8951).

Thailand: 29-30 Queen's Gate, London SW7 5JB (☎ 0207-589 2944).

Tonga: 36 Molyneaux Street, London W1H 6AB (☎ 0207-724 5828).

Trinidad and Tobago: 42 Belgrave Square, London SW1X 8NT (☎ 0207-245 9351).

Turkey: 43 Belgrave Square, London SW1X 8PA (☎ 0207-393 0202).

Uganda: Uganda House, 58-59 Trafalgar Square, London WC2N 5DX (☎ 0207-839 5783).

Ukraine: 60 Holland Park, London W11 3SJ (☎ 0207-727 6312).

United Arab Emirates: 30 Prince's Gate, London SW7 1PT (☎ 0207-581 1281).

United States of America: 24 Grosvenor Square, London W1A 1AE (☎ 0207-499 9000).

Uruguay: 2nd Floor, 140 Brompton Road, London SW3 1HY (☎ 0207-584 8192).

Venezuela: 1 Cromwell Road, London SW7 2HW (☎ 0207-584 4206).

Yugoslavia: 5 Lexham Gardens, London W8 5JJ (☎ 0207-370 6105).

Zaire: 26 Chesham Place, London SW1X 8HH (☎ 0207-235 6137).

Zambia: 2 Palace Gate, Kensington, London W8 5NG (☎ 0207-589 6655).

Zimbabwe: Zimbabwe House, 429 Strand, London WC2R 0SA (☎ 0207-836 7755).

Tourist Information

British Tourist Authority (BTA), Thames Tower, Black's Road, Hammersmith, London W6 9EL (☎ 0208-846 9000).

British Travel Centre, 12 Regent Street, London SW1Y 4PQ (☎ 0207-730 3400).

English Tourist Board, Thames Tower, Black's Road, Hammersmith, London W6 9EL (☎ 0208-846 9000).

London Tourist Board, Glen House, Stag House, London SW1E 5LT (recorded information service, ☎ 0207-971 0026, ☐ www.londontown. com).

Travel

Association of British Travel Agents, 55-57 Newman Street, London W1P 4AH (☎ 0207-637 2444).

British Airport Authority, Corporate Office, Gatwick Airport, West Sussex RH6 0HZ (☎ 01293-517755).

British Airways, Head Office, Speedbird House, PO Box 10, Heathrow Airport, Hounslow, Middx. TW6 2JA (☎ 0208-897 4000).

British Midland, Donington Hall, Castle Donington, Derby DE7 2SB (☎ 0207-589 5599).

London Transport, 55 Broadway, London SW1H 0BD (☎ 0207-222 5600).

National Express, 13 Regent Street, London SW1 9TP (☎ 0207-824 8461).

P&O, 77-91 New Oxford Street, London WC1A 1PP (☎ 0207-831 1234).

Virgin,

Publications

The Big Issue, 236-240 Pentonville Road, London N1 9JY (☎ 0207-526 3200). Weekly 'street' newspaper.

Evening Standard, Associated Newspapers Ltd., Northcliffe House, London W8 5TT (☎ 0207-938 6000). London's evening newspaper.

Girl About Town, *Midweek*, *Ms London* and *Nine to Five*, Independent Magazines (UK) Ltd., 7-9 Rathbone Street, London W1P 1AF (☎ 0207-636 6651, ☐ www.londoncareers.net). Free weekly careers and recruitment magazines.

The London Magazine, Premier Magazines Ltd., Haymarket House, 1 Oxendon Street, London SW1Y 4EE (☎ 0207-925 2544, ☐ premiermags.co.uk). Monthly real estate and lifestyle magazine.

The London Parents' Guide, 1 Stockwell Terrace, London SW9 0QD (☎ 0207-793 1990/0641). A magazine for families with children aged up to 14 years.

Loot, Loot House, 24/32 Kilburn High Road, London NW6 5TF (☎ 0207-328 1771, 🖳 www.loot.com). Daily newspaper for buying/selling properties privately (and just about everything else) and property rentals in an around London.

Metro London, Associated London Metro Limited, Harmsworth Quays Printing, Surrey Quays Road, Rotherhithe, London SE16 1PJ (☎ 0207-651 5200, 🖳 www.londonmetro.co.uk). Free daily newspaper (Mon-Fri).

Southern Cross Magazine, 14-15 Child's Place, Earls Court, London SW5 9RX (☎ 0207-373 3377, 🖳 www.southerncross.co.uk). Weekly magazine for expatriate Australians and New Zealanders living in London.

Time Out, Time Out Magazine Ltd., Universal House, 251 Tottenham Court Road, London W1P 0AB (☎ 0207-813 3000, 🖳 www.timeout.com). Weekly (Tuesdays) entertainment guide ('London's living guide').

TNT Magazine, 14-15 Child's Place, Earls Court, London SW5 9RX (☎ 0207-373 3377, 🖳 www.tntmag.co.uk). Weekly magazine for expatriate Australians and New Zealanders living in London.

What's On in London, Where to Go Ltd., 180 Pentonville Road, London N1 9LB (☎ 0207-278 4393, ✉ whatson@globalnet.co.uk). Weekly entertainment guide.

Which? magazine, Castlemead, Gascoyne Way, Hertford SG14 1LH (☎ 01992-822800, 🖳 www.which.net). Monthly consumer magazine, available on subscription only.

Miscellaneous

Aliens' Registration Office, 10 Lamb's Conduit Street, London WC1 (☎ 0207-230 1208).

Automobile Association (AA), Fanum House, PO Box 50, Basingstoke, Hampshire RG21 2EA (☎ 01256-20123).

British Council, 10 Spring Gardens, London SW1A 2BN (☎ 0207-930 8466).

British Broadcasting Corporation (BBC), Broadcasting House, Portland Place, London W1A 1AA (☎ 0207-580 4468).

BBC Television Centre, Wood Lane, London W12 7RJ (☎ 0207-743 8000).

British Telecom, 81 Newgate Street, London EC1A 7AJ (☎ 0207-356 6666).

Central Bureau for Educational Exchanges & Visits (☎ 0207-930 8466). Address is c/o the British Council above.

Central Office of Information, Hercules Road, London SE1 7DU (☎ 0207-928 2345).

Confederation of British Industry (CBI), Centre Point, 103 New Oxford Street, London WC1A 1DU (☎ 0207-379 7400).

Consumers' Association, Castlemead, Gascoyne Way, Hertford SG14 1LH (☎ 01992-587773).

Department of Education and Employment, Overseas Labour Service, Moorfoot, Sheffield S1 4PQ (☎ 0114-259 4074).

Driver and Vehicle Licensing Centre (DVLC), Swansea SA99 1AR (☎ 01792-822800).

HM Customs and Excise, New King's Beam House, 22 Upper Ground, London SE1 9PJ (☎ 0207-620 1313).

Inland Revenue, Somerset House, Strand, London WC2R 1LB (☎ 0207-438 6622).

The Stationery Office Ltd., National Publishing, 51 Nine Elms Lane, Vauxhall, London SW8 5DR (☎ 071-873 0011, ⌨ www.the-stationery-office.co.uk).

National Association of Citizens Advice Bureaux, Myddelton House, 115-123 Pentonville Road, London N1 9LZ (☎ 0207-833 2181).

National Consumer Council, 20 Grosvenor Gardens, London SW1 0DH (☎ 0207-730 3469).

National Federation of Women's Institutes, 39 Eccleston Street, London SW1W 9NT (☎ 0207-730 7212).

Office of Fair Trading, Field House, 15-25 Bream's Building, London EC4A 1PR (☎ 0207-242 2858).

Office for National Statistics, 1 Drummond Gate, London SW1V 2QQ (☎ 0207-233 9233).

Public Record Office, Ruskin Avenue, Kew, Richmond, Surrey TW9 4OU (☎ 0208-876 3444).

Royal Automobile Club (RAC), RAC House, Lansdowne Road, East Croydon, Surrey CR9 2JA (☎ 0208-686 2525).

UK Council for Overseas Student Affairs (UKCOSA), 9-17 St Alban's Place, London N1 0NX (☎ 0207-354 5210, ⌨ www.ukcosa.org.uk).

Westminster Reference Library, 35 St Martin's Street, London WC2 (☎ 0207-641 4634, 101m-8pm, Mon-Fri, 10am-5pm Sat).

APPENDIX B: FURTHER READING

There are many useful reference books for anyone seeking general information about Britain and the British. Published annually since 1868, *Whitaker's Almanack* (The Stationery Office) contains a wealth of information about the British government, finances, population, commerce and general statistics of the nations of the world. Another comprehensive publication is *Enquire Within Upon Everything* by Moyra Bremner (Helicon), first published in 1856, and containing information on a multitude of subjects from social behaviour to organisations. Newcomers to Britain may also be interested in *Britain* (The Stationery Office), an annual reference book describing many features of life in Britain, including the workings of the government and other major institutions.

In the list below, the publication title is followed by author's name and the publisher (in brackets). All books prefixed with an asterisk (*) are recommended by the author.

London Tourist Guides

*Access London, Richard Saul Wurman & Lucy Koserski (Access)

American Walks in London, Richard Tames (Interlink Publishing)

*Baedeker Guide: London (AA Publishing)

The Best of London, Andre Gayot (Gault Millau)

Blue Guide: London, Ylva French (A&C Black)

Cadogan London, Andrew Gumbel (Cadogan)

Companion Guide to London, David Piper (Companion Guides)

*David Gentleman's London, David Gentleman (Phoenix)

Essential London, Paul Murphy (AA Publishing)

Everybody's Historic London, Jonathan Kiek (Quiller Press)

Everyman Guide to London (Everyman)

Explorer London, Christopher Catling (AA Publishing)

*Eyewitness Travel Guides: London, Michael Leapman (DK Publishing)

The Faber Book of London, A.N. Wilson (Faber & Faber)

*Fodor's London Companion, Louise Nicholson (Fodor)

Fodor's Up Close London (Fodor)

Frommer's London from $70 a Day (Macmillan Reference)

In and Around London (Pitkin Unichrome)

*Let's Go London (St Martin's Press)

*London, England – A Daytripper's Travelogue from the Coolest City in the World, Derek Hammond (Mainstream)

London for Free, Peter & Richard Harden (Harden's Guides)

London for Free, Brian Butler (Mustang)

*London: The Rough Guide, Rob Humphreys (Rough Guides)
London Step by Step, Christopher Turner (Independent Traveller)
*Lonely Planet: London, Pat Yale (Lonely Planet)
*Michelin Green Tourist Guide: London (Michelin)
*The National Geographic Traveller: London (National Geographic)
Rick Steves' London, Rick Steves & Gene Openshaw (John Muir)
Secret London, Andrew Duncan (New Holland)
*Time Out London Guide (Penguin)

Special Guides

*The Art & Architecture of London, Anne Saunders (Phaidon)
*Capital BYOs: A Guide to London's Bring Your Own Wine Restaurants, Victoria Alers (Hankey VBAH)
*Cheap Eats in London, Sandra A. Gustafson (Chronicle)
*Evening Standard Children's London, Linda Conway (Prentice Hall)
*Evening Standard London Pub and Bar Guide, Edward Sullivan (Simon & Schuster)
*Evening Standard London Restaurant Guide, Nick Foulkes (Simon & Schuster)
*Frommer's Born to Shop London, Suzy Gershman (IDG Books)
Gay London, Will McLoughlin (Ellipsis)
*Guide to Ethnic London, Ian McAuley (Immel Publishing)
The Heinz Guide to Days Out with Kids: South East, Janet Bonthron (Bon Bon)
Holistic London, Kate Brady (Brainwave)
*London Restaurants: The Rough Guide, Charles Campion (Rough Guides)
*The Serious Shoppers' Guide to London, Beth Reiber (Prentice Hall Press)
Zagat Survey 1999: London Restaurants (Zagat)

Living & Working

**Buying a Home in Britain, David Hampshire (Survival Books)
Guide to Good Living in London (Francis Chichester)
**Living and Working in Britain, David Hampshire (Survival Books)
*Living in London, Karen Howes (Editions Flammarion)
London Living, Lisa Lovatt-Smith & Paul Duncan (Weidenfeld)
London Living (Ramboro Books)
*The New London Property Guide, Carrie Seagrave (Mitchell Beazley)

Summer Jobs in Britain (Vacation Work)
*Where to Live in London, Sarah McConnell (Simon & Schuster)

Miscellaneous

*Access in London, Gordon Couch (Quiller Press)
*A-Z Big Street Atlas of London (Geographers A-Z Map Co.)
The Bookshops of London, Matt Jackson (Mainstream)
*The English, Jeremy Paxman (Michael Joseph)
*Enquire Within Upon Everything, Moyra Bremner (Helicon)
Focus on London '99, Office for National Statistics
*Geographers' London Atlas (Geographers A-Z Map Co.)
*How to be a Brit, George Mikes (Andre Deutsch)
*In and Around London Pathfinder Guide (Jarrold/Ordnance Survey)
*Notes From a Small island, Bill Bryson (Doubleday)
*On Your Bike, Guide to Cycling in London (London Cycling Campaign)
*The Penguin London Mapguide, Michael Middleditch (Penguin)
*Residence in Britain: Notes for People from Overseas (Central Office of Information)
*The State We're In, Will Hutton (Vintage)
*Top Towns (Guiness Publishing)
Which London School, Derek Bingham (John Catt)
*Whitaker's Almanack (The Stationery Office)

APPENDIX C: WEIGHTS & MEASURES

Officially Britain converted to the international metric system of measurement on 1st October 1995, although many goods have been sold in metric sizes for many years. The use of imperial measures was officially due to finish at the end of 1999 but has been given a reprieve until end of 2009. Therefore you can expect to find goods sold in imperial (and other old British measures), metric or marked in both metric and British measures. Many foreigners will find the tables on the following pages useful. Some comparisons shown are approximate only, but are close enough for most everyday uses.

Women's clothes:

Continental	34	36	38	40	42	44	46	48	50	52
UK	8	10	12	14	16	18	20	22	24	26
USA	6	8	10	12	14	16	18	20	22	24

Pullovers: Women's   Mens

Continental	40	42	44	46	48	50	44	46	48	50	52	54
UK	34	36	38	40	42	44	34	36	38	40	42	44
USA	34	36	38	40	42	44	Sm	Medium	large			exl

Note: sm = small, exl = extra large

Men's Shirts

Continental	36	37	38	39	40	41	42	43	44	46
UK/USA	14	14	15	15	16	16	17	17	18	

Men's Underwear

Continental	5	6	7	8	9	10
UK	34	36	38	40	42	44
USA	small	medium	large	extra large		

Children's Clothes

Continental	92	104	116	128	140	152
UK	16/18	20/22	24/26	28/30	32/34	36/38
USA	2	4	6	8	10	12

Children's Shoes

Continental	18	19	20	21	22	23	24	25	26	27	28
UK/USA	2	3	4	4	5	6	7	7	8	9	10

Continental	29	30	31	32	33	34	35	36	37	38
UK/USA	11	11	12	13	1	2	2	3	4	5

Shoes (Women's and Men's)

Continental	35	35	36	37	37	38	39	39	40	40
UK	2	3	3	4	4	5	5	6	6	7
USA	4	4	5	5	6	6	7	7	8	8

Continental	41	42	42	43	44	44
UK	7	8	8	9	9	10
USA	9	9	10	10	11	11

Weights:

Avoirdupois	Metric	Metric	Avoirdupois
1 oz	28.35 g	1 g	0.035 oz
1 pound	454 g	100 g	3.5 oz
1 cwt	50.8 kg	250 g	9 oz
1 ton	1,016 kg	1 kg	2.2 pounds
1 tonne	2,205 pounds		

Note: g = gramme, kg = kilogramme

Length:

British/US	Metric	Metric	British/US
1 inch =	2.54 cm	1 cm =	0.39 inch
1 foot =	30.48 cm	1 m =	3.28 feet
1 yard =	91.44 cm	1 km =	0.62 mile
1 mile =	1.6 km	8 km =	5 miles

Note: cm = centimetre, m = metre, km = kilometre

Capacity:

Imperial	Metric	Metric	Imperial
1 pint (USA)	0.47 l	1 l	1.76 UK pints
1 pint (UK)	0.568 l	1 l	0.265 US gallons
1 gallon (USA)	3.78 l	1 l	0.22 UK gallons
1 gallon (UK)	4.54 l	1 l	35.211 fluid oz

Note: l = litre

Temperature:

Celsius	Fahrenheit	
0	32	freezing point of water
5	41	
10	50	
15	59	
20	68	
25	77	
30	86	
35	95	
40	104	

The Boiling point of water is 100° Celsius, 212° Fahrenheit.

Oven temperature:

Gas	Electric	
	°F	°C
-	225-250	110-120
1	275	140
2	300	150
3	325	160
4	350	180
5	375	190
6	400	200
7	425	220
8	450	230
9	475	240

For a quick conversion, the Celsius temperature is approximately half the Fahrenheit temperature.

Temperature Conversion:

Celsius to Fahrenheit: multiply by 9, divide by 5 and add 32.
Fahrenheit to Celsius: subtract 32, multiply by 5 and divide by 9.

Body Temperature:

Normal body temperature (if you're alive and well) is 98.4° Fahrenheit, which equals 37° Celsius.

INDEX

U

V

W

SUGGESTIONS

Please write to us with any comments or suggestions you have regarding the contents of this book (preferably complimentary!). We are particularly interested in proposals for improvements that can be included in future editions. For example did you find any important subjects were omitted or weren't covered in sufficient detail? What difficulties or obstacles have you encountered which aren't covered here? What other subjects would you like to see included?

If your suggestions are used in the next edition of *Living and Working In London*, you will receive a free copy of the Survival Book of your choice as a token of our appreciation.

NAME: _____

ADDRESS: _____

_____

_____

Send to: Survival Books, PO Box 146, Wetherby, West Yorks. LS23 6XZ, United Kingdom.

My suggestions are as follows (please use additional pages if necessary):

LIVING AND WORKING IN BRITAIN

Living and Working in Britain is essential reading for anyone planning to spend some time there including holiday-home owners, retirees, visitors, business people, migrants, students and even extraterrestrials! It's packed with over 500 pages of important and useful information designed to help you **avoid costly mistakes and save both time and money.** Topics covered include how to:

- find a job with a good salary
- obtain a residence permit
- avoid and overcome problems
- find your dream home
- get the best education
- make the best use of public transport
- endure motoring in Britain
- obtain the best health treatment
- stretch your pounds further
- make the most of your leisure time
- enjoy the British sporting life
- find the best shopping bargains
- insure yourself against most things
- use the post office and telephones
- do numerous other things

Living and Working in Britain is the most comprehensive and up-to-date source of practical information available about everyday life in Britain. It isn't, however, a boring text book, but an interesting and entertaining guide written in a highly readable style.

Buy this book and discover what it's <u>really</u> like to live and work in Britain.

Order your copies today by phone, fax, mail or e-mail from Survival Books, PO Box 146, Wetherby, West Yorks. LS23 6XZ, United Kingdom (☎/🖷 +44-1937-843523, ✉ orders@survivalbooks.net, 🖳 www.survivalbooks.net).

ORDER FORM – ALIEN'S/BUYING A HOME

Qty.	Title	Price (incl. p&p)			Total
		UK	Euro.	World	
	The Alien's Guide to America	Winter 2000-01			
	The Alien's Guide to Britain	Spring 2000			
	The Alien's Guide to France	£5.95	£6.95	£8.45	
	Buying a Home in Abroad	£11.45	£12.95	£14.95	
	Buying a Home in Britain	£11.45	£12.95	£14.95	
	Buying a Home in Florida	£11.45	£12.95	£14.95	
	Buying a Home in France	£11.45	£12.95	£14.95	
	Buying a Home Greece/Cyprus	Spring 2000			
	Buying a Home in Ireland	£11.45	£12.95	£14.95	
	Buying a Home in Italy	£11.45	£12.95	£14.95	
	Buying a Home in Portugal	£11.45	£12.95	£14.95	
	Buying a Home in Spain	£11.45	£12.95	£14.95	
	Rioja and its Wines	Spring 2000			
				Total	

Order your copies today by phone, fax, mail or e-mail from Survival Books, PO Box 146, Wetherby, West Yorks. LS23 6XZ, United Kingdom (☎/🖷 +44-1937-843523, ✉ orders@survivalbooks.net, 🖳 www.survivalbooks. net). If you aren't entirely satisfied, simply return them to us within 14 days for a full and unconditional refund.

Cheque enclosed/please charge my Delta/Mastercard/Switch/Visa card

Card No. _ _ _ _   _ _ _ _   _ _ _ _   _ _ _ _

Expiry date _____ Issue No. (Switch only) _____

Signature _____ **Tel. No.** _____

NAME _____

ADDRESS _____

_____

ORDER FORM – LIVING AND WORKING

Qty.	Title	Price (incl. p&p)			Total
		UK	Euro.	World	
	Living & Working in Abroad	Winter 2000-01			
	Living & Working in America	£14.95	£16.95	£20.45	
	Living & Working in Australia	£14.95	£16.95	£20.45	
	Living & Working in Britain	£14.95	£16.95	£20.45	
	Living & Working in Canada	£14.95	£16.95	£20.45	
	Living & Working in France	£14.95	£16.95	£20.45	
	Living & Working in Germany	Summer 2000			
	Living & Working in Italy	Autumn 2000			
	Living & Working in London	£11.45	£12.95	£14.95	
	Living & Working in N.Z.	£14.95	£16.95	£20.45	
	Living & Working in Spain	£14.95	£16.95	£20.45	
	Living & Working in Switz.	£14.95	£16.95	£20.45	
				Total	

Order your copies today by phone, fax, mail or e-mail from Survival Books, PO Box 146, Wetherby, West Yorks. LS23 6XZ, United Kingdom (☎/🖨 +44-1937-843523, ✉ orders@survivalbooks.net, 🖳 www.survivalbooks. net). If you aren't entirely satisfied, simply return them to us within 14 days for a full and unconditional refund.

Cheque enclosed/please charge my Delta/Mastercard/Switch/Visa card

Card No. _ _ _ _   _ _ _ _   _ _ _ _   _ _ _ _

Expiry date _____ Issue No. (Switch only) _____

Signature _____ **Tel. No.** _____

NAME _____

ADDRESS _____

_____

A NEW LIFE
ABROAD!

How often have you pictured yourself living abroad? Enjoying a brand new lifestyle somewhere new and different?

It's an ambition you share with lots of people, of all ages and backgrounds.

But most fall at the first hurdle, unsure where to start and daunted by the prospect of cutting through all the red tape and bureaucracy that is involved. What a pity they didn't know about First Point International.

Whether you'd like to work, run your own business or even spend your retirement abroad, First Point will secure that crucial visa and provide all the advice and practical assistance you're likely to need.

YOUR NEXT STEP

To find out how you could soon be on your way to a new life abroad, call or send for our Information Pack today.

+44 (0)20 7724 9669

(24 Hours.) Please quote ref. LWL

www.firstpointinter.com
info@firstpointinter.com